Springer Proceedings in Business and Economics

Springer Proceedings in Business and Economics brings the most current research presented at conferences and workshops to a global readership. The series features volumes (in electronic and print formats) of selected contributions from conferences in all areas of economics, business, management, and finance. In addition to an overall evaluation by the publisher of the topical interest, scientific quality, and timeliness of each volume, each contribution is refereed to standards comparable to those of leading journals, resulting in authoritative contributions to the respective fields. Springer's production and distribution infrastructure ensures rapid publication and wide circulation of the latest developments in the most compelling and promising areas of research today.

The editorial development of volumes may be managed using Springer Nature's innovative EquinOCS, a proven online conference proceedings submission, management and review system. This system is designed to ensure an efficient timeline for your publication, making Springer Proceedings in Business and Economics the premier series to publish your workshop or conference volume.

This book series is indexed in SCOPUS.

More information about this series at https://link.springer.com/bookseries/11960

Rabi Narayan Subudhi · Sumita Mishra ·
Abu Saleh · Dariush Khezrimotlagh
Editors

Future of Work and Business in Covid-19 Era

Proceedings of IMC-2021

Springer

Editors
Rabi Narayan Subudhi
School of Management
KIIT University
Bhubaneswar, Odisha, India

Sumita Mishra
School of Management
KIIT University
Bhubaneswar, Odisha, India

Abu Saleh
School of Management, BGL
University of Canberra
Canberra, ACT, Australia

Dariush Khezrimotlagh
Pennsylvania State University
Harrisburg, PA, USA

ISSN 2198-7246 ISSN 2198-7254 (electronic)
Springer Proceedings in Business and Economics
ISBN 978-981-19-0356-4 ISBN 978-981-19-0357-1 (eBook)
https://doi.org/10.1007/978-981-19-0357-1

This Springer imprint is published by the registered company Springer Nature Singapore Pte Ltd.
The registered company address is: 152 Beach Road, #21-01/04 Gateway East, Singapore 189721, Singapore

Preface

The first wave of COVID-19, which was declared a pandemic by WHO in March 2020, created much panic world over, as nobody, not even scientists, knew then a solution or how to prevent or check the disease. Global and local shutdowns and micromanagement followed, as casualties increased everywhere. Within next 5–7 months, the virus spread all over the world like wildfire and all economic activities came to a grinding halt. Not only countries, but even small local governments, including village panchayats, sealed their respective borders, effectively stopping all movements across. COVID-19 changed the way of life as we knew it, and it also changed the way we lived and managed our life and livelihood.

It was in this backdrop that KIIT University School of Management thought of having a formal academic deliberation, on issues of 'future of business and management' and the future of our 'way of our future life and livelihood', in the form of an international conference.

Thus the International Management Conference, IMC-2021, was organized at School of Management, KIIT Bhubaneswar, during February 2021. There were two-day long deliberations which had huge participation by scholars, teachers and industry practitioners; over 170 research papers were presented and spread over 14 parallel sessions. After screening and blind review, selection committee finally recommended 30 articles for publication in this proceedings, spread across five functional areas.

We are very much thankful to KIIT University administration, for providing all technical and financial support. In particular, we are thankful to founder, Prof. (Dr.) Achyutananda Samanta, and all colleagues of School of Management, headed by Director, Prof. S. K. Mahapatra.

We are thankful to all members of program committee and organizing committee of IMC-2021, all chairpersons and invited speakers of each of the 14 sessions. We are grateful to all the reviewers of the papers who took time off to go through them and give critical comments, making real value addition to this final proceedings.

We express our sincere thanks to the entire team of Springer Nature, particularly Ms. Nupoor Singh and Mr. Daniel Joseph Glarance, for making this (IMC-2021 proceedings) book publication smooth and successful. We shall take special mention of Ms. Nupoor who guided and coordinated with us since beginning.

The real architects of success of any book projects are its contributing authors. We thank all authors for their valuable academic contribution, and more particularly their patience and cooperation, during this long journey of selection process and editing.

This proceedings has five broad sections, dividing the chapters according to functional areas.

In ***finance and economics area***, there are six papers. The first chapter is on 'Test of Efficient Market Hypothesis, Relating to Cryptocurrency', where a detailed analysis has been presented by authors on EMH. Next article presents an 'Evolving Economy Outlook', in COVID era. In this section, two articles, 'Foreign Direct Investment of India' and 'Poverty and Income Distribution' during COVID-19, present very contrasting financial sentiments. The other two articles, in this section, are on 'Green Accounting' and 'Behavioural Finance'.

In ***human resources*** (HR) area, two very important aspects, like 'Maintaining Employee Motivation During COVID-19 Pandemic' and 'Role of Supervisory Leadership', have been discussed. It is observed, and mentioned above, companies and institutions were majorly successful in motivating their employees during this unprecedented pandemic and maintain productivity wherever possible to do so via an online mode of functioning.

In ***marketing section***, this proceedings contains eight useful chapters, carefully selected. It covers consumers' behaviour during this unprecedented pandemic, when most of us had to transact online and engage in social media with greater involvement. Papers, particularly on 'Consumerism Through E-Commerce Portals', 'Grandparents' Influence on Consumption Intention', 'Online Product Recommendation System', 'Consumer Behaviour During COVID-19', 'Mobile Banking Service Quality Dimensions Using Multi-Criterion Decision Making', would be of great academic interest for researchers. This section also has an interesting study on 'Social Media during COVID-19 and Vaccine Hesitancy among People', explaining how social media helped in dispelling initial hesitancy, thus motivating eligible people demanding to get vaccinated. The most expected topic on use of virtual platform is covered in the chapter on 'Adoption of Cloud-Based Video Conferencing Platform'.

This proceedings has highest contribution in the area of ***sociology and entrepreneurship*** including education sector, tourism, social and firm growth and rights issue. On education sector, chapters on 'learning continuity in the realm of Education 4.0, in higher education', 'pedagogical shift in education sector', 'educational technology during pandemic', 'intelligent approaches in Indian education system during COVID-19', 'technological renovation in online second language teaching' would be of great interest to academia.

Bhubaneswar, India — Rabi Narayan Subudhi
Bhubaneswar, India — Sumita Mishra
Canberra, Australia — Abu Saleh
Harrisburg, USA — Dariush Khezrimotlagh

Contents

About the Editors

Rabi Narayan Subudhi is a Senior Professor at KIIT School of Management, KIIT University, India. With over 34 years of teaching experience, he has published 10 books and over 70 research papers in the area of quantitative research methodology. He had received a senior research fellowship (SRF) award from CSIR, Government of India, for his doctoral research. He was chapter president of ORSI. He is presently the Editor of KIIT Management Research Journal, *Parikalpana.*

Sumita Mishra is a Professor at KIIT School of Management, KIIT University, India. Her research on organizational culture, organization design, group culture and social psychology has been published in several reputable journals, such as *Asian Case Research Journal, Indian Journal of Industrial Relations*, and *Management Review.*

Abu Saleh is Associate Professor at Canberra Business School, University of Canberra, Australia. He was a postdoc fellow, Queensland University of Technology, Australia and has published about 50 papers in internal journals of repute.

Dariush Khezrimotlagh is Assistant Professor of Computer Science and Mathematics at Penn State University, Harrisburg, Pennsylvania. He was previously an Assistant Professor of Statistics at the University of Malaya, Malaysia, and Visiting Researcher at University Technology Malaysia. He served as the Director of the Studies and Information Center, Commercial Aviation Organization in Iran, and has more than 20 years of experience as an educator. He earned his MS in Pure Mathematics and his Ph.D. in Applied Mathematics, specializing in Operations Research and DEA. Dr. Khezrimotlagh is a committee member of the Data Envelopment Analysis International Conference (DEAIC), a member of INFORMS, Mathematical Association of America (MAA) and American Mathematical Society.

Reinventing the Future of Work and Business in the COVID-19 ERA: Challenges, Opportunities and the Path Ahead

Rabi N. Subudhi and Sumita Mishra

1 Introduction

The greatest danger in times of turbulence is not the turbulence—it is to act with yesterday's logic.—Peter Drucker.

Coronavirus (COVID-19) disease reported first in the Chinese city of Wuhan in December 2019 and recognized by China as a new virus in the third week of January 2020 (Izumi et al. 2021).[1] The World Health Organization (WHO) finally recognized COVID-19 as a pandemic on the 11th of March 2020 (WHO 2020).[2] The US, India and Brazil experienced the highest numbers of daily cases, while the rest of the world attempted a transition back to a life that was known earlier. The grim prognosis is that while tens of thousands of people remain infected with the virus, a similar number of people may also die. In an interconnected world, the pandemic has had a devastating effect on life and work in general as governments around the world declared prolonged periods of lockdown ceasing almost all forms of human contact (Dwivedi et al. 2020).[3] This cessation had unprecedented impact on personal and organizational life. These impacts created the concept of a *new normal* within the COVID-19 era which required people to totally rethink the way the interacted and operated within the organization (Griffin and Denholm 2020).[4] While many companies have shut down operations, organizations that continued were forced to work with changing requirements, new processes and practices influenced by

R. N. Subudhi (✉) · S. Mishra
School of Management, KIIT University Bhubaneswar, Bhubaneswar, India

S. Mishra
e-mail: sumita.mishra@ksom.ac.in

[1] Izumi et al. (2021).

[2] WHO (2020).

[3] Dwivedi et al. (2020).

[4] Griffin and Denholm (2020).

R. N. Subudhi et al. (eds.), *Future of Work and Business in Covid-19 Era*,
Springer Proceedings in Business and Economics,
https://doi.org/10.1007/978-981-19-0357-1_1

social distancing requirements. Organizations have been coerced to envisage newer, leaner, and sustainable methods of conducting their business. Future has arrived faster than anticipated as most companies have shifted to remote working style and most activities are being carried out on digital platforms.

For majority business leaders and managers, COVID-19 emerged as the most disruptive world-changing event in recent history. Managers are coerced to take decisions amidst tremendous uncertainty. For example, uncharacteristic human behavior, irrational patterns in financial markets, extreme volatility of the economy, lack of data measuring lockdown impact and unknown outbreak of the virus lead to incomplete information (Izumi et al. 2021). To cope with these unforeseen challenges, organizations move in with efforts to integrate information technology and artificial intelligence (AI) to better understand data and make more compatible decisions in a digital economy. Taking cues from the *new normal*, organizations recognize that agility is the key to deal with massive disruptions such as the COVID-19 pandemic. With significant rise in social media and remote working platforms, the demand for key products such as Zoom, WebEx, Microsoft Teams has risen exponentially. In the *interim normal*—one that is predicted to last till the end of 2021 (as rightly stated by Izumi et al. 2020)—the huge demand for homeworking and the necessary change in the infrastructure to accommodate this will have lasting impacts on the work processes and habits in the foreseeable future.

All sectors of work and business along with core functional verticals have experienced sweeping changes during the pandemic. As organizations institutionalize lessons learned through trial and error, an effort is required to document these efforts. Tremendous amount of research was published in the previous year noting the impact of COVID-19 in various sectors. The following sections in this chapter provide a succinct overview of the drastic changes experienced in diverse verticals of management.

2 Impact of COVID-19 on Work and Business

The COVID-19 (C-19) has presented a paradox like none other. While many organizations were forced shut down operations, C-19 helped organizations to think in terms of innovations and alternate business models (Seetharaman 2020).[5] The following subsections present an exposition of the influences of C-19 on varied prominent functional verticals of business such as (1) human resources, (2) marketing/consumer behavior, (3) financial markets, (4) innovation and entrepreneurship and (5) supply chain management.

[5] Seetharaman (2020).

2.1 *Influence of C-19 on Managing Human Resources*

The influence of C-19 on human resource management has been tremendous and all pervasive. The following areas in human resource management (HRM) are at the forefront of change (Vnouckova 2020).[6]

1. As the nature of work keeps changing, online education and training of managers equip them to work better in a virtual environment. Thus, digital tools used to map performance in the current environment are particularly useful.
2. The prolific use of online tools for recruitment and retention assumes importance. Database screening has been in use to effectively screen and complete the recruitment process. In contrast to recruitment, fewer digital tools for retention are used, and hence, HR practitioners need to invest further on discovering the optimal use of digital tools for employee retention.
3. The use of online tools has ushered digital pedagogies in training-related organizational activities. While practitioners do understand the limitations of digital pedagogies, they also give credence to their need while working remotely. Digital pedagogies require differing competencies from both the trainees and the trainers alike.
4. While much has already been spoken about the generational capacity to adhere to technology, COVID-19 has brought these issues to the forefront. Organizations need to equip their employees (of varied generations) to singularly adopt to technology to work remotely.
5. Massive utilization of technologies places a huge demand on information and data security. The greatest impediment to security issues is a lack of employee awareness about the same. Hence, organizational initiatives on provision of adequate training to employees in matters of information security are imperative.
6. In the new normal, as organizations shift to a hybrid working environment combing the best aspects of the physical and the digital, adherence to safety norms and helping employees maintain a safe working atmosphere takes precedence.
7. Lowered salaries, reduction in total compensation and muted increments have been common organizational occurrences during the pandemic. Hence, while organizations struggle to bring in revenue, they also need to invest to build the morale and engagement of their employees.
8. While remote working conditions have helped organizations cope with the onset of the pandemic, employers need to be aware about the psychological distance between employees and the organization. A close psychological distance will help alleviate the pressure of work hours and maintain a better quality of occupational mental health. Hence, constant updates on safety norms, changing work hours, work protocols and transparent communication channels will help in reducing the psychological distance.

---

[6] Vnouckova (2020).

9. The psychological aspects due to COVID-19 such as fear, depression, lack of social contact, high risk of job loss, uncertain work conditions and failing health issues have been devastating. Hence, organizations need to open regular channels for psychological counseling of their employees to help them adjust to these numerous changes.

2.2 *Influence of C-19 on Marketing and Consumer Behavior*

The pandemic has equally affected marketing management as traditional marketing philosophies and practices were rendered ineffective in the new normal. There have been suitable changes in marketing, advertisements, promotional engagements and the media (Yas and Alsaud 2020).[7] Most businesses are engaged in promoting their marketing and advertisements on online platforms as it is relatively hard to engage in traditional channels during the pandemic.

As all of marketing is anchored to patterns of consumption, it is necessary to evaluate the changes in consumer behavior amidst the pandemic. Consumption patterns are anchored to time and location and hence have experienced sweeping changes from the onset of the pandemic. Yas and Alsaud (2020) highlight many of these changes:

1. There is a tendency in consumers to hoard essential items resulting in temporary stockouts and shortages during an emergency and prolonged periods of lockdown as was predominant during the pandemic. The extra demand created by hoarding also encourages marketing of counterfeit products.
2. Due to a crisis of this magnitude, there was an improvisation or "*Jugaad*" in consumers to deal with shortages in required product and services. Even for tradition-bound services such as weddings and funerals, the creativity of consumers was observed in sidewalk weddings or Zoom funeral services. Improvisation in consumption patterns also offers exciting vistas for further research.
3. While there was a tendency to hoard on essential products, consumers generally postponed the consumption of products such as large-scale durable products like homes, automobiles, etc. and discretionary services such as concerts, bars and restaurants. Hence, pent-up demand is a familiar outcome when access to market is denied for prolonged periods of time due to pandemic. The nature and scope of pent-up demand can also be researched upon in marketing management.
4. Influence of digital technologies is all pervasive in a consumer's daily life during the pandemic. The largest population to be found now are the Facebook, WhatsApp and the YouTube. A fast-growing area of research are the influential marketeers. The pandemic has witnessed the largest growing adoption of digital media during a compressed cycle. Hence, a worthwhile outlet of research can address

[7] Yas and Alsaud (2020).

whether this digital boom will lead to near permanent changes in consumption patterns.

5. Due to complete lockdown in many different parts of the world, the stores have entered the homes of consumers along with work and education. Hence, with online delivery services and streaming giants like Netflix, Amazon, etc., the habit of going to brick-and-mortar places has taken a setback. Research can focus on how home consumption impacts consumer impulse buying behaviors.
6. Consumers are mostly confined to their homes with many discrete tasks to implement such as working, learning, shopping and socialization. Thus, there is a blurring and intermingling of boundaries between work and home and between tasks and chats.
7. The cultural and sociological associations of consumption practices also need a focus on. The pandemic took a huge toll on social contact in gatherings but also helped connect with distant relatives at a regular basis through Zoom calls. The universal adoption of technologies to maintain social contact may leave long-term impact on consumption patterns.

The managerial implications of these changes are manifold. Some of the more important implications as pointed out by Yas and Alsaud (2020) related to businesses concentrating on building an omni-channel delivery. Secondly, organizations need to match their demand and supply due to hoarding in consumption patterns in lockdowns during the pandemic. Thirdly, customer experience in the virtual world and post-purchase support both would require significant investments from organizations.

2.3 *Influence of C-19 on Financial Markets.*

The influence of COVID-19 on financial markets, on financing and costs of capital and finally on banking and insurance has been huge. COVID-19 as a global pandemic is differing in its intensity from any other disaster like a nuclear attack. While a nuclear attack is largely localized and the chances of human survival are next to nil, the impact of COVID-19 has been on a global scale and is also survivable. Thus, the value of financial markets remains extremely relevant (Goodell 2020).[8] Regarding firm financing, COVID-19 is likely to increase the cost of equity capital (Goodell 2020). Future research may explore questions such as whether there will exist long-term shift in costs of equity or will firms adopt less of leverage.

COVID-19 also raises implications for banking and insurance. Banks become vulnerable during economic downturns due to possibilities of increase in non-performing loans. Thus, one question that requires further research efforts is how long would banks maintain a more conservative leading policy post the pandemic (Goodell 2020). Similarly, even though COVID-19 has had tremendous global impact and precipitated economic crisis on a huge scale, it cannot be treated as an unforeseeable event. As such events can be predicted, it is beneficial to make them insurable.

[8] Goodell (2020).

But once again further research needs to address that how would these insurance policies affect the bottom of the pyramid (Goodell 2020).

2.4 *Influence of C-19 on Innovation and Entrepreneurship*

The outbreak of C-19 has led to the collapse of many a brick-and-mortar businesses and supply chains as consumers simply postponed their purchases or cult down on their demand altogether. Hence, under the onslaught of this crisis, firm's survival is guaranteed on their ability to innovate. Li-Ying and Nell (2020)[9] in their paper provide an interesting description of market opportunities for entrepreneurs during the pandemic under the heads of testing, tracking, isolation, and treatment. Firstly, given the importance to testing of infectious diseases, new opportunities for companies emerge to produce test kits and face shields. Secondly, robust surveillance techniques are required to contain the spread of the virus. As countries are debating on restrictions on social gatherings, surveillance becomes even more important. Once reopening of schools, colleges, restaurants becomes inevitable, new age solutions such as drones, tracking apps and artificial intelligence (AI) will raise opportunities for organizations. Thirdly, people under isolation and treatment require psychological support to remain motivated. While these requirements open opportunities for relevant service providers, banks and other public services need to creatively design their operations to meet the demands of consumers under isolation. Fourthly, treatment in the form of drugs and vaccines has raised a host of opportunities for pharmaceutical and vaccine companies. Li-Ying and Nell (2020) also highlight the qualities that firms need to imbibe to innovate for competitive advantage during and beyond the pandemic, i.e., customer-centric creativity, agility, resilience and the ability to reinvest and restructure.

Ratten (2020)[10] highlights three other areas that need to be taken into consideration, i.e., changing lifestyle and work, cultural entrepreneurship and lifestyle entrepreneurship. The increase in the gig economy and temporariness of the workforce has created space for digital nomads who can work from any location. These nomads rely on the gig economy and are alike to micro-entrepreneurs. Similarly, cultural entrepreneurship highlights business opportunities resulting from cultural considerations of COVID-19. As entrepreneurial behavior is influenced by culture, businesses need to consider cultural consideration while reimagining their products and services. Lifestyle entrepreneurs are people who start businesses on lifestyle values resulting out of COVID-19. They emphasize on social values and financial benefits. These entrepreneurs can typically be found in art and craft industries apart from tourism and hospitality sectors. During the pandemic, many traditional industries in arts and crafts were severely affected leaving artisans devoid of income. Hence, research efforts on entrepreneurial efforts in these sectors are desirable.

---

[9] Li-Ying and Nell (2020).

[10] Ratten (2020).

2.5 *Influence of C-19 on Supply Chain Management*

In the backdrop of the magnitude of COVID-19, on February 21, 2020, Fortune (2020)[11] reported that 94% of businesses included in the Fortune 1000 list experienced supply chain disturbances. An apparent and serious consequence of the pandemic has been the reduction in demand for goods and services due to partial or absolute lockdown in different parts of the world. The pandemic led to unprecedented job losses lowering the demand for goods further and leaving businesses in many sectors (such as hospitality and tourism) almost bankrupt. Disruption in the work of schools and colleges, government institutions, closure of restaurants, stores, cafes, etc. to prevent interaction among people and contain the spread of the virus interrupted global supply chains halting activities of multinational companies and declining revenues (Grida et al. 2020).[12] Supply chains were affected either in demand or in supply or logistics. Maximum research has focused on the negative effects of the pandemic on supply chains (Grida et al. 2020). The biggest challenge faced by companies in mitigating these negative effects on their supply chains is determining the optimal amount of demand for their goods and services. However, supply chains always susceptible to pandemics have witnessed an unprecedented impact of the COVID-19 due to its very reach and magnitude. While researchers studied the possibilities of alternative supply chains for important medical equipment such as face shields (Shokrani et al. 2020)[13]; Cappelli and Cini (2020)[14] in their study stated that food supply chains and local productions were minimally affected by international policies as they were located closest to the consumer. Hence, supply chains in varied industries require a systematic examination to fully comprehend the impact of COVID-19.

All sectors of work and business along with core functional verticals have experienced sweeping changes during the pandemic. As organizations institutionalize lessons learned through trial and error, an effort is required to document these efforts. Tremendous amount of research was published in the previous year noting the impact of COVID-19 in various sectors. Notwithstanding the importance of these research efforts, the International Management Conference (IMC) 2021 was hosted at KIIT DU on the 27th and 28th of February 2021 to collectively gather insights on the future of work and business encompassing varied industries, businesses, countries and core management functions such as strategy, organization behavior, human resource management, production and operations, higher education, economics, finance and sustainability initiatives. The thrust of this conference was different as we sought to gather a holistic picture of the lessons derived during the pandemic hardship. Selected papers presented in the conference and published in the book provide readers with an idea of the new normal in various domains of management across industries and organizations.

---

[11] Fortune. (2020).

[12] Grida et al. (2020).

[13] Shokrani et al. (2020).

[14] Cappelli and Cini (2020).

References

Cappelli, A., and E. Cini. 2020. Will the COVID-19 pandemic make us reconsider the relevance of short food supply chains and local productions? *Trends in Food Sciences and Technology* 99: 566.

Dwivedi, Y., D.L. Hughes, C. Coombs, et al. 2020. Impact of COVID-19 pandemic on information management research and practice: Transforming work, education and life. *International Journal of Information Management.* 55: 102211.

Fortune. 2020. 94% of the Fortune 1000 are seeing coronavirus supply chain disruptions: Report. https://fortune.com/2020/02/21/fortune1000-coronavirus-china-supply-chain-impact/ (Accessed on 10 July 2021).

Goodell, J.W. 2020. COVID-19 and finance: Agendas for further research. *Finance Research Letters* 35: 101512.

Grida, M., R. Mohamed, and A.N.H. Zaied. 2020. Evaluate the impact of COVID-19 prevention policies on supply chain aspects under certainty. *Transportation Research Interdisciplinary Perspectives* 8: 100240.

Griffin, D., and Denholm, J. 2020. *This isn't the First Global Pandemic, and it Won't be the Last. Here's What We've Learned From 4 Others Throughout History* (https://theconversation.com/this-isnt-the-first-global-pandemic-and-it-wont, Accessed on 19 July, 2021).

Izumi, T., V. Sukhwani, A. Surjan, and R. Shaw. 2021. Managing and responding to pandemics in higher educational institutions: Initial learning from COVID-19. *International Journal of Disaster Resilience in the Built Environment* 12 (1): 51–66.

Li-Ying, J., and Nell, P. 2020. Navigating opportunities for innovation and entrepreneurship under COVID-19. *California Management Review*. https://cmr.berkeley.edu/2020/06/innovation-entrepreneurship/.

Ratten, V. 2020. COVID-19 and entrepreneurship. *Journal of Small Business and Entrepreneurship* 32 (5): 503–516.

Seetharaman, P. 2020. Business model shifts: Impact of COVID-19. *International Journal of Information Management* 54. https://doi.org/10.1016/j.ijinfomgt.2020.102173.

Shokrani, A., Loukaides, E.G., Elias, E., and Lunt, A.J., 2020. Exploration of alternative supply chains and distributed manufacturing in response to COVID-19; a case study of medical face shields. *Materials and Design* 108749.

Vnouckova, L. 2020. Impact of COVID-19 on human resource management. *Relias* 3 (1): 18–21.

WHO. 2020. *COVID-19 Public Health Emergency of International Concern: Global Research.*

Yas, H., and A.B. Alsaud. 2020. The impact of COVID-19 on supply chain and human resource management practices and future marketing. *International Journal of Supply Chain and Inventory Management* 9 (5): 1681–1685.

Cryptocurrency Response to COVID-19: A Test of Efficient Market Hypothesis

Brajaballav Kar and Chandrabhanu Das

1 Introduction

The World Health Organization (WHO) declared COVID-19 as a pandemic on March 11, 2020. The announcement sent financial markets into turmoil and negative sentiment as evident from reactions of global stock markets. Prices of gold, considered a safe haven for investors, dropped. Therefore, it is imperative to study how different financial instruments attracted the attention of investors. The cryptocurrency market has been an emerging phenomenon with much interest among technocrats for blockchain technology, and investors for the associated arbitrage opportunities.

The cryptocurrency market has grown tremendously with the Bitcoin price from $0 in 2009 to $7000 in 2020. The dramatic rise in prices has questioned the hedging potential of these groups of assets (Chan et al. 2019). Market regulators and policymakers have cautioned against its use due to possible manipulation and instability. Investment in gold has been considered as a better investment during a stock market plunge (Baur and Lucey 2010). Financial markets are interrelated and are likely to move in the same direction. In such a situation, any asset that has a negative correlation with traditional investment can act as a better asset, especially during financial turmoil. Thus, cryptocurrencies provide a plausible alternative. However, studies have argued about the adverse nature of cryptocurrencies as a mode of diversification (Liu 2019; Conlon and McGee 2020).

Despite the skepticism, speculators and investors have been interested in cryptocurrencies as an asset class. Prior studies have evaluated bitcoin as a speculative commodity (Selgin 2015; Baeck and Elbeck 2015). The limited number of investors, market, and acceptability to the regulators and policymakers warrant an investigation concerning the market efficiency aspect of cryptocurrencies. If the cryptocurrency market is inefficient in responding to any information, an investor may select a

B. Kar (✉) · C. Das
School of Management, KIIT University, Bhubaneswar, India

R. N. Subudhi et al. (eds.), *Future of Work and Business in Covid-19 Era*,
Springer Proceedings in Business and Economics,
https://doi.org/10.1007/978-981-19-0357-1_2

mispriced asset (Narayan et al. 2016). This study takes the turbulent market situation of COVID-19 and examines how different cryptocurrencies have reacted to information to test the efficient market hypothesis (EMH).

2 Literature Review

A growing body of literature has examined the price movements of cryptocurrencies during COVID-19 (Mariana et al. 2021; Umar and Gubareva 2020). Researchers have debated the nature of cryptocurrencies and their suitability for investment. Dyhrberg (2016) identifies the role of Bitcoin as a hedging mechanism. Similarly, Beneki et al. (2019) have suggested the cryptocurrency Ethereum as a safe haven for investment. A contrary strand of literature argued high volatility and imminent danger associated with Bitcoin investment (Smales 2019; Chaim and Laurini 2019; Geuder et al. 2019).

Economic recessions affect financial assets of different classes and erode investor wealth. The COVID-19 pandemic is one such event, and the recovery is still being debated. The socioeconomic consequences of the pandemic have been severe. Stock markets of different countries reacted by a sharp decline in prices. The declining stock market presented a disincentive to investment. Meanwhile, regulators and policymakers have disapproved of the use of cryptocurrency due to instability and manipulation issues (Foley et al. 2019; Gandal et al. 2018).

Lahmiri and Bekiros (2020) in their study on the impact of the COVID-19 pandemic on equity and cryptocurrency markets argued that cryptocurrencies have a higher risk than equities. Umar and Gubareva (2020) provided evidence that cryptocurrency as a hedging mechanism may not succeed at times of global crisis. However, Corbet et al. (2020) advocated cryptocurrency as a safe haven investment similar to gold, at times of crisis.

Given that this asset class is new, it is plausible that there may be a time dependency on its efficiency to respond to information. Bariviera (2017) observes that Bitcoins exhibited inefficiency up to 2014 and afterward they have become more efficient. However, Wei (2018) claimed that Bitcoins are becoming efficient compared to other cryptocurrencies. Prior studies applied tools and techniques similar to exchange currencies and stock markets on cryptocurrencies. Tiwari et al. (2019) find that Litecoin has been an effective hedging route against the risk of the Standard and Poor (S&P 500) index. Bouri et al. (2017) argued Bitcoin to be a better investment in times of crisis than gold and commodities. However, Conlon and McGee (2020) mention Bitcoin price movement in tandem with S&P 500 index. Thus, the asset class or a particular asset has been tested on different parameters taken for investment. The EMH is an accepted basis to test the efficiency of the financial market as well as assets and therefore suitable for testing the efficiency of cryptocurrencies as well.

The primary objective of this study is to ascertain if the price movement of cryptocurrencies reflected the information flow during the COVID-19 pandemic. We try to analyze this behavior using the Efficient Market Hypothesis (EMH) test. The EMH identifies a market as efficient if prices display the impact of available information. The weakest form of EMH claims the market is efficient if historical information cannot be used to predict future prices (Hu et al. 2019). Caporale et al. (2018) discussed inefficiency of Bitcoin, Litecoin, Ripple, and Dash while Zhang et al. (2018) identified the inefficiency in twelve cryptocurrencies. Charfeddine and Maouchi (2019) documented the inefficiency of Bitcoin, Litecoin, Ripple, and Dash. Numerous tests of market efficiency were conducted on Bitcoin, a cryptocurrency with the largest market capitalization (Urquhart 2016; Kristoufek 2018; Sensoy 2019).

The EMH of cryptocurrencies during COVID-19 is still evolving and this study contributes to understanding the behavior of cryptocurrencies during the COVID-19 pandemic. It applied statistical techniques used to test the EMH in stock markets to assess the price movements in different major cryptocurrencies. Such an approach is unique to consider price movements like the price movement of stocks and is a contribution to literature.

3 Data and Methodology

The daily exchange prices of ten major cryptocurrencies by market capitalization were extracted from a dedicated website for cryptocurrencies (coindesk.com) and were converted to INR on the prevailing exchange rate. The name (symbol) of the following were considered for this study: (1) Cardano (ADA), (2) Bitcoin Cash (BCH), (3) Binance Coin (BNB), (4) Bitcoin (BTC), (5) Ethereum (ETH), (6) Chainlink (LINK), (7) Litecoin (LTC), (8) Tether (USDT), (9) Stellar (XLM), and (10) Ripple (XRP). The prices were taken from January 1, 2020, to December 31, 2020, to accommodate the pandemic effect. The daily returns were calculated using the formula (1):

$$\text{Daily returns} = \frac{\text{Price}_t}{\text{Price}_{t-1}} - 1 \tag{1}$$

where Price_t is the price on date t and Price_{t-1} is the price on the previous day.

The method used by Vasileiou et al. (2021) to test EMH in stock markets was applied for the selected cryptocurrencies. To account for different information related to the pandemic, the initial seven months of the pandemic were divided into five time zones (TZ).

TZ 1 (01.01.2020–29.01.2020)—Notice related to COVID-19 by WHO.

TZ 2 (30.01.2020–21.02.2020)—Public health emergency declaration.

TZ 3 (22.02.2020–10.03.2020)—Turbulence in Financial markets.

TZ 4 (11.03.2020–18.03.2020)—Pandemic declaration and a sharp decline in financial markets.

TZ 5 (19.03.2020–31.07.2020)—Declaration of relief programs and gradual easing of lockdowns.

The cumulative returns and standard deviation for each time zone were calculated by the formula (2).

$$\text{Cumulative returns} = \left[\prod_{\mathrm{i}=1}^{\mathrm{N}} (1 + \mathrm{r_i})\right]^{-1} \tag{2}$$

where r_i = daily returns of cryptocurrencies from day 1 to day N. Here N is the specified time zone.

$$\text{Standard deviation} = \sqrt{\frac{\sum_{i=1}^{N} (r_i - r_{\text{mean}})^2}{N - 1}} \tag{3}$$

where r_{mean} = mean return during the specified period.

We studied the leverage effect to examine the return and volatility dependence on positive or negative price movements during the specified time zones. The EMH is tested based on how the returns respond to events specified as time zones. The GARCH family models are widely used in financial econometrics to identify how the returns behave to calendar anomalies in form of time zones. We used a model similar to Derbali and Hallara (2016) which examined calendar effects in the Tunisian stock market. This study also examined the leverage effect and asymmetric nature of volatility.

The EGARCH (1, 1) model is specified as follows:

$$r_t = i_t r_{t-1} + e_t \tag{4}$$

$$\begin{aligned} \ln\left(\sigma_t^2\right) = {} & \mathrm{C}1 + \S 1 \ln\left(\sigma_{t-1}^2\right) + \alpha 1 |\theta_{t-1}/\sigma_{t-1}| + \gamma 1 (\theta_{t-1}/\sigma_{t-1}) \\ & + \beta 1 T1 + \beta 2 T2 + \beta 3 T3 + \beta 4 T4 + \beta 5 T5 \end{aligned} \tag{5}$$

Equations (4) and (5) represent the return and variance equations.
where

σ_t^2 conditional variance.

r_t mean equation.

$\theta_{t-1}/\sigma_{t-1}$ leverage effect. $T1$,$T2$, $T3$, $T4$, and $T5$ are dummy regressors for the time zones. i_t is the pandemic information at time t and C1 is the constant.

4 Results and Discussion

The cumulative return for these currencies for the time zones and entire period was calculated (Table 1).

Table 1 Cumulative returns of cryptocurrencies

Symbol	Period 1	Period 2	Period 3	Period 4	Period 5	Whole
ADA	−0.69	0.13	0.47	−0.37	−0.05	0.83
BCH	−0.20	0.55	0.56	−0.32	0.13	1.12
BNB	0.22	−0.05	−1.60	−0.80	0.16	0.46
BTC	0.12	0.34	1.88	−31.40	0.12	−0.13
ETH	0.27	0.50	0.71	−0.70	0.18	0.83
LINK	−1.44	0.10	−0.05	−0.57	0.26	0.01
LTC	0.17	0.40	−0.04	−0.46	0.16	0.76
USDT	0.73	0.22	0.08	−3.04	0.01	−0.43
XLM	−0.89	−2.22	0.04	0.32	0.03	1.03
XRP	0.47	0.25	3.37	−0.15	0.39	−1.61

Source SPSS output table, compiled by author

Except for Bitcoin, Tether, and Ripple, other cryptocurrencies exhibited positive returns for the entire period. Following are major observations and plausible explanations:

Period 1—Four out of ten cryptocurrencies have negative returns. Differential assimilation of pandemic-related information can cause differences in return during the period.
Period 2—Interestingly, most cryptocurrencies have given positive returns during the period after the declaration of emergency. It is to be noted here that various stock indices across the world reported positive returns during the period as well.
Period 3—This period marks a negative market return but a positive return from cryptocurrencies. The EMH of stock markets and cryptocurrencies are contradictory in this period and could indicate market inefficiency in the case of cryptocurrencies.
Period 4—This period was marked by an increase in COVID-19 cases and deaths and declaration of the pandemic. The currency returns also fell in line with global indices with the most negative returns for Bitcoin. Therefore, contrary to the assumption of safe haven, the cryptocurrencies also moved similar direction with the stock markets, indicating market efficiency.
Period 5—The period coincides with various stimulus measures announced by various governments and positive returns in most cryptocurrencies. The positive returns suggested a possible market efficiency.

We estimated the volatility by the standard deviation of these currencies for different time zones and the entire period (Table 2).

Table 2 indicates almost the same level of volatility for the entire period. Specific time zone volatility is interpreted as follows:

(a) Period 1—The range of standard deviation of returns remained 0.01 to 0.08. Over the different time zones, USDT maintained the lowest standard deviation.

Table 2 Standard deviation of cryptocurrencies

Symbol	Period 1	Period 2	Period 3	Period 4	Period 5	Whole
ADA	0.05	0.04	0.05	0.17	0.05	0.06
BCH	0.08	0.05	0.06	0.17	0.04	0.05
BNB	0.04	0.05	0.05	0.17	0.04	0.05
BTC	0.03	0.03	0.03	0.15	0.04	0.04
ETH	0.04	0.05	0.05	0.17	0.04	0.05
LINK	0.04	0.06	0.06	0.18	0.05	0.07
LTC	0.05	0.05	0.06	0.16	0.04	0.05
USDT	0.01	0.01	0.01	0.03	0.01	0.01
XLM	0.04	0.04	0.05	0.14	0.04	0.06
XRP	0.04	0.04	0.05	0.14	0.03	0.06

Source SPSS output table, compiled by author

(b) Period 2—During this time zone, the range of standard deviation remained 0.01 to 0.06 but, the volatility of Chain link increased.
(c) Period 3—Interestingly, in contrast to stock market changes, the volatility of cryptocurrencies remained at similar levels compared to the previous time zone. Contrarian volatility to the stock market possibly indicates inefficiency in cryptocurrency markets.
(d) Period 4—During this time zone, volatility increased across all cryptocurrencies.
(e) Period 5—During this time zone, volatility reduced compared to the previous time zone and the period was marked by declaration of relief measures by different governments. The reduction in volatility can be considered to assimilate reforms related information, thus exhibiting market efficiency.

The final test of EMH is done by exploring whether the market is really efficient or anomaly exists in form of reaction to events. Shiller (1981) argued about the herd mentality of investors through stocks' overreaction to events in form of price volatility. Several researchers have applied GARCH family models to identify the patterns in volatility clustering (Corrado et al. 2005; Karmakar 2007; Guidi et al. 2011). GARCH models have been applied to test EMH in financial markets (Narayan et al. 2016). We studied, the leverage effect, whether the responses of cryptocurrencies are different from good or bad news. The leverage effect in GARCH models explains that negative news affects volatility to a greater extent than positive news (Almeida and Hotta 2014).

The leverage effect was explored to identify the impact of events in form of the time zones identified. We employed the variance equation of the EGARCH model equivalent to the model for calendar anomalies by Derbali and Hallara (2016). For identifying the conditional variance, an autoregressive conditional heteroscedasticity) test was conducted. The presence of ARCH effects necessitated the GARCH family volatility modeling. Table 3 displays the ARCH effects test for select

Table 3 Test of ARCH effects

Sl. No.	Symbol	Chi-square	P-value	ARCH disturbance
1	ADA	5.253	0.0219	Yes
2	BCH	1.595	0.2067	No
3	BNB	1.064	0.3022	No
4	BTC	1.343	0.2465	No
5	ETH	5.402	0.0201	Yes
6	LINK	3.043	0.0811	No
7	LTC	16.622	0.000	Yes
8	USDT	75.683	0.000	Yes
9	XLM	20.695	0.000	Yes
10	XRP	17.468	0.000	Yes

Source SPSS output table, compiled by author

cryptocurrencies.

From Table 3 indicated ARCH effects for Cardano, Ethereum, Litecoin, Tether, Stellar, and Ripple. The null hypothesis of no ARCH effects at a 5% significance level was rejected.

Subsequently, we proceeded with the EGARCH models for identifying the leverage effect. Table 4 presents the EGARCH model for return and volatility estimation.

We observe (Table 4) that the past returns influence the mean returns thereby indicating that the market is inefficient. The positive significance of §1 coefficient for all cryptocurrency returns indicates that past volatility has a very high influence on present volatility. The dependency of current volatility on past volatility indicates the risk associated with cryptocurrency investment. Further, this behavior indicates that the cryptocurrency market is not efficient, even in the weak form of EMH since past information affects future prices. Similarly, the $\gamma 1$ parameter examines the leverage effect and almost all cryptocurrencies exhibit a higher leverage effect. The relatively higher significant coefficient of $\gamma 1$ for Stellar and Ripple reveals destabilizing effect due to new information. Asymmetric information has stronger effect in these two currencies as evident by the larger value of $\gamma 1$ than $\alpha 1$. The pandemic has severely affected the volatility of currencies as seen by the significance of time zone T4. However, the announcement of relief measures by various governments has a very less significant influence on Cardano, Ethereum, and Litecoin. This is seen by the value of time zone T5. The T5 influence is insignificant on other cryptocurrencies.

Table 4 EGARCH (1,1) model for cryptocurrencies

Parameters	ADA		ETH		LTC	
	Coefficient	p-value	Coefficient	p-value	Coefficient	p-value
□	−0.0004	0.603	0.0067	0.000	0.0025	0.013
r_{t-1}	−0.1063	0.027	−0.1194	0.000	−0.1714	0.001
C1	−1.3011	0.026	−0.1897	0.000	−0.2465	0.000
$\alpha 1$	−0.0084	0.911	0.1193	0.000	0.1577	0.000
§1	0.7722	0.000	0.9694	0.000	0.9606	0.000
$\gamma 1$	0.3986	0.000	0.0817	0.053	0.0103	0.820
T1	0.0190	0.024	0.0088	0.124	0.0113	0.015
T2	0.0057	0.105	0.0085	0.177	0.0013	0.825
T3	−0.0037	0.727	−0.0586	0.000	−0.0576	0.000
T4	−0.1341	0.000	−0.0541	0.000	−0.0032	0.857
T5	0.0135	0.000	0.0024	0.354	0.0043	0.007
Parameters	USDT		XLM		XRP	
	Coefficient	p-value	Coefficient	p-value	Coefficient	p-value
□	0.0001	0.006	0.0021	0.465	0.0009	0.211
r_{t-1}	−0.3188	0.000	−0.9484	0.194	−0.1072	0.050
C1	−0.3978	0.040	−1.9854	0.002	−1.8570	0.000
$\alpha 1$	0.0142	0.773	0.0491	0.502	0.0056	0.937
§1	0.9611	0.000	0.6584	0.000	0.6875	0.000
$\gamma 1$	0.4480	0.000	0.7543	0.000	1.0299	0.000
T1	0.0001	0.772	0.0144	0.057	0.0219	0.000
T2	−0.0001	0.962	0.0073	0.401	0.0061	0.001
T3	0.0026	0.012	−0.0053	0.606	0.0031	0.694
T4	0.0132	0.000	−0.1133	0.000	−0.1073	0.000
T5	−0.0003	0.127	−0.0015	0.717	−0.0009	0.665

Source SPSS output table, compiled by author

5 Conclusion

The study identified that most of the cryptocurrency returns are market inefficient during the COVID-19 pandemic. Lack of market efficiency in the lowest form raises a question about the ability of cryptocurrencies for investment and as a hedge against risk. The conditional volatility modeling also provided evidence of market inefficiency. A higher leverage effect was observed in cryptocurrency returns. Findings will help policymaking and regulations in cryptocurrency investment with different investors' perspectives. Future research can also consider how different attributes and associated characteristics of each cryptocurrency influence its price and volatility.

References

Baek, Chung, and Matt Elbeck. 2015. Bitcoins as an investment or speculative vehicle? A first look. *Applied Economics Letters* 22 (1): 30–34.

Bariviera, Aurelio F. 2017. The inefficiency of Bitcoin revisited: A dynamic approach. *Economics Letters* 161: 1–4.

Baur, Dirk G., and Brian M. Lucey. 2010. Is gold a hedge or a safe haven? An analysis of stocks, bonds and gold. *Financial Review* 45 (2): 217–229.

Beneki, Christina, et al. 2019. Investigating volatility transmission and hedging properties between Bitcoin and Ethereum. *Research in International Business and Finance* 48: 219–227.

Bouri, Elie, et al. 2017. On the hedge and safe haven properties of Bitcoin: Is it really more than a diversifier? *Finance Research Letters* 20: 192–198.

Caporale, Guglielmo Maria, et al. 2018. Persistence in the cryptocurrency market. *Research in International Business and Finance* 46: 141–148.

Charfeddine, Lanouar, and Youcef Maouchi. 2019. Are shocks on the returns and volatility of cryptocurrencies really persistent? *Finance Research Letters* 28: 423–430.

Chaim, Pedro, and Marcio P. Laurini. 2019. Is Bitcoin a bubble? *Physica a: Statistical Mechanics and Its Applications* 517: 222–232.

Chan, Wing Hong, Minh Le, and Yan Wendy Wu. 2019. Holding Bitcoin longer: The dynamic hedging abilities of Bitcoin. *The Quarterly Review of Economics and Finance* 71: 107–113.

Conlon, Thomas, and Richard McGee. 2020. Safe haven or risky hazard? Bitcoin during the COVID-19 bear market. *Finance Research Letters* 35: 1–5.

Corbet, Shaen, Yang Greg Hou, Yang Hu, Charles Larkin, and Les Oxley. 2020. Any port in a storm: Cryptocurrency safe-havens during the COVID-19 pandemic. *Economics Letters* 194: 109377.

Corrado, Charles J., and Thomas W. Miller Jr. 2005. The forecast quality of CBOE implied volatility indexes. *Journal of Futures Markets: Futures, Options, and Other Derivative Products* 25 (4): 339–373.

de Almeida, Daniel, and K Luiz Hotta. 2014. The leverage effect and the asymmetry of the error distribution in GARCH-based models: The case of Brazilian market related series. *Pesquisa Operacional* 34 (2): 237–250.

Derbali, Abdelkader, and Slaheddine Hallara. 2016. Day-of-the-week effect on the Tunisian stock market return and volatility. *Cogent Business and Management* 3 (1): 1147111.

Dyhrberg, Anne Haubo. 2016. Bitcoin, gold and the dollar—A GARCH volatility analysis. *Finance Research Letters* 16: 85–92.

Foley, Sean, J.R. Karlsen, and T.ālis J. Putniņš. 2019. Sex, drugs, and bitcoin: How much illegal activity is financed through cryptocurrencies? *The Review of Financial Studies* 32 (5): 1798–1853.

Gandal, Neil, et al. 2018. Price manipulation in the Bitcoin ecosystem. *Journal of Monetary Economics* 95: 86–96.

Geuder, Julian., Harald. Kinateder, and Niklas. F. Wagner. 2019. Cryptocurrencies as financial bubbles: The case of Bitcoin. *Finance Research Letters* 31.

Guidi, Francesco, Rakesh Gupta, and Suneel Maheshwari. 2011. Weak-form market efficiency and calendar anomalies for Eastern Europe equity markets. *Journal of Emerging Market Finance* 10 (3): 337–389.

Karmakar, Madhusudan. 2007. Asymmetric volatility and risk-return relationship in the Indian stock market. *South Asia Economic Journal* 8 (1): 99–116.

Kristoufek, Ladislav. 2018. On Bitcoin markets (in) efficiency and its evolution. *Physica a: Statistical Mechanics and Its Applications* 503: 257–262.

Lahmiri, Salim, and Stelios Bekiros. 2020. The impact of COVID-19 pandemic upon stability and sequential irregularity of equity and cryptocurrency markets. *Chaos, Solitons and Fractals* 138: 109936.

Liu, Weiyi. 2019. Portfolio diversification across cryptocurrencies. *Finance Research Letters* 29: 200–205.

Mariana, Christy Dwita, Irwan Adi Ekaputra, and Zaäfri Ananto Husodo. 2021. Are Bitcoin and Ethereum safe-havens for stocks during the COVID-19 pandemic? *Finance Research Letters* 38: 101798.

Narayan, Paresh Kumar, Ruipeng Liu, and Joakim Westerlund. 2016. A GARCH model for testing market efficiency. *Journal of International Financial Markets, Institutions and Money* 41: 121–138.

Selgin, George. 2015. Synthetic commodity money. *Journal of Financial Stability* 17: 92–99.

Sensoy, Ahmet. 2019. The inefficiency of Bitcoin revisited: A high-frequency analysis with alternative currencies. *Finance Research Letters* 28: 68–73.

Shiller, Robert J. 1981. The use of volatility measures in assessing market efficiency. *The Journal of Finance* 36 (2): 291–304.

Smales, Lee A. 2019. Bitcoin as a safe haven: Is it even worth considering? *Finance Research Letters* 30: 385–393.

Tiwari, Aviral Kumar, Ibrahim Dolapo Raheem, and Sang Hoon Kang. 2019. Time-varying dynamic conditional correlation between stock and cryptocurrency markets using the copula-ADCC-EGARCH model. *Physica a: Statistical Mechanics and Its Applications* 535: 122295.

Umar, Zaghum, and Mariya Gubareva. 2020. A time–frequency analysis of the impact of the Covid-19 induced panic on the volatility of currency and cryptocurrency markets. *Journal of Behavioral and Experimental Finance* 28: 100404.

Urquhart, Andrew. 2016. The inefficiency of Bitcoin. *Economics Letters* 148: 80–82.

Vasileiou, Evangelos, et al. 2021. Health risk and the efficient market hypothesis in the time of COVID-19. *International Review of Applied Economics* 35 (2): 210–223.

Wei, Wang Chun. 2018. Liquidity and market efficiency in cryptocurrencies. *Economics Letters* 168: 21–24.

Yang, Hu., Harold Glenn A. Valera, and Les Oxley. 2019. Market efficiency of the top market-cap cryptocurrencies: Further evidence from a panel framework. *Finance Research Letters* 31: 138–145.

Zhang, Wei, Pengfei Wang, Xiao Li, and Dehua Shen. 2018. The inefficiency of cryptocurrency and its cross-correlation with Dow Jones industrial average. *Physica a: Statistical Mechanics and Its Applications* 510: 658–670.

Business Revolution in Post-COVID Era: An Evolving Economy Outlook

Jonika Lamba and Esha Jain

1 Introduction

COVID19 has transformed the communal and business landscape globally and it can be noticed in the way businesses shifted to the E-commerce business model. The economy of the country has been badly impacted due to disturbance in the global supply change, turbulent market conditions, and swift demand and supply of products and services. The policies, procedures, and strategies have been modified to match the modern and much-needed ways of working. Digitalizahtion is one of the business solutions opted by every successful entrepreneur and big boon industrialist to accelerate the business operations which can be digitalized. The pandemic proves out to be bountiful for digital leaders and contributed to the field of machine learning, cloud computing, artificial intelligence, distributed cloud, and automation, etc. The need of the hour for business is to continuously monitor the market stimulations and remain focused on rapid innovation by meeting the demands of people, to provide a seamless digital user experience. The economy of the nation was falling, and it was expected India might enter a phase of recession. India's GDP is expected to contract by 7.7% in the fiscal year 2020–21. The 7.7% contraction if it materializes, would mark India's worst economic performance since 1961–62. With a different degree of sternness, the turbulent market situations have inserted undue pressure on the companies to continuously monitor the uncertain consumer demands and frame policies, procedures, and strategies accordingly. Post-COVID-19 must have an extremely egalitarian comprehensive knowledge, transformative, and politics at its center (Leach et al. 2021). The new normal depends on innovative and rousing business improvement and the transformation of business operations is the only way to survive this pandemic phase. The COVID19 influence is going to have a long-lasting impact on customer's psychology (Jain and Lamba 2020). The pandemic

J. Lamba (✉) · E. Jain
The NorthCap University, Gurugram, India

R. N. Subudhi et al. (eds.), *Future of Work and Business in Covid-19 Era*,
Springer Proceedings in Business and Economics,
https://doi.org/10.1007/978-981-19-0357-1_3

transmits an enormous sequential implication, by being situated at the convergence of numerous organized global changing aspects, e.g., emergency for the supportable environment, healthcare systems, and industrial economics (Kamal 2020).

2 Review of Literature

2.1 *Influence of COVID19 on Financial Markets*

COVID-19 connected impetus and bailouts, with the attendant rise in government-backed funding amenities for counterparties (Caldecott 2020). The stockholders do not want to capitalize in the share market because everyone wants liquidness (Jain 2020). Growing financial disparity and the decrease of generous egalitarianism are elements shared to both industrialized and developing nations (Murshed 2020).

2.2 *Transformation of Tourism and Travel Sector Amid COVID19*

The COVID-19 plague hit the travel business brutally. Brouder (2020) talked about vital notions in evolutionary fiscal layout, especially track necessity/formation and recognized inertia/invention, showed distinctions in ways for tourism and travel in an aftermath COVID-19 pandemic world that the travel business may transmute into a novel worldwide fiscal order categorized by maintainable tourism, humanity's well-being, weather action, and the contribution of domestic societies. Studies outlined four bulbous aspects for building resilience in commerce–consumer–employee confidence, technology innovation, government response, and local belongingness (Sharma et al. 2020).

2.3 *Impact of COVID19 on the Education Industry*

B-schools in Republic of India are formulating themselves to overwhelm with short-range tasks confronted due to COVID-19 and transmuting themselves through long-standing approaches (Rana et al. 2020). The phase of learning was continued without any disruption during COVID19 and there was continuous upgradation of skills of teachers and students by the adoption of the online education system (Jain and Lamba 2020). Jain and Lamba (2021) also talked about the initiative of MHRD Innovation cells which helped in boosting the entrepreneurial skills in the period of COVID-19.

2.4 The Emergence of Digital Technology Amid COVID19

The upsurge of the Internet of Things (IoT) has been widely used in COVID19 phase to meet emerging technology's needs (Allam and Jones 2021). Supporting the capability of governments, commerce, and broader humanity to endure to function and role within the COVID-19 plague is a dependence on IS expertise (Dwivedi et al. 2020). Organizational complexity and employee burnout remain the biggest hurdle to progress. The five vital detections for the post-pandemic commercial countryside can be digital revolution was at no time just about the technology, the human component is the key to success, the traumatic strain had commandeered business approach, few will do it unaccompanied, and well-being and safety are novel solutions to sustainability (Anderson et al. 2020). Narula et al. (2021) aimed to identify and classify the noteworthy tests connected with application of Industry 4.0 (I4.0) know-hows in the health industry and planned a mind map and theoretical prototype of ladder and interdependences of trials linked with the digital revolution of the medical maneuver industry towards Industry 4.0. The influence of digitalization is probable to be transversal to each area and will inspire the development of novel digital products and facilities built on the belief of elasticity. Cybersecurity and confidentiality will become two key fundamentals that will back the integrated growth of IoT technology resolutions, artificial intelligence, big data, and robotics (Almeida et al. 2020). Diverse forms of AI (mechanical, thinking, and feeling) might open distinct research streams at the connection of health crises and hotel administration, considering the COVID-19 pandemic (Jiang and Wen 2020). The development of energy capability in digitalization is approving financial growth but repentantly also the energy stresses the custom (Klemeš et al. 2020). COVID-19 is seen as a prospect for tough change, which appeals novel data practices athwart a range of balances of communal action (Milne and Costa 2020). Even the customers from the banking sector prefer e-banking during and post-COVID-19 (Jain and Lamba 2021).

2.5 Outlook of Human Resource Department in Pandemic Period

COVID-19 has persuaded a changeover to telework, looming office design and conformation reversals, and office working decorum re-engineering. Management approaches imitate ranking choices between work-related health and safety versus economic returns. Beyond official accountability reports, office management approach and rationales will become substantially observable and answerable to office staff and other gatherings (Parker 2020). There is a need to rebuild our social paradigms through SDGs after the COVID-19 pandemic to recognize the new possibilities of development focused on human factors (Contipelli and Picciau 2020). Arora and Suri (2020) provided the basis for dealing with the COVID-19 contagion associated with administrative working. Digital expertise decays, trials, and improves work toward supreme efficiency and authorizes workforces that involve in fluid work preparations and take custody of expertise, their education, and their life paths (Wang et al. 2020).

2.6 Post-COVID 19 Global Business Revolution

The pandemic timeframe has elevated the necessity for a grave discussion on the imminent future of the worldwide dogmatic order (Bukhari and Bukhari 2020). McNamara and Newman (2020) struggled that globalization desires to be seen not just as a distributional game of champions and failures but rather a more intensely revelational game that redesigns selves, creates new places for contentious politics and redefines systems of power and authority. Transformative travel and tourism as an ever-growing drift appear to be a significant standard through which these artistic creatives reinvent themselves and the ecosphere, they live in. The dream of relating regenerative agriculture and transformative tourism is accessible to rearrange the worldwide tourism system for good (Ateljevic 2020). Defiance accepted toward the disaster, the faces of the business and the businessperson, the associations with institutions, human and social capital, and strategic management can be measured in working out programs for resilient entrepreneurs (Castro and Zermeño 2020). There is an opportunity to treatise some of the weakness of globalization through an additional provincially built international budget offering an improved equilibrium between national and global prosperities, and flexibility in international supply chains, efficiency and between, exhaustiveness, equity bearings, and expansion (Enderwick and Buckley, 2020). Ferrannini et al. (2021) contended that a revolving fact on the construction between industrial policy, development, and sustainability has been grasped, permanenting the necessity to reconsider its theoretic fundamentals as well as its domination and application procedures for a novel role in the Post-COVID 19 cultures. Ibn-Mohammed et al. (2020) identified the hazard of trusting on COVID-19 affiliated aids in attaining sustainable development goals and highlighted a necessity for a pivotal, important structural alteration to the subtleties of how we live. The micro, small and medium enterprises (MSMEs) have the potential to support the economy in the period of global downfall and liquidity crisis as they can produce in large quantum at relatively less investment (Lamba and Jain 2020). Globalization desires to be seen not just as a distributional game of champions and failures but rather a more intensely revelational game that redesigns selves, creates new places for contentious politics, and redefines systems of power and authority (McNamara and Newman 2020). Many of the teachings that arose from the pandemic can be functional to policies to contract with the weather change (Prideaux et al. 2020; Zahra 2021). Supply Chain Network Viability (SCV) is the chief principle for dealing with buyer–supplier rapport and ornamental survivability of SSCs throughout and post-COVID-19 conditions (Sharma et al., 2020).

3 Objectives for the Study

The study has been taken on to accomplish the below-mentioned objectives:

1. To study the role of digital leaders in facilitating technology-related transformation.
2. To examine the hardship faced by different sectors in the COVID19 contagion and what remedial actions have been taken in wake of a pandemic.
3. To explore the post-pandemic opportunities for businesses.

4 Materials and Methods

The information collected in this study has been taken from reliable springs of secondary data collection including former studies. The study is a descriptive analysis of the post-COVID-19 opportunities for enterprises and the role of digital leaders in the transformation of business.

5 Role of Digital Leaders in COVID19 Pandemic

Change is the only thing in the world that is constant. The transformation initiatives of the digital leaders are opening new business opportunities in terms of strengthening customer relationships and partnering avenues. Business leaders should learn from disruption in the economy, continuously changing customer needs and an unprecedented pace of revolution. The leaders in the phase of COVID19 should prioritize their requirements for speed and litheness. Timely capture of opportunities is the only mantra for success and survival in tough times of pandemic. The leaders should capitalize on the digital competencies of the corporates and meet the expectations of the consumers. COVID19 created a sagacity of urgency around digital transformation. Changes made by big organizations in wake of the COVID19 pandemic are as follows:

- Enhanced process mechanization.
- Paradigms shift to Digitalization of business operations.
- Swing to cloud-based business operations.
- Attuned to their tactic to change management.
- Eternal changes made to business strategies.
- Positive attitude toward crisis management.
- Managing enterprise agility.
- Focusing on new product development and identifying new product markets.
- Growing partnering networks

6 Survival Strategies for Significant Industries in Post-COVID 19 Pandemic Period

1. Automobile Industry

Rapid response has been undertaken by the automobile sector to deal with current disruption and declining sales. The potential risk should be identified and dealt with precautions to adapt to the new normal phase.

- Companies should maintain relations with their customers via mobile and online channels.
- Reconsidering sales models for the future, espousal digital networks as well as considering direct turnover models.
- In the wake of the post-pandemic period, there will be undue pressure on the dealers to reduce the stock and the price of the models will also witness a sharp decline. The business managers should analyze monetary incentives in the form of discounts that can be given to stabilize the sales and maintain the brand image.
- Contactless sales should be fostered to meet health and hygiene safety requirements.
- Virtual Car events should be promoted to compensate for the loss suffered due to the cancelation of trade shows.

2. Banking Industry

The banking sector has been hard hit due to financial distress in the economy during COVID19 pandemic. People were not able to repay their loans on time due to delays in salary and layoffs. Outside India, banks in foreign countries created provisions in the rest of nonperforming assets considering prevailing financial catastrophe. Banks need substantial, analytical, and personalized credit management to help customers, satisfy the stakeholders and facilitate the transformation process in the economy. The following actions can be taken by banks to maintain balance in the economy:

- With the assistance of automation, data, and analytics banks will be able to address the real risk of each customer's business and environment.
- Machine learning mechanism should be used to render esteemed (high net worth and corporate) client's high-end treatment.
- Framing policies to quickly manage the upcoming credit wave due to less cash flow during the period of lockdown.
- Acclimating credit and collection policies to contemplate a broad range of aspects rather than concentrating only on asset recovery.

3. Tourism Industry

The tourism sector is one of the biggest economic contributors in the world. The people are fond of traveling but during COVID19 pandemic the tourism sector saw a drastic decline due to novel coronavirus. People chose to stay at home instead of going outside. Post-pandemic recovery is full of uncertainty. The travel companies have responded in the following ways to relinquish the impact of novel coronavirus.

- Frame an agile, vision-rich enterprise while mitigating costs and enhancing operational efficiencies with constant and repeatable processes.
- Providing flexibility into ways of doing work that turn out to be effective and efficient leading to a satisfied workforce. The workforce will be able to adapt to changing situations.
- Formulate a retail marketing appliance and front-end stands to encompass products and services, rationalize purchases, spread income, and build trustworthiness.
- Giving vouchers and discounts to loyal customers in wake of financial hardship.
- Recuperate astronomical customer involvements across travel journey from dream and book to vacation, trustworthiness, and beyond.
- Shift from old IT systems to cloud-based designs and use technology to break silos, decrease costs, boost elasticity, and expand performance.

4. Healthcare Industry

The foremost sector which required utmost attention during COVID-19 is the health care sector. With everything going digital health services were also offered online with emerging mobile-based applications such as Practo, MFine, and Healthians. The global pandemic greatly accelerated the adoption of digital healthcare services to meet the norms of contactless meetings. With most in-person care visits on hold, the use of online care services exploded during the crises. To flatten the curve on the behavioral health crisis, the population should be encouraged to prefer virtual health channels in wake of novel coronavirus.

- Emerging Information techniques such as cloud computing should be a business concern in modern health systems for the future.
- Forward rational health players are using near-term revolutions to redefine their business and functional models for novel coronavirus and aftermath.

5. Education Industry

The various e-learning apps such as BYJU'S, Unacademy, Udemy, and edX students have now got rid of the outmoded approaches of learning, i.e., textbook and white-board culture. The concerned e-learning app has now fetched video lectures and enlightening games which aid the pupils in inspiring their minds and get further absorbed in the learning.

- Online teaching is a platform that is removing the geographical barriers, teachers at any corner of the world can deliver lectures to the students located dispersedly.
- In the era of technology, the use of advanced emergent tools and techniques brings new energy to the medium of communication. Multimedia is growing in every assorted field to improve the impact of messages. It facilitates the transformation of information that is stored, diffused, and treated digitally.
- The advancement in multimedia systems in the pandemic phase leads to integrated audio and video with the aid of digital computing. Multimedia learning has eased the process of delivery of lectures in schools and colleges more competently. The use of digital technology in the education industry has transformed the learning process and methods.

- There is a need to establish a practical teaching system that is appropriate for practical universities in preschool schooling, use multimedia expertise to regulate practical teaching purposes from unresolved topographies, concentrating on capacity structure, and increasing investment.

6. Telecom and Communication Industry

After the eruption of the COVID-19 catastrophe, telecom companies have played a pivotal role in keeping the world linked, employed, and well-versed. Communication service providers (CSP) have augmented the level of faith patrons place in them. They have recouped fame as patrons recognize that the services, they render facilitate their financial and communal well-being. It provides clear guidance for digital leaders in the telecom industry on how to best outflank ambiguity at this crucial phase of the COVID19 crisis as they moved from rapid response to future business bounciness. The communication sector is focused on increasing revenue and growth drivers, enriching the customer experience, edifice a digital workforce, seizing the potential of the persistent network, and leveraging the supremacy of the cloud across the entire business to sustain CSPs to emerge stronger from novel coronavirus pandemic.

- The Telecom sector has entered a partnership with the government of India to extend, accelerate and enhance connectivity.
- The pervasive networks have saved costs through digital platforms and Artificial Intelligence-powered networks.
- It has created incremental revenue opportunities leveraging 5G and cloud computing technologies.
- The communication sector must revisit mission and vision statements to incorporate the changing business scenario due to deadly disease novel coronavirus.
- Bring next-generation retail omnichannel experience and quicken customer relocation to digital with immersive Computer-generated Store.
- It has redesigned customer operations to facilitate remote working.
- It has enabled the work from the home economy with increased connectivity, security, and remote working solutions.
- It has played a tactical role in the progress of connected businesses (telemedicine, public service, education).

Findings

- In the wake of a novel coronavirus, businesses need to be transformed into digital businesses to support enterprise sales and profitability.
- The focus should be to maintain continuous liaison with the customers via online channels.
- COVID19 pandemic has augmented the trend toward e-commerce rather than brick-and-mortar sales.
- Contactless sales should be fostered to meet health and hygiene safety requirements.
- Adapting to changing business scenarios is the mode of survival and success in the COVID19 pandemic period.

- The strategies, policies, and procedures should be redefined in the wake of novel coronavirus to meet changing customer preferences.
- Shift from old IT systems to cloud-based designs and use technology to break silos, decrease costs, boost elasticity, and expand performance.
- Giving vouchers and discounts to loyal customers in wake of financial hardship.
- It was found that the communication sector has played a crucial role to uplift other sectors in the economy. It has kept people connected during a period of crisis.
- The contraction of GDP can be rectified by an enhanced government fiscal deficit.
- COVID19 has augmented the espousal of fully digitized methods to re-create the greatest of in-person learning through real-time videos and communal sharing.
- The digital transformation makes it likely to gauge learning efforts in a more lucrative way and licenses greater personalization for beginners and in turn superior efficacy.
- The healthcare sector had led to telehealth technology, teletherapy, virtual fitness, and gyms.
- COVID19 pandemic has led to branchless banking, parametric insurance, and contactless payments.
- In the wake of the COVID-19 pandemic e-learning start-ups are emerging and reported substantial growth in the crisis period.

7 Solutions and Recommendations

COVID-19 has badly influenced the Indian economy and it will take time to stabilize the situation. It requires the support of regulatory bodies and the public to fight against this situation of economic catastrophe. Businesses are required to set up a professional crisis management plan that includes proactive measures to handle the financial distress and control anxiety of individuals. The foremost priority of any business should be the well-being of its employees that includes alternative working infrastructure (i.e., work from home) and proper medical support in the time of hardship. Commercial organizations need to prepare themselves for the unexpected such as disruption in supply chains, it can be overcome by formulating recovery plans, leverage digital ecosystems, reimagine the supply chain model, and frame policies to work even in the time of disruption supply chains. Due to financial distress, there is a need to keep backups for budget deficits by making business financial plans more agile and companies should look for near-term capital raising, refinancing of loans, and credit support from the government and banks. Adoption of proactive communication leads to the reduction of penal liabilities associated with the customer obligations. Business continuity plans and the adoption of the digital revolution will help in overcoming this pandemic outbreak.

8 Conclusion

The study has enlightened how businesses have transformed their operations in the wake of the COVID-19 pandemic. Learning and development (L&D) have provided immense opportunities to corporates to capitalize and exploit them in the best manner. The crisis has created an atmosphere that can be viewed as frightening and electrifying. The pandemic has created the need for rethinking, reflecting, and re-engineering. There is uncertainty when this pandemic slows down or end, business needs to keep themselves ready to meld their business operations in wake of financial distress. In businesses from health care to teaching to investment to engineering, lockdown, and social distancing norms are forcing companies to adopt a digital platform to reimagine nearly every facet of their business operations. The pathway to recovery was difficult to determine in the initial phase of COVID19 but continuous efforts of government and support of technocrats have provided relief in tough times. The need of the hour for business is to continuously monitor the market stimulations and remain focused on rapid innovation and try to meet the demands of people in the post-COVID19 eras, to provide a seamless digital user experience. The new normal depends on innovative and rousing business improvement. As the process of vaccination is about to start and resurrecting begins in fits and starts, businesses would be thriving in a post-COVID-19 world.

References

Allam, Zaheer, and David S. Jones. 2021. Future (post-COVID) digital, smart and sustainable cities in the wake of 6G: Digital twins, immersive realities and new urban economies. *Land Use Policy* 101: 105201.

Almeida, Fernando, José Duarte. Santos, and José Augusto. Monteiro. 2020. The challenges and opportunities in the digitalization of companies in a post-COVID-19 world. *IEEE Engineering Management Review* 48 (3): 97–103.

Anderson, Cindy, Christian Bieck, and Anthony Marshall. 2020. How business is adapting to COVID-19: Executive insights reveal post-pandemic opportunities. *Strategy and Leadership*.

Arora, Pallvi, and Divij Suri. 2020. Redefining, relooking, redesigning, and reincorporating HRD in the post Covid 19 context and thereafter. *Human Resource Development International* 23 (4): 438–451.

Ateljevic, Irena. 2020. Transforming the (tourism) world for good and (re) generating the potential 'new normal.' *Tourism Geographies* 22 (3): 467–475.

Brouder, Patrick. 2020. Reset redux: Possible evolutionary pathways towards the transformation of tourism in a COVID-19 world. *Tourism Geographies* 22 (3): 484–490.

Bukhari, Shahid Hussain, and Syed Mussawar Hussain. Bukhari. 2020. The post-corona world and international political landscape: Emerging challenges. *Journal of Business and Social Review in Emerging Economies* 6 (2): 453–461.

Caldecott, Ben. 2020. Defining transition finance and embedding it in the post-Covid-19 recovery. *Journal of Sustainable Finance and Investment* 1–5.

Contipelli, Ernani, and Simona Picciau. 2020. *Post-COVID-19: Rebuilding Our Paradigms Through Sustainable Development Goals and the Sufficiency Economy Philosophy*. IndraStra Global.

Castro, May Portuguez, and Marcela Georgina Gómez Zermeño. 2020. Being an entrepreneur post-COVID-19–resilience in times of crisis: a systematic literature review. *Journal of Entrepreneurship in Emerging Economies.*

Dwivedi, Yogesh K., et al. 2020. Impact of COVID-19 pandemic on information management research and practice: Transforming education, work and life. *International Journal of Information Management* 55: 102211.

Enderwick, Peter, and Peter J. Buckley. 2020. Rising regionalization: Will the post-COVID-19 world see a retreat from globalization?. *Transnational Corporations Journal* 27(2).

Ferrannini, Andrea, et al. 2021. Industrial policy for sustainable human development in the post-Covid19 era. *World Development* 137: 105215.

Ibn-Mohammed, T., et al. 2020. A critical review of the impacts of COVID-19 on the global economy and ecosystems and opportunities for circular economy strategies. *Resources, Conservation and Recycling* 105169.

Jain, Esha. 2020. Analysing the impact of covid-19 on stock market using Fibonacci retracements. *ACADEMICIA: an International Multidisciplinary Research Journal* 10 (5): 249–265.

Jain, Esha, and Jonika Lamba. 2020. COVID 19 and e-banking: Psychological impact on customer preferences in India. *Psychology and Education Journal* 57 (8): 1160–1169.

Jaromír Klemeš, Jiří, Yee Van Fan, and Peng Jiang. 2020. COVID-19 pandemic facilitating energy transition opportunities. *International Journal of Energy Research.*

Jain, Esha, and Jonika Lamba. 2021. MHRD's initiative IIC contribution towards innovation in higher educational institutions during COVID 19. *IARS' International Research Journal* 11 (1): 63–69.

Jain, Esha, and Jonika Lamba. 2021. Management and digitalization strategy for transforming education sector: an emerging gateway persuaded by COVID-19. In *Emerging Challenges, Solutions, and Best Practices for Digital Enterprise Transformation*, pp. 69–83. IGI Global.

Jiang Yangyang, and Jun Wen. 2020. Effects of COVID-19 on hotel marketing and management: A perspective article. *International Journal of Contemporary Hospitality Management.*

Kamal, Muhammad Mustafa. 2020. The triple-edged sword of COVID-19: Understanding the use of digital technologies and the impact of productive, disruptive, and destructive nature of the pandemic. *Information Systems Management* 37 (4): 310–317.

Kathleen R. McNamara, and Abraham L. Newman. 2020. The big reveal: COVID-19 and globalization's great transformations. *International Organization* 1–19.

Lamba, J., and E. Jain. 2020. Covid-19 pandemic-bountiful for MSMES and Indian economy. *Purakala Journal* 31 (33): 89–94.

Leach, Melissa, et al. 2021. Post-pandemic transformations: How and why COVID-19 requires us to rethink development. *World Development* 138: 105233.

Lee D. Parker, 2020. The COVID-19 office in transition: Cost, efficiency and the social responsibility business case. *Accounting, Auditing and Accountability Journal.*

Milne, Richard, and Alessia Costa. 2020. Disruption and dislocation in post-COVID futures for digital health. *Big Data and Society* 7 (2): 2053951720949567.

Newman, A.O. 2020. Covid, cities and climate: Historical precedents and potential transitions for the new economy. *Urban Science* 4 (3): 32.

Prideaux, Bruce, Michelle Thompson, and Anja Pabel. 2020. Lessons from COVID-19 can prepare global tourism for the economic transformation needed to combat climate change. *Tourism Geographies* 22 (3): 667–678.

Sanjiv Narula, et al. 2021. Modeling and analysis of challenges for industry 4.0 implementation in medical device industry to post COVID-19 scenario. *International Journal of Supply and Operations Management.*

Sharma, Manu, et al. 2020. Developing a framework for enhancing survivability of sustainable supply chains during and post-COVID-19 pandemic. *International Journal of Logistics Research and Applications* 1–21.

Sudhir Rana, et al. 2020. A perspective on the positioning of Indian business schools post COVID-19 pandemic. *International Journal of Emerging Markets.*

Wang, Blair, et al. 2020. Beyond the factory paradigm: Digital nomadism and the digital future (s) of knowledge work post-COVID-19. *Journal of the Association for Information Systems* 21 (6): 10.

Zahra, Shaker A. 2021. International entrepreneurship in the post Covid world. *Journal of World Business* 56 (1): 101143.

Green Accounting in India as a Measure of Attaining Sustainable Development Goals

Meghna Chotaliya

1 Introduction

Green accounting also called environmental accounting is an accounting term used to measure the environmental accounting to incorporate the natural and environmental assets of the firm and its resources. The process commences with identification of the environmental parameters of a business, defining the environmental parameters, specifying the environmental targets to be achieved, developing the environment performance indicators, measuring the environmental performance results through various means and finally reporting the environmental performance results. The environmental clearance from state government has taken a central stage. As per the Indian Constitution, Article 51A of directive principles of state policies says that it is the duty of every citizen of India to protect and improve natural environment, which includes forests, lakes, rivers and all natural resources and wildlife. This fundamental duty is enforced by means of various legislations which exist in India.

Moreover, the Ministry of Environment and Forests at both state and central level issues guidelines to existing and new projects to obtain environmental and anti-pollution clearance before the commencement of the business. However, the ground reality is different as only a handful of businesses in India actually provide adequate information about the environmental issues. With respect to the Millennium Declaration signed in September 2000 by 189 countries gathered at the United Nations headquarters, the commitment to achieve a set of eight measurable goals that range from halving extreme poverty and hunger to promoting gender equality and reducing child mortality was undertaken by the target date of 2015 which were then converted into "Sustainable Development Goals (SDGs)" by the participating member countries, and various measures were undertaken by the government of these countries

Meghna Chotaliya (✉)
Assistant Professor, R.D. National College, Bandra West, Mumbai, India
e-mail: meghna.chotalia@rdnational.ac.in

R. N. Subudhi et al. (eds.), *Future of Work and Business in Covid-19 Era*,
Springer Proceedings in Business and Economics,
https://doi.org/10.1007/978-981-19-0357-1_4

starting from 2000 and were given a deadline of 15 years to achieve these goals by 2015. This paper seeks to understand the impact of sustainable development measures with reference to selected variables of environment for selected nations from 2015 so as to understand the success rate of these measures by the government of these countries in mitigating environmental degradation while undertaking economic development.

2 Review of Literature

Numerous studies in the past have been carried out on green accounting/environmental accounting in India and other countries with emphasis on different aspects such as methods of environmental accounting and impact of green accounting. According to Jui-Che and Huang, green accounting will lead to a proactive environmental planning through reduction on environmental cost and have stated that unlike financial accounting which is mandatory and is costly; green accounting is voluntary and has become mainstream under the popular demand of CSR. However, green accounting has led to additional 86 costs which is related to environmental recovery. Negash (2012) has examined whether IFRS can be used for monitoring environmental degradation, and by referring the case of three environmentally sensitive companies found that the sustainability reports produced by companies contained information and also propaganda and so also the size and adequacy of the contribution of these companies toward sharing of costs of environment related to decommissioning, rehabilitation and restoration was not disclosed. Craig and Glasser (2017) have analyzed the transfer models for green accounting as an approach to environmental policy analysis for decisions making, and this model has emphasized on both stocks and flows as a framework to green accounting stressing on the need for sustainable utilization of forest and other resources.

Very few studies have been undertaken to measure Sustainable Development Goal achievement by green accounting aspects of countries across the world due to the fact that these practices vary from country to country, and there are no uniform practices to measure the same across the globe.

3 Objective of the Study

This study is undertaken to fulfill the following objectives:

(i) To study the impact of sustainable development measures on energy-related CO_2 emissions of selected countries from 2015 to 2019
(ii) To study the impact of sustainable development measures on greenhouse gas emissions of selected countries from 2015 to 2019

(iii) To study the impact of sustainable development measures on forest resource stocks of selected countries from 2015 to 2019

4 Research Methodology

The present study seeks to examine the impact of sustainable development measures taken by selected countries in view of the Millennium Development Goals (MDGs). Though 191 United Nations member countries aimed to achieve the Millennium Development Goals, for this study selected countries are taken as a sample, namely India, China, Brazil, USA and UK. The study is done to compare the impact of sustainable development measures as a result of implementation of MDGs. Since the Millennium Development Goals were adopted in the year 2015, the period selected for this study comprises the years 2015 and 2019 so as to analyze the impact of MDGs on sustainable development by measuring different environmental variables before the implementation and post-implementation till 2019, the latest year for which data is available.

1. **Variables used**: The variables selected for this study pertaining to sustainable development and environmental accounting are:
   - Cumulative carbon emissions (CO_2)
   - Greenhouse gas emissions
   - Forest resource stocks (cubic meters, millions).

     Further, an analysis of CO_2 emissions of Annex countries and non-Annex parties is done. Annex parties are those which include the industrialized countries that were members of the OECD in 1992 and also countries in transition, whereas non-Annex parties are mostly the developing countries like India
2. **Statistical method used**: The statistical techniques used for hypothesis testing are: mean, standard deviation and t-test (one-tailed) for testing the significance of growth in different variables
3. **Sources of data**: Secondary data was collected for the study from various published sources such as Government of India (GOI) reports on Environment, viz. EnviStats India 2019 and other journals, magazines and newspapers.

5 Hypotheses of the Study

The following hypotheses were framed for the study:

H_1: There is no significant impact of the Sustainable Development Goals on levels and growth of CO_2 emissions from 2015 to 2019 for the selected countries.

H_2: There is no significant impact of the Sustainable Development Goals on levels and growth of greenhouse gas emissions from 2015 to 2019 for the selected countries.

H_3: There is no significant impact of the Sustainable Development Goals on levels and growth of CO_2 emissions of Annex countries as compared to non-Annex countries from 2015 to 2019.

H_4: There is no significant impact of the Sustainable Development Goals on levels and growth of forest resources stocks from 2015 to 2019 for the selected countries.

6 Data Analysis and Hypothesis Testing Using t-test of Significance (One-Tailed)

The data collected for emissions of CO_2 for the selected five countries is presented in Table 1, and average and standard deviation of the data on emissions are found so as to compute the value of *t*-test.

1. **H_1**: There is no significant impact of the Sustainable Development Goals on levels and growth of CO_2 emissions from 2015 to 2019 for the selected countries. To test this null hypotheses, we compare the *t* value (as shown in Table 1) with the table value for *t* for 8 degree of freedom $(5-1)+(5-1)=8$ at 5% (0.05) level of significance, and it is found that the *t* value 0.6342 is less than the table value (1.860) for one-tailed test and hence the difference cannot be considered to be significant.

   Hence, the null hypothesis stands accepted that there is no significant growth and change in carbon emissions of selected countries post-implementation of sustainable development measures. It signifies that these measures were having an impact on controlling the growth of CO_2 emissions from 2015 to 2019.
2. **H_2**: There is no significant impact of the Sustainable Development Goals on levels and growth of greenhouse gas emissions from 2015 to 2019 for the selected countries. To test this null hypothesis, we compare the *t* value (as shown in Table 2) with the table value for *t* for 8 degrees of freedom $(5-1)+(5-1)=8$ at 5% (0.05) level of significance, and it is found that the *t*

Table 1 Table showing energy-related emissions cumulative CO_2 emissions of select countries in the pre- and post-implementation period of Millennium Development Goals (MDGs)

Country	2015	2019
India	1,523,766.56	2,100,849.73
China	4,057,617.00	11,895,765.00
Brazil	756,663.68	1,027,739.00
United States	7,216,645.32	6,638,132.74
Europe	716,796.65	511,273.61
Average	*2,854,297.842*	*4,434,752.016*
Std Dev	*2,793,624.278*	*4,821,050.76*
T-test	*0.6342*	

Source SPSS output table, compiled by author

Table 2 Table showing greenhouse gas emissions in the pre- and post-implementation period of the MDGs

Country	2015	2019
India	905	2066
China	3284	9085
Brazil	299	451
United States	5605	4998
United Kingdom	3224	2641
Average	*2663.4*	*3848.2*
Standard deviation	*2123.369*	*3351.143*
T-test	*0.6678*	

Source SPSS output table, compiled by author

value 0.6678 is less than the table value (1.860) for one-tailed test and hence the difference cannot be considered to be significant. Hence, the null hypothesis stands accepted that there is no significant growth and change in greenhouse gas emissions of selected countries post-implementation of sustainable development measures. It signifies that these measures were having an impact on controlling the growth of greenhouse gas emissions from 2000 to 2015.

3. $\mathbf{H_3}$: There is no significant impact of the Sustainable Development Goals on levels and growth of CO2 emissions from 2000 to 2015 for the selected countries. To test this null hypothesis, we compare the t value (as shown in Table 3) with the table value for t for 8 degrees of freedom $(2 - 1) + (2 - 1) = 2$ at 5% (0.05) level of significance, and it is found that the t value 0.6678 is less than the table value (2.92) for one-tailed test, and hence, the difference cannot be considered to be significant. Hence, the null hypothesis stands accepted that there is no significant growth and change in greenhouse gas emissions of Annex member countries post-implementation of sustainable development measures. It signifies that these measures were having an impact on controlling the growth of CO_2 emissions from of these two categories of countries from 2015 to 2019
4. $\mathbf{H_4}$: There is no significant impact of the Sustainable Development Goals on levels and growth of forest carbon stocks from 2015 to 2019 for the selected countries. To test this null hypothesis, we compare the t value (as shown in Table 4) with the table value for t for 8 degrees of freedom (2 − 1) + (2

Table 3 Table showing energy-related emissions cumulative CO_2 emissions of Annex and non-Annex parties in the pre- and post-implementation period of Millennium Development Goals (MDGs)

Countries	2015	2019
Annex parties	13,560	12,407
Non-Annex parties	9101	18,701
Average	*11,330.5*	*15,554*
Standard deviation	*3152.989*	*4450.53*
T-test	*1.0951*	

Source SPSS output table, compiled by author

Table 4 Table showing forest carbon stocks (in cubic meters in millions) for selected countries in the pre- and post-implementation period of Millennium Development Goals (MDGs)

Country	2015	2019
India	4662.00	5167.00
China	12,348.30	16,002.40
Brazil	100,804.10	
United States	35,556.00	40,699.00
United Kingdom	480.00	652.00
Average	*30,770.08*	*15,630.1*
Standard deviation	*41,431.12*	*17,910.97*
t-test	*0.75003*	

Source SPSS output table, compiled by author

− 1) = 2 at 5% (0.05) level of significance, and it is found that the t value 0.75003 is less than the table value (1.860) for one-tailed test, and hence, the difference cannot be considered to be significant. Hence, the null hypothesis stands accepted that there is no significant growth and change in forest carbon stocks of selected countries post-implementation of sustainable development measures. It signifies that these measures did not have a major impact on the growth of forest stock resources.

7 Conclusion

It is a well-accepted fact that economic development and ecology do not go hand in hand, and some amount of environmental degradation is inevitable in the process of commercial development. However, the purpose of Sustainable Development Goals is to reduce if not totally mitigate the harmful impact of environmental resource degradation and misuse to the maximum possible extent. Due to the fact that environmental accounting is at the nascent stage across the world though some countries do comply with the environmental protection laws. For sustainable development, a proper accounting procedure for environmental resources is a must. The findings of this study are presented by means of hypotheses testing in the table below:

Hypothesis (null hypothesis)	Status
H_1	Accepted
H_2	Accepted
H_3	Accepted
H_4	Accepted

The above table shows that there is a significant impact of the execution of Sustainable Development Goals on different resources of the countries under study for the said period under study. However, much remains to be done to this end to achieve the SDGs as can be seen from the above analysis with regard to these important environmental variables. However, the major limitation of this study is the selection of limited environmental variables due to time and constraint; however, there are other important environmental variables such as forest cover, freshwater resources, livestock, land resources among others which need attention as these have a major impact on environment. Also there are other countries which are not taken into consideration in this study—both developed and developing due to time constraints. Significant policies and measures and its strict implementation by the government of major countries is a major step which can ensure sustainable development.

References

Chen, Y.S., S.B. Lai, and C.T. Wen. 2006. The influence of green innovation performance on corporate advantage in Taiwan. *Journal of Business Ethics* 67: 331–333.

Clarkson, P.M., Li, Y., Richardson, G.D., and Vasvari, F.P. 2008. Revisiting the relation between environmental performance and environmental disclosure: an empirical analysis. *Accounting, Organizations and Society*, 303–327

Craig, Paul P., and Harold Glasser. (1994). Transfer models for "Green Accounting": An approach to environmental policy analysis for sustainable development. *Assigning Economic Value to Natural Resources.* National Academics of Science, Engineering and Medicine.

Environmental Protection Agency. 1995. *An Introduction to Environmental Accounting as a Business Management Tool: Key Concepts and Terms.* Office of Pollution Prevention and Toxics, EPA 742-R-95–001.

Negash, Minga. 2012. IFRS and environmental accounting. *Management Research Review* 35 (7): 577–601.

Tarun, and Ramu. (2018). A study of green accounting: A way to sustainable development. *International Journal of Pure and Applied Mathematics* 119 (17): 509–518

Tu, Jui-Che, and Hsieh-Shan Huang. 2015. Analysis of the relationship between green accounting and green design for enterprises. *Sustainability*, 6264–6277

United States Environmental Protection Agency. 1995. *An Introduction to Environmental Accounting as a Business Management Tool: Key Concepts and Terms.* Washington.

Forecast of Foreign Direct Investment of India Through ARIMA Under COVID-19 Pandemic

Ronismita Mishra and Swapnamoyee Palit

1 Introduction

A batch of occurrence of pneumonia of exotic elements around the downtown of Wuhan (Hubei territory of China) was disclosed to the World Health Organisation (WHO) on 31 December 2019. In January 2020, this exotic new virus was recognized and consequently named the Novel Coronavirus 2019. In February 2020, this Novel Coronavirus (nCov) was named Coronavirus Disease 2019 (COVID-19) by the World Health Organization. This virus is attributed to SARC-COV-2, and the related disease is COVID-19. This COVID-19 was declared as a pandemic by the WHO and worldwide support, and coordination was needed to stop the spread of this virus. Around 162 countries are fixedly impelled into lockdown since then and trade across the globe merged in the panic of a crash approaching the Global Financial Markets. This gave rise to stagnant economic growth and extremely volatile market conditions in developing countries like India spiralled by an increasing rate of interest, unemployment rate, and fiscal deficit. The fuel to this fire was added by sending tremors down the Indian trade market reliant on China for import following the worldwide mobility restrictions. In India, approximately 55% of the electronic items are imported from China, and due to this outbreak of COVID-19 and continuous lockdown, this import declined to 40%. On the other hand, in the exportation of raw materials like mineral fuels, organic chemicals, cotton, etc. China is considered the third-biggest export partner of India, and this pandemic and subsequent lockdown drive to trade arrears for India. Nearly, 70% of Active Pharmaceutical Ingredients (APIs) is imported from China, which is an important raw material for many Indian pharmaceutical manufacturing companies in the country. As there was no sufficient

R. Mishra (✉) · S. Palit
Department of Economics, KIIT University, Bhubaneswar, India

S. Palit
e-mail: spalitfhu@kiit.ac.in

R. N. Subudhi et al. (eds.), *Future of Work and Business in Covid-19 Era*,
Springer Proceedings in Business and Economics,
https://doi.org/10.1007/978-981-19-0357-1_5

APIs to manufacture medicines, the trade and the market perceived catapulting prices. Similarly, with the suspension of visa and continuous shut down to tourist flow, entire restaurants, hotels, agents, and sectors related to tourism value chain is anticipated to incur a huge loss in thousands of crores. Another notable fact is that after the declaration of tourist visa suspension by the Government of India, airlines started functioning under huge pressure with the cancellation of around 600 international flights over an indefinite period. Nearly, 90% of domestic flights have been cancelled, showing a decline in airline fares, and several of them running into huge losses were propelled to go for mass retrenchment, wage cut, and non-payment being weighed down by the economic yoke. The pandemic has hard hit several sectors with closures or slowed down activities and most importantly the flow of financial capital through the Foreign Direct Investment (FDI). This paper makes a focussed analysis of the compositional and directional impact of the on-going pandemic on the FDI of India in several sectors. It forecasts FDI using ARIMA for the next 10 years to throw light on its future potentiality and buoyancy.

2 Review of Literature

Relating to the impact of India's FDI policy on sector-specific issues, Masharu and Nasir (2018) find that the liberalization of the Indian economy has provided sustainable development and diversification to the economy of India. This has been beneficial in general to the service sector and retail sectors in particular. They recommend the provision of an unrestrictive investment environment for more FDI inflows to all sectors for the growth of the Indian economy. Jana et al. (2019) investigated the impact, focusing on sector-wise FDI inflows rather than the overall inflow. They find that inward FDI does not contribute to the growth rate of agricultural output, but observed a reverse causality where the growth rate in the agricultural sector attracts FDI inflows. They recommend the rejuvenation of the primary sector through appropriate policy measures. Similarly, it is found to contribute to a positive growth rate in the manufacturing sector and observed a two-way causality in the case of the service sector.

Some interlinking factors exist between the inward and outward FDI of India as is evident from the fact that most of the top FDI sectors were found to be common between them. These factors are like the government's FDI policies towards these sectors, the performance of these sectors over the years, the market size, etc. Thus, the sectors which are capable of investing overseas are mostly those which show a domestic performance over the years. Thus, adequate government policies towards developing the identified potential sectors are the road to enable the country to emerge as a global leader in overseas investment (Palit 2019).

India's apt move to amend the FDI policies during the pandemic to prevent opportunistic takeovers by financially hegemonistic and global dominance desirous nations though would go a long way to prevent such overt attempts, but the actual impact in terms of preventing these investments routed through third party countries or other economic garb remains to be observed with time (Saxena 2020).

The eruption of pandemic COVID-19 as brought the social as well as economic life to a dead end. Chaudhary et al. (2020) attempted to examine the impact of COVID-19 on the different spheres of the economy like tourism, aviation, capital market, retail, oil, and Micro, Small, and Medium Enterprises (MSME). Internal and external mobility are restrained, and the total revenue provoked by the tourism and travel was 9.2% of the GDP. Revenue generated by aviation was reduced by USD 1.56 billion and from oil it was reduced to USD 22 per barrel. Foreign Portfolio Investors have restrained their investments around USD 571.4 million in India. It leads to a deficit in the current account and depreciation of the Indian rupee. Due to this pandemic, many people lost their jobs, daily ration, and avenues of social securities. Despite the negative effect, every pandemic comes with new opportunities to restore the path of development for communities, society, and human beings. COVID-19 provides opportunities for self-reliance, sustainable development, environment-friendly and inclusive frameworks. Poddar and Yadav (2020) analysed the relationship between the outbreak of COVID-19 and its impact on the Indian economy, and they found that there is a consequential relationship between the occurrence of COVID-19 and the decline in the Indian economy. India is failing to meet its growth rate expected in the last two financial years. The consequence of COVID-19 is exaggerating the financial condition of the country even more than decay. As a result of this pandemic, India will rack up USD 348 million on its trade and this figure will increase even further with the extension of the period of lockdown, locally as well as globally.

In their study, authors Aneja and Ahuja (2020) examines the significance of COVID-19 on the society as well as the overall sphere of the Indian economy by taking primary, secondary, and tertiary sector accompanying with health, poverty, environment, information sector, job losses, and migrants. All the spheres of the economy have been immensely affected, and the loss is extravagant. At the same time, society has to sacrifice a lot in terms of mental illness, job losses, and increased domestic violence. There is also some positive effect observed during this pandemic in the form of improved air and water quality, the sustainability of wildlife, people's good habits, and environment-friendly attitudes.

As the whole world is in the clench of coronavirus, various economic hardships and acute ramification ought to be standing by the Indian firms in this deteriorating pecuniary condition. Rakshit and Paul (2020) analysed the business survival strategies to overwhelm this stiff situation and the basis on which the Indian economy can be benefited during this pandemic. Business strategies are adopted by industries to cope up with the adverse situation, and every industry should fortify for the challenges and uncertainties which are trimming off due to this pandemic. They required catching and arresting apparent forthcoming changes in business, and to strive and thrive, they should identify the opportunities.

Das and Patnaik (2020) analysed the impact of COVID-19 on the GDP growth rate in India by applying various statistical tools and techniques. From their finding, it is observed that India's GDP reduced its bottom in over 6 years during 2019–20, and GDP for next year (2020–21) is anticipated in between 5.3% to 5.7%. In the current situation, COVID-19 deprived 4% permanent change to real GDP in India, the sustenance of the numerous employees is at peerless hazard, and much more have lost their jobs.

Dev and Sengupta (2020) analysed the economic system of India in pre-COVID-19 periods, investigated the significant strike of COVID-19 over different sections of the nation, and examined the strategy that has been declared by the federal and state government and RBI to rectify the fiscal shocks. The unreliable conditions of the economy, especially in the financial sector and the dependence on periodical lockdowns and social distancing measures, are revolved to be a huge risk. At the same time, policymakers are required to prepare effective policies to minimize the adverse impact of the COVID-19 both on the informal and on the formal sectors and for uninterrupted recovery.

FDI procreates maximum job possibilities in the tertiary sector compared with any other sector in India, the major lead taken by banking and insurance sector followed by the telecommunication sector. The consequences of this research indicate that the job creation in India over the past couple of decades is relatively observable, and at the same time, inflows of FDI might not be contemplated as a substantial component for this growth rate. Consequently, the Indian authorities have adopted several governmental measures to enthral job possibilities in India primarily the informal sector. India ought to stimulate its legislative framework by promoting its monetary and fiscal policies. India needs to adopt affirmative business climates for appealing further FDI in India (Mishra and Palit 2020).

3 Methodology

This paper uses secondary data from various sources like Reserve Bank of India, United Nation Conference on Trade and Development (UNCTAD)'s handbook of statistics, World Bank, and various online journals. The data analysis is done using econometrics and statistical softwares packages of R studio and eviews for forecasting and other analysis. It has used time series FDI data from 1980 to 2020 for forecast using ARIMA modelling.

4 Findings of the Study

The findings of the study are presented in this section divided into two parts with the analysis of the impact of the COVID-19 pandemic on the direction and composition of FDI in India in Sect. 4.1, while Sect. 4.2 makes the forecast of FDI and discusses its implications.

4.1 *Analysis of the Impact on Direction and Composition of FDI Flows in India*

There is an extensive interruption to FDI inflows, particularly in developing countries following COVID-19, disrupting the benefits of economic globalization. Market demand and supply are in turmoil following the adoption of containment measures. As a result, global production channels are being disturbed on a massive scale, never observed, and attested before. Interruption to FDI flows, which is a major part of economic globalization, became obvious fallout. Since the starting of the COVID-19 crisis in late march 2020, a declaration made by the International Monetary Fund (IMF) shows that investors had detached USD 83 billion from developing countries which is a huge capital crush ever reported. According to the UNCTAD, world FDI flows are anticipated to reduce by 30% to 40% during the period 2020–21. It will ultimately affect all the sectors in the economy with the economic adversities particularly hitting the consumers' supply chain like restaurants, hotels, airlines, manufacturing industries, and the energy sectors due to the sharp decline in FDI to these sectors. As per the data released by the Organisation for Economic Cooperation and Development (OECD), global FDI rose in 2019, but the rate grappled due to COVID-19. In comparison with 2017, FDI flows have reduced by 15% as per the drift ascertained since 2015. FDI influx to the OECD countries improved by 6% since 2005, and effusions from OECD countries improved by 62% in 2019 as USA outlets were restored at a positive level. However, FDI inflows to non-OECD G-20 countries reduced by 9% and outflows reduced by 19% due to discontinuance and decline in capital flows from and to China. Despite grasping favourable outcomes from economic support and public health measures taken by the governments to handle the situation of the pandemic, FDI flows are anticipated to decrease by 30% in 2020 across the globe. According to the OECD database, FDI is anticipated to reduce, and this leads to emphasizing and stimulating the substantial reduction of FDI stocks realized in the last five years due to the decline in reinvested earnings. There are mainly two factors that determine the amount of reinvested earnings which are (i) the earnings of direct investments in industries and (ii) the share that the direct investor chooses to reinvest. The earnings of large Multi-National Companies (MNCs) are anticipated to reduce during the first and second quarter of 2020, but the impact varies in different sectors. The information collected by Definitive-2020 for companies in S&P 500 including the largest MNCs in the globe shows that there is a decline in earnings in the consumer discretionary sector, energy, materials, and industrial sectors. The share of earnings investor chooses to reinvest is also expected to reduce during the COVID-19 crisis. Due to the financial crisis, the share of earnings that were invested decreased from 45% in 2007 to 24% in 2008 due to some industries "constant amount of earnings, and some other industries" distributed high share of earnings to support other parts of the MNCs. That is why, it is anticipated that the share of earnings that are invested will decline in the first half of 2020 in the globe.

India's FDI policy is more flexible than the world, and in this pandemic, the country could captivate more than USD 22 billion value of FDI as per the announcement made by Amitabh Kant, CEO of NITI Aayog on 8 August 2020. He also announced that about 90% of the 22 billion US dollars' worth of FDI in India over this pandemic is channelised by the Automatic Route. It has appeared as a pre-eminent destination for FDI as per the research carried out by the Confederation of Indian Industries (CII) for MNCs. This survey revealed that India is likely to become one of the leading three favourable terminuses for FDI flows by the year 2025. As per this survey, around 67% of the MNC appellants regarded India as their top preference for future investments, whereas more than 25% of foreign MNC appellant regarded India as their first choice for future investment. According to this survey, 80% of all the appellants and 71% of non-India appellants decided to invest globally by the year 2023 and about 30% of the enterprises are decided to invest more than ₹3,700 Cr (USD 500 million). As the pandemic beat sthe economy, the influx of FDI has, however, endured delicately. As per the statistics revealed by the Department for Promotion of Industry and Internal Trade (DPIIT), India's FDI inflows reduced by 60% year-by-year to USD 6.56 billion (₹49,820 Cr) from 16.33 billion US dollar over April–June quarter. Therefore, it is anticipated that FDI inflows in India may reduce accordingly during the financial year 2021 due to the lockdown.

Table 1 shows that during the year 2019–2020, India has obtained the highest FDI of 49.9 billion US dollars since 2009–10. Also reflected in Fig. 1, this has been an increase of 11.02% over 2018–19. This was preceded by falling percentages from an increase of 25.75% in 2015–16 to 2.90% in 2018–19 followed by negative growth of 0.90% in 2018–19. After the starting of the United Progressive Alliance (UPA)'s second stretch, India's FDI inflows have been observing an adrenaline-changed structure. However, the FDI contribution in GDP persists to endure in the reach of 1.6% to 1.7% for the past 3 years.

Table 2 depicts the month-wise FDI inflows in India in pre-pandemic and Pandemic period. It is reflected that the FDI inflows were high in March than February

Table 1 FDI Inflows in India 2010–2020

Year	FDI inflows (USD billion)	% change over the previous years
2009–10	25.8	–
2010–11	21.4	−20.56
2011–12	35.1	39.031
2012–13	22.4	−56.70
2013–14	24.3	7.82
2014–15	29.7	18.18
2015–16	40.00	25.75
2016–17	43.5	8.04
2017–18	44.8	2.90
2018–19	44.4	−0.90
2019–20	49.0.9	11.02

Source DPIIT and UNCTAD data compiled in excel

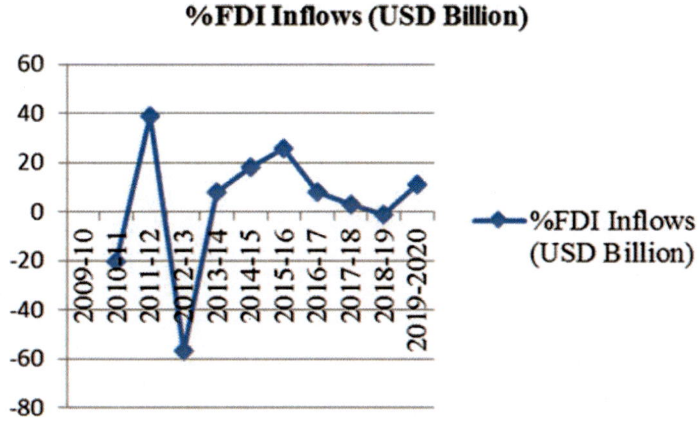

Fig. 1 % change of FDI inflows over the during the period previous years in India (2010–2020). *Source* DPIIT and UNCTAD database

Table 2 Depiction of month-wise FDI inflows in India in pre-pandemic and pandemic period

Months	Jan	Feb	Mar	Apr	May	Jun	Jul	Aug	Sep	Oct	Nov	Dec
2018–19 (in USD billion)	4.4	2.9	3.6	5.4	4.5	2.9	2.8	2.5	4.6	4.7	1.7	4.4
2019–20 (in USD billion)	5.6	3.4	4.3	5.2	3.8	7.3	4.5	2.5	2.7	3.2	2.8	4.6

Source DPIIT and UNCTAD database

2020 despite a one-week lockdown. The financial year 2020 began with a decline in FDI inflows month by month, with the second month attending a downfall. During September and October 2020, FDI inflows reported a decline of 41% and 32%, respectively.

India has occupied an eighth place in terms of being a destination nation for receiving inward FDI in 2019 with a 14.28% increase relative to the inflows in 2018 (Table 3).

India is proceeding with an eighth place in the globe in the year 2019, whereas France and Canada interchanged their position as seventh and ninth in 2018 and 2019. Canada and Germany gave an immense contention to India for the eighth place.

Analysing the impact on the direction of inward FDI during the pandemic period relative to its earlier position, some changes are observed as is shown in Table 4. However, it would be worth mentioning here that these changes are not only a fall out of the current pandemic situation and adopted coping strategies, but also a consequence of the FDI policies adopted by the government preceding the pandemic year, whose effect is observed in subsequent years.

After the implementation of the India–Mauritius Treaty, Cayman Island is replaced by Singapore as the topmost roots of FDI in India. Over the year 2019, Singapore bestowed a double of FDI received from Mauritius and it decreased a little in 2020. During the same period, Cayman Island and Cyprus intensified their position over the year. Singapore became apparent as the highest root of FDI in India

Table 3 India's position in terms of FDI inflows (2018–19)

Country	2018 (USD billion)	2019 (USD billion)	FDI Growth in % (2019 over 2018)
USA	254	251	−1.19
China	139	140	0.71
Singapore	78	110	29.09
Brazil	60	75	20
UK	65	61	−6.55
Hong Kong	104	55	−89.09
France	37	52	28.85
India	42	49	14.28
Canada	43	47	8.51
Germany	12	40	70

Source DPIIT and UNCTAD database

Table 4 Top FDI investing countries in India (in USD billion during 2017–2020)

Country	2017–18	2018–19	2019–2020
Singapore	12.2	16.2	14.7
Mauritius	15.1	8.1	8.2
Netherlands	2.8	3.9	6.5
USA	2.1	3.1	4.2
Cayman islands	1.2	1.0	3.7
Japan	1.6	2.9	3.2
France	0.5	0.5	1.9
UK	0.8	1.3	1.4
Cyprus	0.4	0.3	0.9
Germany	1.1	0.9	0.5

Source DPIIT and UNCTAD database

amounting to 14.67 billion US dollar investments during the last financial year. It has now been pursued by Mauritius with 8.24 million US dollars, the Netherlands with 6.5 billion US dollar, the USA with 4.2 billion US dollar, Cayman Island with 3.7 billion US dollar, Japan with 3.2 billion US dollar, and France with 1.89 billion US dollar. FDI becomes paramount as the nation needs huge investment to modernize its infrastructure sector to improve its growth.

In terms of the impact on the composition of FDI, it is observed that the sector which captivates more FDI inflows in India during the period 2019–20 includes the service sector with 7.85 billion US dollar, computer software and hardware with 7.67 billion US dollar, telecommunication with 4.44 billion US dollar, trading with 4.57 billion US dollar, the automobile with 2.82 billion US dollar, construction with 2 billion US dollar and chemical with 1 billion US dollar as per the data released by DPIIT. The service sector together with computer software and hardware attracted

Table 5 Sector-wise FDI inflows in India during 2017–2020 in USD Billion

Sectors	2017–18	2018–19	2019–2020
Service	6.7	9.1	7.85
Computer software and hardware	6.1	6.4	7.67
Telecommunication	6.2	2.7	4.44
Trading	4.3	4.5	4.57
Automobile	2.1	2.6	2.82
Construction	2.7	2.2	2.00
Chemicals	1.3	1.9	1.00

Source DPIIT database

31% of FDI in India during the pandemic situation (Table 5). The pandemic has unrevealed several new areas of foreign investment as well as the expansion potentialities of several pre-existing sectors and organizations. Some of these emerging and opportunity exploring features are as follows:

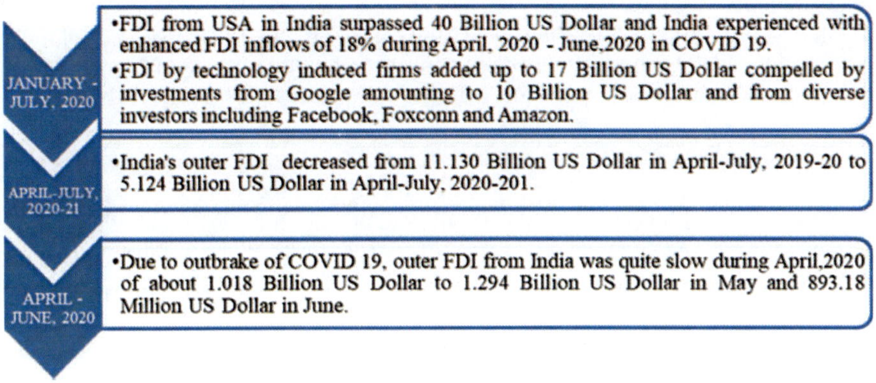

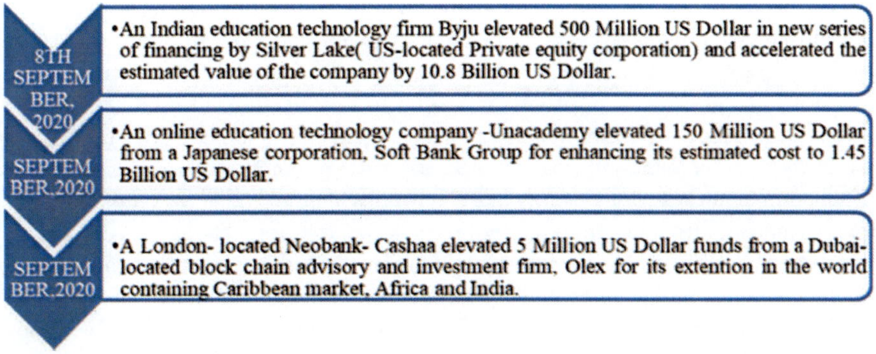

Indian government made some changes in FDI policy to check the excessive takeovers and investment by Chinese capitalists like Xiaomi, Tencent, and Alibaba in Ola, Bigbasket, Paytm, Byju's, Dream11, MakeMy Trip, and Swiggy towards follow-financing. This is also anticipated to decrease the investment inflows in mergers and acquisitions along with new industries in the country. There are mainly three approaches through which Chinese capital enters into India, which are 100% FDI in establishing manufacturing plants or getting shares in listed or unlisted Indian companies or a share through Foreign Institutional Investor (FII). India's policy adoption towards Chinese FDI into the country during the pandemic may twist the Chinese investment into India. As per the notification released by India's authorized trade and investment regulatory body, the Department of Promotion for Industry and Internal Trade (DPIIT), India is now effecting mandatory formal endorsement for whole overseas investment from riparian countries. This step was taken by the Indian Government after realizing China's intention to obtain capital in core industries around the globe, as nations strive during pandemic COVID-19. At the same time, India is appearing as a strong opportunity to China for investment in sourcing and manufacturing industries. Germany, European Union, Australia, Spain, Italy, and France have earlier taken steps to retaliate against this drive by constricting their overseas investment policies. Additionally, DPIIT notified that transmit of appurtenance of any existing or perceptive FDI in an entity in India either expressly or implicitly will need mandatory approvals from the government, and investors of neighbouring countries of India will require government's approvals for taking forwards their investments in the country in future.

Up to December 2019, aggregate investment of China in India increased by USD 8 billion and with the adoption of a new strategic partnership, it is expected that the new restricted investment policy could disturb the bilateral trade relations and foreign investments in the country. But as expert believes that, this change may not affect the industry in the long run. It is essential to know that, FDI from China is not outlawed, but a scan approach has now been proposed to evaluate the significance of investment, as all nations over the globe are attempting to handle the difficulties raised by the pandemic by ensuring security and economic stability.

India's decision may hamper liquidation in Indian firms, exclusively in the start-ups and indigenous unicorns. A minimum of 18 out of 23 of India's new businesses including Snapdeal, Ola, Paytm, Zomato, Swiggy, and Big basket are supported by foremost Chinese investors as Ant Financial, Alibaba, and Tencent. At the same time, India is appearing as a feasible investment terminus for foreign companies as a further investor is trying to escape from China due to COVID-19 and political management issues. About 1000 foreign companies are actively involved in discussion with the Indian government and an estimated 300 foreign companies are ensuring their production plans in various sectors like electronics, medical devices, synthetic fabric, textiles, and smartphones in India. India has initiated different strategies comprising three stratagems for electronic manufacturing worth 6 billion US dollars to expand its internal manufacturing, to captivate overseas investments, and to appear as a prime production and manufacturing centres, hoisting a silver lining even in this gloom stricken global economic ambiguity. Its apt steps to armour against opportunistic

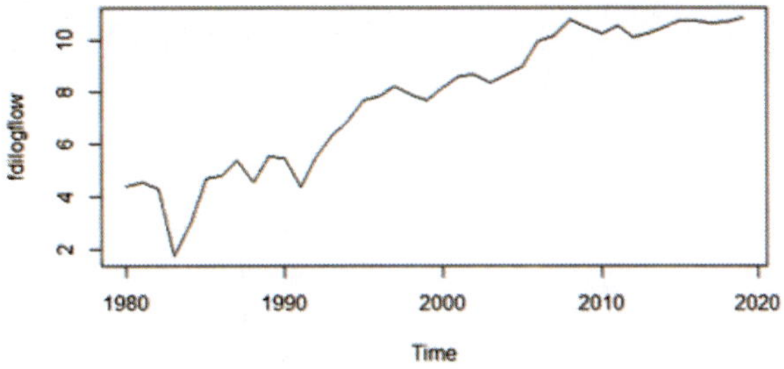

Fig. 2 Non-stationary FDI data (log transformation): 1980–2020. *Source* UNCTAD data, compiled in R studio

shadowing of its companies by competing nations during the pandemic are the right move. Also, it has to tap all the existing and emerging areas which possess the potential to attract and absorb huge foreign investment for development. The following sections make a forecast of the FDI flow into India to anticipate its extent of resilience over the future years.

4.2 *Forecasting by ARIMA Model of FDI in India*

The data analysis in this section is done by using the R studio. It has used the time series FDI data from 1980 to 2020 to forecast for the next 10 years. The FDI data are the inward annual Foreign Direct Investment flows in US dollars at current prices in millions, available in UNCTAD Handbook of Statistics 2019–20. The log transformation of the FDI data (lnFDI) was taken to handle the heteroskedasticity presence in time series data. The lnFDI variable is found to be non-stationary as reflected in Fig. 2, displaying a trend upward.

The non-stationary feature of this time series data is supported by the autocorrelation function (ACF) and the partial autocorrelation function (PACF) tests conducted. Figure 3 shows the presence of significant autocorrelation as the spikes are crossing over the blue lines till almost 15 years lag period. As for the PACF (in Fig. 4), it shows the significant autocorrelation for the first lag period.

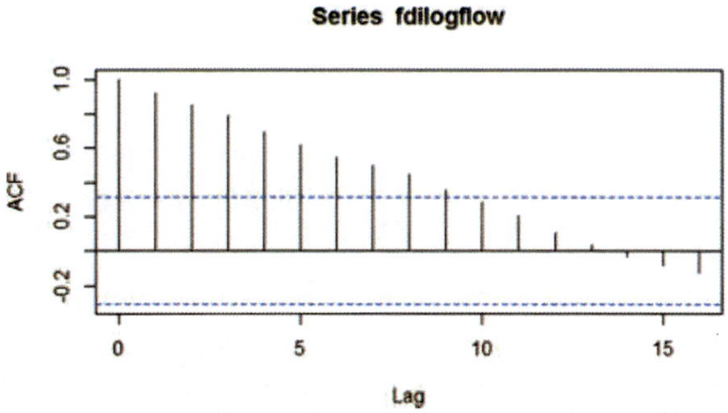

Fig. 3 ACF for autocorrelation test *Source* UNCTAD data, compiled in R studio

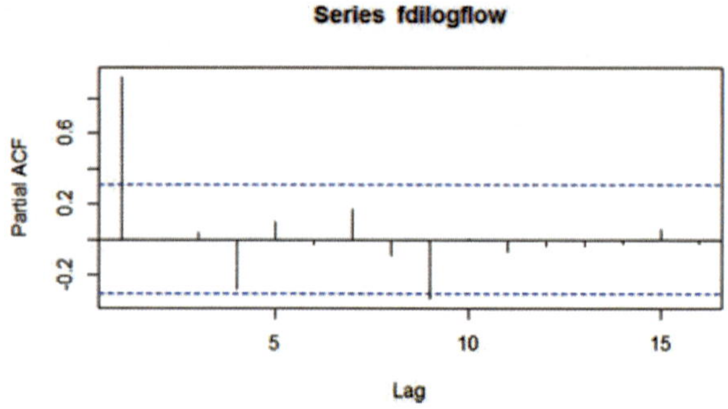

Fig. 4 Partial autocorrelation test *Source* compiled in R studio

The Augmented Dickey–Fuller Test (ADF) also shows p value >0.05, and thus, we fail to reject the null hypothesis that 'time series of FDI is non-stationary'.

[Dickey–Fuller = −1.9658, Lag order = 3, p value = 0.5869 (alternative hypothesis: stationary)].

The ARIMA model to forecast the future values of FDI requires the data to be stationary. The data were observed to be stationary after the first-order differencing. The log-transformed FDI values are used to fit the model. It has been worked out using the R studio. The best ARIMA model identified is ARIMA (0, 1, 0) with drift which has the lowest Akaike Information Criteria (AIC) value as shown below (Table 6).

The features of the best-fitted model, ARIMA (0, 1, 0) with drift is as follows: The model identified is a random walk with drift. Thus, the predicted values are represented by the model:

$$Y_t' - Y_{t-1} = \mu$$

or

$$Y_t' = \mu + Y_{t-1},$$

Table 6 Best ARIMA model identified by R studio

ARIMA models	AIC value
ARIMA(2,1,2) with drift	Inf
ARIMA(0,1,0) with drift (Best model)	**87.2122**
ARIMA(1,1,0) with drift	88.97043
ARIMA(0,1,1) with drift	88.73069
ARIMA(0,1,0)	87.31779
ARIMA(1,1,1) with drift	Inf

Source compiled by R studio

where Y_t' represents the predicted Y values as a function of its own past values lagged by 1 with coefficient 1, plus a drift (μ) which represents the average of the period to period change, that is the long-term drift in Y_t values. Thus, it can be regarded as a special case of AR (1) model. Given the following information,

Coefficients: drift 0.1656 (s.e. 0.1126), our model can be represented as

$$Y_t' = 0.1656 + Y_{t-1}$$

Sigma^2 estimated as 0.5075: log likelihood = -41.61; AIC = 87.21 AICc = 87.55 BIC = 90.54.

The stationarity of this best-fitted ARIMA model with drift is shown in Figs. 5 and 6 with the same ACF and PACF test repeated. Now, all the spikes are found to be within the blue lines except the first period lag of the residuals. The PACF test shows no significant autocorrelation with any lag periods in Fig. 6.

Forecast of the FDI with the best-identified ARIMA with drift (0,1,0) model is shown in the following Table 7 with the lower and higher confidence level limits at 95% confidence level.

The plot of the forecasted FDI data is given in Fig. 7 which shows an increase over the years from 2020 to 2029. This obviously is a silver lining showing the potentiality of the country to expect the inward flow of the FDI. However, a clearer analytical expectation can be drawn from Fig. 8 which shows the plot of the log reconverted

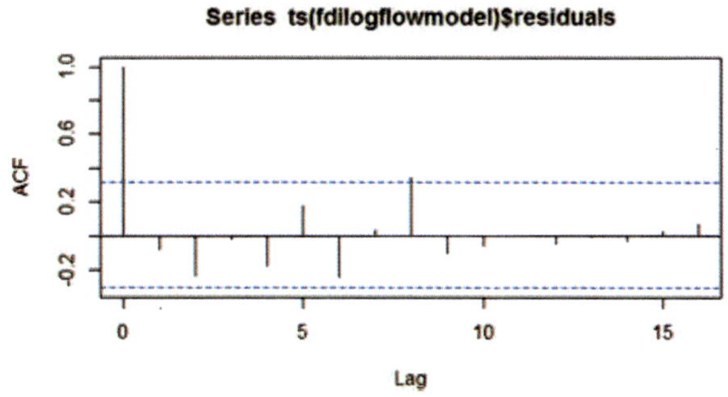

Fig. 5 ACF of the ARIMA with drift mode *Source* UNCTAD data, compiled in R studio

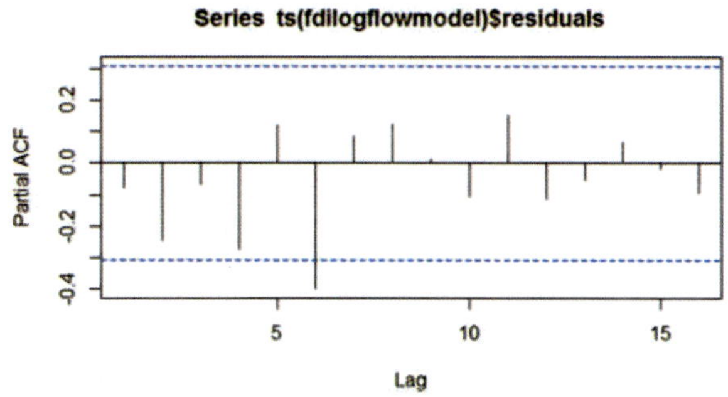

Fig. 6 PACF of the ARIMA with drift model *Source* compiled in R studio

Table 7 Forecast of 10 years from 2020 to 2029 using ARIMA with drift (0, 1, 0)

Forecast years	Forecast (in log)	Lower limit at 95%	Higher limit at 95%	Actual FDI values (log reconverted)	Actual FDI values, log reconverted (at 95% lower limit)	Actual FDI values, log reconverted (at 95% higher limit)
2020	10.99	9.60	12.39	59,658.54	14,766.72	241,024
2021	11.16	9.18	13.14	70,404.50	9773.24	507,185
2022	11.33	8.91	13.75	83,086.90	7400.05	932,879
2023	11.49	8.70	14.28	98,052.89	6007.35	1,600,426
2024	11.66	8.54	14.78	115,714.61	5098.75	2,626,125
2025	11.82	8.40	15.24	136,559	4466.59	4,175,062
2026	11.99	8.29	15.68	161,156.61	4007.69	6,480,378
2027	12.15	8.21	16.10	190,184.86	3664.81	9,869,692
2028	12.32	8.13	16.51	224,444.04	3403.61	14,800,313
2029	12.49	8.07	16.90	264,871.9	3202.33	21,908,136

Source compiled in R studio

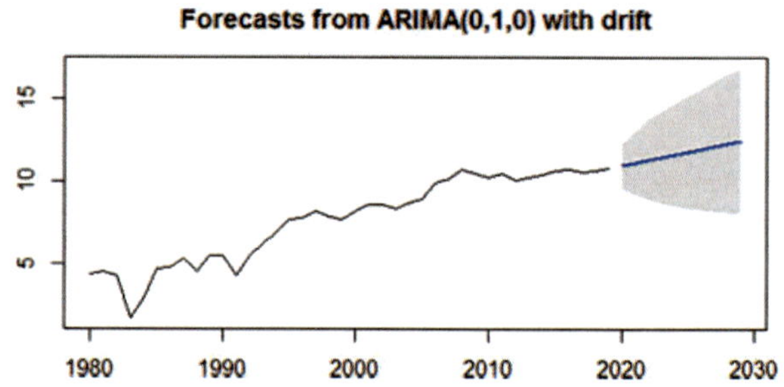

Fig. 7 Forecast of FDI inflow of India from 2020 to 2029 by ARIMA with drift (0,1,0) *Source* UNCTAD data, compiled in R studio

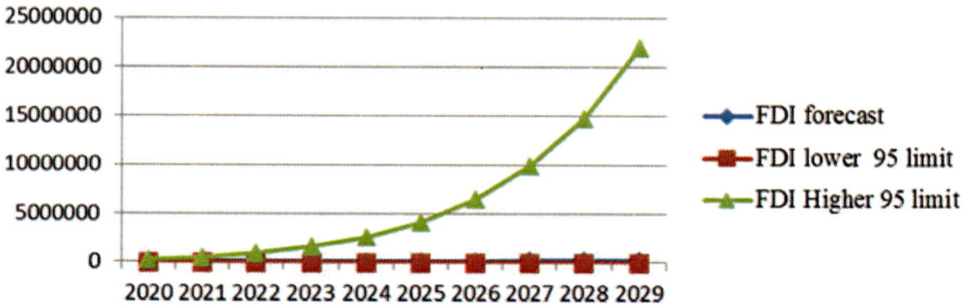

Fig. 8 Depiction of actual FDI forecast against its lower and upper limits at 95% confince interval. *Source* compiled in excel

Table 8 Box–Ljung test results for validating the forecasted FDI values

X-squared	6.0304	15.948	16.222	18.728	25.998
Df (lags)	5	10	15	20	30
P value	0.3033	0.1011	0.3675	0.5396	0.6752

Source compiled in R studio

forecast values relative to its upper and lower limits at 95% confidence interval. It can be observed that though the forecast may show a hope but the FDI trend values are almost merged with the lower limiting values of the forecast. This signals the necessity of streamlined and substantial policy strategies to tap and promote the buoyancies of the FDI inflow so that it can be realized at least towards its upper limits, if not beyond.

To validate the result of the forecast with the best-identified model, the Box-Ljung test is used as shown below. A p value of 0.05 would show the presence of autocorrelation still in the fitted model. The test was done at different lag periods of 5, 10, 15, 20 and 30 years. In case of all tested lag periods, it is found to be greater than 0.05 showing no autocorrelation in the data and thus validating the forecasted results (Table 8).

5 Conclusions

The impact of COVID-19 in India has been troublesome. According to the statistics released by the Ministry of Statistics, India's progress in the last three months of the financial year 2020 goes down to 3.1%. Hence, after the declaration of economic packages in the middle of May, the GDP rate in India was degraded even negatively indicating a recession. Unemployment increased from 6.7% on 15 March to 26% on 19 April. Throughout the lockdown, around 14 crores people lost their occupations and numerous others have experienced the problem of a salary cut. Major industries in India such as Bharat Forge, Tata Motors, Aditiya Birla Group, BHEL, Ultra Tech Cement, Grasim Industries, and Larsen and Toubro have decreased their operations for an indefinite period. The Government of India declared several policy measures to deal with this situation from food security measures, the extra funding for the healthcare services to the states, and tax deadline extensions. However, regardless of the adverse transitory shocks from COVID-19, aggregate FDI inflows into India have continued resilient. FDI by technology-based firms have reached 17 billion US dollar in the first seven months of 2020, supported by new investment made by Google worth of 10 billion US dollar in the middle of July 2020, and other global technology-based firms like Amazon, Facebook, and Foxconn have agreed for new large investment in India by this year. A significant positive aspect for India is its large and rapidly growing bourgeois, which helps to stimulate expenditure on consumer durables, and aggregate household expenditure in India is anticipated to improve by

42%, betweent 2020 and 2025. The digital revolution of India can be expected to boost the progress of the retail consumer market and e-commerce over the next ten years. This helps to captivate prime global MNCs in high-tech and e-business in the Indian market.

Though the long-run forecast over the next 10 years throws a silver lining of a continuation of the upward trend of the inward FDI inflows in India, the fact that it is more skewed towards its lower limits signals the need for streamlined and substantial policy strategies to tap and promote its buoyancies to realize its trend towards the upper limit if not beyond.

References

Aneja, R., and V. Ahuja. 2020. An assessment of the socioeconomic impact of COVID-19 pandemic in India. *Journal Public Affairs* e2266. https://doi.org/10.1002/pa.2266.

Chaudhary, Monika, P.R. Sodani, and Shankar Das. 2020. Effect of COVID-19 on economy in India, some reflections for policy and programme. *Journal of Health Management* 22 (2): 169–180. https://doi.org/10.1177/0972063420935541.

Das, Kishore Kumar, and Shalini Patnaik. 2020. The impact of covid-19 in Indian economy—An empirical study. *International Journal of Electrical Engineering and Technology*, 11(3), 194–202. http://www.iaeme.com/IJEET/issues.asp?JType=IJEET&VType=11&IType=3.

http://www.oecd.org/investment/FDI-in-Figures-April-2020.pdf.

https://auto.economictimes.indiatimes.com/news/industry/india-attracts-usd-22-billion-fdi-during-covid-19-amitabh-kant/77436521.

https://corporate.cyrilamarchandblogs.com/2020/06/fdi-in-brownfield-pharma-will-covid-19-be-the-catalyst-for-policy-reforms/.

https://economictimes.indiatimes.com/news/economy/indicators/indian-economy-set-for-post-covid-19-rebound-as-fdi-remains-buoyant-hismarkit/articleshow/77127090.cms?from=mdr.

https://en.wikipedia.org/wiki/Economic_impact_of_the_COVID-19_pandemic_in_India.

https://inc42.com/resources/effects-of-coronavirus-outbreak-in-the-investment-sector/.

https://indianexpress.com/article/explained/explained-india-forex-reserves-covid-19-economic-crisis-6448701/.

https://niti.gov.in/covid-19-india-swot-analysis.

https://physio-pedia.com/Coronavirus_Disease_(COVID-19).

https://scroll.in/article/963879/Indias-restrictions-on-Chinese-FDI-to-protect-domestic-firms-is-likely-to-backfire.

https://thewire.in/economy/new-FDI-norms-in-time-of-covid-geopolitics-or-for-the-real-economy.

https://unctad.org/system/files/official-document/wir2020_en.pdf.

https://www.business-standard.com/article/current-affairs/67-mncs-see-india-among-top-choices-for-fdi-says-cii-ey-survey-120101301271_1.html.

https://www.business-standard.com/article/economy-policy/fdi-policy-changes-to-impact-investments-from-china-amid-covid-19-lockdown-120042.

https://www.business-standard.com/article/economy-policy/statsguru-fdi-inflows-revive-in-fy20-but-face-covid-19-test-in-fy21-120060700984_1.html.

https://www.businesstoday.in/opinion/columns/coronavirus-impact-companies-businesses-jobs-indian-economy-profits-revenues-covid-19-pande.

https://www.cnbctv18.com/politics/covid19-impact-govt-tweaks-fdi-policy-to-regulate-chinese-investments-into-india-5950901.htm.

https://www.ey.com/en_gl/news/2020/05/businesses-remain-optimistic-on-foreign-direct-investment-plans-despite-covid-19-concerns.

https://www.financialexpress.com/economy/covid-19-pandemic-may-be-good-news-for-indias-economy-or-may-be-bad-for-china/1954207/.

https://www.firstpost.com/india/changes-in-fdi-rules-necessary-to-ensure-no-indian-entity-is-shortchanged-during-covid-19-pandemic-especially-by-opportunist-china-8274721.html.

https://www.globaltimes.cn/content/1193101.shtml.

https://www.hindustantimes.com/business-news/india-needs-rs-50-60-lakh-cr-fdi-to-bolster-covid-hit-economy-gadkari/story-93Wtt96WVoCd0QF9.

https://www.ibef.org/economy/foreign-direct-investment.aspx.

https://www.india-briefing.com/news/will-indias-fdi-policy-change-impact-chinese-investments-post-covid-19-20256.html/.

https://www.investindia.gov.in/siru/government-indias-measures-boost-business-improve-eodb-welcome-fdi-during-covid-19.

https://www.lexology.com/library/detail.aspx?g=9c19ff1d-66e6-4799-9a05-2f4867827358.

https://www.livemint.com.

https://www.mondaq.com/india/corporate-and-company-law/922366/impact-of-covid-19-on-fdi-regimes.

https://www.mondaq.com/india/financing/923078/covid-19-impact-government-of-india-amends-foreign-direct-investment-policy-to-regulate-chinese-investments-into-india?signup=true.

https://www.oecd.org/coronavirus/policy-responses/foreign-direct-investment-flows-in-the-time-of-covid-19-a2fa20c4/.

https://www.policycircle.org/opinion/india-must-fortify-fdi-screening-rules-to-escape-wto-scrutiny/.

https://www.sundayguardianlive.com/news/consequences-covid-19-indian-economy.

https://www.thehindu.com/business/Industry/fdi-in-india-jumps-13-to-record-4998-bn-in-2019-20/article31695470.ece.

https://www.weforum.org/agenda/2020/06/coronavirus-covid19-economics-fdi-investment-united-nations/.

Jana, S.S., Nath Tarak, and K.D. Pandey. 2019. Foreign direct investment and economic growth in India. *Asia-Pacific Journal of Management Research and Innovation* 15(1–2). https://doi.org/10.1177/2319510x19849731.

Mahendra Dev, S., and Rajeswari Sengupta. 2020. *Covid-19: Impact on the Indian Economy*. http://www.igidr.ac.in/pdf/publication/WP-2020-013.pdf.

Masharu, U., and M.A. Nasir. 2018. Policy of foreign direct investment liberalisation in India—Implications for retail sector. *International Review of Economics* 65: 465–487. https://doi.org/10.1007/s12232-018-0306-y.

Poddar, Ajay, and Brijendra Yadav. 2020. Impact of COVID-19 on Indian economy—A review. *Journal of Humanities and Social Sciences Research* 2.15–22. https://doi.org/10.37534/bp.jhssr.2020.v2.nS.id1033.p15.

Rakshit, Debdas, and Ananya Paul. 2020. Impact of COVID-19 on sectors of Indian economy and business survival strategies. *International Journal of Engineering and Management Research* 10(3). www.ijemr.net https://doi.org/10.31033/ijemr.10.3.8.

Ronismita Mishra, and Swapnamoyee Palit. March 2020. Role of FDI on employment scenario in India. *International Journal of Recent Technology and Engineering (IJRTE)* 8(6). ISSN: 2277-3878. https://doi.org/10.35940/ijrte.F7777.038620.

Saxena, Abhisek. 2020. India: Covid 19 impact—Government of India amends foreign investment policy to regulate Chinese investments into India. *Article of Phoenix Legal*. Accessed at:mondaq.com/india/financing/923078.

Swapnamoyee P. Palit. Sep–Oct 2019. Strategic management of foreign direct investment: Potential markets analysis. *Journal of Mechanics of Continua and Mathematical Sciences* 14(5) 819–831. ISSN (Print) 0973-8975.

Ronismita Mishra has 6 years of teaching experience at UG and PG level. She has a first class career. Besides, she has publications in national level journals as well as participations in such level conferences.

Swapnamoyee Palit has 14 years of teaching experience at UG and PG level. She has a first class career throughout from ICSE to M. Phil and has her Ph.D. in Health Economics. She also has a professional degree in MBA in Finance from Pondicherry Central University. She is also UGC (NET) qualified in Economics. Besides, she has publications in various national and international journals as well as participations in such level conferences.

Applying Behavioural Finance Approach to Investment Decisions: Determinants of Investment

Sunil Kumar, Sanjay Guha, and Sattar Ali

1 Introduction

Modern finance assumes that markets are efficient and that agents know the probability distribution of future market risk (Markowitz 1952; Merton 1969; Fama 1970). The traditional theory of finance and investment assumes that investors are rational and all investments are as per information's available in the market. But there are many instances where this assumption is not true always. Most of the time investors take investment decisions on the basis of his/her behavioural factors. Behavioural aspects and psychology often affects the investor's decisions (Yuh et al. 2015), which are evident from irrational decisions under the influence of overreaction, underreaction, overconfidence, group behaviour, etc. In recent years, many researchers in the area of finance and investment have been very active in behavioural finance, and many of their research works have been accepted in the top journals in the field of financial economics (Henker et al. 2006). This shows that behavioural finance (Yuh et al. 2015) is becoming an increasingly significant area for research.

S. Kumar (✉) · S. Guha
Department of Management, Bhilai Institute of Technology, Durg (C.G.) Pin-491001, India
e-mail: s.kushwaha@bitdurg.ac.in

S. Guha
e-mail: sanguha@bitdurg.ac.in

S. Ali
Axis Bank Ltd, Chandigarh Pin-160002, India

R. N. Subudhi et al. (eds.), *Future of Work and Business in Covid-19 Era*,
Springer Proceedings in Business and Economics,
https://doi.org/10.1007/978-981-19-0357-1_6

1.1 Prospect Theory of Behavioural Finance

Luong and Ha (2011) described the event through finance that has been researched for thousands of years, and a completely fresh region is behavioural finance that sees individual activities in finance. Psychologically oriented behavioural finance models tried to comprehend how feelings and remembering mistakes affect the behaviour of personal shareholders.

Alquraan et al. (2016) financial theory surveys have been evolving over the past centuries; this research is attempting to comprehend investor sensibility in financial markets through the use of fresh designs. It was observed that when stakeholders make business choices about the securities, they have no trouble as they are well versed, cautions and coherent (Subramaniam and Velnampy 2017). Analysed the data via suitable procedures and techniques created an ultimate choice depend upon the outcomes of the assessment and needed which always changed the scenarios fresh data. Mostly, people are saving wealth for upcoming utilization purposes and investing the accumulated wealth with the goals of caring the factual importance of money and making extra income.

Maheswari (2016) conducted research which analyses the behavioural factors which influences the saving and investment patterns of rural family (Shinde and Zanvar 2015). Explored various demographic factors which affect the decision of investors during investment involved with a higher-risk profile (Akerele 2013). Collected data from small-scale farmers of Benue state located in Nigeria with a purpose to study the pattern used by the farmers for investment and their saving and conducted survey to examine the respondent's views about the investment pattern which covered urban as well as rural area. The data was collected for survey purpose, and the method for the data collection used was personal interview (Sharma and Goyal 2014). Conducted a research to study the behaviour of a particular group of individuals belongs from middle-class group for investment. They tried to find out how the middle-class groups manage their investment after having such a less amount of income.

1.2 Behavioural Determinants

Mahesh et al. (2017) explored the perception of investor and the risk involved while investing in different type of commodities (Kaufmann 2015). Has taken the European countries to compare the investors from those who are from non-formal education and to understand the investment instruments chosen by the investors by taking an appropriate decision, which is suitable for them to invest. (Ogbonna et al. 2015). Has showed evidence that the investor invested an average amount in arable crop production in Umuahia capital territory of Abia State, Nigeria. The study researched about investment pattern, income and savings of small holders of arable crop farmers.

Kengatharan and Kengatharan (2014). Done the research in Colombo stock exchange to study whether the behavioural factor influences the investment decisions and tried to find out those behavioural factors which impacts the performance of an individual investor (Zhou and Phan 2014). Analysed the dynamic behaviour of the individual investors repeatedly changes as per the scenario. As per paper, psychological factors influence the behaviour of the investor for taking decision towards investment in stock market (Jagongo and Mutswenje 2014). Found that sole investment behaviour is characterized as purchasing decisions with his/her own considerations of tiny quantities of stock. Judgement on investment is frequently backed by decision-making aid. It is presumed that the composition of data and business variable will methodically affect business choices of people as well as business results.

Chaffai and Medhioub (2014) examined that behavioural finance tries to provide various reasons for the security markets emotional and social variables that influence financer actions and marketplace competence. It was found that the existence of cognitive partiality on the Tunisian security market by looking at an example of 193 shareholders and by one-dimensional and multidimensional study.

Ngoc (2014) seeked to explore variables in the securities companies in Ho Chi Minh City, Vietnam, that influence personal shareholder choice. The Ho Chi Minh Stock Exchange has five personal shareholder cognitive factors: grouping, market, view, misleading notion of audaciousness risk and partial of anchoring ability.

Through the literature review, factors affecting investment decisions were explored and then relationships of these determinants with investment decisions were identified using regression analysis.

2 Research Methodology

The present study was undertaken in two distinct phases. During the first phase of study, attempt was made to identify the factors for development of behavioural model towards investment pattern for different income groups using exploratory factor analysis approach.

2.1 Research Hypothesis

H_{01}: There is no significant prediction of investment pattern by factors which influence investors.

Ha_1: There is significant prediction of investment pattern by factors which influence investors.

2.2 Research Design

The study has been focused on exploring factors responsible for investment patterns of investors and then developing model for the mentioned cities using confirmatory factor analysis approach. It means there would be cause-and-effect relation, so causal research design has been applied to accomplish the study.

Data has been collected directly from investors of selected cities, the population and sample group in the area of investigation. Data on opinions and behavioural factors of investors will be derived from a questionnaire (five-point Likert scale).

Since study is based on multivariate analysis, self-designed structured questionnaire has been used along with five-point Likert scale data for psychographics and nominal scaled data for demographics.

3 Results and Discussion

3.1 Exploratory Factor Analysis

This study follows the research methodology based on previous research in related areas, and a questionnaire was constructed to measure, and a 5-point Likert scale is used. A pilot study on a small group of individual is used, and 531 respondents' data are collected. Exploratory factor analysis (EFA) statistical technique is used to identify the factors (Table 1).

KMO value is 0.822 which is greater than 0.6 thus confirms that sample is adequate for exploratory factor analysis (Kaiser 1974). This indicates that correlations are comparatively compact which will yield distinct factors (Field 2000). Bartlett's test of sphericity is significant as p-value is less than 0.05. Thus, it can be concluded that correlation matrix (R-Matrix) is not an identity matrix.

Anti-image correlation is analysed to check the data adequacy for each statement. KMO value for each statement is greater than 0.6; therefore, data is sufficient for each statement used. Communalities for statement "Investment is Tough Task but it is a Must" are less than 0.5; therefore, this statement is removed as it can produce inflated value of variance (Gorsuch 1990). Again KMO and Bartlett's test are performed to

Table 1 KMO and bartlett's test

Kaiser–Meyer–Olkin measure of sampling adequacy		0.822
Bartlett's test of sphericity	Approx. χ^2	8065.43
	Df	780
	Sig	0.000

Source IBM Corp. Released 2015. IBM SPSS Statistics for Windows, Version 23. Armonk, NY: IBM Corp analyse the changes because of omission of one statement as stated above and found adequate.

From eigenvalues, component-1 has 25.04% of total variance explained, while component-2 has 11.9% of total variance explained and so on. Under extraction sums of Squared Loadings, only components having eigenvalues greater than "1" are listed; there are ten such components which account to 68.43% of total variance explained. Rotation of the factor axis leads to restructuring of total variance explained. The restructured factors have now changed variance as Factor 1 explains 10.01% of total variance while Factor 2 explains 9.97% of total variance, whereas Factor 10 explains 3.59% of total variance (Table 2).

Figure 1 scree plot also confirmed the number of factors explored through exploratory factor analysis. By examining the graph of the eigenvalues and looking for natural bend of the graph, it can be seen that there are ten numbers of factors which are required to be retained, as after point 10 the curve gets flattened (Velicer and Jackson 1990).

The identified factors through PCA are analysed through rotated component matrix for grouping of statements. All 39 statements are grouped in ten factors, and their reliability is analysed using Cronbach's Alpha test for reliability and internal consistency. Further considering the factor loadings and reliability, further factors are reduced from 10 to 7. Rotated component matrix shows the loadings of seven identified factors extracted. Higher the absolute value of the loading represents more contribution is by the factor for the variables identified. The loading less than 0.4 is suppressed (Fig. 2).

The above figure shows the conceptual framework for sustainable development of tourism in the state of Chhattisgarh after exploring factors using exploratory factor analysis (EFA): Financial Security (FS), Risk Appetite (RA), Life Style (LS), Awareness (AW), Investment Avenues (IA), Assured Returns (AR), Secured Returns (SR).

The identified factors through PCA is analysed through rotated component matrix for grouping of statements. All 39 statements are grouped in 7 factors, and their reliability is analysed using Cronbach's Alpha test for reliability and internal consistency. The below table shows rotated component matrix loadings of seven identified factors extracted. Higher the absolute value of the loading represents more contribution is by the factor for the variables identified. The loading less than 0.4 is suppressed (Table 3).

For estimating the relationships between the dependent variable "Investment Pattern (IP)" and independent variables as explored, Financial Security (FS), Risk Appetite (RA), Life Style (LS), Awareness (AW), Investment Avenues (IA), Assured Returns (AR) and Secured Returns (SR) regression analysis are used (Table 4).

The model was constituted seven explanatory variables. These seven constructs explain 48.2% variance of the model. There is no sign of autocorrelation as Durbin–Watson statistics is 1.935 as the value is between range of 0 to 4 (Durbin and Watson 1950) (Table 5).

At 95% confidence level, the association is statistically significant as the p-value is less than or equal to the significance level; it is concluded that there is a statistically

Table 2 Total variance explained

Component	Initial eigenvalues			Extraction sums of squared loadings			Rotation sums of squared loadings		
	Total	% of variance	Cumulative %	Total	% of variance	Cumulative %	Total	% of variance	Cumulative %
1	9.76	25.04	25.04	9.76	25.04	25.04	3.90	10.01	10.01
2	4.64	11.91	36.95	4.64	11.91	36.95	3.89	9.97	19.98
3	2.33	5.99	42.93	2.33	5.99	42.93	3.26	8.35	28.34
4	2.06	5.29	48.22	2.06	5.29	48.22	3.19	8.18	36.52
5	1.56	3.99	52.21	1.56	3.99	52.21	2.99	7.67	44.19
6	1.49	3.83	56.04	1.49	3.83	56.04	2.61	6.68	50.88
7	1.42	3.64	59.68	1.42	3.64	59.68	2.26	5.80	56.68
8	1.19	3.05	62.73	1.19	3.05	62.73	1.72	4.41	61.09
9	1.14	2.92	65.65	1.14	2.92	65.65	1.46	3.76	64.85
10	1.08	2.78	68.43	1.08	2.78	68.43	1.40	3.59	68.43

Source IBM Corp. Released 2015. IBM SPSS Statistics for Windows, Version 23. Armonk, NY: IBM Corp
Extraction Method: Principal Component Analysis

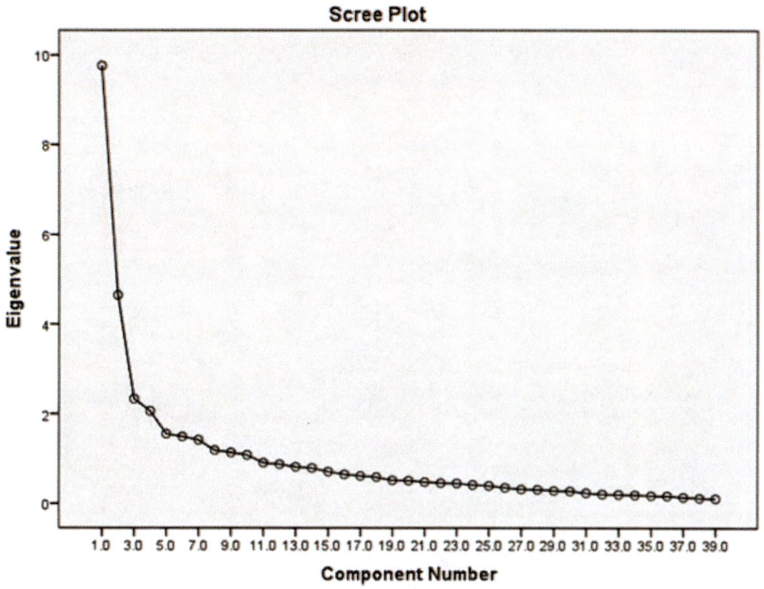

Fig. 1 Scree plot *Source* IBM Corp. Released 2015. IBM SPSS Statistics for Windows, Version 23. Armonk, NY: IBM Corp

significant association between the independent variable and dependent variable, i.e. there is significant association between "Investment Pattern (IP)" and independent variables as explored Financial Security (FS), Risk Appetite (RA), Life Style (LS), Awareness (AW), Investment Avenues (IA), Assured Returns (AR) and Secured Returns (SR). The histogram of the residuals shows the distribution of the residuals for all observations which is normal distribution (Table 6).

From the coefficients of the above table, out of seven explanatory variables, namely Financial Security (FS), Life Style (LS), Awareness (AW), Investment Avenues (IA), Assured Returns (AR), Secured Returns (SR) are found to have significant impact on investment pattern (IP). While Risk Appetite (RA) is found to be statistically insignificant at 95% confidence interval as the p-value is 0.687 which is greater than 0.05.

The collinearity index shows that there are no chances of collinearity as the maximum VIF(variance inflation factor) value of independent variables in the model fit is 1.919 which is much less than 10 (Rawlings and Pantula 1998). Collinearity diagnostics supports the same (Table 7 and Fig. 3).

The above plot is a check on normality; the plotted points should follow the straight line. Serious departures would suggest that normality assumption is not met. Here we have no major cause for concern and thus can be concluded that graphically the dependent variable investment pattern (IP) is well explained by the independent variables.

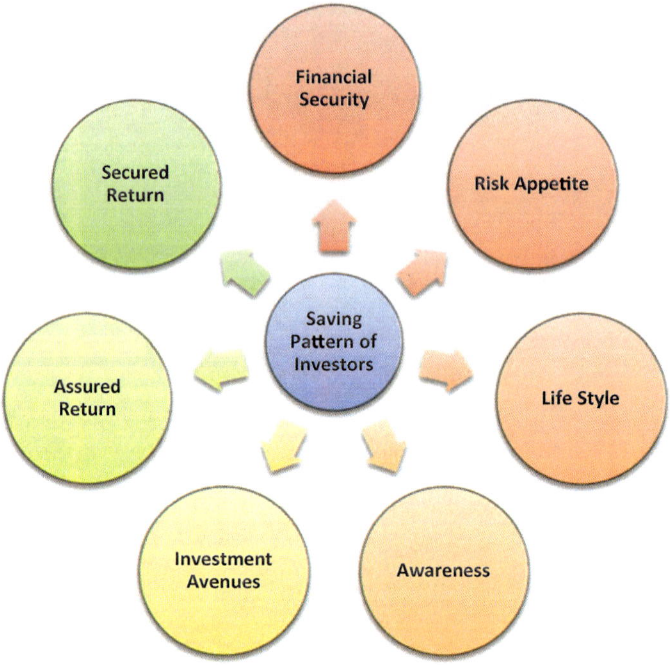

Fig. 2 Conceptual model for sustainable development of tourism *Source* Author's Conceptual Model (NO Referencing required)

3.2 Predictions

In order to get a investment pattern (IP) for particular *independent variables,* values we can use the fitted equation.

$$Y = -0.112 - 0.122\ X_{01} + 0.1X_{03} + 0.386X_{04} \\ + 0.126X_{05} + 0.228X_{06} + 0.335X_{07} + 0.661$$

where

Y = Investment Pattern (IP); X_{01} = Financial Security (FS); X_{03} = Life Style (LS); X_{04} = Awareness (AW); X_{05} = Investment Avenues (IA); X_{06} = Assured Returns (AR); X_{07} = Secured Returns (SR).

Table 3 Principle component analysis

Factors	Items	Factor loadings	Cronbach's alpha (α)	Total variance explained (%)	Eigenvalues
Financial security (FS)	F10	0.83	0.698	12.3	4.79
	F11	0.76			
	F12	0.76			
	F13	0.72			
	F14	0.71			
	F15	0.67			
	F16	0.49			
	F17	0.42			
Risk appetite (RA)	F20	0.72	0.805	11.9	4.63
	F21	0.64			
	F22	0.63			
	F23	0.6			
	F24	0.59			
	F25	0.59			
	F26	0.57			
	F27	0.56			
	F28	0.51			
	F29	0.47			
Life style	F30	0.67	0.753	9.7	3.79
	F31	0.64			
	F32	0.61			
	F33	0.52			
	F34	0.51			
Awareness	F40	0.78	0.667	8.8	3.43
	F41	0.72			
	F42	0.71			
	F43	0.66			
	F44	0.63			
Investment avenues	F50	0.770	0.649	8.6	3.36
	F51	0.760			
	F52	0.720			
	F53	0.660			
Assured return	F60	0.62	0.835	4.3	1.68
	F61	0.57			
	F62	0.46			
Secured investment	F71	0.54	0.696	4.1	1.59

(continued)

Table 3 (continued)

Factors	Items	Factor loadings	Cronbach's alpha (α)	Total variance explained (%)	Eigenvalues
	F72	0.49			

Source IBM Corp. Released 2015. IBM SPSS Statistics for Windows, Version 23. Armonk, NY: IBM Corp

Table 4 Model summary

Model	R	R square	Adjusted R square	Std. Error of the Estimate	Durbin–Watson
1	0.694[a]	0.482	0.475	0.66114	1.935

Source IBM Corp. Released 2015. IBM SPSS Statistics for Windows, Version 23. Armonk, NY: IBM Corp
[a]Predictors: (Constant), X01, X02, X03, X04, X05, X06, X07.; [b]Dependent Variable: Y

Table 5 ANOVA

Model		Sum of squares	Df	Mean square	F	Sig
1	Regression	212.104	7	30.301	69.321	0.000[b]
	Residual	228.168	522	0.437		
	Total	440.272	529			

Source IBM Corp. Released 2015. IBM SPSS Statistics for Windows, Version 23. Armonk, NY: IBM Corp
[a]Dependent Variable: Y
[b]Predictors: (Constant), X01, X02, X03, X04, X05, X06, X07

Table 6 Coefficients

Model		Unstandardized coefficients		Standardized coefficients	T	Sig	Collinearity statistics	
		B	Std. error	Beta			Tolerance	VIF
1	(Constant)	−0.112	0.200		−0.558	0.046		
	X01	−0.122	0.028	−0.164	−4.378	0.000	0.706	1.417
	X 02	−0.013	0.033	−0.015	−0.403	0.687	0.749	1.335
	X 03	0.100	0.036	0.107	2.767	0.006	0.659	1.517
	X 04	0.386	0.049	0.345	7.963	0.000	0.530	1.887
	X 05	0.126	0.047	0.118	2.702	0.007	0.521	1.919
	X 06	0.228	0.035	0.226	6.475	0.000	0.818	1.223
	X 07	0.335	0.038	0.335	8.887	0.000	0.700	1.429

Source IBM Corp. Released 2015. IBM SPSS Statistics for Windows, Version 23. Armonk, NY: IBM Corp
[a]Dependent Variable: Y

Table 7 Collinearity diagnostics

Model	Dimension	Eigenvalue	Condition Index	Variance proportions							
				(Constant)	X01	X02	X03	X04	X05	X06	X07
1	1	7.682	1.000	0.00	0.00	0.00	0.00	0.00	0.00	0.00	0.00
	2	0.119	8.025	0.00	0.61	0.01	0.02	0.01	0.02	0.00	0.00
	3	0.059	11.380	0.00	0.18	0.61	0.01	0.03	0.00	0.03	0.09
	4	0.044	13.227	0.02	0.04	0.30	0.07	0.03	0.00	0.04	0.49
	5	0.039	14.057	0.01	0.03	0.07	0.28	0.00	0.01	0.52	0.11
	6	0.028	16.603	0.05	0.01	0.00	0.57	0.12	0.09	0.31	0.00
	7	0.017	21.531	0.82	0.00	0.00	0.05	0.01	0.30	0.09	0.06
	8	0.012	24.812	0.10	0.13	0.00	0.00	0.79	0.58	0.00	0.24

Source IBM Corp. Released 2015. IBM SPSS Statistics for Windows, Version 23. Armonk, NY: IBM Corp

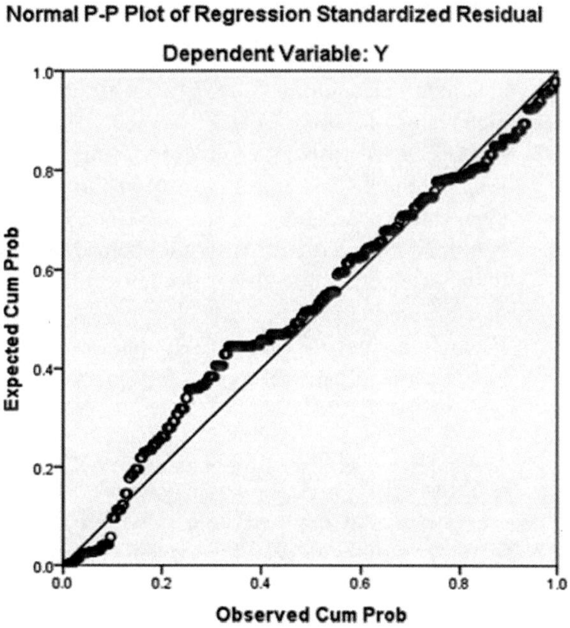

Fig. 3 Normal plot *Source* IBM Corp. Released 2015. IBM SPSS Statistics for Windows, Version 23. Armonk, NY: IBM Corp

3.3 Findings

Through various literatures as well as through data analysis, it is evident that different locations have different saving and investment pattern. The present study has identified certain factors which can be considered as drivers of investment by investors. After factor extraction method, and rotated component matrix 7 factors have been extracted that accounts to 61.09% of the variation expressed. Identified factors were rotated, and thus, the total variations expressed by those factors were calculated.

By observing the scree plot having the eigenvalues, it can be observed that the seven factors are required to be considered as after 7 factors there is natural bend in the plot and after point 7 the curve gets flattened thus confirming the number of identified factors to be considered.

The Seven identified Factors are

a. Factor 1: **Financial Security (FS)** is considered as first factor which consists of eight statements accounting to 12.3% of the total variation having the calculated eigenvalue of 4.79.
b. Factor 2: **Risk Appetite (RA)** considered as second factor which consists of ten statements accounting to 11.89% of the total variation having the calculated eigenvalue of 4.6.
c. Factor 3: **Life Style (LS),** considered as third factor which consists of five statements accounting to 9.76% of the total variation having the calculated eigenvalue of 3.79.
d. Factor 4: **Awareness (AW),** considered as fourth factor which consists of five statements accounting to 8.79% of the total variation having the calculated eigenvalue of 3.43.
e. Factor 5: **Investment Avenues (IA),** considered as fifth factor which consists of four statements accounting to 8.6% of the total variation having the calculated eigenvalue of 3.36.
f. Factor 6: **Assured Returns (AR)** considered as sixth factor which consists of three statements accounting to 4.3% of the total variation having the calculated eigenvalue of 1.68.
g. Factor 7: **Secured Returns (SR)** considered as seventh factor which consists of two statements accounting to 4.07% of the total variation having the calculated eigenvalue of 1.58.

To develop psychological model towards saving decisions and for estimating the relationships between the dependent variable "Investment Pattern (IP)" and independent variables as explored, Financial Security (FS), Risk Appetite (RA), Life Style (LS), Awareness (AW), Investment Avenues (IA), Assured Returns (AR) and Secured Returns (SR) regression analysis were used. These seven constructs explain 48.2% variance of the model.

All explored factors have significant impact on investment pattern except Risk Appetite (RA) which found to be statistically insignificant at 95% confidence interval as the p-value is 0.687 which is greater than 0.05. The factor Financial Security (FS) has negative coefficient of 0.122, while factors Life Style (LS), Awareness (AW), Investment Avenues (IA), Assured Returns (AR) and Secured Returns (SR) have positive coefficient with standard error of 0.661.

4 Summary and Conclusion

This part explains the findings which justify the objectives identified for the research undertaken.

5 Conclusion

The above study concludes that the investment pattern is explained through various investors and savers; for this, the conceptual model was framed using seven identified factors through rotated component matrix approach; investment pattern is a behavioural variable, and it requires efforts from all stakeholders and psychological science to define the pattern, but primary responsibility is to device a framework for this which includes parameters like Financial Security (FS), Risk Appetite (RA), Life Style (LS), Awareness (AW), Investment Avenues (IA), Assured Returns (AR) and Secured Returns (SR) which will govern according to the options of saving and investment.

The identified factors and their relationship with dependent variable, i.e. investment pattern of the work, will help an individual to invest in those avenues and financial instruments which comfort their psychological behaviour with respect to their risk appetite to increase their saving returns. The identified factors and their relationship with dependent variable, i.e. investment pattern, will help financial product managers/agents to reformulate their product as per the psychology of an individual, considering active or passive saving thus better saving strategies and management.

The companies can evaluate the performance of their financial product by using the outcome of the proposed model and can strategize towards continuations/ discontinuation and improvisations which will help them to enhance the marketability of their product.

5.1 Limitations

The proposed work associated with many limitations that led to certain changes to the planned research design. Few of the constraints are described below:

a. The proposed research topic was very vast, and there was need to access wide scope of primary and secondary data for in-depth analysis. In this study, work relied on the primary data collected using external who visited banks or in contacts, which may have intervened their comfort level.
b. The feedback taken considered self-administered questionnaire among the savers and investors under study contains questions and was very lengthy, which could have affected the interest of the investment and saving to give feedback in the research process.

c. Some of the investors under study have not participate in the feedback process as they get worried about the confidentiality of their feedback, which could have exposed to the other investors and expected to face comparison among peer groups.
d. Sample size was very limited and was collected using convenience sampling which could have included biasness in their response to the administered questions.

5.2 *Scope of the Study*

Further work in the area of investment pattern can be conducted in order to cover the present discussion among many researchers and scholars. In the present study, an endeavour has been made to approach the research questions in as much depth and details as possible, but still the aspect of content is very intensive & broad and is beyond the scope of the present work.

Therefore, further study is required to find the effect of various identified factors as well as other factors on investment patterns of investors. To find out their causal effect can be defined through controlled experiment. Studies can be undertaken to evaluate the effect of each parameter and identified factors on each and every investment parameters. The present model developed through regression model to establish relationship between dependent and independent variables.

However, no study is complete in itself, and scope for further exploration and improvement will be there. This remains true with the present study, and so during the research tenure, the researcher has identified few areas where the present study can be extended to, as mentioned below:

- Future study should include more factors.
- Shifting from convenience sampling to probability sampling to improve model fit.
- The study can further be extended to understanding the behaviour of investors and their concerns.
- Measure the impact of policy rates and other market forces on investment pattern.

References

Akerele, S.O., et al. 2013. Saving and investment pattern of small-scale farmers of. *Global Journal of Human Social Science*.

Alquraan, Talal, Ahmad Alqisie, and Amjad Al Shorafa. 2016. Do behavioral finance factors influence stock investment decisions of individual investors? (Evidences from Saudi stock market). *American International Journal of Contemporary Research* 6 (3): 159–169.

Chaffai, Mustapha, and Imed Medhioub. 2014. Behavioral finance: An empirical study of the Tunisian stock market. *International Journal of Economics and Financial Issues* 4 (3): 527–538.

Durbin, James, and Geoffrey S. Watson. "Testing for serial correlation in least squares regression: I." *Biometrika* 37, no. 3/4 (1950): 409–428.
Fama, Eugene F. 1970. Efficient capital markets: A review of theory and empirical work. *The Journal of Finance* 25 (2): 383–417.
Field, A. 2000. *Comparing Several Means: ANOVA (GLM 1)*. 1st ed. London; A. Field. *Discovering Statistics Using SPSS for Windows*. 1st ed. 243–294. London: SAGE Publications Ltd.
Gorsuch, R.L. 1990. common factor-analysis versus component analysis—Some well and little known facts. *Multivariate Behavioral Research* 25 (1): 33–39.
Henker, J., T. Henker, and A. Mitsios. 2006. Doinvestors herd intraday in Australian equities? *International Journal of Managerial Finance* 2 (3): 196–219.
Huang, Jim Yuh, J.C.P. Shieh, Littlejohn Allison, and Y.-C. Kao. 2015. Starting points for a new researcher in behavioural finance. *International Journal of Managerial Finance* 12 (1): 92–103.
Jagongo, Ambrose, and Vincent S. Mutswenje. 2014. A survey of the factors influencing investment decisions: The case of individual investors at the NSE. *International Journal of Humanities and Social Science* 4 (4): 92–102.
Kaiser, H.F. 1974. An index of factorial simplicity. *Psychometrika* 39 (1): 31–36.
Katrin Kaufmann. 2015. Non-formal education in international comparison: Patterns of participation and investment in selected European countries. *International Journal for Research in Vocational Education and Training (IJRVET)*.
Navaneethakrishnan Kengatharan, and Lingesiya Kengatharan. 2014. The influence of behavioral factors in making investment decisions and performance: Study on investors of Colombo stock exchange, Sri Lanka. *Asian Journal of Finance and Accounting*.
Luong, Le Phuoc, and Doan Thi Thu. Ha. 2011. *Behavioral Factors Influencing Individual Investors' Decision-Making and Performance A Survey at the Ho Chi Minh Stock Exchange*. Sweden: Umeå School of Business.
Mahesh, B.S., K.S. Shilpashree, and AkshathaPrabhu. 2017. The investment patterns of investors in different financial products in Dakshina Kannada. *International Journals of Science Technology and Management*.
Maheswari, T. 2016. Saving and investment behavior of rural household (With special reference to Coimbatore district). *International Journal of Multidisciplinary Research and Development*.
Markowitz, Harry. 1952. Portfolio selection. *The Journal of Finance* 7 (1): 77–91.
Merton, Robert C. 1969. Lifetime portfolio selection under uncertainty: The continuous-time case. *The Review of Economics and Statistics* 51 (3): 247–257.
Ngoc, Luu Thi Bich. 2014. Behavior pattern of individual investors in stock market. *International Journal of Business and Management* 9 (1): 1–16.
Ogbonna, S.I., K.C. Obike, and C.K. Osondu. 2015. Savings, income and investment patterns and its determinants among small holder arable crop farmers in Umuahia capital territory, Abia state Nigeria. *Territory, Abia State Nigeria*.
Rawlings, John O., Sastry G. Pantula, and David A. Dickey, eds. *Applied regression analysis: a research tool*. New York, NY: Springer New York, 1998.
Sharma, Dr. Anukrati, and Megha Goyal 2014. A study of investment behavior of middle income group towards different kinds of investment avenues. *IOSR Journal of Business and Management (IOSR-JBM)*.
Shinde, C.M., and Priyanka Zanvar. 2015. A study of investment pattern on the basis of demographic traits. *Internation Journal of Research-Granthaalayah*.
Subramaniam, V.A., and T. Velnampy. 2017. Rationality: A central point between traditional finance and behavioural finance. *International Journal of Research-Granthaalayah* 5 (6): 2394–3629.
Velicer, W.F., and D.N. Jackson. 1990. Component analysis versus common factor-analysis—Some further observations. *Multivariate Behavioral Research* 25 (1): 97–114.
Zhou, Jian, and Khoa Cuong Phan. 2014. Factors influencing individual investor behavior: An empirical study of the Vietnamese stock market. *American Journal of Business and Management*.

Poverty and Income Distribution Amid Covid-19: An Analysis of India

Veena Tripathi and Deepti Ahuja

1 Introduction

The catastrophe through the advent of coronavirus has become the global concern due to its impact on the global health and economy. The countries are facing various challenges in drafting policy framework during this pandemic time. Social distancing is the only tool to alleviate the spread of novel coronavirus in the lack of inadequate system, poor infrastructure and absent of vaccines. The prolonged lockdown of production of household and non-essential products has been considered as an advisory under distance measures policy. These policies impose a breakdown in economy which consequently resulted as an unequal impact on the different segment of the society. The recommended protection measures of complete shutdown of factories and production of non-essential items for a prolonged period deviated to downturn in economy for a long duration. Policy-makers have drafted positive health measures, but it is not in proportion with economic costs, which accentuated poverty and income inequality in India.

This paper examines the impact of the COVID-19 containment measures on poverty and income inequality in India. Section 2 describes a brief literature review of Poverty and Income Distribution before Covid-19 lockdown in India. Section 3 discusses Social Protection Policy. Section 4 describes the implication of Covid-19 policy measures. Section 5 summarizes and concludes, delineating the importance of health and social protection policies as a potent strategy that could cushion the impact of the health crisis.

V. Tripathi (✉)
Jaipuria Institute of Management, Ghaziabad, India

D. Ahuja
Business Manager, Publicis Media, Gurgaon, India

R. N. Subudhi et al. (eds.), *Future of Work and Business in Covid-19 Era*,
Springer Proceedings in Business and Economics,
https://doi.org/10.1007/978-981-19-0357-1_7

2 Poverty and Income Distribution Before Covid-19 Lockdown

India has witnessed the major trajectory path of economy post the liberalization. The social policies implemented from last 30 years stimulate the Indian economy, though it also led to inequality for disadvantaged communities (Jha 2012). The social policies kept getting addressed as per the need and rights of the diverse states across the India. Yet, the global inequality was falling down, and national inequality was rising (Sumner 2019).

Indian development economists defined the growth of India under two categories of income distribution, where the prolific segment represents the opulence, while the remaining huge populations are representing the category of unequal distribution of basic services such as income, wages, education, sanitation, healthcare, electricity and transportation (Dreze and Sen 2013). The economists concluded an unfavourable approach, that India's problems can't be solved with a sudden economic growth alone, where deep inequalities in the policies had been designed (Dreze and Sen 2013).

To control political and economic instability, welfare states have been designed under the liberal economy to control the inequality in the income (Swank and Betz 2003), which is implemented successfully in the emerging economics countries. The flexible labour markets, equal distribution of income and economy stability are the key features of social policy in the global market. The systematic implementations of redistributive policies are being allotted by the democratic electoral parties of India (Bardhan 2009).

The caste, gender, tribe and regional segregation are the varied facets for social and economic inequalities, which led to the poverty and income distribution in the country (Nayak et al. 2002). The major population of the country is raising their income from agriculture, family business and informal economy to sustain their livelihood. These major social reform policies have been implemented majorly after advanced liberalization, where the legislative innovations had been designed under the National Rural Employment Guarantee Act, 2005 (Harriss 2013). During the end of twentieth century, the absolute poverty was reduced, but the unequal distribution of income between rural and urban cities and economic inequality among the states of the country have been raised as a key concern in social policy framework (Deaton and Dreze 2002).

The economic unequal distribution among the states of the country led to "labour mobility", where more than three million people migrated from Uttar Pradesh, Bihar and Kolkata to Maharashtra and Punjab in 1990s (World Bank 2009). This mobility uncovers the poverty reduction inequality and raises a doubt on State's social and economic protection measures. Poverty measures are being considered as state social protection measures. There has always been discussion by different committees in defining the National Poverty line in the country. National poverty lines defined the threshold of income or consumption under which the citizen's basic physical quality of life index, i.e. clothing, nutritional and shelter lives cannot be met in the respective country.

As per the statistical data by Labour Force Survey in 2017–18, 415 million are being counted as informal workers under the 90% of the total workforce, while 28 million workers held under rural-to-urban workers segment who are specifically from the background of small farmers, labourers, domestic workers, fishermen, weavers and artisans, forest gatherers, construction labourers, manufacturing workers (factories/industries/workshops), street vendors, transport workers and waste pickers (Chen 2020). As per the Periodic Labour Force Survey (PLFS) of 2017–18, more than 70% non-agriculture workers enlist as migrant workers, who are not having a documented job contract details while among them 55% are not eligible for leave entitlements and 50% are not entitled for social security benefits (Government of India 2020).

The income distribution cannot be uniformed designed and justified in the absence of needs, welfare, poverty relief, security and social protection measures of the workers. Under the wave of Covid-19, the sluggish development of economy would only worsen the poverty and income distribution of the country.

3 Social Protection Policy

Social protection has been primarily defined as "public actions taken in response to levels of vulnerability, risk, and deprivation, which are deemed socially unacceptable within a given polity and society" (Conway et al. 2000). Till the early 1990s, the developmental role of social protection remained limited to either social security measures of wealthy nations or social insurance programs for workers in the modern world (Merrien 2013). For instance, the International Labour Organization (ILO) emphasized on extending social coverage to workers but did not incorporate the informal section of the population. Only minimum safety nets were kept for the soially vulnerable groups because non-contributory social measures were considered as a burden on government budget (Merrien 2013).

However, in the late 1990s, in the wake of the economic crises in Asia and Latin America, structural adjustment programme and globalization and increased awareness of the negative effects of global poverty, social protection emerged as an important component of poverty reduction strategies and stabilization policies especially in developing countries (Gentilini and Were 2014; Merrien 2013). The literature on social protection had further grown and flourished during the 2000s when social protection covered all aspects of development under a holistic and forward-looking perspective, as against its passive and narrow role played in the 1990s (Devereux 2003; Holzmann 2001). It was during this period that international organizations formulated social protection policy frameworks (DRID 2005; Sabates-wheeler and Devereux 2004; World Bank 2001). The outburst of pandemics such as Spanish flu (1918), Asian flu (1957), H1N1 flu (2009) and Zika virus (2015) has conventionally resulted with human losses and a downturn in global economy (Sharma et al. 2020.) which further underlined the importance of social protection as an economic and social necessity (International Labor Organisation 2011).

Several measures were taken by emerging countries well before the global crisis to expand social protection to foster inclusive growth in the short term and build human capital in the longer run. High rate of economic growth since 2000 helped these countries to build fiscal space and broaden the revenue base which in turn contributed towards the expansion of social protection. Indeed, in the absence of such measures, the impact of crisis on unemployment, poverty rates and household's disposable income would have been much higher (International Labor Organisation 2011). Eichhorst et al. (2010) show that social protection in particular unemployment benefits, minimum income support and progressive taxation reduced the depth and duration of the current crisis in EU member states and stabilize labour markets and consumption. The study further found that on one hand, social protection provides safety nets to the vulnerable group that have been hit hardest by the crisis and on other hand, it has a stabilizing effect on the overall demand of goods and services in the economy. Fiszbein et al. (2014) argue that social protection must be an integral part of the post-2015 framework. They found that social protection programmes have resulted in significant reduction in poverty in developing world. According to them, social protection programmes are currently preventing 150 million people from falling into poverty.

Further, social protection measures help to reduce income inequality. For instance, Fig. 1 shows the correlation between the social protection expenditure and inequality (as expressed by the Gini coefficient) in Asian countries. The results illustrate that the correlation is negative, suggesting that higher levels of social protection expenditure are associated with lower levels of inequality. This clearly indicates that social protection not only helped in poverty reduction but also narrowed the gap between rich and poor that has increased significantly in developing countries.

However, the recent novel coronavirus (2019) has paralyzed the global economy as it dragged the policy-makers to design new social protection policies. The impact of Covid-19 in terms of human loss and economy disruption is higher in developing countries such as India because of poor infrastructure, unemployment, significant

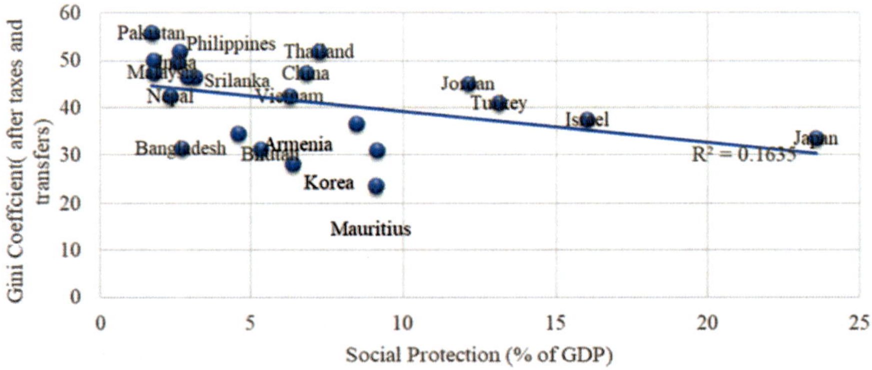

Fig. 1 Correlation between social expenditure and income inequality (as a % of Gini coefficient) *Source* SPSS output, compiled by author

population, poverty and low growth rate. This clearly emphasizes the need of robust health infrastructure and social protection policy to control the spread due to shortages of beds, health personnel and hospitals.

Post the first confirmed case of Covid-19 in India, India began taking precautionary measures from thermal screening of passengers at airports. Government stopped issuing new visas and suspended all the issued visas till 13 March 2020. Government of India issued the 21-day nation-wide lockdown to flatten the speedily rising curve of Covid-19. Under this first lockdown, the 1.3 billion populations needed to be at their home, while the shutdown of all non-essential items had been announced. Government capitalized nudge of nationalism to implement their social distance measures through public policy implication, led to huge economic and unemployment costs. The workers from permitted essential services were allowed under the first lockdown to continue their work services. The first lockdown imposed in India brought an economic shock in the country.

India's US$2.9 trillion economy is being dependent upon more than 90% of workforce enlisted as uprooted informal workers (Sengupta and Jha 2020). The most vulnerable community workers are from unorganized sector and contractual migrants due to the lockdown. The immediate effect of pandemic resulted to collapse of informal sector. The effectiveness of adequate policy measures is not being implemented for a prolonged period due to the unpredictability of Covid-19 contained duration in the country.

The steepest economic downturn in GDP of India to 2.5% rose careful weighing of policy interventions (Business Today 2020). Government of India announced new policy measures to synchronize with 1% of GDP through relief measures such as reducing interest rate in loans & EMIs, reducing the CRR and extending the realization period of export proceeds (Sharma et al. 2020). The structural reforms and concentrated policy measures are yet not been identified to yield significant improvement in the economy. The lockdown and quarantine policies affected millions of migrant workers, who are dependent upon daily wages. The optimal policy measures are significantly not successful in improvising the poverty and income distribution (Kumar et al. 2021).

4 Implications of Covid-19 Policy Measures

India was witnessing a sluggish growth before the outburst of Covid-19 to 4.7% from the year 2018. The country was facing unemployment at a 45-year high, where the major core sectors contributing in Indian economy grounded down by 5.2% from the year 2018 (Mukharji 2020). Post the implementation of first lockdown in India, the country faced a huge still in the economy. The social distancing measures led to a massive collapse under the "Great Lockdown" and counted as the worst economic plunge (Gopinath 2020).

Manufacturing and services sectors (hospitality, healthcare, retails, hotels, recreation, media, education, real estate and others) affected immensely by the lockdown in the country. While the policy-makers were only measuring lockdown and social distancing as a measure to control the spread, the Indian economy resulted a huge loss. The country had already implemented policies to recover its huge fiscal deficit before the outburst of Covid-19, which depicts that India is not ready for any over-spend to support the economy (Goyal 2020). Under such circumstances, designing the new social policies post Covid-19 raised the momentum of poverty and unequal distribution.

Tourism industry accounted for more than 9.2% of GDP. The sector is a backbone for more than 26.7 million jobs in the country and considered as 8th largest country due to its accountability in GDP (JaganMohan 2020). While the tourism industry was expected to employ more than 53 million at the end of year 2029, the social distance measures policy had a significant impact on unemployment and income distribution. This counted as a potential loss of more than 70% of workforce (KPMG 2020).

The retail industry of the country contributes more than 10% of GDP and provides 8% of employment. The shutdown of manufacturing industry and slowdown of supply chain for a prolonged time reflected as a steep down curve in the employment while the country received 30% growth in online retail in last year (National Investment Promotion and Facilitation Agency 2020). The shut-down of manufacturing industries for a prolonged lockdown resulted as demand shocks and inflation. This led to a deep recession in the economy with a higher unemployment rates and millions have been shifted towards poverty. India's 50% population is dependent on agriculture land where majorly belongs to subsistence sector (Chaudhary et al. 2020). They don't fall under the category of social security net. The insecurity raised migration from one state to another and increases the poverty of migrated workers.

The slowdown of economy escalated the income distribution, where employers are either losing their jobs or not getting paid with the full income. The domestic workers and contractual workers faced a huge traumatic effect of income distribution (Deshpande 2020). CMIE report (2020) states the jump of unemployment from 21 to 28% in mid of April only, while as a summation the unemployment rose from 7.03% May' 2019 to 23.98% May 2020. The devastation in unemployment raised the poverty and migrant workers from informal economy shifted at a higher risk (Chen 2020).

According to the World Economic Outlook report (IMF), the percentage of people living below the poverty line would surge in India from 80 million in 2018 to 120 million in 2020. Moreover, income inequality within countries is expected to increase as the pandemic affects low-income individuals disproportionately. Further, the Global Hunger Index (2020) placed India at 94th position (of 107 countries) with a score of 27.2, which is far below the neighbouring countries Sri Lanka, Bangladesh and Pakistan. In 2008, the global hunger score of India was 38.9 that declined to 27.2 in 2020. This clearly reflects how Covid-19 has worsened the situation in the country.

5 Conclusions

The epidemiological models identify that validity of assumptions of policy measures is always questionable in the absence of understanding of disease and human response. The authorities need to identify the policy measures, which are developing a bridge between the social & behavioural and economic impact on the citizens. The trajectory of Covid-19 impacts for the long term on the economic fallout. The lockdown measures that India has taken to control the spread of novel coronavirus have impacted the lower strata of the society, leading to unequal distribution of income. With lack of education and high risk of having no income, this segment would witness the real income shock that could further endanger the food security of these households. Although the government has announced various social protection measures, they are not enough to cater the basic need of the unprivileged classes. In such a grim situation with further lockdown and limited support from the government, the low-income groups will be left with the choice between employment with the acceptance of risk getting infected or unemployment and starvation, despite any official lockdown measures.

The observations from the previous pandemics in the country can serve as a foundation in developing policies. The historic patterns of poverty and income distribution can be identified with the long-term impact on the employment and economy. The authorities must plan to recover the losses through economic reforms. The new policy must consider stimulus package to mitigate the risk of Covid-19 social distance measures to control the unemployment, poverty and unequal income distribution. In the face of globalization, developing countries such as India need to make such expenditure more progressive so that it can actually target the lower strata of society, thus reducing the gap between haves and have-not and support the vulnerable sections of the society during the economic and health crisis.

References

Bardhan Pranab. 2009. Notes on the political economy of India's tortuous transition. *Economic and Political Weekly* 31–36.

Business Today. 2020. *Coronavirus: Moody's Cuts India's 2020 GDP Growth Forecast to 2.5%.*

Chaudhary, Monika, et al. 2020. Effect of COVID-19 on economy in India: Some reflections for policy and programme. *Journal of Health Management* 22 (2): 169–180.

Chen, M. 2020. To die from hunger or the virus. An all too real dilemma for the poor in India and (Elsewhere). *WIDER Blog.*

Conway, Tim. et al. 2000. *Social Protection: New Directions of Donor Agencies.*

KPMG. 2020. *Coronavirus: India's GDP Growth May Fall below 3% If Lockdown Extends.* https://www.businesstoday.in/current/economy-politics/coronavirus-india-gdp-growth-may-fall-below-3-if-lockdown-extends-says-kpmg-report/story/400135.html.

Deaton, Angus, and Jean Dreze. 2002. Poverty and inequality in India: A re-examination. *Economic and Political Weekly* 3729–48.

Deshpande, Ashwini. 2020. Early effects of lockdown in India: Gender gaps in job losses and domestic work. *The Indian Journal of Labour Economics* 63 (1): 87–90.

Devereux, Stephen. 2003. Policy options for increasing the contribution of social protection to food security. *Forum for Food Security in Southern Africa.*

Dreze, Jean, and Amartya Sen. 2013. *An Uncertain Glory: India and Its Contradictions.* Princeton University Press.

DRID. 2005. *Social Transfers and Chronic Poverty: Emerging Evidence and the Challenge Ahead.*

Eichhorst, Werner. et al. 2010. The role of social protection as an economic stabiliser: Lessons from the current crisis. *Institute for the Study of Labor (IZA)* (31).

Fiszbein, Ariel. et al. 2014. Social protection and poverty reduction: Global patterns and some targets. *World Development* 61:167–77. https://doi.org/10.1016/j.worlddev.2014.04.010. Elsevier Ltd.

Gentilini, Ugo, and Steven Were. 2011. Social protection 2.0: Exploring issues, evidence and debates in a globalizing world. *Food Policy* 36 (3):329–40. https://doi.org/10.1016/j.foodpol.2011.03.007. Elsevier Ltd.

Gopinath, Gita. 2020. *The great lockdown: Worst economic downturn since the great depression.*

Government of India. 2020. *Periodic Labour Force Survey 2017–18.*

Goyal, A. 2020. *Containing the Economic Impact of Covid.* https://www.magzter.com/article/Newspaper/The-Hindu-Business-Line/Containing-The-EconomicImpact-Of-Covid?utm_source=whatsapp&utm_medium=whatsapp_art_campaign&dt=1586044800.

Harriss, John. 2013. Audacious reforms? India's new rights agenda: An introduction. *Pacific Affairs* 86 (3): 561–568.

Holzmann, Robert. 2001. Social risk management: A new conceptual framework for social protection and beyond. *International Tax and Public Finance* 8 (4): 529–556.

International Labor Organisation. 2011. *Social Security for Social Justice and a Fair Globalization.*

JaganMohan, M. 2020. *Travel and Tourism Industry in India, Statistics and Facts.* https://www.statista.com/topics/2076/travel-and-tourism-industry-in-india/.

Jha, M.K. 2012. State, space and political subjects: A case of special economic zones. *The Indian Journal of Social Work* 73 (2): 157–176.

Kumar, Anand. et al. 2021. Response to the COVID-19: Understanding implications of government lockdown policies. *Journal of Policy Modeling* 43 (1): 76–94.

Merrien, Francois-Xavier. 2013. Social protection as development policy: A new international agenda for action. *International Development Policy, Revue Internationale de Politique de Developpement* 4.2:89–106.

Mukharji, A. 2020. *Coronavirus: India's Bailout May Not Be Enough to Save Economy.* https://www.bbc.com/news/world-asia-india-52117704.

National Investment Promotion and Facilitation Agency. 2020. *Invest India.* https://www.investindia.gov.in/sector/retail-e-commerce.

Nayak, Radhika, et al. 2002. ***Reaching the Poor: The Influence of Policy and Administrative** Processes on the Implementation of Government Poverty Schemes in India.* London: Overseas Development Institute.

Sabates-Wheeler, Rachel, and Stephen Devereux. 2004. *Transformative Social Protection.* 232.

Sengupta, Sohini, and Manish Jha. 2020. Social policy, covid-19 and impoverished migrants: Challenges and prospects in locked down India. *The International Journal of Community and Social Development* 2 (2): 152–172.

Sharma, Gagan Deep, et al. 2020. Policy Response to the Economic Challenge from Covid-19 in India: A Qualitative Enquiry. *Journal of Public Affairs* 20 (4): e2206.

Sumner, Andy. 2019. Global poverty and inequality: Change and continuity in late development. *Development and Change* 50 (2): 410–425.

Swank, Duane, and Hans-Georg. Betz. 2003. Globalization, the welfare state and rightwing populism in Western Europe. *Socio-Economic Review* 1 (2): 215–245.

World Bank. 2001. *Social Protection Sector Strategy: From Safety Net to Springboard.*

World Bank. 2009. *World Development Report 2009. Reshaping Economic Geography.* https://openknowledge.worldbank.org/handle/10986/5991.

Maintaining Employee Motivation During COVID-19 Pandemic

Pallavi Padhy and Madhusmita Dash

1 Introduction

Recently the whole globe is very much concerned about the pandemic and its effect which is spread over the world. Fachriansyah (2020), said that the whole working culture of all workers or staff members of the companies got disturbed by the outbreak of this COVID-19 pandemic. On the other hand, organization to maintain their income from the business, adopt the ways that the employee can work properly in this situation. To maintain the employees' motivation the companies faced a great challenge to manage it in a good way. According to Syakriah, (2020a) and Grima et al. (2020), the organization is specially focused to have proper equipment and knowledge in order to have appropriate security for the employees due to the outbreak of this corona virus pandemic.

The corona virus spread or transfers among the Humans, which is the major factor that the employees of the organization need to keep safe and their security is a key role for the organization (Kampf et al. 2020). For this, the companies need to have focused on the system of 'work from home' facility for the employees and with the provision of equipment provide to them (Desk 2020).

Even the organization faces the difficulty to maintain the motivation of the employees as the outbreak of this pandemic negatively affects the emotions and creates anxiety among them (Assor et al. 2005). Alternatively, the employees can work if they are fully satisfied with their basic needs to manage their motivation (Amiot et al. 2013). In another way, the employees can be motivated through their own capability of fulfilling their needs to allow their responsibilities as member of the organization (Humala 2017).

P. Padhy (✉) · M. Dash
Siksha O Anusadhan Deemed to be University, Bhubaneswar, Odisha, India

M. Dash
e-mail: madhusmitadash@soa.ac.in

R. N. Subudhi et al. (eds.), *Future of Work and Business in Covid-19 Era*,
Springer Proceedings in Business and Economics,
https://doi.org/10.1007/978-981-19-0357-1_8

The main reason of this research is to widen the ways to motivate the employees in this pandemic situation to work safely for the organization through reviewing various literatures and to support this with the help of qualitative methodologies.

2 Literature Review

Employee to work in the organization mainly reflects the motivation for achieving goal or objective to satisfy the basic needs and desires (Wiradendi et al. 2019). Now in the literature, we found that there are many theories of motivation, which supports the employee's wellness but in this study it only focuses on the theory of Abraham H. Maslow for examining the present exertions with suggestions that needed for the organizations.

According to the theory of Abraham H. Maslow, motivation is the reason for which one acts according to the need, want and desires. In this theory of motivation, it mainly comprises five stages of need. The need that required for basic living needs represents the first need like shelter, food and cloth. Next, come to the need of safety and security. Then the third need is about the social identification in the society and the importance of their living. Then the need of position, status and prominence of their existence represents the fourth need. Ultimately, self-actualization is the fifth need as required by the people for the progress of their prospective view towards the achieving of goals (Maslow 1954). The fundamental nature of this theory suggests that if the need at the base level will be fulfilled then the upper need can be attained according and that go on according to the hierarchy of the needs. Therefore, in the organization the managers need to understand that the needs of the workers and employees required to fulfil in order to motivate them to work properly (Maslow 1954).

3 Methodology

This study purely focuses on reviewing systematically using the technique of 'PRISMA' which is Preferred Reporting Items for Systematic Reviews and Meta-analysis by following certain research procedure. This method of research mainly stresses on evaluation, identification, investigation of past studies, which must relate to the present research (Perry and Hammond 2002; Wolor et al. 2020). Here the information presents mainly relevant to inclusive and impartial findings. This study is purely an approach of qualitative study where it aims on framing, evaluating and offering the inclusive explanation to retain employee motivation towards work during the outbreak of this COVID-19 pandemic (Berkah and Sawarjuwono 2019). From various journals, articles are taken to impose the ways to motivate the employees and their performance during this extreme situation of COVID-19 with the help of literatures of various authors (Moreno et al. 2017).

4 Discussion

In an organization where employees feel the security and safety, they perform better than usual for the organization (Christian et al. 2009; Mensah and Tawiah 2016). Moreover, if the employees do not have the sense of safety and security of their job, they will not perform towards the objective of the organization (O'Rourke et al. 2011). During any unfavourable situation or any pandemic, the management needs to think to adopt some motivational ways in their policies and procedures to support the employees to keep them working well (Anderson et al. 2016; Balda and Mora 2017). Thus, the employees of the organization have the support from the management as it considers as a central role of the organization (Eisenberg and Krishnan 2018; Martins et al. 2004).

During the outbreak of the corona virus pandemic, the organizations take responsibility of acquiring all the functional needs through extrinsic motivation. This extrinsic motivation is mainly referred to the extra bonus or compensation to the employees for their overtime work and their physical presence that need in this high time of pandemic. As well as the companies know the fact that this form of motivation will not last as the situation can turn to less performance of the employees or employee turnover. Subsequently, the organization should recognize the effort and accomplishment of the employees and provide short-term rewards in order to make them motivated (Cameron et al. 2001; May et al. 2014; Reitman 1998).

According to Maslow (1954) there are five hierarchal needs of Human Being, and same as the needs of the employees in the organization. Out of these needs, the employees do not require the societal need, status need and self-actualization need as the employee remain isolated for this pandemic for their safety. Even the organizations allow the employees to remain in their home in order to follow the necessary precaution for this corona virus pandemic (Fachriansyah 2020; Kampf et al. 2020; Syakriah 2020b). As a result, the physiological needs and the safety need are the two basic needs required by the employees to sustain in this situation.

This study mainly focuses to provide some suggestion for motivating the employees to retain in this condition of corona virus outbreak specifically, work from home and suitable work shifts.

Work from home: To provide the security to employees, the organization creates a virtual platform that the employees can perform their work in their safe zone and complete their assigned job. This makes an employee to feel secure in this pandemic situation and get motivated to balance a healthy work life (Felstead and Henseke 2017; Humala 2017; Robey et al. 2003). In addition, in the same way there may be a possibility of misinterpretations that may be generated due to less interpersonal contact among employees and conflicts (Morley et al. 2015). This leads to the problems for the leader to manage the inconvenience that create in this situation of virtual working. According to Geister and Hertel (2006) and Humala (2017), this is very difficult to solve this misunderstanding among the employees as they will not present actually in the organization and direct contact or face to face communication may not be possible to avoid this misinterpretation. However, there are ways to resolve this problems and motivate employees through video conference among the employees and with the managers and leaders (Humala 2017; Raghuram et al. 2019; Verburg et al. 2013). Certain approaches need to be taken care for applying work form by the organizational guidance specially.

First, in the company's rules and regulations, it has been implemented the strategy of work from home to increase the motivation of the employees. Through these policies employee can feel safe from the outer environment due to this outbreak of corona virus (Morley et al. 2015; Verburg et al. 2013).

Second, through this latest operating standards, there should be proper communication between the employees through online or digital media to perform task easily can improve the motivation also (Raghuram et al. 2019). However, there are many ways to communicate between employees but it is required to have better flow of knowledge and information (Morley et al. 2015).

Work shifts: Companies like manufacturing, distribution and shipping do not have virtual platform to work as it only depends on the physical present of the employees. For this reason, the companies need to adopt some strategy to motivate employees to work in the situation of this corona virus pandemic. The organizations must involve good suitable work shifts to employee according to their comfort zone for accomplishment to their job. However, the organization must implement the strategy of suitable work shift by considering certain things explicitly

First, companies should not entail long work shift for employees due to this outbreak of pandemic as it slows down the performance of the employees. As well as it must take care of suitable work shifts for employees in which they feel safe as for this corona virus, workers need to maintain social distance while working (Ackah 2014; Ayed et al. 2015). Framing a suitable work shift according to the need of the employees for the completion of work in order to keep them safe and secure will definitely boost their motivation (Hooi and Su 2017).

Second, the basic equipment that required by the employees for the safety purpose like sanitizer, face mask, hand gloves etc. are the essential necessities should be given by the companies (Nea et al. 2017; Syakriah 2020a). Therefore, the organization must take care of the health of the employees in this outbreak of the pandemic to motivate them for good performance.

Third, the companies must identify and recognize the work and efforts of the employees as they work in this pandemic without thinking of their health and give them some intrinsic motivational benefits to enhance their performance in terms of some monetary rewards (Hooi and Su 2017; Shen and Dicker 2008).

Fourth is group work among the employees in the same work shift (Hooi and Su 2017). Employees in the same team can help each other during this situation can improve the motivation of the employees (Kaul et al. 2017; Martins et al. 2004).

5 Conclusion

To meet the daily needs, the employees require to work regularly by own choice. In addition to this, the main need of the employees is to have safety and security in this pandemic situation because health is the main thing to take care of. The organization needs to incorporate the policies and procedures of safety measures of the employees. From this study we only give attention to the ways where employee can feel safe to work and can secure their job by accomplishing their task freely. As we, all know that the globe demands that the human resource need to work according to their comfort and feel secure. That is why the organization should consider the policies to keep them motivated through suitable work shifts and working from home.

References

Ackah, D. 2014. The Impact of Motivation on Employee Performance in the Manufacturing Industry in Ghana. *Global Journal of Management Studies and Researches* 1 (5): 291–310.

Amiot, C.E., S. Sansfaçon, and W.R. Louis. 2013. Investigating the motivations underlying harmful social behaviors and the motivational nature of social norms. *Journal of Applied Social Psychology* 43: 2146–2157. https://doi.org/10.1111/jasp.12167.

Anderson H.J., J.E. Baur, J.A. Grif, and M.R. Buckley. 2016. What works for you may not work for (Gen) Me: Limitations of present leadership theories for the new generation. *The Leadership Quarterly* 1–16. https://doi.org/10.1016/j.leaqua.2016.08.001.

Assor, A., H. Kaplan, Y. Kanat-maymon, and G. Roth. 2005. Directly controlling teacher behaviors as predictors of poor motivation and engagement in girls and boys: The role of anger and anxiety. *Learning and Instruction* 15: 397–413. https://doi.org/10.1016/j.learninstruc.2005.07.008.

Ayed, A., A.S. Thulth, and S. Sayej. 2015. Impact of night shift and training development factors on performance of professional nurses in north west bank governmental hospitals. *Journal of Education and Practice* 6 (27): 50–61.

Balda, J.B., and F. Mora. 2017. Adapting leadership theory and practice for the networked, millennial generation. *Journal of Leadership Studies* 5(3).

Berkah, D., and T. Sawarjuwono. 2019. Inheritance wealth distribution model and its implication to economy. *Humanities and Social Sciences Reviews* 7 (3): 1–10.

Cameron, J., K.M. Banko, and D. Pierce. 2001. Pervasive negative effects of rewards on intrinsic motivation: The myth continues. *The Behavior Analyst* 24: 1–44.

Christian, M.S., J.C. Bradley, J.C. Wallace, and M.J. Burke. 2009. Workplace safety: A meta analysis of the roles of person and situation factors. *Journal of Applied Psychology* 94 (5): 1103–1127. https://doi.org/10.1037/a0016172.

Desk, N. 2020. No lockdown for Indonesia, Jokowi insists as COVID-19 cases continue to rise. The Jakarta Post. Retrieved from https://www.thejakartapost.com/news/2020/03/24/no-lockdown-for-indonesia-jokowiinsists-as-covid-19-cases-continue-to-rise.html.

Eisenberg, J., and A. Krishnan. 2018. Addressing virtual work challenges: Learning from the field addressing virtual work challenges. *Organization Management Journal* 15 (2): 78–94. https://doi.org/10.1080/15416518.2018.1471976.

Fachriansyah, R. 2020. Work-from-home policy in effect at major Jakarta companies over virus concerns. *The Jakarta Post*. https://www.thejakartapost.com/news/2020/03/15/work-from-home-policy-in-effectat-major-jakarta-companies-over-virus-concerns.html.

Felstead, A., and G. Henseke. 2017. Assessing the growth of remote working and its consequences for effort, well-being and work-life balance. *New Technology, Work and Employment* 195–212. https://doi.org/10.1111/ntwe.12097.

Geister, S., and G. Hertel. 2006. Effects of process feedback on motivation, satisfaction, and performance in virtual teams. *Small Group Research* 37 (5): 459–489. https://doi.org/10.1177/1046496406292337.

Grima, S., R. Dalli Gonzi, and I.E. Thalassinos. 2020. The impact of COVID-19 on malta and its economy and sustainable strategies. Available at SSRN: https://ssrn.com/abstract=3644833 or https://doi.org/10.2139/ssrn.3644833.

Hooi, L.W., and A.S.Y. Su. 2017. Motivational factors of shift workers in the chemical industry in Malaysia. *International Journal Management Practice* 4(2). https://doi.org/10.1504/IJMP.2010.033692.

Humala, I. 2017. Typology on leadership toward creativity in virtual work. *Interdisciplinary Journal of Information, Knowledge, and Management* 12: 209–243.

Jones, N.B., and C.M. Graham. 2015. Virtual teams in business and distance education: Reflections from an MBA class. *Journal of Business and Economic Policy* 2 (1): 49–59.

Kampf, G., D. Todt, S. Pfaender, and E. Steinmann. 2020. Persistence of corona viruses on inanimate surfaces and their inactivation with biocidal agents. *Journal of Hospital Infection* 104 (3): 246–251. https://doi.org/10.1016/j.jhin.2020.01.022.

Kaul, S., N. Pande, and V. Ahuja. 2017. Virtual team effectiveness: An empirical study using SEM. *Procedia Computer Science* 122: 33–41. https://doi.org/10.1016/j.procs.2017.11.338.

Martins, L.L., L.L. Gilson, and M.T. Maynard. 2004. Virtual teams: What do we know and where do we go from here? *Journal of Management* 30 (6): 805–835. https://doi.org/10.1016/j.jm.2004.05.002.

Maslow, A.H. 1954. *Motivation and Personality*. Harper and Row.

May, D.R., C. Li, J. Mencl, and C.C. Huang. 2014. The ethics of meaningful work: Types and magnitude of job-related harm and the ethical decision-making process the ethics of meaningful work: Types and magnitude of job-related harm and the ethical decision-making process. *Journal of Business Ethics* 121 (4): 651–669. https://doi.org/10.1007/s10551-013-1736-9.

Mensah, E.B.K., and K.A. Tawiah. 2016. Employee motivation and work performance: A comparative study of mining companies in Ghana. *Journal of Industrial Engineering and Management* 9 (2): 255–309. https://doi.org/10.3926/jiem.1530.

Moreno, F.M., J.G. Lafuente, F.Á. Carreón, and S.M. Moreno. 2017. The characterization of the millennials and their buying behavior. *International Journal of Marketing Studies* 9 (5): 135–144. https://doi.org/10.5539/ijms.v9n5p135.

Morley, S., K. Cormican, and P. Folan. 2015. An analysis of virtual team characteristics: A model for virtual project managers. *Journal of Technology Management and Innovation* 10 (1): 188–203.

Nea, F.M., L.K. Pourshahidi, J. Kearney, M.B.E. Livingstone, C. Bassul, and C.A. Corish. 2017. A qualitative exploration of the shift work experience the perceived barriers and facilitators to a healthier lifestyle and the role of the workplace environment. *Journal of Occupational and Environmental Medicine* 59(12). https://doi.org/10.1097/JOM.0000000000001126.

O'Rourke, D.J., R.E. Smith, F.L. Smoll, and S.P. Cumming, 2011. Trait anxiety in young athletes as a function of parental pressure and motivational climate: Is parental pressure always harmful? *Journal of Applied Sport and Psychology* (August 2010): 398–412. https://doi.org/10.1080/10413200.2011.552089.

Perry, A., and N. Hammond. 2002. Systematic reviews: The experiences of a Ph.D. student. *Psychology Learning and Teaching* 2 (1): 32–35.

Raghuram, S., N.S. Hill, J.L. Gibbs, and L.M. Maruping. 2019. Virtual work: Bridging research clusters. *Academy of Management Annals* 13 (1): 1–34.

Reitman, D. 1998. The real and imagined harmful effects of rewards: Implications for clinical practice. *Journal of Behavior Therapy and Experimental Psychiatry* 29(May 1997): 101–113.

Riyadi Slamet. 2011. Pengaruh Kompensasi Finansial, Gaya Kepemimpinan, dan Motivasi Kerja Terhadap Kinerja Karyawan pada Perusahaan Manufaktur di Jawa Timur. *Jurnal Manajemen Dan Kewirausahaan.*

Robey, D., K.S. Schwaig, and L. Jin. 2003. Intertwining material and virtual work. *Information and Organization* 13: 111–129. https://doi.org/10.1016/S1471-7727(02)00025-8.

Shen, J., and B. Dicker. 2008. The impacts of shiftwork on employees. *The International Journal of Human Resource Management* 19 (2): 392–405.

Syakriah, A. 2020a. What about us? Domestic workers feel neglected amid virus outbreak. The Jakarta Post. Retrievedfrom https://www.thejakartapost.com/news/2020/03/18/what-about-us-domestic-workers-feel-neglected-amid-virusoutbreak.html.

Syakriah, A. 2020b. Jakarta declares emergency, but doubts persist over compliance with social distancing directive.The Jakarta Post. Retrieved from https://www.thejakartapost.com/news/2020/03/22/jakarta-declares-emergencybutdoubts-persist-over-compliance-with-social-distancing-directive.html.

Verburg, R.M., P. Bosch-Sijtsema, and M. Vartiainen. 2013. Getting it done: Critical success factors for project managers in virtual work settings. *International Journal of Project Management* 31 (1): 68–79. https://doi.org/10.1016/j.ijproman.2012.04.005.

Wiradendi, C., Y. Supriyati, and D. Purwana. 2019. The effect of work stress, compensation and motivation on the performance of sales people. *International Journal of Innovation, Creativity and Change* 9 (5): 252–269.

Wolor, C.W., A. Pratama, S. Aditya, and D. Purwana. 2020. Adversity quotient in improving millennial generation salespeople's performance in the industrial revolution. *Humanities and Social Sciences Reviews* 8 (1): 220–226.

Restructuring the Green Consumerism Through e-commerce Portals: A Behavioural Congruence During Post-Covid-19

Indrajit Ghosal, Bikram Prasad, and Bijoy Gupta

1 Introduction

The deadly virus (COVID-19) hits globally the e-commerce business in the world; it has denaturized the essence of industry and reported to investigation that 52% of customers are refusing to go brick and mortar shops and huddled places. Moreover, 36% fear brick and mortar shops until they get the coronavirus vaccine. Coronavirus has different effects on different product characteristics, which means that different products have been infected by COVID-19 in various ways (Andrienko 2020). In this research paper, researchers have framed an outlook on consumer behaviour with respect to online green goods. A consumer is a person who identifies a need or desire in the consumption process, makes a purchase and then disposes of it. The use of agricultural and industrial products, values, housing and wealth depends on the use of a typical customer (Grundey 2009). Consumers are already conscious of quality and wellness, so they are willing to pay an incredible amount for eco-friendly goods and services.

1.1 Green Marketing

In the modern business climate, green marketing is a sizzling phenomenon. According to (Polonsky 1994), green marketing is also called ecological marketing

I. Ghosal (✉)
Poornima University, Jaipur, India

B. Prasad
Seacom Skills University, Bolpur, West Bengal, India

B. Gupta
Raniganj Institute of Computer and Information Sciences, Raniganj, West Bengal, India

R. N. Subudhi et al. (eds.), *Future of Work and Business in Covid-19 Era*,
Springer Proceedings in Business and Economics,
https://doi.org/10.1007/978-981-19-0357-1_9

or environmental marketing that is bring up to any form of advertising that presents or intimate an environmental advantage. There is a non-appearance of a general meaning of "green marketing". However, the term eco-friendly items is known to the buyers; still, it is a rising stage in India that needs to redirect the purchasers' recognition and the advertisers towards choice for buying green items through online mode. It alludes to an adjustment in the creation cycle, bundling, marking and promoting of the items that cause less harmful to climate and strength of the individuals. Purchasers are more mindful of this new term, feeling that it is not just the responsibility of the administration to control the ecological issues yet in addition their responsibility to spare the green planet. With the expansion in the well-being-related issues such as impurity, skin illness, there is increasing trend of concern among the buyers about the shift conventional methodology of manufacturing technology towards a sustainable direction (Mishra and Devakumar 2018).

In the present investigation, researchers also figure out that consumers will change their consumption patterns permanently because of lockdown and social distancing, or will they return to their old habits once the global crisis is over? Can new purchasing habits be acquired via local kirana shops due to new legislation related to green vegetables and green products? Will any psychographic factors affect the consumer's online purchasing of the item? Consumers are very conscious of the items they purchase in this consumer-oriented era, the services they use and the world they live in. This has given rise to many businesses that have started to develop goods and services that are environmentally friendly.

1.2 Consumer Buying Behaviour on Green Marketing

In the new world of industry, green marketing is a sizzling phenomenon. A universal concept of "green marketing" is missing. Green marketing adoption also helps the organization to reduce production costs in the long run. Green marketing has benefited both corporations and the environment; it helps to reduce costs for the organization and provides a positive image for clients. According to Yeng and Yazdanifard (2015), green marketing serves as a marketing technique to improve the competitive edge. In an empirical study undertaken by (Ali et al. 2017) on the perception of Bangladeshi young consumers towards green practice, the authors developed that young people, i.e. showed more interest in eco-friendly products and are exceedingly satisfied with the use of green products. A theoretical analysis conducted by Bhalerao (2014) on green marketing concluded that current customers are highly concerned with the climate and the environmental changes. This leads to a shift in the development process of the industry, compelling the introduction of "Go Green Strategy" in all areas of the industry, so that their purchasing behaviour shifts to eco-friendly goods. He and Zhu (2020) examined minimizing the risk of low-quality green goods sold by the e-marketer, encouraging customers to work together in quality observation work and nurture their consciousness of safeguarding. However, in light of above discussion, few questions in research have been generated according to their purchase intention towards green marketing approach via online. How to extract the factor/factors affecting the perception of the consumers' towards purchase of green products online during post-COVID-19? How to identify the impact of specific factors that has affected the purchase intention of the consumers towards online green products during post-COVID-19?

With the aim of answering the above questions, the researcher used a positivist approach to understand green consumers' buying intentions on a statement-by-statement basis through factor analysis and regression model. Therefore, this study has a novelty to know about the psychographic attributes of the consumers living in the Kolkata city, West Bengal (India). Now, this research is classified as follows: Section 2 describes the theoretical framework on consumer buying behaviour on green marketing, consumer shopping behaviour through online, impact of digital marketing during post-COVID-19; methodological part is explained in Sect. 3; data analysis and interpretation have been defined in Sect. 4; findings, theoretical implications, managerial implications and limitation are described in Sect. 5.

2 Theoretical Framework

2.1 Online Shopping Behaviour of Consumer

For social science researchers, consumer behaviour has been a field of major concern. A study is done by Butu et al. (2020) about the impact of COVID-19 crisis on the consumer buying behaviour of fresh vegetables from the local market in the area of Suceava (Romania). The results of their study reveal that before declaring the state of emergency, only 12% of respondents from quarantined area prefer online buying vegetables from local market, while 60% of respondents chose online purchase of products post-declaration of emergency in Romania. Sheth (2020) examined the impact of COVID-19 on the consumer purchasing behaviour and concluded that as consumers spent a prolonged time period in their home during the lockdown period, they learn new advance technology which makes their work easier and consumption in a conductive approach. Vijai and Nivetha (2020) analysed in their study the consumer buying behaviour at the time of pandemic in the city Chennai. The study found that 39.5% of the selected respondents adopted online mode for making payments; 50% of the selected respondents spent their income in buying essential goods and spending a major part of their income in buying health and hygiene products.

2.2 *Pandemic-Driven Consumer Behaviour During COVID-19*

Hassen et al. (2020) inspected the effect of immediate COVID-19 pandemic on buyers' awareness, attitude with respect to food consumption. The authors observed that the consumers shifted towards healthier foods, preferred domestic products, moved to online store for acquiring grocery items in the time of pandemic crisis. Mehta et al. (2020) conducted a study on the consumer behaviour during COVID-19 pandemic situation and in subsequent lockdown time. Major findings of their study are that 76% of the Indian consumer out of the sample agreed to spent their income very carefully and cut their expenditure on purchase. Consumers place a high value on personal safety, family safety and public health in general.

2.3 *Impact of Digital Marketing During Post-COVID-19*

Digital marketing capabilities have a significant impact on innovation capabilities, digital marketing capabilities have a significant consequence on marketing performance, and innovation capabilities have a significant outcome on marketing performance said by Utomo and Susanta (2020). A study did by Habes et al. (2020) has investigated about the function of online advertisement in the dissemination of knowledge of COVID-19 and its potential for attitudinal change. The results of their study have showed that "knowledge Sharing", "healthcare ads" and "healthcare literacy" are the main predictors of COVID-19 awareness in digital media advertising.

Many eminent academicians and research scholars have deep insight into the "green marketing" and contributed significant hypothetical ideas in the current phenomenon. Yet, there are restricted exploration works or studies that revealed the variables which could change the outlook of the buyer (customer) towards green products through online shopping portals. This examination urges the creators to make an endeavour to discover the factor/factors that influence the customers' decision to purchase green products through web portals. The paper examines the impact of COVID-19 in Kolkata Municipal Corporation area of West Bengal in order to provide government and practitioners with a better understanding of why the adoption of green marketing practices through digital mode is necessary in order to improve green consumer behaviour which can help in sustaining pro-environmental attitude among the consumers.

3 Design/Methodology/Approach

3.1 Research Design

Empirical and descriptive approach was applied in this investigation.

3.2 Population and Sample of the Study

In this investigation, online mode was used to administer the questionnaire wherein the questionnaire was sent to 130 respondents among the online green item buyers in the various regions of Kolkata local among male and female with no discrimination. For this investigation, convenience sampling was used to collect the data. Among 130 reactions, researcher has gathered 100 real respondents on the basis of inclusion criteria of purchase of the green items through web portal. The method of convenient sampling has been heavily used in recent literatures. Bornstein et al. (2013) have studied the use of sampling method in five prominent development science journals from the period of 2007 to 2011. The study has indicated that in the cases where sampling strategy could be conclusively determined, they have used the method of convenient sampling. The study has indicated that 92.5% of the study has used convenience sampling method. Only 5.5% of the study has used the method of probability sampling. Hence, this valid literature has indicated clearly that the method of convenience sampling can be used.

3.3 Questionnaire Design and Pilot Testing

Structure questionnaire constructed using interval and nominal scale was used to collect the data. The five point Likert scale has been utilized with 20 questions from the dynamic respondents where 1 alluded to as "strongly agree" and 5 alluded to as "strongly disagree".

3.4 Tools for Data Analysis

The primary data from respondents was obtained using the survey process, which was analysed using statistical techniques such as exploratory factor analysis through SPSS 23 software. A measurable instrument factor analysis has been utilized to recognize the factors. After examination, six elements specialist again utilized regression analysis for predicting the effect of explicit factor/factors.

3.5 *Time Period*

For the fulfilment of the examination, researchers have taken around 4 months; the excursion has been started from first September 2020 to 28th December 2020.

4 Data Interpretation and Analysis

4.1 *Reliability and Validity Testing*

The Cronbach's alpha was used to assess the degree of reliability among the multiple proportions of each factor. It measures the inter-item accuracy of a scale created from a variety of objects. The result of Cronbach's alpha value, which is 0.795, indicates adequate results for data reliability, and sample adequacy according to this empirical study research researcher has obtained (Gliem and Gliem 2003). The KMO measure of sampling adequacy is 0.799, and Bartlett test of spehericity has extracted the Df value of 180 and $p < 0.000$.

4.2 *Factor Analysis*

Factor analysis with statistical tool SPSS 23 was used to test Objective 1 in order to identify the factor/factors influencing the consumer's online purchasing of green products during post-COVID-19. The factors obtained are depicted in Table 1 along with their respective value of cumulative explained variance (%), eigen value, factor loading (average), Cronbach's alpha. The factors obtained are: (a) quality and attributes of the product, (b) reasonable price of the eco-labelled product with certification, (c) online shopping portals related attributes, (d) pro-environmental consumer behaviour and (e) consumers' preferences according to vernacular culture along with principal component analysis (PCA).

4.3 *Regression*

In particular, the regression model estimates the explanatory variables that serve as a latent variable behind the extracted factors. The use of the regression model has been used in this study to identify the impact of specific factor/factors which influence consumer to change their buying attitude towards online green products (Table 2).

Table 1 Name of the factors along with their respective value of cumulative explained variance (%), eigen value, factor loading (average), Cronbach's alpha

Serial number	Name of factor	Cumulative explained variance (%)	Eigen value	Factor loading (average)	Cronbach's alpha
1	Quality and attributes of the product	51.651	0.641	0.583	0.872
2	Reasonable price of the eco-labelled product with certification	62.311	4.809	0.763	0.911
3	Online shopping portals-related attributes	75.891	3.870	0.805	0.920
4	Pro-environmental consumer behaviour	61.252	3.675	0.771	0.872
5	Consumers' preferences according to vernacular culture	76.121	3.713	0.857	0.921

Source Self-compiled by the authors from the data analysis

Table 2 Model summary

Model	R	R^2	Adjusted R^2	Std. error of the estimate
1	0.901[a]	0.840	0.817	0.6889
2	0.902[b]	0.849	0.816	0.6758

Source SPSS output-result table, compiled by author
[a]Predictors: (constant), reasonable price of the eco-labelled product with certification
[b]Predictors: (constant), reasonable price of the eco-labelled product with certification, consumers' preferences according to vernacular culture
[c]Dependent variable: satisfaction

5 Findings of the Study and Discussion

The factors that have been extracted through factor analysis are: (a) quality and attributes of the product, (b) reasonable price of the eco-labelled product with certification, (c) online shopping portals-related attributes, (d) pro-environmental consumer behaviour and (e) consumers' preferences according to vernacular culture. The quality and attributes of the product encompass the attributes of the products like quality and reliability. The acceptability of the end product as mentioned with the specific information in the website has been entrusted in this factor. The factor "reasonable price of the eco-labelled product with certification" is fabricated with the eco-label certifications like ecomark. It also emphasizes the environmentally friendliness claim as well as well as category of accreditation like single attribute certifications, multiple attribute certifications or life cycle-based certifications. The other attributes manifested through these factors are VOC emissions, use of recycled content and use of energy efficient strategy and technology. The factor "online shopping portals-related attributes" terms of underlines the serviceability of the online shopping portals in terms of delivery within scheduled time, reasonable price and user-friendly websites. Furthermore, this factor has been invigorated by the facilitation of flexibility in financial transaction, maintenance of the privacy and confidentiality of the consumers. The factor "pro-environmental consumer behaviour" is constituted of the variables like environmental responsibility, public sphere behaviour and private sphere behaviour and ecological view of the consumers, environmental concerns, attitudes towards recycling, recycling behaviour and adoption of sustainable innovation. The other factor which has been stated as "consumers' preferences according to vernacular culture" is composed of the attributes that underline environmental preservation, individualism-collectivism attributes (IND-COL). It also encompasses the "the country-of-origin effect". The effect of the cultural values, norms, attitudes and gastronomic culture, consumption subcultures, beliefs, values and consumption has also been included in it. The effect of acculturation, assimilation and multiculturalism on the purchase intention has also been included in this factor. After observing five factors through EFA, the researcher has employed the regression analysis which predicts the exact factor or factors which influence to consumer towards buying green products through web portal. Here, authors noticed two important factors such as "reasonable price of the eco-labelled product with certification" and "consumers' preferences according to vernacular culture" have higher impact on consumer (Fig. 1).

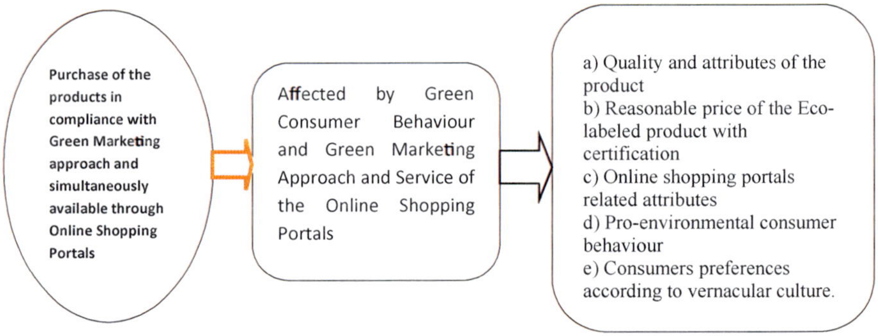

Fig. 1 Refined model indicating the factors that affect the purchase intention of the products which are in compliance with the green marketing approaches and simultaneously sold through online shopping portals *Source* Own conceptualization by author

5.1 Theoretical Implications

The research has provided both theoretical as well as managerial implications. In terms of theoretical research, this research adds value to the existing literatures about the concern of the consumers towards green products. It unearthed a strong evidence-based research regarding the green consumerism specifically during the period of COVID-19. The results of this research are strong proponent of the shift of the consumer behaviour towards sustainable modes of the business. In addition, this research offers a theoretical basis for predicting the consumer behaviour towards green products and their proclivity towards products sold through green marketing approaches. Previous researches (Mishra and Devakumar 2018; Ali et al. 2017) have explored about the buying behaviour of the consumers towards buying environment-friendly products from business organizations that are involved environment-friendly practices. This research has explored the buying behaviour of this products prepared and sold through green marketing approaches from online shopping portals. Hence, the results of this research is advanced literature on the increasing inclination of consumers towards green consumerism through online shopping portals.

5.2 Managerial Implications and Discussion

In India, setting the implied findings of this research will help the organization to understand about the purchase intention of consumers. The organization can understand and respectively target the various segments of the green consumer, viz. true values, green back greens, sprouts, grousers and apathetic. The findings of this paper would assist both the companies and the consumers' to create a win–win environment wherein the business firms would be able to minimize the cost, build a positive goodwill with the consumers. Thus, this strategy helps the consumers, business house and environment. The implied findings of this research will help to promote the sale of the products that were promoted through green marketing approach and simultaneously available at ecommerce portals.

5.3 Conclusion

Thus, this empirical study contributed on multiple perspectives. In case of theoretical front, it has extracted the factors affecting the online buying behaviour of the products sold through green marketing approaches (before this research, these dimensions of consumer behaviour were implicitly studied and empirically tested in a less pertinent manner). In empirical front, it has used the method of exploratory factor analysis (EFA) and regression analysis. In case of methodological front, it has answered the call for measuring the online buying behaviour of the products sold through green approaches by considering this trend of green consumerism through online portals in research design. This discussion provides a deep insight that the extraction of the factors affecting the purchase intention of products sold through green marketing approach is a novel contribution of this research to the current field. In order to test this dimension of consumer behaviour, data has been collected from 100 respondents and tested empirically. The factors that have been extracted through factor analysis are: (a) quality and attributes of the product, (b) reasonable price of the eco-labelled product with certification, (c) online shopping portals-related attributes, (d) pro-environmental consumer behaviour and (e) consumers' preferences according to vernacular culture. Regression analysis has been used to extract the most influential factor among them. Implications for theory and managers were discussed.

5.4 Limitation and Future Research Agenda

The study considers the respondents from Kolkata city, West Bengal. A more representative sample covering various parts of the country would offer more relevant results for the marketers on online buying system of green products. The sample size of study can be extended. The study can be subjected qualitative data analysis methods and mixed methods research design to extract better insight about the consumer behaviour.

References

Ali, Md Julfikar, Md Julfikar Ali Jony, and Ahnaf Shakil. 2017. Consumer perception towards green practice: An empirical study on young consumer from Bangladesh perspective. *Journal of economics and Sustainable Development* 8: 23.

Andrienko, O. 2020. *Ecommerce and Consumer Trends During Coronavirus.*

Ben Hassen, Tarek, Hamid El Bilali, and Mohammad S Allahyari. 2020. Impact of COVID-19 on food behavior and consumption in Qatar. *Sustainability* 12 (17): 6973.

Bhalerao, S. 2014. Green marketing: A new marketing strategy for environmentally compatible products. *International Journal of Development Research* 4 (8): 1531–1538.

Bornstein, Marc H., Justin Jager, and Diane L. Putnick. 2013. Sampling in developmental science: Situations, shortcomings, solutions, and standards. *Developmental Review* 33 (4): 357–370.

Butu, Alina, et al. 2020. The impact of COVID-19 crisis upon the consumer buying behavior of fresh vegetables directly from local producers. Case study: The quarantined area of Suceava County, Romania. *International Journal of Environmental Research and Public Health* 17 (15): 5485.

Gliem, Joseph A., and Rosemary R. Gliem. 2003. Calculating, interpreting, and reporting Cronbach's alpha reliability coefficient for Likert-type scales. In *Midwest Research-to-Practice Conference in Adult, Continuing, and Community Education, 2003.*

Grundey, Dainora. 2009. Consumer behavior and ecological agri-business: Some evidence from Europe. *Economics and Sociology* 2 (1a): 157–170.

Habes, Mohammed, et al. 2020. The relation among marketing ads, via digital media and mitigate (COVID-19) pandemic in Jordan. *International Journal of Advanced Science and Technology* 29 (7): 12326–12348.

He, Hui, and Lilong Zhu. 2020. Online shopping green product quality supervision strategy with consumer feedback and collusion behavior. *PloS One* 15 (3): e0229471.
Mehta, Seema, Tanjul Saxena, and Neetu Purohit. The new consumer behaviour paradigm amid COVID-19: Permanent or transient? *Journal of Health Management* 22 (2): 291–301.
Mishra, P., and G. Devakumar. 2018. Factors influencing consumer preference intention of organic apparel products-A structure review. *Pacific Business Review International* 11–6: 130–146.
Polonsky, Michael Jay. 1994. An introduction to green marketing. *Electronic Green Journal* 1 (2).
Sheth, Jagdish. 2020. Impact of Covid-19 on consumer behavior: Will the old habits return or die? *Journal of Business Research* 117: 280–283.
Utomo, Humam Santosa, and Susanta Susanta. 2020. The effect of digital marketing capability against marketing performance with innovation as mediation (study on batik SMEs during the covid-19 pandemic). In *Proceeding of LPPM UPN "Veteran" Yogyakarta Conference Series 2020–Political and Social Science Series,* vol. 1, no. 1.
Vijai, C., and P. Nivetha. 2020. A study on coronavirus (COVID-19) impact of consumer buying behavior with special reference to Chennai City. In *International Conference on COVID-19 Studies, 2020.*
Yeng, Wong Fui, and Rashad Yazdanifard. 2015. Green marketing: A study of consumers buying behavior in relation to green products. *Global Journal of Management and Business Research.*

Social Media During the COVID-19 and Vaccine Hesitancy Among People

Amir Hafizullah Khan, Rijuta Joshi, and Kimsy Gulhane

1 Introduction

COVID-19 is a novel coronavirus that causes infectious disease of severe acute respiratory syndrome (WHO 2020). COVID-19 has become a serious health issue worldwide. COVID-19 was declared a pandemic by the World Health Organization (WHO) in March, 2020. Researchers have reported that social media was found to be an effective tool in elevating public knowledge towards health issues and influencing public behaviour in meeting individual health needs (Korda and Itani 2013). Limited studies have been conducted to record the role and impact of social media on health awareness related to pandemic infections (Korda and Itani 2013). COVID-19 and social media carries the same viral effect in a different manner but it will be interesting to know whether social media has lessened the hazardous impact of COVID-19 or not. Social media is not only playing an important role in running campaigns against COVID-19 but also contributing towards the acceptance of vaccine among people. The utility of social media can be broadened with better understanding of its data related to public awareness and their reaction (Freberg et al. 2013). Social media is proved to be an effective tool in disseminating real-time information to the public related to taking precautions against infectious diseases (Al-Dmour et al. 2020). It helps in creating a conducive environment where useful information can be created and disseminated among the people with the help of the wide reach of social media (Laranjo et al. 2015; Kouri et al. 2017).

Social media has opened many doors of opportunities to disseminate health-related information for the general public irrespective of the geographical limits of various countries (Al-Dmour et al. 2020). It is important to mention here that

A. H. Khan (✉) · R. Joshi · K. Gulhane
Shri Ramdeobaba College of Engineering and Management, Nagpur, India
e-mail: khanah@rknec.edu

R. N. Subudhi et al. (eds.), *Future of Work and Business in Covid-19 Era*,
Springer Proceedings in Business and Economics,
https://doi.org/10.1007/978-981-19-0357-1_10

social media was the route to internet usage among many locations in India specifically rural areas of India wherein people have very low literacy rate. This trend was facilitated by the wide acceptance and usage of mobile phones. It was also observed that social media penetrated much better than other ground level activities and campaigns of health awareness by Government (Dubey et al. 2016). It has been observed in a significant number of researches that people tend to spend more time online during the pandemic in order to access much needed information, feel less lonely, participate in the discussion and exchange their opinions (Person et al. 2004; WHO 2019; Nabity-Grover et al. 2020). The chances of spreading rumours, fake news, social stigma and distorted information cannot be ignored in places like India where the population is very huge; internet and mobile phones have become reasonably affordable for every segment and usage of social media is growing very rapidly among public. It is also worthwhile mentioning here that the utility of social media is not explored much in the context of health services to the public. Thus, the current research aims to study the following objectives:

- To study the role of social media in raising public awareness towards the perils of COVID-19.
- To study the reaction and action of social media users towards COVID-19.
- To study COVID-19 vaccine hesitancy among social media users.
- To study the overall impact of social media during the COVID-19 pandemic.

2 Literature Review

Social media has been used tremendously by the health organizations, government authorities and the WHO in order to stress the issues pertaining to the public health (Freberg et al. 2013). Cinelli et al. (2020) mentioned that the effectiveness of countermeasures taken by the government during COVID-19 can be affected by spreading of information on social media and strong influence on people's behaviour. It was discovered by Cinelli et al. (2020) that diffusion of information hardly matters to the users which are present on mainstream platforms. It was further discussed that the shift from the traditional sources to social media has majorly influenced social perception, political communication, public debate and policy making (Del Vicario et al. 2016; Schmidt et al. 2017). Social media has a very wide scope in educating people related to the topic such as self-medication habits among public, antimicrobial resistance issues, controlling the spread of misinformation among public etc. Self-medication without consulting doctors have become a rampant practice especially among patients who are turning to internet for their health problems. Jamhour et al. (2017) emphasized that educating the general population about proper antibiotics use and discouraging self-medication are among the WHO's recommendations. Researchers have suggested that the mortality associated with drug resistance can be reduced through collaborative research work at the international level and by spreading more awareness among the general population about self-medication and the side effects of antibiotic overuse (Gould and Bal 2013; Spellberg and Gilbert

2014). During this time of the COVID-19 pandemic, people are largely dependent on social media in order to maintain human interaction and connectivity so that they can feel less lonely and also to share health-related information about COVID-19 (Limaye et al. 2020). People who want to use social media look for unique ways of communicating their views, opinions and insights so that their message will resonate with people (Llewellyn 2020). Increased usage of social media has changed the trusted sources of information among people. They rely and trust more on their peer network available on social media for the authenticity of the information and seek more information from such network (Limaye et al. 2020). This trusted source paves the way for creating authentic source of information (Allgaier and Svalastog 2015). Social media shapes the perception of people towards any matter through its viral impact. People can perceive any matter as true if it is supported, accepted and propagated by majority. Thus, the overall perception of public depends on the way information is communicated to them through social media. Consequently, this triggers the reaction among social media users. Similarly, people react on the discussion of their social media forums in the form such as comments, likes, share or dislike. They also like to participate in the opinion polls, ongoing discussions or share their views on the topic. This in turn leads them to take informed decisions either in favour of the information propagated or against the information. In order to improve the accuracy and credibility of the information, World Health Organization (WHO) has urged medical health professionals to participate aggressively in disseminating correct information more frequently on public forums of social media, so that the guided decision can be persuaded among the people and misinformation can be curtailed to a larger extent (Al-Dmour et al. 2020). Similarly, the best possible solution to fight with fake news on social media is to load as much accurate information as possible which should resonate with the common man and be logical, easy to comprehend and share. It should address questions of users and should be much more in volume compared to the fake posts or misinformation (Llewellyn 2020). The information and misinformation spreading are dependent on the combined effect of the characteristics of the audience and their interaction pattern on social media. Similarly, it has been observed that the type of platform plays major role in spreading fake news and content consumption timing among their audience (Cinelli et al. 2020). Cinelli et al. (2020) suggested that social media interaction among the users are driven by the interaction paradigm imposed by the specific social media platform and the specific pattern of interaction of users with the topic of that specific social media platform. Cinelli et al. (2020) further suggested that in order to design more affective epidemic model of communication during the time of crisis, it is important to understand the social dynamics of each social media platform and its content consumption pattern. Social media ensures that the trust and accountability should be maintained in the highest possible manner with transparency while giving citizens an opportunity to voice their opinion (Song and Lee 2016; Guo et al. 2019). Social media companies have shown social concern and decided to regulate information related to COVID-19 and during the pandemic (Shu and Schieber 2020). Because of its unique features like transparency, commonality, participatory and openness, social media is able to create a bridge between Government and its citizens for interactive communication (Chen et al. 2020). Researcher suggested an active involvement of important social entities such as social media companies, political and Government leaders, and healthcare services providers in the right use of social media for facilitating the correct useful information as its essential civic responsibility and prevent it from being utilized for distrustful interest of the antisocial element (Limaye et al. 2020). In the situation of pandemic, it becomes an utmost important responsibility of all the concerned members of the global community who are directly or indirectly related to the dissemination of information related to COVID-19 that they should disseminate accurate information, strengthen the resilience among community members and take preventive measures against fake information by quickly identifying it and curbing misinformation at the earliest. It also becomes an urgent need for the Government agencies to collaborate with the social media companies to form a partnership of regulating information dissemination by regularly checking information whether it is outdated, fake, in order to protect public health information system from getting it collapsed (Garrett 2020).

Researchers have found that certain group of users are more prone to content led misinformation about vaccination and COVID-19 which includes people with low levels of literacy, older age, lower digital literacy and cognitive impairment (Betsch et al. 2012; Callender 2016). They also get affected because of their biased personal beliefs including political, religious, ethno-cultural and social (Jones et al. 2012; Buller et al. 2019; Dubé et al. 2019). Vaccine hesitancy can be defined as reluctance among people towards acceptance of vaccine which can be demotivated by factors ranging from previously held views to the extent of spreading of rumours among public who can be categorized as outright rejectors or cautious acceptors (Wilson et al. 2014; Callender 2016; Carrieri et al. 2019). There are many factors which are affecting vaccine acceptance among public like unsubstantiated rumours, extensive posting of misinformation from unauthentic sources on every platform leading to loss of satisfaction and trust on Government and, move towards vaccination against SARSCoV-2 (Mills et al. 2020; Devine 2021; Kreps and Kriner 2020; Figueiredo et al. 2020). It has been observed in the research works that people having similar sentiments share more content on social media related to vaccination compared to those having different opinions (Yuan et al. 2019). Thus, it seems to give an impression that delusion of opinion is supported by such platforms but in reality, instead of accepting new ideas people tend to support previously held notions. Such kind of behaviour among people limit the potential of social media from promoting vaccination (Puri et al. 2020). The acceptability of vaccine can be achieved more effectively if the health campaigns are designed according to the need and requirement of platforms and their users. Some of successful practices include using powerful imagery, emotive language, vivid narratives, keeping balanced information, timely responding to the queries and comments of the people, having a well-regulated content monitoring system in place and avoiding excessive text, scientific jargons, pushy posts, etc. (Shelby and Ernst 2013; Chen and Dredze 2018). Youth are found to be most important group in terms of promoting vaccine among their family members as they carry certain level of influence on them and are also found to be heavy consumers of social media. They can also be converted into advocates of vaccine and Government backed campaign (Kortum et al. 2008). Additionally, the acceptability of message can be further enhanced among people if it is aligned with the attitude of individual person (Giese et al. 2019).

Based on the above literature, below mentioned model is proposed in the current study.

The conceptual model presents the guided path of persuading informed decision among public in any uncertain situation specifically related to health issues. The model emphasizes on how to move social media users from the awareness stage to the action stage (Cinelli et al. 2020; Nabity-Grover et al. 2020). It describes the better utility of social media by disseminating correct information among public related to COVID-19 precautions and reducing vaccine hesitancy for further protection (Limaye et al. 2020; Li et al. 2020; Allington et al. 2020; Cauberghe et al. 2021). It highlights that when social media users come across the health-related information across various platforms, they develop either favourable or unfavourable perception towards the information depending on the way information reaches to them (Nabity-Grover et al. 2020; Cauberghe et al. 2021; Li et al.2020). Based on this perception, people react in different manners such like they like, dislike, comment and share the information with others (Cinelli et al. 2020; Limaye et al. 2020; Islam et al. 2020; Li et al. 2020) The reactions of people lead them to the actions whether to follow the instruction, guidelines, suggestions or not (Hooi and Cho 2014; Cheung et al. 2015). If the information comes from a trusted source, then it improves the favourable behavioural change among public (Liu et al. 2016; Crabtree and Pillow 2018; Puri et al. 2020). Thus, the model proposes that the health centres and institutes should have a very strong presence over social media and they should propagate correct information more frequently among the social media users which might help in reducing vaccine hesitancy among public. Hence the research assumes the following hypotheses.

Hypotheses

H1: Social media positively and significantly contribute in raising public awareness towards the perils of COVID-19 and reducing vaccine hesitancy among people.

H2: Social media positively and significantly improve the favourable perception among public towards the prevention of COVID-19 and acceptance of the vaccine.

H3: Social media positively and significantly persuade public to take favourable action towards the prevention of COVID-19 and acceptance of the vaccine.

3 Research Methodology and Descriptive Statistics

The study is descriptive in nature as it shows the impact of social media usage on taking preventive actions against COVID-19 and reducing vaccine hesitancy among people. The construct of the study was developed using an extensive literature review and inductive method, i.e. by incorporating the views of experts (Schriesheim et al. 1993). After delineating the construct (domain) of the study (Haynes et al. 1995; Raykov and Marcoulides 2011), the pool of 25 positively written instrument items were conceptually hypothesized which consisted of five dimensions. The five dimensions were the Social Media Usage (SMU) 1, Awareness related to prevention of COVID-19 and reducing Vaccine hesitancy (A1), Perception related to prevention of COVID-19 and Vaccine acceptance (P1), Reaction (R1) and Action (A1). The deductive and inductive methods were used to identify the dimensions of the domain. The data collected in the form of online questionnaire were analysed for content validity. It was necessary to judge the content effectiveness of the dimensions of the construct after identifying 32 instrument items, thus the panel of two experts from academics and two experts from hospital industry were involved to deliberate upon the selection of the construct, dimensions and instruments items for preparing questionnaire (Liu et al. 2019). The instrument items of 32 were reduced to 28 after careful comprehensive induction and analysis by panel of expert. Statements were formed for the above-mentioned parameters using Likert scale in the questionnaire. The five-point rating scale (1 = Strongly Disagree to 5 = Strongly Agree) was also approved by the panel. The responses were collected from the current 500 users of social media platforms including the followers of various social media pages related to health, COVID-19 and vaccine against COVID-19. Social media platforms were selected based on their popularity among the public such as Facebook, Instagram, Twitter, WhatsApp and YouTube. The respondents include 61% male and 39% female. It was revealed that 58% respondents belong to the age group of 18–30 years. It was further found that 31% respondents were students while 24% have mentioned their occupation as businessmen (Business owner). The result showed that 48% respondents belong to the income group of 8–15 lakhs per annum. Furthermore, the analysis revealed that 38% respondents rated their social media usage as highly active whereas 5% respondents rated their usage as least active. The respondents have ranked "Facebook" as the most popular social media platform with 39% responses, "Instagram" as the second most popular among them with 23% responses followed by "WhatsApp" with 19% responses and "YouTube" with 11% responses. The statistical tool such as exploratory factor analysis and structural equation modelling were used to test the goodness of fit for the proposed conceptual model. In order to test the internal consistency and validity of the data, Cronbach's alpha and average variance extracted (AVE) were used.

4 Analysis and Result

Exploratory Factor Analysis (EFA) was used to purify the dimensions which showed that three items were not fulfilling the requirement of statistical significance (Kaiser 1960). Those three items, i.e. I accept whatever is currently happening on social media; I only use social media to stay updated with information about my family and friends' lives; Social Media is way ahead in providing true and detailed information by COVID-19 and vaccine, were deleted and the remaining 25 items were retained after showing the acceptable range of factor loading (Stevens 1992; Liu et al. 2019).

The construct of the conceptual model was tested for internal consistency and validity of the data using Cronbach's alpha and average variance extracted. The standard value suggests that the average variance extracted (AVE) should be higher than 0.5 for convergent validity of the data whereas values of Cronbach's alpha greater than 0.7 show high degree of reliability (Nunnally 1978). All the parameters were found to be having Cronbach's alpha value greater than 0.7 which satisfied the criteria of high reliability. Similarly, composite reliability values were calculated to be more than 0.7 which fulfilled discriminant validity of the construct whereas average variance extracted (AVE) resulted in greater than 0.5 which ensured convergent validity of the model (Fornell and Larcker 1981). Thus, the high value of AVE and composite reliability showed that the construct validity of the proposed model was established (Table 1; Figs. 1 and 2).

*Awareness related to prevention of COVID-19 and reducing the vaccine hesitancy.

**Perception towards the role of social media in taking preventive measures against COVID-19 and building vaccine acceptance among public.

Reaction-Response in the form of like, dislike, comment and share towards the social media information related to COVID-19 and Vaccine hesitancy or acceptance.

Action-Taking preventive measures against the COVID-19 and willingness for vaccination against COVID-19 (Tables 2 and 3).

The proposed model is also tested using the goodness of fit indices such as root mean square error of approximation (RMSEA), parsimonious model fit (the ratio of chi-square to degrees of freedom), goodness of fit index (GFI), adjusted goodness of fit index (AGFI), comparative fit index (CFI), normed fit index (NFI), incremental fit index and Tucker–Lewis index (TLI) for the model fitness. All the values showed a very high level of acceptance for the goodness of fit of the model such as parsimonious model fit = 1.159, RMSEA = 0.052, GFI = 0.929, AGFI = 0.910, CFI = 0.967, NFI = 0.945, IFI = 0.958 and TLI = 0.973. Hence the proposed model proved to be the correct construct. Furthermore, the path coefficient and Coefficient of determination (R2) were used to test the validity and hypotheses. The construct showed R2 of "Action" was 36% which means that the 36% of variance in the "Action" were resulted from the social media usage, awareness towards the perils of COVID-19 and reducing the vaccine hesitancy among people, perception towards the role of social media in taking preventive measure against COVID-19 and building vaccine acceptance among people and reaction of the public towards social media posts. The construct also showed that the R2 of "Reaction" of the public towards social media posts related to COVID-19 and Vaccine was 41% which means that the 41% of variance in "Reaction" were explained by social media usage, awareness through social media and perception towards the role of social media. Thus, the above result supported that the hypotheses H1, H2 and H3 can be accepted.

Table 1 Estimated value of exploratory factor analysis and overview of construct validity

Indicators	Statements	loading	Alpha	AVE	Composite Reliability
Social media usage (SMU) 1	I am already following many social media pages which offer health benefits through creatives	0.784	0.80	0.615	0.888
SMU 2	I started following social media pages providing COVID-19 information after pandemic	0.769			
SMU3	I follow Government official social media pages	0.793			
SMU4	I follow WHO and other authentic health institutes pages on social media	0.758			
SMU5	I am also specifically following pages which are providing information about vaccine	0.816			
Awareness related to prevention of COVID-19 and reducing Vaccine hesitancy (A1)	Shared content, health institute pages and ads on social media have provided the initial information to me about the perils of COVID-19 and Vaccine development	0.778	0.79	0.601	0.882
A2	Social Media instantly provides updates related to prevention of COVID-19 and success of vaccine among public	0.744			
A3	Discussion on social media groups and forums prompted me to seek further information about COVID-19 and Vaccine hesitancy among public	0.831			

(continued)

Table 1 (continued)

Indicators	Statements	loading	Alpha	AVE	Composite Reliability
A4	Government and other authentic sources share very less information on social media compared to other private accounts	0.768			
A5	I prefer social media over other medias for COVID-19 and Vaccine related information	0.753			
Perception related to prevention of COVID-19 and vaccine acceptance (P1)	Social media helped me to believe that COVID-19 can be prevented from spread with proper precaution and vaccine can curtail the harm of COVID-19	0.779	0.82	0.627	0.909
P2	Social media provides me with simplified content and trusted information on COVID-19 and vaccine acceptance. Thus, I believe social media should be widely used for such purpose	0.793			
P3	Social media network provides me with mature, rational suggestions and more user generated content for knowing more about COVID-19 and vaccine	0.765			
P4	Special community pages related to health benefits instigated me to redefine my choices for vaccine as well as precautions against COVID-19	0.789			

(continued)

Table 1 (continued)

Indicators	Statements	loading	Alpha	AVE	Composite Reliability
P5	Social media creates curiosity to investigate further about COVID-19 prevention, precautions and vaccine acceptance	0.851			
Reaction (R1)	Social media provides me better communities, platforms and social network to ask about COVID-19 and vaccine	0.752	0.80	0.623	0.908
R2	I frequently like and dislike the content shared on social media depending on its authenticity	0.769			
R3	I actively participate in discussions on social media forums related to COVID-19 and vaccine acceptance	0.798			
R4	I significantly contribute in commenting on social media posts and sharing the useful information among my social media circles	0.779			
R5	I take part in surveys, polls and reviews about my experience related to COVID-19 and Vaccine acceptance	0.842			
Action (A1)	I will take the vaccine when my turn will come after confirming it with my social media circle or forums	0.732	0.78	0.588	0.895

(continued)

Table 1 (continued)

Indicators	Statements	loading	Alpha	AVE	Composite Reliability
A2	I have started taking better precaution against COVID-19 after reading useful information on social media	0.746			
A3	I regularly follow Government guidelines received on social media	0.796			
A4	I rely on authentic social media pages and never try to self-medicate myself if observe any change in my physical or mental well-being	0.777			
A5	I take action/precautions against COVID-19 after confirming with my social media circle or forums	0.824			

Source SPSS output table, compiled by author

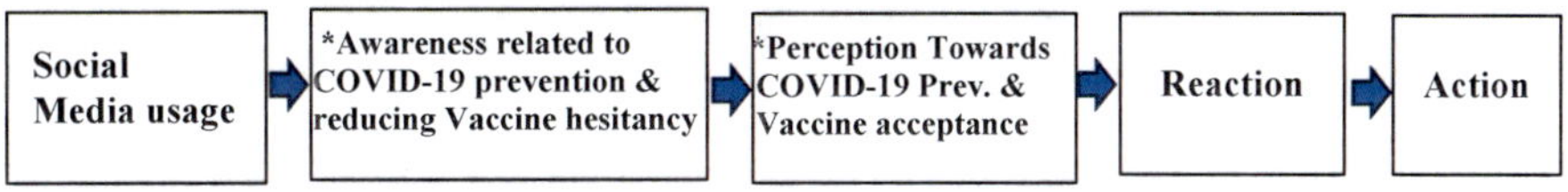

Fig. 1 Conceptual model *Source* Own conceptualization by author

5 Conclusion and Implications

The current study proposes the model on how to use social media for disseminating information among public related to health issues. It emphasizes only on the positive aspect of social media for addressing key issues related to public health. It helps in developing an ecosystem for creating authentic information, disseminating information among public, persuading people to participate in the ongoing discussion and to act in their capacity for favourable change. Result showed that social media positively and significantly contribute in building awareness among the public related to COVID-19 and acceptance of the vaccine. Thus, the model can be used for better utility of social media for health-related issues. The current research also suggests the statistical tools, scales and measures for analysing the impact of social media on

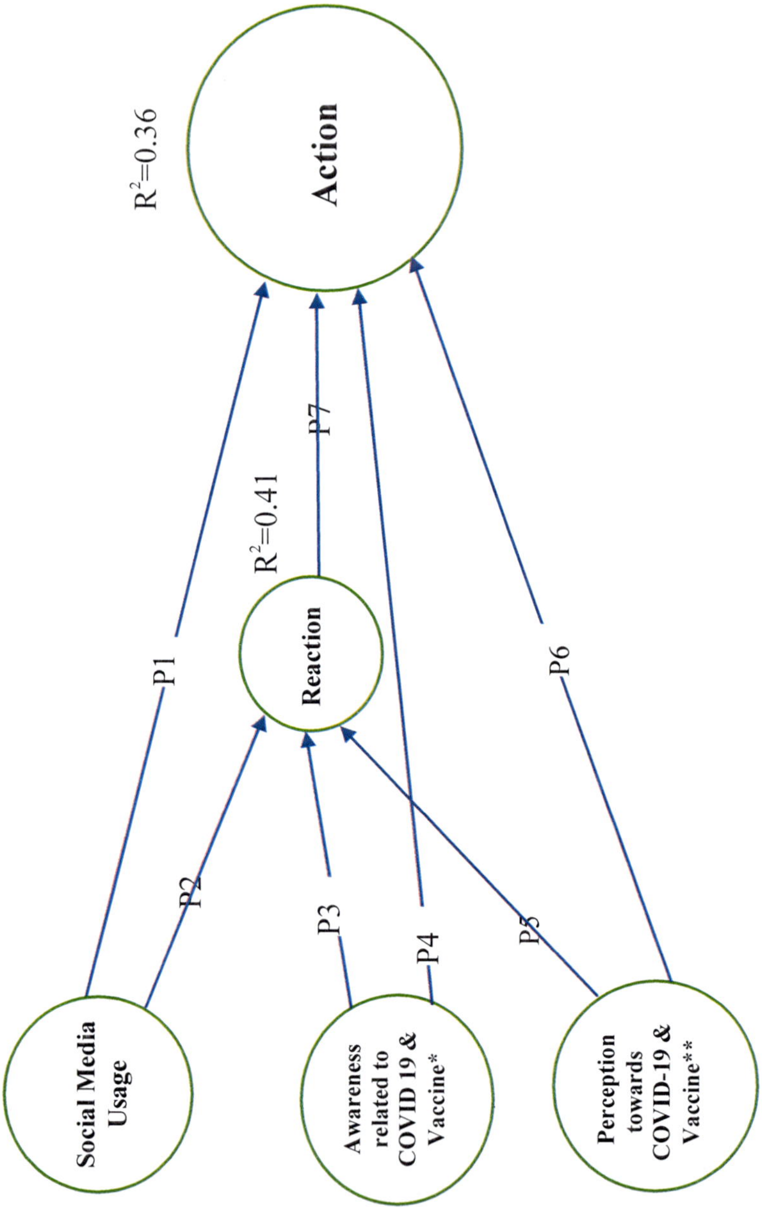

Fig. 2 Estimated values of the proposed model *Source* Own conceptualization by author

Table 2 Path coefficient of the proposed model

Structural paths	Impact (path coefficient)
Path 1	0.38
Path 2	0.41
Path 3	0.44
Path 4	0.39
Path 5	0.48
Path 6	0.33
Path 7	0.37

Source SPSS output table, compiled by author

Table 3 Hypothesis testing

<table>
<tr><th>Structural paths</th><th>R2 (coefficient of determination)</th><th>Hypothesis</th></tr>
<tr><td>Path 2</td><td rowspan="3">41%</td><td rowspan="7">H1 accepted
H2 accepted
H3 accepted</td></tr>
<tr><td>Path 3</td></tr>
<tr><td>Path 5</td></tr>
<tr><td>Path 1</td><td rowspan="4">36%</td></tr>
<tr><td>Path 4</td></tr>
<tr><td>Path 6</td></tr>
<tr><td>Path 7</td></tr>
</table>

Source SPSS output table, compiled by author

public. It also mentions the path coefficient and coefficient of determination were significant in explaining the relationship among the selected parameters. Finally, it stresses on matters like health departments of government, private health centres and other health institutes should have a very strong presence on social media for providing authentic information more frequently to capture the public attention.

References

Al-Dmour, H., R. Masa'deh, A. Salman, M. Abuhashesh, and R. Al-Dmour. 2020. Influence of social media platforms on public health protection against the COVID-19 pandemic via the mediating effects of public health awareness and behavioral changes: Integrated model. *Journal of Medical Internet Research* 22 (8).

Allgaier, Joachim, and Anna Lydia Svalastog. (2015). The communication aspects of the Ebola virus disease outbreak in Western Africa—do we need to counter one, two, or many epidemics? *Croatian medical journal* 56 (5): 496–9. doi:https://doi.org/10.3325/cmj.2015.56.496.

Allington, D., B. Duffy, S. Wessely, N. Dhavan, and J. Rubin. (2020). Health-protective behaviour, social media usage and conspiracy belief during the COVID-19 public health emergency. *Psychological Medicine* 1–7. Advance online publication. https://doi.org/10.1017/S003329172000224X.

Betsch, C., N.T. Brewer, P. Brocard, P. Davies, W. Gaissmaier, N. Haase, J. Leask, F. Renkewitz, B. Renner, and V.F. Reyna. 2012. Opportunities and challenges of web 2.0 for vaccination decisions. *Vaccine* 30 (25): 3727–3733. https://doi.org/10.1016/j.vaccine.2012.02.025.

Buller, D.B., B. J. Walkosz, J. Berteletti, S.L. Pagoto, J. Bibeau, K. Baker, J. Hillhouse, and K.L. Henry. 2019. Insights on HPV vaccination in the united states from mothers' comments on facebook posts in a randomized trial. *Hum Vaccin Immunother* 15 (7–8), 1479–87. doi:https://doi.org/10.1080/21645515.2019.1581555.

Callender, D. 2016. Vaccine hesitancy: More than a movement. *Human Vaccines and Immunotherapeutics* 12 (9): 2464–2468. https://doi.org/10.1080/21645515.2016.1178434.

Carrieri, V., L. Madio, and F. Principe. 2019. Vaccine hesitancy and (fake) news: Quasi-experimental evidence from Italy. *Health Economics* 28 (11): 1377–1382. https://doi.org/10.1002/hec.3937.

Cauberghe, V., I. Van Wesenbeeck, S. De Jans, L. Hudders, and K. Ponnet. 2021. How adolescents use social media to cope with feelings of loneliness and anxiety during COVID-19 Lockdown. *Cyberpsychology, Behavior and Social Networking* 24 (4): 250–257. https://doi.org/10.1089/cyber.2020.0478.

Chen, T., and M. Dredze. 2018. Vaccine images on twitter: Analysis of what images are shared. *Journal of Medical Internet Research* 20 (4): e130. doi:https://doi.org/10.2196/jmir.8221.

Chen, Q., C. Min, W. Zhang, G. Wang, X. Ma, and R. Evans. 2020. Unpacking the black box: How to promote citizen engagement through government social media during the COVID-19 crisis. *Computers in Human Behavior* 110: 106380. https://doi.org/10.1016/j.chb.2020.106380.

Cheung, C., Z.W.Y. Lee, and T.K.H. Chan. 2015. Self-disclosure in social networking sites: The role of perceived cost, perceived benefits and social influence. *Internet Research* 25 (2): 279–299. https://doi.org/10.1108/IntR-09-2013-0192.

Cinelli, M., W. Quattrociocchi, A. Galeazzi, et al. 2020. The COVID-19 social media infodemic. *Science and Reports* 10: 16598. https://doi.org/10.1038/s41598-020-73510-5.

Crabtree, M.A., and D.R. Pillow. 2018. Extending the dual factor model of facebook use: Social motives and network density predict facebook use through impression management and open self-disclosure. *Personality and Individual Differences* 133: 34–40. https://doi.org/10.1016/j.paid.2017.06.017.

Del Vicario, M., A. Bessi, F. Zollo, F. Petroni, A. Scala, G. Caldarelli, H.E. Stanley, and W. Quattrociocchi. 2016. The spreading of misinformation online. *Proceedings of the National Academy of Sciences United States of America* 113 (3): 554–559. https://doi.org/10.1073/pnas.1517441113.

Devine, Daniel, et al. 2021. Trust and the coronavirus pandemic: What are the consequences of and for trust? An early review of the literature. *Political Studies Review* 19(2): 274–285. doi:https://doi.org/10.1177/1478929920948684.

Dubé, E., D. Gagnon, P. Clément, J.A. Bettinger, J.L. Comeau, S. Deeks, M. Guay, S. Mac Donald, N.E. Mac Donald, and H. Mijovic. 2019. Challenges and opportunities of school-based HPV vaccination in Canada. *Human Vaccines and Immunotherapeutics* 15 (7–8): 1650–55. doi:10.1080/ 21645515.2018.1564440

Dubey, B., and P. Dubey, Dubey. 2016. US. Role of media and treatment on an SIR model. *NAMC* 21(2): 185–200.

Figueiredo, A.D., C. Simas, E. Karafillakis, P. Paterson, and H.J. Larson. 2020. Mapping global trends in vaccine confidence and investigating barriers to vaccine uptake: A large-scale retrospective temporal modelling study. *Lancet* 396: 898–908.

Fornell, C., and D.F. Larcker. 1981. Evaluating structural equation models with unobservable variables and measurement error. *Journal of Marketing Research* 18: 39–50. [CrossRef]

Freberg, K., M.J. Palenchar, and S.R. Veil. 2013. Managing and sharing H1N1 crisis information using social media bookmarking services. *Public Relations Review* 39 (3): 178–184.

Garrett, L. 2020. COVID-19: The medium is the message. *Lancet* 395: 942–943.

Giese, H., H. Neth, M. Moussaïd, C. Betsch, and W. Gaissmaier. 2019. The echo in flu-vaccination echo chambers: Selective attention trumps social influence. *Vaccine* 38 (8): 2070–2076. https://doi.org/10.1016/j.vaccine.2019.11.038.

Gould, I.M., and A.M. Bal. 2013. New antibiotic agents in the pipeline and how they can overcome microbial resistance. *Virulence* 4 (2): 185–191.

Guo, B., Y. Ding, L. Yao, Y. Liang, and Z. Yu. 2019. The future of misinformation detection: new perspectives and trends. *ACM Computer Survey* 53. doi:1909.03654.

Haynes, S.N., D.C.S. Richard, and E.S. Kubany. 1995. Content validity in psychological assessment: A functional approach to concepts and methods. *Pyschol Assess* 7: 238–247. https://doi.org/10.1037/1040-3590.7.3.238[CrossRef].

Hooi, R., and H. Cho. 2014. Avatar-driven self-disclosure: The virtual me is the actual me. *Computers in Human Behavior* 39: 20–28. https://doi.org/10.1016/j.chb.2014.06.019.

Islam, M.S., T. Sarkar, S.H. Khan, A.H. Mostofa Kamal, S. Hasan, A. Kabir, D. Yeasmin, M.A. Islam, K.I. Amin Chowdhury, K.S. Anwar, A.A. Chughtai, and H. Seale. 2020. COVID-19-related infodemic and its impact on public health: A global social media analysis. *The American Journal of Tropical Medicine and Hygiene* 103 (4): 1621–1629. https://doi.org/10.4269/ajtmh.20-0812.

Jamhour, A., A. El-Kheir, P. Salameh, P.A. Hanna, and H. Mansour. 2017. Antibiotic knowledge and self-medication practices in a developing country: A cross-sectional study. *American Journal of Infection Control* 45 (4): 384–388.

Jones, A.M., Omer S.B., R.A. Bednarczyk, N.A. Halsey, L.H. Moulton, and D.A. Salmon. 2012. Parents' source of vaccine information and impact on vaccine attitudes, beliefs, and nonmedical exemptions. *Advances in Preventive Medicine* 932741–48. doi:https://doi.org/10.1155/2012/932741.

Kaiser, H.F. 1960. The application of electronic computers to factor analysis. *Educational and Psychological Measurement* 20: 141–151. [CrossRef]

Korda, H., and Z.H. Itani. 2013. Social media for health promotion and behavior change. *Health Promotion Practice* 14 (1): 15–23.

Kortum, P., C. Edwards, and R. Richards-Kortum. 2008. The impact of inaccurate internet health information in a secondary school learning environment. *Journal of Medical Internet Research* 10 (2): e17. doi:10.2196/ jmir.986.

Kouri, P., M. Rissanen, P. Weber, and H. Park. 2017. Competences in social media use in the area of health and healthcare. *Studies in Health Technology and Informatics* 232: 183–193.

Kreps, S.E., and D.L. Kriner. 2020. Model uncertainty, political contestation, and public trust in science: Evidence from the COVID-19 pandemic. *Science Advanves* 6 (43): eabd4563. doi:https://doi.org/10.1126/sciadv.abd4563.

Laranjo, L., A. Arguel, A.L. Neves, A.M. Gallagher, R. Kaplan, and N. Mortimer. 2015. The influence of social networking sites on health behavior change: A systematic review and meta-analysis. *Journal of the American Medical Informatics Association* 22 (1): 243–256.

Li, L., Q. Zhang, X. Wang, J. Zhang, T. Wang, T.-L. Gao, W. Duan, K. Kam-fai Tsoi, and F.-Y. Wang. 2020. Characterizing the propagation of situational information in social media during COVID-19 epidemic: A case study on Weibo. *IEEE Transactions on Computational Social Systems* 7 (2): 556–562. https://doi.org/10.1109/TCSS.2020.2980007.

Limaye, R.J., M. Sauer, J. Ali, J. Bernstein, B. Wahl, A. Barnhill, and A. Labrique. 2020. Building trust while influencing online COVID-19 content in the social media world. *Digital-Health* 2 (6): 277-E278.

Liu, Z., Q. Min, Q. Zhai, and R. Smyth. 2016. Self-disclosure in Chinese micro-blogging: A social exchange theory perspective. *Information and Management* 53: 53–63.

Liu, T., H. Shen, K.Y. Chau, and X. Wang. 2019. Measurement scale development and validation of female employees' career expectations in Mainland China. *Sustainability* 11: 2932. doi:https://doi.org/10.3390/su11102932.

Llewellyn, S. 2020. Covid-19: How to be careful with trust and expertise on social media. *BMJ*. doi:110.1136/bmj.m1160.

Mills, M., C. Rahal, D. Brazel, J. Yan, and S. Gieysztor. 2020. COVID-19 vaccine deployment: Behaviour, ethics, misinformation and policy strategies. *The Royal Society*.

Nabity-Grover, T., C. Cheung, and J.B. Thatcher. 2020. Inside out and outside in: How the COVID-19 pandemic affects self-disclosure on social media. *International Journal of Information Management* 55: 102188. Doi:https://doi.org/10.1016/j.ijinfomgt.2020.102188.

Nunnally, J.C. 1978. *Psychometric Theory*. New York: McGraw-Hill.

Person, B., F. Sy, K. Holton, B. Govert, and A. Liang. 2004. NCID/SARS Community Outreach Team. Fear and stigma: The epidemic within the SARS outbreak. *Emerging Infectious Diseases* 10 (2): 358–363.https://doi.org/10.3201/eid1002.030750.

Puri, N., A. Eric, H.H. Coomes, and K. Gunaratne. 2020. Social media and vaccine hesitancy: New updates for the era of COVID-19 and globalized infectious diseases. *Human Vaccines and Immunotherapeutics* 16 (11): 2586–2593. doi:https://doi.org/10.1080/21645515.2020.1780846.

Raykov, T., and G.A. Marcoulides. 2011. *Introduction to Psychometric Theory*. New York, NY: Routledge, Taylor & Francis Group

Schmidt, A.L., F. Zollo, M. Del Vicario, A. Bessi, A. Scala, G. Caldarelli, H.E. Stanley, and W. Quattrociocchi. 2017. Anatomy of news consumption on facebook. *Proceedings of the National Academic Science United States of America* 114 (12): 3035–3039. https://doi.org/10.1073/pnas.1617052114.

Schriesheim, C.A., K.J. Powers, T.A. Scandura, C.C. Gardiner, and J. Lankau. 1993. Improving construct measurement in management research: Comments and a quantitative approach for assessing the theoretical content adequacy of paper-and-pencil survey-type instruments. *Journal of Management* 19: 385–417. [CrossRef]

Shelby, A., and K. Ernst. 2013. Story and science. *Human Vaccines and Immunotherapeutics* 9 (8): 1795–1801. https://doi.org/10.4161/hv.24828.

Shu, C., and J. Schieber. 2020. Facebook, Reddit, Google, LinkedIn, Microsoft, Twitter and YouTube issue joint statement on misinformation. *TechCrunch*. Accessed March 24, 2020. Available at: https://techcrunch.com/2020/03/16/facebook-reddit-google linkedin-microsoft-twitter-and-youtube-issue-joint-statement-onmisinformation/.

Song, C., and J. Lee. 2016. Citizens' use of social media in government, perceived transparency, and trust in Government. *Public Performance Management* 39: 430–453.

Spellberg, B., and D.N. Gilbert. 2014. The future of antibiotics and resistance: A tribute to a career of leadership by John Bartlett. *Clinical Infectious Diseases* 59 (2): S71–S75.

Stevens, J.P. 1992. *Applied Multivariate Statistics for the Social Sciences*. Hillsdale: Erlbaum.

Wilson, K., K. Atkinson, and S. Deeks. 2014. Opportunities for utilizing new technologies to increase vaccine confidence. *Expert Review of Vaccines* 13 (8): 969–977. https://doi.org/10.1586/14760584.2014.928208.

World Health Organization. 2019. Ebola Virus Disease—Democratic Republic of the Congo. *Geneva, Switzerland: WHO*. Accessed August 8, 2020. Available at: https://www.who.int/csr/don/28-november-2019-ebola-drc/en/.

Yuan, X., R.J. Schuchard, and A.T. Crooks. 2019. Examining emergent communities and social bots within the polarized online vaccination debate in twitter. *Social Media + Society* 5 (3): 205630511986546. doi:https://doi.org/10.1177/2056305119865465. Accessed on February 18, 2021. https://www.who.int/emergencies/diseases/novel-coronavirus-2019/technical-guidance/naming-the-coronavirus-disease-(covid-2019)-and-the-virus-that-causes-it.

An Empirical Analysis into Perception, Attitude, Sentiments and Consumer Behaviour During COVID-19 Lockdown in Odisha

Smruti Malhar Mahapatro, Ankita Agarwal, and Rabi Narayan Subudhi

1 Introduction

The day 24th March 2020 became memorable for everyone because anyone of this generation had not heard about the term "lockdown" before. It was the day when all India went under lockdown. Everything got stopped, like international trade, inter-state and intra-state transportation and trade, production which increased the worriedness of the customers. They worried about getting of the daily consumables like FMCG products, vegetables and health care products during that period, and at the same time, govt. had declared complete shutdown for some days which influenced the customers for panic buying. Because of fear and anxiety worldwide, they began to buy their daily essentials in large quantity to store for future. Increasing mortality and infected rate and communication of health professionals staying at home lead to impulse buying from retail store (Naeem 2020). If we will remind that period, we all have observed one thing which is the scarcity of "sanitizer and masks" at the first phase. When coronavirus came to India, people came to know that "wearing mask and using sanitizer" are the best way to prevent from that virus. Because of fear, everyone started purchasing these in large quantity by thinking whether they might be able to get it later or not, which was reflected at the time of lockdown in case of daily consumables. As customers are worried about catching the virus, so they do not want to go outside more. When they went to the market, they bought in large quantity which is for a week or a month; otherwise, they highly depended on e-commerce. As per (the survey of 3000 consumers by BCG, 17/08/2020; Tandon 2020), it was found that 45% of pre-COVID-19 online buyers increased their online purchases during this period.

S. M. Mahapatro (✉) · R. N. Subudhi
School of Management, KIIT University, Bhubaneswar, Odisha, India

A. Agarwal
BIITM, Bhubaneswar, India

R. N. Subudhi et al. (eds.), *Future of Work and Business in Covid-19 Era*,
Springer Proceedings in Business and Economics,
https://doi.org/10.1007/978-981-19-0357-1_11

Talking about the consumption habit of the customer, it had also changed during the period. Before the lockdown, people who were depending on the other persons (maid, gardener, etc.) for their household works faced a lot of difficulties during that period. As per the (IANS-CVoter; Voter 2020) COVID-19 tracker survey, nearly 43.143.1% of old people those above 60 years of age and 60% of old people those above 60 years of age and 60% of those aged between 25 and 45 years took active part in household chores. They had to get their work done by themselves, as they had a fear of getting virus if they allowed them to their home. During the lockdown as every services (like saloon, beauty parlour, gym, restaurants) were closed, people could not avail the services. So, they started doing such things at their home like got hair cut by themselves, they started cooking tasty food as well as fast food which is more hygiene, and those who always concentrate on their fitness, they also started purchasing gym equipment, so that they can work out at their homes. Some people also had done multiple works in their like work of a carpenter, plumber because of compulsion. The entertainment or amusement of people also gets affected because of permanent closure of movie halls and parks as a result they started streaming online videos, watching movies online. So at that point of time, users online video channels were increased. For meeting people, they used online platforms like Zoom, Google Meet and WhatsApp as they cannot meet them socially. As reported (The Hindu, 20/05/2020; Patra 2020), Google Meet has surpassed 50 million downloads on play store and 3 million new users every day during the lockdown period. And, (CNBC, 26/02/2020; Novet 2020) reported that Zoom also had added 2.22 million monthly new active customers during that period.

The customer priority depends on time and situations. At that time, their first priority was to survive. They did not think about their luxurious life and maintaining image in the society, for which both luxurious and lifestyle sector faced a decline stage and sectors like FMCG and health care grew a lot.

Like everything, this lockdown had also pros and cons. Due to this lockdown and economic crises, many people lost their jobs; at the same time, they got an opportunity to spend time with their family. And, the people also who were working also got an opportunity of work from home. It has also a great pros, i.e. because of working digitally from home, people were able to save their time and money which was earlier spent on communicating to and from office, which enabled them time to do, what they like.

2 Review of Literature

Perception, attitude, sentiments and consumer behaviour during COVID-19 lockdown have been explored through various dimensions as apparent from the literature available.

Chauhan and Shah (2020) studied the sentiments, media consumption habits and consumer behaviour during the coronavirus (COVID-19) outbreak and found that around 80% of consumer had high level of concern over coronavirus, which had a significant impact on media consumption habit of people. Due to lockdown as newspapers were not printed, they used T.V, internet and social media to stay informed about the impact of coronavirus on the lives of the people. People were concerned about staying safe from getting infected of COVID-19. They concerned about social distancing, stay measures and more concerned about the education. Because of staying at home, visit to websites and mobile applications consumed significant hours throughout a day's routine. The overall usage of social media sites ranged between 2 and 5 h per day. According to his study, around 77% people observed that the lockdown has significantly affected the consumer behaviour just like the parrot in the cage. Some of them changed their shopping either willingly or forcibly. And, the fear of getting infected changed their mode of purchase like they shifted from in-store to online. They spent more on basics like groceries, health care products, medicine, fruits and vegetables.

Another study by Loxton et al. (2020) examined the consumer panic buying, herd mentality, changing discretionary spending and the role of media in influencing behaviour during the COVID-19 lockdown. They found during lockdown, panic buying emerges globally. Because of increase in consumer fear and anxiety worldwide, they began to establish categories of products which were essential according to them. But, it is not only limited to rice, dal, flour, sugar, hand sanitizer, mask and gloves but also office equipment and gym equipment, etc. Because of herd mentality of consumers, firm took advantage and extended their business models like various manufacturers move into the production of hand sanitizers. The media influenced changes to customer sentiment for which influenced behavioural trends became notable more self-perpetuating as news outlets continued to repot the behaviour.

Naeem (2020) examined customer psychology of impulse buying during COVID-19 pandemic. He found the increasing usage of social media had not only increased the engagement of customers in sharing of information but also influenced the buying behaviour of customers. Work from home and social distancing encouraged people to become more connected and engaged using social media. The messages of social media related to COVID-19 precautions lead to buy extra so that consumers can stay at home. The statistical report of increasing death rates and communication of health professionals staying at home changed the consumer behaviour and leads to impulse buying from retail stores. The situation made people to buy more stock because of fear of unavailability due to COVID-19 pandemic. And, the key contribution is rumours and misleading information over social media that created perception of risk, for which customers started buying impulsively so that they could stay home for a long period.

Sheth (2020) in his study explored the impact of lockdown on the old habits of customers, i.e. will they return or die. According to his study, all consumptions became time bound and location bound. As people work, study and relax at home, the work life boundaries are now blurred. As the consumers are unable to go to the store, the store has come to the consumers. The consumers were adopted new technologies which facilitate wok, study and consumption in a more convenient manner as they are house arrested for a prolonged period.

A study by Sood (2020) found that the lockdown of COVID-19 pandemic affected the global economy and altered the consumer preferences, behaviour and purchasing behaviour like consumers postponed their purchase decisions. Many consumers adopted digital technology so that they did not have to go anywhere. Digital gaming, live streams and video apps have gained popularity.

Madani et al. (2020) explored that there has been increase in the usage of over the top platforms (OTT) during the lockdown. People who were under work from home during lockdown were also spending more time on OTT platforms. The average hours spent on OTT increased from 0–2 h to 2–5 h.

3 Objective and Methodology

The after-effect of COVID-19 pandemic is relatively a new, virgin area in research. This paper aims at studying consumer behaviour during extended lockdowns. As a part of descriptive empirical research study, the main objective of this paper is to investigate and analyse if consumer behaviour changed significantly because of severe mobility restrictions.

It also proposes to study if there was significant change in perception, attitude and sentiment of consumers, particularly for FMCG products.

For this, because of paucity of time, continuous sampling method has been adopted and circulated a structured questionnaire, both online and offline among consumer–respondents of different age group within Odisha.

For this study, a structured questionnaire was circulated both in online and offline modes to around 300 consumer–respondents, by convenience sampling method. Details of valid responses are mentioned in Table 1. Total questionnaires received in online mode are 98, and in offline mode, it was 22. Finally, only the valid and completed questionnaires were accepted for analysis. From online mode, 98 responses, while from offline mode, only 15 responses were collected, mostly because of restrictions of mobility due to COVID-19 lockdowns.

Table 1 Sample size

	Questionnaire sent	Questionnaire received	Complete questionnaire accepted
Online	150	98	98
Offline	100	22	15
Total	250	120	113

Source Primary data, collected by authors

4 Data Analysis

The first part of the analysis describes about the demographic details of the study, and the rest part analyses about the responses of consumers.

Figure 1 shows that the number of responses of different age groups. The highest numbers of responses collected from the age group of 25–35 years is 34%. The second highest number, i.e. 28% responses collected from the age group of <25 years and the sample size of age groups 35–44 years and 45–54 years is closely equal which is 16% and 17%, respectively. The least percentage of responses collected from >55 years is only 5%.

Figure 2 shows the information about the occupation of the collected responses. The highest number of responses is collected from job holders which is 54% (more than half). The second highest is 33% collected from student, 5% are home maker, 3% are entrepreneurs, other 3% are retired, and rest 2% are others.

Based on the analysis of questionnaire, following are the major findings of the study:

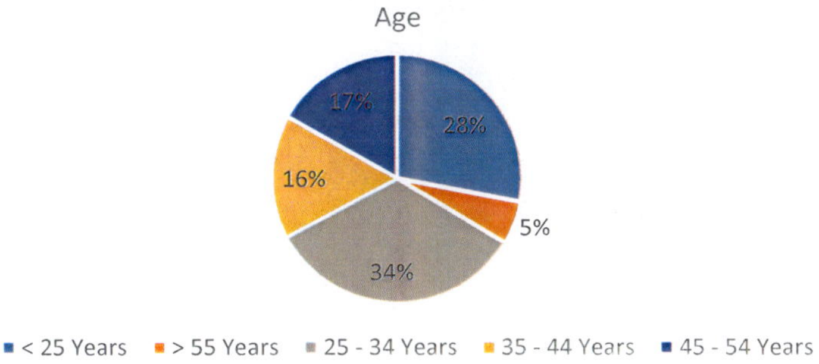

Fig. 1 Age *Source* SPSS graphical output, compiled on primary data, collected by authors

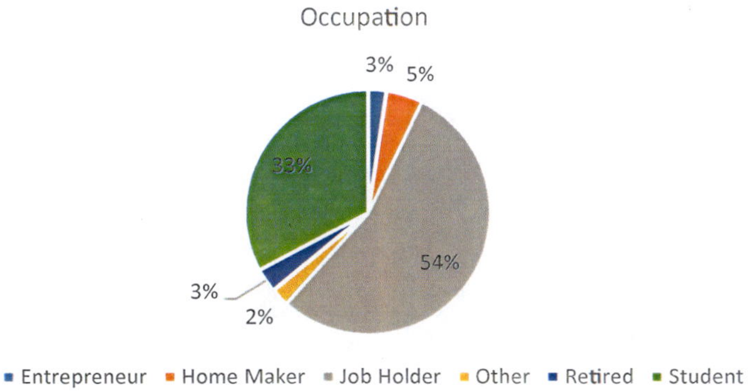

Fig. 2 Occupation *Source* SPSS graphical output, compiled on primary data, collected by authors

- Talking about time spent on news, majority of the sample, i.e. 78% spent more time, 22% per cent spent less time, 18% spent same time, and for only 2%, it is not applicable.
- Fig. 3 shows more than half of the sample size, which is 71% people spent more time on social media during that period, whereas 10% people spend less time, 17% people spend same time, and only 2% said it is not applicable for them.
- Online essential shopping was increased during the lockdown. Here, Fig. 4 shows that in our survey, half of the respondents mention that they spent more time on online essential shopping, 19% spent same time, 21% spent less time, and 10% said it is not applicable for them as they are from the rural areas, they were not aware about that.

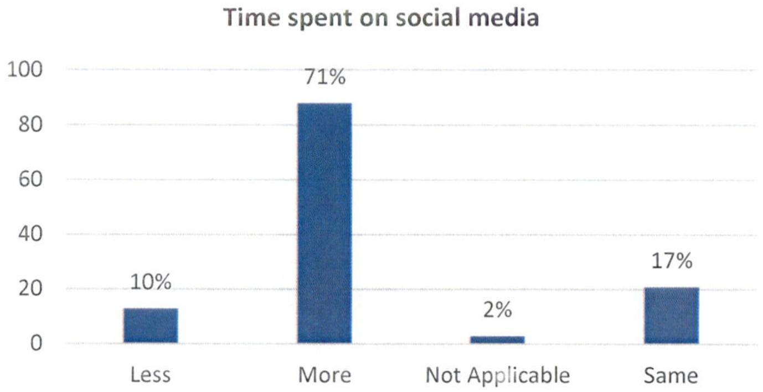

Fig. 3 Time spent on social media *Source* SPSS graphical output, compiled on primary data, collected by authors

Fig. 4 Online essential shopping *Source* SPSS graphical output, compiled on primary data, collected by authors

1. **Impact on experience-based activities**

Because of fear of catching coronavirus, people were very careful at the time of meeting people like friends and neighbours socially. In the survey, it was found that 25% people never met anyone during that period, 30% met once in a month, 30% met once in a week. Only 14% people met daily or regularly as they had no fear of catching virus in their area.

Consumers when asked about the frequency of going to shopping malls and retail shops 38% said they never went, 36% said they went once in a month, 20% said once in a week, whereas only 6% went regularly or daily. Interestingly, when they asked about attending events, 70% respondents said they had never attended the event by overseeing the rules and guidelines of the government and also for the fear of catching virus. But, rest of them attended once in a month, once in a week and regular basis.

2. **Impact on personal and Lifestyle aspects**

Due to lockdown, people were stayed at their homes and got time to spend with their family members. So, when they ask about what impact did the lockdown had on the time spent with family, 90% among them had positive impact, 7% had no impact, and 3% had negative impact.

Regarding reading, watching series, etc. out of the total sample size, 77% told it had positive impact, whereas 21 % had no impact, and only 2% had negative impact.

When they asked about sleeping pattern, more than half of the respondents, i.e. 54% said that they had positive impact, 27% had no impact, and 19% had negative impact.

Talking about the mental health, Figure 5 shows that 38% mentioned that they had positive impact, 37% mentioned negative impact, 23% had no impact, and 2% cannot say. Due to fear of catching virus, people always try to keep them physically fit and keep their immune system strong. So, the 41 % of the total respondents told they had positive impact, 33% said they had negative impact, and only 1% mentioned that they cannot say about it.

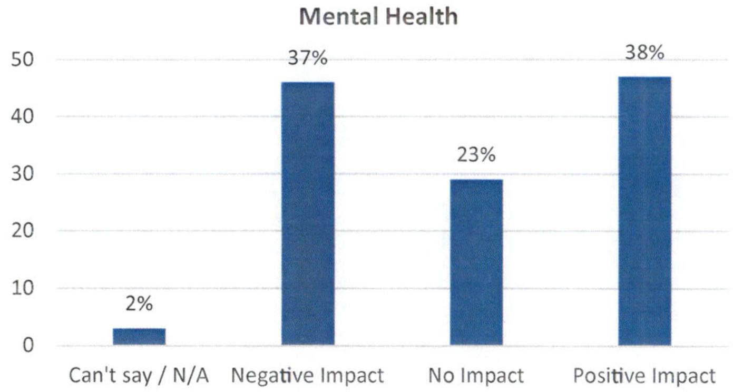

Fig. 5 Mental health *Source* SPSS graphical output, compiled on primary data, collected by authors

During the lockdown period, maid/servants were not allowed to home. The people did their indoor/outdoor activities themselves. Interestingly, when they asked about that, 61% told they had a positive impact on doing all their work themselves, 18% mentioned no impact, 16% told negative impact, only 5% told it is not applicable for them.

Due to COVID-19 outbreak, many people lost their jobs. In the survey when the consumers or respondents asked about the impact on their job or business, half of the respondents said they had negative impact, 23% had no impact, 18% had positive impact, and 9% would not say about it.

3. **Worriedness of consumers**

Coronavirus has spread all across the world, and millions of people were affected by this, which became the main cause of tension among the consumers. So based on the survey, Figure 6 shows that 65% of respondents were extremely worried about them or their family member catching the virus, 20% were less worried about it, 9% were not at all worried, and for 6%, it is not applicable.

In the study regarding the price rise of essential and others, 46% said they were extremely worried about this, 40% were less worried, 11 % were not at all worried, while 3% told it is not applicable for them.

Talking about need of increased savings, in the survey, it was found that 47% among all the respondents were extremely worried about it, whereas 27% were less worried, 19% were not at all worried, and for 7%, it is not applicable.

During the lockdown, many people lost their jobs, many people lost their relatives because of affected by coronavirus. Many people who stayed away from their family could not come, which may cause increased tension and stress level. In this survey, 40% of the total respondents were extremely worried about increased mental tension/stress/depression, 30% were less worried, 21% were not at all worried, while only 3% mentioned it is not applicable to them.

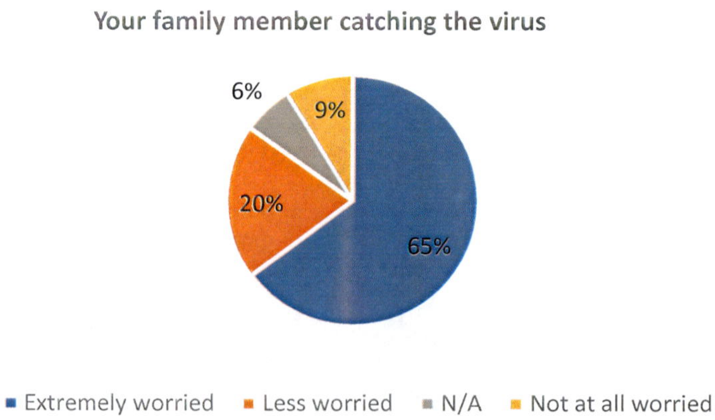

Fig. 6 Your family member catching the virus *Source* SPSS graphical output, compiled on primary data, collected by authors

4. **Impact on eating habits**

To increase or strengthen the immune system during the lockdown, people started eating healthy food like homemade food, nutritious and balanced diet. During the survey, 73% consumer told they were eating more healthy food, whereas 27 % were eating same amount as before.

Interestingly, when they asked about eating outside food, 69% told they were consuming outside food less than before, whereas 4% were consuming more, and another 4% were consuming same amount as before. But surprisingly for 23% of respondents, it is not applicable means they were not consuming outside food.

The chi-square analysis has been done by using SPSS for the study. Following are the results (Tables 2 and 3).

Based on the output of the SPSS, it can be concluded that time spent on social media is significantly associated with age group with 5% significance level (Tables 2 and 3).

The above result shows that there is a significant relationship between age group and shopping online from e-market places (Tables 4 and 5).

Here, it can be concluded that shopping online from e-market place has a significant relationship with occupation of the respondents (Tables 6 and 7).

In generalization, there is a significant association of mental health with age group and occupation but is not verified in our study.

Here, T test has been done with the null hypothesis. In shopping online, female and male have same choices and preferences (Table 8).

Table 2 Crosstab result

		Age group				Total
		25–34 years	35–44 years	45–54 years	> 55 years	
Time spent on social media like WhatsApp, Twitter, Facebook	Less	2	5	0	6	13
	More	27	32	15	14	88
	Same	5	5	5	6	21
	N/A	1	0	0	2	3
Total		35	42	20	28	125

Source Primary data, collected by authors

Table 3 Pearson chi-square test

	Value	*Df*	Asymptotic significance (2-sided)
Pearson chi-square	21.355[a]	12	0.045
Likelihood ratio	21.550	12	0.043
No. of valid cases	125		

Source Primary data, collected by authors

[a]Fourteen cells (70.0%) have expected count less than 5. The minimum expected count is 0.17

Table 4 Crosstab result

		Age group				Total
		25–34 years	35–44 years	45–54 years	> 55 years	
Shopping online e-market place	Daily/regularly	9	9	4	4	26
	Once in a week	16	11	4	9	40
	Once in a month	10	16	6	4	36
	Never	0	6	6	11	23
	Total	35	42	20	28	125

Source Primary data, collected by authors

Table 5 Chi-square test

	Value	*Df*	Asymptotic significance (2-sided)
Pearson chi-square	25.959[a]	12	0.011
Likelihood ratio	31.745	12	0.002
No. of valid cases	125		

Source Primary data, collected by authors
[a]Eight cells (40.0%) have expected count less than 5. The minimum expected count is 1.29

Table 6 Crosstab result

		Occupation					Total
		Student	Job holder	Homemaker	Retired	others	
Shopping online e-market place	Daily/regularly	7	18	0	0	1	26
	Once in a week	20	16	0	3	1	40
	Once in a month	12	19	1	1	3	36
	Never	2	15	5	0	1	23
Total		41	68	6	4	6	125

Source Primary data, collected by authors

Table 7 Chi-square test

	Value	*Df*	Asymptotic significance (2-sided)
Pearson chi-square	33.606[a]	12	0.001
Likelihood ratio	32.509	12	0.001
No. of valid cases	125		

Source Primary data, collected by authors
[a]Twelve cells (60.0%) have expected count less than 5. The minimum expected count is 0.74

Table 8 Two-sample *T* test assuming equal variances

	Female	Male
Mean	19	12.25
Variance	24.667	20.9167
Observations	4	4
Pooled variance	22.79	
Hypothesized mean difference	0	
Df	6	
t stat	1.999	
$P\ (T < \ = t)$ one tail	0.0462	
t critical one tail	1.943	
$P\ (T < \ = t)$ two tail	0.092	
t critical two tail	2.447	

Source Primary data, collected by authors

In this result, by taking 10% as significance level, it was found that p value is less than 0.1, so it is significant. Thus, the null hypothesis will be rejected, and alternative hypothesis will be accepted. It can be concluded that the choice and preferences of male and female are different.

5 Limitation of the Study

Due to unprecedented pandemic shutdowns and lockdowns, the study could not cover a large, and geographically diverse sample size. This study attempted to cover consumption pattern and behaviour of daily essential consumables, particularly in FMCG sector, used during covid lockdown. This had a larger, diverse basket of products. Specific focus was not given to particular items. This had a limitation of studying specific consumer behviour.

6 Findings and Conclusion

Due to COVID-19, government imposed lockdown for 21 days for safety measure on March 24, 2021 which was extended till May 3, 2021. Due to lockdown and shutdown, the retail shops, malls and brick and mortar stores remained closed. Some shops were opened for a short time. But, they started purchasing their essential products through online mode. In our study, it was also found that people preferred online more for purchasing their essentials. During the lockdown, the internet use increased significantly, as found in this study. People were using social media more frequently, as compared to other media. During COVID-19, people started eating healthier and hygiene food and reduce the consumption of outside food. As a result, there is a positive impact on their physical health condition. But, many people lost their jobs, and because of fear of getting virus, their mental stress level was increased. During our study, we have also found out that time spent on social media and online shopping was significantly associated with the age group of the respondents. The online shopping also had a significant relationship with occupation.

7 Contribution to the Society

As the study examined the consumer behaviour during the lockdown period of COVID-19 pandemic, it will be helpful to the FMCG companies, retail stores and malls, and thus, to the society at large. It has been found that people use more e-commerce sites for purchasing essentials. This study suggests healthy eating habits, sustainable consumption, sustainable stress free living habits, through empirical survey data.

References

Bandyopadhyaya, V., and R. Bandyopadhyaya. 2021. Understanding the impact of COVID-19 pandemic outbreak on grocery stocking behaviour in India: A pattern mining approach. *Global Business Review* p.0972150921988955.

Chauhan, V., and M.H. Shah. 2020. An empirical analysis into sentiments, media consumption habits, and consumer behaviour during the coronavirus (COVID-19) outbreak. *Purakala with ISSN* 0971–2143.

Hall, M.C., Prayag, G., Fieger, P., and D. Dyason. 2020. Beyond panic buying: Consumption displacement and COVID-19. *Journal of Service Management.*

Jaravel, X., and M. O'Connell. 2020. High-frequency changes in shopping behaviours, promotions and the measurement of inflation: Evidence from the great lockdown. *Fiscal Studies* 41 (3): 733–755.

Lang, B., Dolan, R., Kemper, J., and G. Northey. 2020. Prosumers in times of crisis: Definition, archetypes and implications. *Journal of Service Management.*

Lee, K., Sahai, H., Baylis, P., and M. Greenstone. 2020. Job loss and behavioural change: The unprecedented effects of the India lockdown in Delhi. In *University of Chicago, Becker Friedman Institute for Economics Working Paper, 2020–65.*

Loxton, M., R. Truskett, B. Scarf, L. Sindone, G. Baldry, and Y. Zhao. 2020. Consumer behaviour during crises: Preliminary research on how coronavirus has manifested consumer panic buying, herd mentality, changing discretionary spending and the role of the media in influencing behaviour. *Journal of Risk and Financial Management* 13 (8): 166.

Madnani, D., Fernandes, S., and N. Madnani. 2020. Analysing the impact of COVID-19 on over-the-top media platforms in India. *International Journal of Pervasive Computing and Communications.*

Naeem, M. 2020. Understanding the customer psychology of impulse buying during COVID-19 pandemic: Implications for retailers. *International Journal of Retail and Distribution Management* 10. Accessed January 12, 2021. URL: International Journal of Retail & Distribution Management | Emerald Insight.

Novet, Jordan. Zoom has added more videoconferencing users this year than in all of 2019 thanks to coronavirus, Bernstein says. *CNBC* (26 Feb 2020). Accessed January 12, 2021. https://www.cnbc.com/2020/02/26/zoom-has-added-more-users-so-far-this-year-than-in-2019-bernstein.html.

Patra, Ishan. Google Meet sees 30-fold growth since January. *The Hindu* (20 May 2020). Accessed January 12, 2021. https://www.thehindu.com/sci-tech/technology/internet/google-meet-sees-30-fold-growth-since-january/article31631115.ece.

Sheth, J. 2020. Impact of Covid-19 on consumer behaviour: Will the old habits return or die? *Journal of Business Research* 117: 280–283.

Sood, S. 2020. Impact of COVID-19 on consumer behaviour in India. In *Conference: Sustainable Management Practices and Economic Slowdown in India held at Delhi.*

Tandon, Suneera. 2020. Covid drives surge in online shoppers, sellers. *Mint* (21 Aug 2020). Accessed January 12, 2021. https://www.livemint.com/industry/retail/covid-drives-surge-in-online-shoppers-sellers-11598003861237.html.

Voter, C. National. 2020. Amid lockdown, 43.1% old people chipped in with household chores. *Daily world* (16 May 2020). Accessed January 12, 2021. https://www.dailyworld.in/news-detail.php?seq=31559&news=Amid%20lockdown%20%2043%201%20%20old%20people%20chipped%20in%20with%20household%20chores.

Assessing Mobile Banking Service Quality Dimensions Using Multi-Criteria Decision Making

Ashwarya Kapoor, Rajiv Sindwani, and Manisha Goel

1 Introduction

Businesses are stressing on building information technology an essential fragment of their functioning to survive and compete in dynamic world markets (Oliveira et al. 2014; Ahmad et al. 2019). Both developed and emerging countries have gained from the growth of information and communication technology (ICT). It has led to tremendous difference in the manner banks deliver their services (Patel and Patel 2018; Ahmad et al. 2019). Click and portal system has replaced brick and mortar system in order to offer personalised banking services to customers (Shaikh and Karjaluoto 2015). Development in information and communication technology facilitated banks to switch from traditional banking to m-banking these days. M-banking is a means to deliver various banking services to users via mobile devices like smartphone, tablet and mobile phone (Barnes and Corbitt 2003; Shankar et al. 2019). It does not require physical contact between users and bank staff (Jun and Cai 2001). The use of technology is greatly advantageous for banks as it can standardise service delivery, expand the options for provision of services, reduce costs, and leads to less pressure on branches. For consumers, technology banking delivers value in form of anywhere and anytime banking. It provides consumers with an extensive variety of services such as fund transfer, bill payment, management of fixed deposit, account inquiry, investment in stock and cheque book order (Tan et al. 2000). The growing adoption of m-banking systems and rising consumers' expectations have led to severe competition among banks. Building competitive advantage and retaining customers require offering superior quality m-banking services to consumers (Jayawardhena 2004; Makanyeza and Chikazhe 2017). As service quality impacts business performance, and assists in enhancing competitive advantage and profitability, evaluating and managing service quality turn out to be major area of interest for researchers, managers and practitioners

A. Kapoor (✉) · R. Sindwani · M. Goel
J. C. Bose University of Science and Technology, YMCA, Faridabad, India

R. N. Subudhi et al. (eds.), *Future of Work and Business in Covid-19 Era*,
Springer Proceedings in Business and Economics,
https://doi.org/10.1007/978-981-19-0357-1_12

(Al-Hawari et al. 2005; Sindwani and Goel 2016). Although literature has studies that analysed various m-banking service quality dimensions but there is hardly any study that identifies critical/key mobile banking service quality dimensions among users and prioritised these dimensions using multi-criteria decision-making method, i.e. best worst method. So, aim of the current study is to figure out and prioritise the critical dimensions of m-banking service quality among users.

Rest of the study is arranged as follows. The following section consists of an in-depth review of studies pertaining to service quality of mobile banking among consumers. Key m-banking service quality dimensions are proposed in this section. Next, the paper discusses the best worst method methodology covering the various steps in the approach. Illustration section describes the evaluation and prioritisation of m-banking service quality dimensions utilising BWM. Further, the conclusion of the paper is presented. Finally, limitations and future scope are discussed.

2 Identification of Mobile Banking Critical Service Quality Dimensions

To find out service quality dimensions of mobile banking, authors adhered to Preferred Reporting Items for Systematic Reviews and Meta-Analyses (PRISMA) guidelines of Moher (2009). Ultimate objective of PRISMA is to report literature review in a clear and transparent manner. It has been used in various fields like health, technology and environment (Hughes-Morley et al. 2015). Based on these guidelines, a review protocol was developed. The protocol covered search strategy, criteria for excluding articles and evaluation of quality.

Search Strategy: Authors consulted Google Scholar for systematic review of literature. Various combinations of keywords related to electronic banking service quality were used to extract papers from database. Authors have keyed the search terms carefully for identification of relevant studies. Search resulted in 562 relevant articles. Articles were screened based on exclusion criteria as shown in Table 1. Totally, 379 articles that came under exclusion criteria were removed. To extract pertinent articles related to m-banking service quality, authors conducted review of abstracts for 183 articles. Based on that, authors selected 76 articles for full text review.

Table 1 Exclusion criteria

Exclusion criteria	
Exclusion 1	Articles in language other than english
Exclusion 2	Articles not in peer-reviewed journal like conference papers, book chapters etc.
Exclusion 3	Duplicate articles
Exclusion 4	Articles where electronic banking service quality is not the major theme

Source Own compilation by authors

Table 2 Quality assessment criteria

Code	Criteria
C1	**Problem statement**: The research objectives are properly explained and well-motivated
C2	**Research design**: Studies related to m-banking service quality having robust research design
C3	**Data Collection**: Data collection and measures are adequately described
C4	**Data analysis**: Data analysis used in the study is unambiguous
C5	**Conclusions**: Findings are clearly reported and supports result

Source Own compilation by authors

Evaluation of Quality: The detailed examination of full text of shortlisted studies was done by researchers for their quality assessment. It helped in analysing their thoroughness, credibility and relevance. It was conducted on the basis of quality assessment criteria (refer Table 2).

The criteria mentioned in Table 2 was adapted from Nguyen-Duc et al. (2015). Every criterion had four possible scores: entirely fulfilled (3), sufficiently fulfilled (2), little fulfilled (1) and completely unfulfilled (0). After that, all shortlisted studies were arranged on the basis of their score. Lastly, authors shortlisted 41 articles having quality score greater than 2 (Nguyen-Duc et al. 2015). Various service quality dimensions identified from the shortlisted articles were discussed at length with an academician who is doing research on electronic banking service quality from the last decade. Dimensions which are both relevant and critical in context of m-banking are considered. Based on systematic literature review and discussion with expert academician, authors propose eight key dimensions to measure mobile banking service quality. The proposed key dimensions are exhaustive in context of m-banking service quality. It has been presented in Table 3. Diagrammatic representation of critical m-banking service quality dimensions has been shown in Fig. 1.

These factors are briefed below.

2.1 *Efficiency*

Users believe m-banking to be efficient when the system is organised well, simple to use and need minimum data input from users (Sharma and Malviya 2011; Ketema 2020). They expect 24/7 accessibility of error-free services over m-banking platform, consistent working of m-banking platform even with slow internet connection, automatic update of their personal information and new features on m-banking platform (Shankar et al. 2020). Precisely, efficiency is about how quickly users adapt to system's interface and how timely system responds to users' transactions (Ganguli and Roy, 2011). Previous studies in literature consider efficiency as a crucial measure for determining overall online banking service quality (Amin 2016; Shankar et al. 2019, 2020; Ketema 2020).

Table 3 Proposed mobile banking service quality dimensions

S. No.	Dimensions	Authors and year
1	Efficiency	(Sharma and Malviya 2011; Ganguli and Roy 2011; Amin 2016; Shankar et al. 2019, 2020; Ketema 2020)
2	Empathy	(Ganguli and Roy 2011; Lau et al. 2013; Wilson et al. 2012; Khan et al. 2018; Shankar et al. 2019)
3	Aesthetics	(Jun and Palacios 2016; Taherdoost 2019)
4	Reliability and security	(Parasuraman et al. 2005; Orel and Kara 2014; Nisha 2016; Sindwani and Goel 2016; Zoghlami et al. 2018; Shankar and Jebarajakirthy 2019; Mostafa 2020; Ketema 2020; Khatoon et al. 2020; Zhou et al. 2021)
5	Responsiveness	(Parasuraman et al. 2005; Lin 2013; George and Kumar 2014; Jun and Palacios 2016; Hammoud et al. 2018; Tsai et al. 2018; Nazeri et al. 2019; Khatoon et al. 2020; Kapoor et al. 2020)
6	Personalisation	(Parasuraman et al. 2005; Loonam and O'loughlin 2008; Sindwani and Goel 2015a; Al-Hawari 2011; Tong et al. 2012; Rocha 2012; Wang et al. 2017; Tsai et al. 2018; Albashrawi and Motiwalla 2017)
7	Convenience	(Davis 1989; Jun and Palacios 2016; Sindwani and Goel 2014; Sindwani and Goel 2015b; Nazeri et al. 2019; Huang et al. 2019; Ahmed et al. 2020; Mostafa 2020; Ketema 2020)
8	Information quality	(Cao et al. 2005; Jung et al 2009; Dwivedi et al. 2013; Zhou 2013; Nisha 2016; Zoghlami et al. 2018; Sharma and Sharma 2019)

Source Own compilation by authors

2.2 *Empathy*

Empathy is having caring attitude towards users regarding communication, individualised attention and understanding of service offered (Wilson et al. 2012). Empathy makes consumers feel unique and special. In context of m-banking services, users always admire attentive and helpful environment. Genuine interest, seriousness and enthusiasm shown by banks will lead users to use mobile banking services (Ganguli and Roy 2011). M-banking service providers can make consumers feel empathetic by politeness and sound behaviour. Past studies outline that empathy positively impacts performance expectancy (Lau et al. 2013) and customer satisfaction (Khan et al. 2018). Shankar et al. (2019) found it as one of the critical dimensions in explaining overall m-banking service quality.

Fig. 1 Critical mobile banking service quality dimensions *Source* Own conceptualization by author

2.3 Aesthetics

Aesthetics refer to appearance and attractiveness of m-banking application. It is linked with the looks and feel of the application. Jun and Palacios (2016) in their study revealed "Aesthetics" among the essential dimensions of mobile base banking application quality. Taherdoost (2019) found it as an essential characteristic to attain high quality e-service.

2.4 Reliability and Security

Reliability refers to accurate technical functioning of m-banking services and providing precise services regularly. Security is the degree to which the m-banking is secure from intrusion (Parasuraman et al. 2005; Sindwani and Goel 2016). M-banking requires interchanging confidential data. Hence, it is necessary for the bank's site to be reliable and secure. When it comes to transacting online, security is must in order to build trust among customers since there is no in person contact between customer and staff. Online service providers should have a transparent security policy that assists in retaining consumers (Orel and Kara 2014; Shankar and Jebarajakirthy 2019). Literature shows that reliability and security positively impacts user's intention to purchase and loyalty (Nisha 2016; Zoghlami et al. 2018; Mostafa 2020; Ketema 2020; Khatoon et al. 2020; Zhou et al. 2021).

2.5 Responsiveness

Responsiveness is associated with rapid reply regarding queries and problems related to mobile banking services (Parasuraman et al. 2005). It is willingness to assist customers and enhancing the level of service. It covers aspects like speed, providing timely services, notifying customers the precise service time and providing services in order to meet customer's demand (Kapoor et al. 2020). George and Kumar (2014) in their research analysed that responsiveness of banks can enhance customers' satisfaction (Nazeri et al. 2019). The faster the response of service providers, more will be the satisfaction perceived by the customers (Lin 2013; Jun and Palacios 2016; Hammoud et al. 2018; Tsai et al. 2018; Nazeri et al. 2019; Khatoon et al. 2020).

2.6 Personalisation

It is the degree to which m-banking services can be customised/modified according to individual consumer's preferences (Parasuraman et al. 2005; Sindwani and Goel 2015a). Many researchers have taken this factor into account in their study regarding automated services. Automated services can be personalised according to user's requirements (Al-Hawari 2011). Personalised services assist in performing financial transactions easily and quickly. It might raise the satisfaction level of customers as it makes customers more systematised and rational (Albashrawi and Motiwalla 2017). It can be used for evaluation, comparison and improving methodology of a website's quality (Rocha 2012). Past literature studies have analysed the impact of personalisation on service quality (Loonam and O'loughlin 2008; Tong et al. 2012; Wang et al. 2017; Tsai et al. 2018).

2.7 Convenience

It is the extent to which consumers think that operating a system will be simple and straightforward (Davis 1989). In context of mobile banking, it is the extent a customer utilises mobile banking services comfortably as per his/her level of information capabilities and knowledge (Nazeri et al. 2019). According to Huang et al. (2019), online customer services focusing on ease of use should provide customers with straightforward operation and understandable interface for contents. An easy to understand interface like convenient login and navigation helps in retaining existing customers and building new customer base (Jun and Palacios 2016). Association between convenience and service quality in context of technology banking has been well established in literature by many researchers (Sindwani and Goel 2014; Sindwani and Goel 2015b; Ahmed et al. 2020; Mostafa 2020; Ketema 2020).

2.8 *Information Quality*

Information quality includes system characteristics like accuracy, timeliness and relevancy (Dwivedi et al. 2013; Sharma and Sharma 2019). It is related to the degree to which mobile banking service providers offer users with relevant, correct and up-to-date information. Quality information increases user's perception of electronic services capabilities. Thus, information provided should be error-free, precise and relevant (Cao et al. 2005). It is one of the key dimensions affecting users' attitude towards technology (Jung et al. 2009; Sharma and Sharma 2019). Lack of information quality leads to operational difficulties as it needs efforts in information dissection from users' side (Zhou 2013). Nisha (2016) reported positive association between information quality and performance expectancy of m-banking services. Zoghlami et al. (2018) and Sharma and Sharma (2019) outline positive influence of information quality on e-trust and e-loyalty.

3 Best Worst Method (BWM) Methodology

Various methods were employed in literature for prioritising dimensions. Multi-criteria decision making (MCDM) is among strong tools considerably utilised for tackling with unstructured problems consisting of manifold contrary objectives (Lee and Eom 1990). Several approaches have been proposed by researchers in their studies for resolving MCDM problems such as AHP, DEA, TOPSIS, PROMETHEE, fuzzy AHP, MOORA and fuzzy TOPSIS. (Yadav and Kapoor 2018; Raut et al. 2020). BWM is a robust novel tool used for the purpose of evaluation and prioritisation. BWM is a powerful tool in comparison to other MCDM techniques such as DEMATEL, ELECTRE, AHP, TOPSIS and VIKOR (Gupta and Barua 2017; Kaushik et al. 2020). It employs lesser pairwise comparison and utilises smaller data samples as compared to AHP which is a broadly used technique for prioritisation. Moreover, results derived from BWM are more authentic and consistent as compared to the results of other MCDM techniques as it utilises easy to understand and structured way to collect the required data for pairwise comparison. Such data can be revised to enhance consistency (Kaushik et al. 2020). BWM is used by researchers for selection of green suppliers (Gupta and Barua 2017), assessment of supply chains social sustainability (Ahmadi et al. 2017), assessment of airline industry based on service quality (Gupta 2018), measurement of the logistics performance index indicator's relative importance (Rezaei et al. 2018), prioritisation of risk factors related to lower back pain (Khan et al. 2019), prioritisation of online apparel return factors (Kaushik et al. 2020), prioritisation of determinants influencing university-industry collaboration (Mosayebi et al. 2020) , establishing a decision support system in mining equipment manufacturing for logistics service provider (Sarabi and Darestani 2021)and assessment of manufacturing organisations capability to control internal barriers (Gupta and Barua 2021). The steps of BWM applied for the current research are explained below (Rezaei 2015, 2016; Ahmadi et al. 2017; Kaushik et al. 2020).

Step 1 Determination of set of evaluation criteria. In this step, evaluation criteria $\{C_1, C_2, \ldots, C_n\}$ is determined for taking decisions. Set of n criteria is identified on the basis of extensive review of literature.
Step 2 Out of the set of criteria finalised in step 1, best and worst criteria are decided by experts. The best criterion denote the most influential criteria and the worst criterion represent the least influential criteria.
Step 3 Thereafter, each expert is asked to give rating on a scale of 1–9 for the best criterion finalised in the above step. Score 1 represents equal preference between the best criterion and all other criteria whereas score 9 represents supreme preference of the best criterion over all other criteria. The resulting best to other vector would be $A_B = \{a_{B1,}a_{B2,}a_{B3}, \ldots, a_{Bn}\}$, where a_{Bj} represents the preference for best criterion B over criteria j. Here, $a_{BB} = 1$.
Step 4 Subsequently, experts take the rating of all criteria with worst criterion on a scale of 1 to 9. Score 1 represents equal preference and 9 represent that criterion in question has higher preference than least preferred criterion. The resulting others to worst vector would be $A_W = \{a_{1W}, a_{2W}, a_{3W}, \ldots, a_{nW}\}^T$, where a_{jW} shows preference of criteria j over the worst criterion W and $a_{WW} = 1$.
Step 5 Next, optimised weights $(w_1^*, w_2^*, \ldots, w_n^*)$ for all criteria are computed

To get optimum weights, maximum absolute differences for all j could be minimised for $\{|w_B - a_{Bj} w_j|, |w_j - a_{jW} w_W|\}$. Given below minimax model will be derived:

$$\begin{aligned} & \min \max\{|w_B - a_{Bj} w_j|, |w_j - a_{jW} w_W|\} \\ & s.t. \sum_j w_j = 1 \\ & w_j \geq 0, \quad \text{for all } j \end{aligned} \tag{1}$$

For obtaining better results, Model (1) has been modified into a linear model. The model has been presented below:

$$\begin{aligned} & \min \xi^L \\ & s.t. \\ & |w_B - a_{Bj} w_j| \leq \xi^L, \quad \text{for all } j \\ & |w_j - a_{jW} w_W| \leq \xi^L, \quad \text{for all } j \end{aligned}$$

$$\sum_j w_j = 1$$

$$w_j \geq 0, \quad \text{for all } j \tag{2}$$

For obtaining optimal weights ($w1^*$, $w2^*$, …, wn^*) and optimal value ξ^L, Model (2) could be solved. Consistency (ξ^L) of criteria comparisons near 0 is preferred (Rezaei 2016).

4 Application of Proposed Methodology

This section discusses the application of BWM approach for prioritising m-banking service quality dimensions. 08 proposed m-banking service quality dimensions are considered for analysis.

4.1 Data Collection

After finalisation of dimensions, importance weight of the dimensions using BWM has been evaluated. Data in the form of opinion was collected from 4 experts (2 academicians having a doctorate degree in area related to e-services quality, 2 customers who are heavy users of mobile banking services).

4.2 Determination of the Best and the Worst Criterion

Best criterion represents the most important mobile banking service quality dimension chosen by experts whereas worst criterion represents the least important mobile banking service quality dimension based on experts' opinion.

4.3 Critical Mobile Banking Service Quality Weights Calculation Using Best Worst Method

Experts are requested to rate best and worst mobile banking service quality dimension on a scale of 1–9 used in this study and explained in the methodology. The interpretation of scale has been described in Table 4 (Gupta et al. 2017). Experts were requested to rate best to others and others to worst dimension for m-banking service quality. The ratings obtained by experts have been shown in Table 5. After getting all the ratings from each expert, weights have been determined for m-banking

Table 4 Pairwise comparison scale

Intensity of importance	1	2	3	4	5	6	7	8	9
Definition	Equal importance	Weak	Moderate importance	Moderate plus	Strong importance	Strong plus	Very strong importance	Very, very strong importance	Extreme importance

Source Gupta and Gupta (2017)

Table 5 Pairwise comparison of critical mobile banking service quality dimensions

Experts	Best criteria	Efficiency	Empathy	Aesthetics	Reliability and security	Responsiveness	Personalisation	Convenience	Information quality
Best to others for 4 respondents									
Expert 1	Reliability and security	6	4	8	1	2	7	3	5
Expert 2	Convenience	7	6	8	2	4	5	1	3
Expert 3	Reliability and security	8	5	7	1	3	6	2	4
Expert 4	Reliability and security	7	6	8	1	3	5	2	4

Experts	Expert 1	Expert 2	Expert 3	Expert 4
Others to worst for 4 respondents				
Worst criteria	Aesthetics	Aesthetics	Efficiency	Aesthetics
Efficiency	2	3	1	3
Empathy	4	7	5	4
Aesthetics	1	1	2	1
Reliability and security	8	8	7	8
Responsiveness	6	4	6	5
Personalisation	3	2	3	2
Convenience	7	6	8	7
Information quality	5	5	4	6

Source Primary data, collected by authors

Table 6 Aggregate weights of critical mobile banking service quality dimensions for all the experts

S. No	Factor	Weight	Ranking
1	Efficiency	0.055	7
2	Empathy	0.080	5
3	Aesthetics	0.037	8
4	Reliability and security	0.295	1
5	Responsiveness	0.145	3
6	Personalisation	0.073	6
7	Convenience	0.210	2
8	Information quality	0.106	4

Source Primary data, collected by authors

service quality dimensions using Eq. (2). Subsequently, aggregated weights of all dimensions have been calculated by using Eq. (2). Average consistency (ξ^L) value was found to be 0.094 which is near zero. Thus, the comparisons are reliable. Aggregate weights calculated for the ratings given by experts have been shown in Table 6.

5 Discussion and Implications

Present study identified and ranked major mobile banking service quality dimensions. Findings revealed reliability and security as the top most dimension determining mobile banking service quality. Banks must give due emphasis towards the security of their users' confidential information shared over m-banking platform. To upgrade the safety of private information and financial transactions conducted using m-banking, banks should offer technical support services, data encryption and electronic signatures (Mostafa 2020). Bank should offer unique identification numbers to users. For enhancing reliability of services, banks must provide timely and up-to-date information to its customers. Convenience has been ranked as second critical dimension. Users use m-banking for performing financial transactions when they observe its simplicity against other alternatives. Service providers should design user-friendly apps which are simple to operate and easy to use. Responsiveness has got third position in ascertaining service quality of mobile banking. Service providers must emphasise on providing speedy and courteous services to customers. They should address users' queries politely on time. Quick respond to users' queries led to a favourable perspective towards service providers. Information quality has been placed as fourth key dimension impacting m-banking service quality. Banks need to focus on giving precise and complete information regarding users' transactions. Up-to-date information will assist in building users' loyalty towards banks. Empathy is prioritised as fifth major m-banking service quality dimension. Offering attention to individual customers and understanding their specific needs, providing supportive customer care can enhance m-banking service quality. Personalisation, efficiency and aesthetics influence service quality of mobile banking but these factors have been ranked lower in present study. Customising services as per users' preference makes them reluctant to switch to other alternatives. In order to increase efficiency, banks should make certain the size of their app so that it could work with slow internet connection. Additionally, service providers can make their apps attractive by improving existing features and bringing in new features to make users enjoy m-banking services.

6 Conclusion

The motive of the research was to pick out and prioritise major m-banking service quality dimensions among users. Authors have proposed 08 key dimensions namely efficiency, empathy, aesthetics, reliability and security, responsiveness, personalisation, convenience and information quality. Linguistic ratings are provided by experts to the factors. Best Worst Method has been applied to aggregate the ratings and thus prioritising key dimensions. Prioritisation is useful in determining the relative importance of dimensions, which in turn provides a pathway to managers in developing strategies for enhancing service quality. "Reliability and security" has emerged as the most important dimension to focus for improving m-banking service quality followed by convenience, responsiveness, information quality, empathy, personalisation, efficiency and aesthetics. This research contributed remarkably to the academics and industry by proposing a structure to evaluate and prioritise major service quality dimensions in context of mobile banking using BWM.

7 Limitations and Future Scope

A bigger group of decision makers including more domain experts may be taken for evaluating service quality dimensions. It will help in obtaining more holistic results. Experts' opinion might be biased. To overcome subjectivity in experts' opinion, findings might be lined up and contrasted with secondary data on popular players in m-banking industry. In future, studies may be conducted by researchers to figure out whether the identified critical dimensions are exhaustive in other electronic services context. Further, study can be performed to prioritise the key m-banking service quality dimensions by taking sub-factors of all dimensions. BWM provides priority ranking but cannot define association between variables. In future, DEMATEL could be used to segment mobile banking service quality dimensions into cause and effect group. Other MCDM techniques like AHP, TOPSIS can also be used for prioritising mobile banking service quality dimensions, and the results obtained may be compared with results of present study. Similar research could be conducted on other domains like e-commerce, m-commerce, etc.

References

Ahmad, Sheraz, Sabeen Hussain Bhatti, and Yujong Hwang. 2019. E-service quality and actual use of e-banking: Explanation through the technology acceptance model. *Information Development* 36 (4): 503–519.

Ahmadi, Badri, Hadi, Simonov Kusi-Sarpong, and Jafar Rezaei. 2017. Assessing the social sustainability of supply chains using best worst method. *Resources, Conservation and Recycling* 126: 99–106.

Albashrawi, Mousa, and Luvai Motiwalla. 2017. Privacy and personalization in continued usage intention of mobile banking: An integrative perspective. *Information Systems Frontiers* 21 (5): 1031–1043.

Al-Hawari, Mohammad Ahmad. 2011. Automated service quality as a predictor of customers' commitment. *Asia Pacific Journal of Marketing and Logistics* 23 (3): 346–366.

Al-Hawari, Mohammed, Nicole Hartley, and Tony Ward. 2005. Measuring banks' automated service quality: A confirmatory factor analysis approach. *Marketing Bulletin* 16.

Amin, Muslim. 2016. Internet banking service quality and its implication on e-customer satisfaction and e-customer loyalty. *International Journal of Bank Marketing* 34 (3): 280–306.

Barnes, Stuart J., and Brian Corbitt. 2003. Mobile banking: Concept and potential. *International Journal of Mobile Communications* 1 (3): 273.

Cao, Mei, Qingyu Zhang, and John Seydel. 2005. B2C E-commerce web site quality: An empirical examination. *Industrial Management & Data Systems* 105 (5): 645–661.

Davis, Fred D. 1989. Perceived usefulness, perceived ease of use, and user acceptance of information technology. *MIS Quarterly* 13 (3): 319.

Demirci Orel, Fatma, and Ali Kara. Supermarket self-checkout service quality, customer satisfaction, and loyalty: Empirical evidence from an emerging market. *Journal of Retailing and Consumer Services* 21 (2): 118–129.

Dwivedi, Yogesh K. et al. 2013. RFID Systems in Libraries: An empirical examination of factors affecting system use and user satisfaction. *International Journal of Information Management* 33 (2): 367–377.

Ganguli, Shirshendu, and Sanjit Kumar Roy. 2011. Generic technology-based service quality dimensions in banking. Ed. Sally McKecnie. *International Journal of Bank Marketing* 29 (2): 168–189.

George, Ajimon, and G.S. Gireesh Kumar. 2014. Impact of service quality dimensions in internet banking on customer satisfaction. *Decision* 41 (1): 73–85.

Gupta, Himanshu. 2018. Evaluating service quality of airline industry using hybrid best worst method and VIKOR. *Journal of Air Transport Management* 68: 35–47.

Gupta, Himanshu, and Mukesh K. Barua. 2017. Supplier selection among SMEs on the basis of their green innovation ability using BWM and fuzzy TOPSIS. *Journal of Cleaner Production* 152: 242–258.

Gupta, Parmarth, Sanjeev Anand, and Himanshu Gupta. 2017. Developing a roadmap to overcome barriers to energy efficiency in buildings using best worst method. *Sustainable Cities and Society* 31: 244–259.

Gupta, Himanshu, and Mukesh Kumar Barua. 2021. Evaluation of manufacturing organizations ability to overcome internal barriers to green innovations. *Greening of Industry Networks Studies* 139–160.

Hammoud, Jamil, Rima M. Bizri, and Ibrahim El Baba. 2018. The impact of e-banking service quality on customer satisfaction: Evidence from the Lebanese banking sector. *SAGE Open* 8 (3): 215824401879063.

Huang, Zhengwei, Yin Luo, and Dong Wang. 2019. Online customer service quality of online shopping: Evidence from dangdang.com. *Cluster Computing* 22 (S6): 15285–15293.

Hughes-Morley, Adwoa et al. 2015. Factors affecting recruitment into depression trials: Systematic review, meta-synthesis and conceptual framework. *Journal of Affective Disorders* 172: 274–290.

Jayawardhena, Chanaka. 2004. Measurement of service quality in internet banking: The development of an instrument. *Journal of Marketing Management* 20 (1–2): 185–207.

Jun, Minjoon, and Shaohan Cai. 2001. The key determinants of internet banking service quality: A content analysis. *International Journal of Bank Marketing* 19 (7): 276–291.

Jun, Minjoon, and Sergio Palacios. 2016. Examining the key dimensions of mobile banking service quality: An exploratory study. *International Journal of Bank Marketing* 34 (3): 307–326.

Jung, Yoonhyuk, Begona Perez-Mira, and Sonja Wiley-Patton. 2009. Consumer adoption of mobile TV: Examining psychological flow and media content. *Computers in Human Behavior* 25 (1): 123–129.

Kapoor, Ashwarya, Rajiv Sindwani, and Manisha Goel. 2020. Mobile wallets: Theoretical and empirical analysis. *Global Business Review* 097215092096125.

Kaushik, Vineet et al. 2020. Modelling and prioritizing the factors for online apparel return using BWM approach. *Electronic Commerce Research.*

Ketema, Eyob. 2020. The impact of M-banking quality service on customers satisfaction during Covid-19 lock down: The case of Bank of Abyssinia, Ethiopia. *African Journal of Marketing Management* 12 (2): 21–37.

Khan, Abdul Gaffar, Reshma Pervin Lima, and Md Shahed Mahmud. 2018. Understanding the service quality and customer satisfaction of mobile banking in Bangladesh: Using a structural equation model. *Global Business Review* 22 (1): 85–100.

Khan, Noor Zaman et al. 2019. Prioritization of lower back pain risk factors among industrial workers using the best–worst method. *International Journal of Occupational Safety and Ergonomics* 27 (2): 544–551.

Khatoon, Sadia, Xu Zhengliang, and Hamid Hussain. 2020. The mediating effect of customer satisfaction on the relationship between electronic banking service quality and customer purchase intention: Evidence from the Qatar banking sector. *SAGE Open* 10 (2): 215824402093588.

Lau, Mei Mei, et al. 2013. Measuring service quality in the banking industry: A Hong Kong based study. *Contemporary Management Research* 9 (3): 263–282.

Lee, Sang M., and Hyun B. Eom. 1990. Multiple-criteria decision support systems: The powerful tool for attacking complex, unstructured decisions. *Systems Practice* 3 (1): 51–65.

Lin, Hsiu-Fen. 2013. Determining the relative importance of mobile banking quality factors. *Computer Standards & Interfaces* 35 (2): 195–204.

Loonam, Mary, and Deirdre O'Loughlin. 2008. Exploring e-service quality: A study of irish online banking. *Marketing Intelligence and Planning* 26 (7): 759–780.

Makanyeza, Charles, and Lovemore Chikazhe. 2017. Mediators of the relationship between service quality and customer loyalty. *International Journal of Bank Marketing* 35 (3): 540–556.

Moher, David. 2009. Preferred reporting items for systematic reviews and meta-analyses: The PRISMA statement. *Annals of Internal Medicine* 151 (4): 264.

Mosayebi, Alireza, Shahryar Ghorbani, and Behzad Masoomi. 2020. Applying fuzzy Delphi and best-worst method for identifying and prioritizing key factors affecting on university-industry collaboration. *Decision Science Letters* 107–118.

Mostafa, Rania B. 2020. Mobile banking service quality: A new avenue for customer value co-creation. *International Journal of Bank Marketing* 38 (5): 1107–1132.

Nazeri, Ali et al. 2019. The effect of the internet banking service quality on customer satisfaction (case study: Refah Bank in Tehran). *International Journal of Services and Operations Management* 34 (1): 65.

Nguyen-Duc, Anh, Daniela S. Cruzes, and Reidar Conradi. 2015. The impact of global dispersion on coordination, team performance and software quality—A systematic literature review. *Information and Software Technology* 57: 277–294.
Nisha, Nabila. 2016. Exploring the dimensions of mobile banking service quality. *International Journal of Business Analytics* 3 (3): 60–76.
Oliveira, Tiago et al. 2014. Extending the understanding of mobile banking adoption: When UTAUT meets TTF and ITM. *International Journal of Information Management* 34 (5): 689–703.
Parasuraman, A., Valarie A. Zeithaml, and Arvind Malhotra. E-S-QUAL. *Journal of Service Research* 7 (3): 213–233.
Patel, Kiran J., and Hiren J. Patel. 2018. Adoption of internet banking services in Gujarat. *International Journal of Bank Marketing* 36 (1): 147–169.
Raut, Rakesh D. et al. 2020. Supplier selection and performance evaluation for formulating supplier selection strategy by MCDM-based approach. *International Journal of Business Excellence* 20 (4) (2020): 500.
Rezaei, Jafar. 2015. Best-worst multi-criteria decision-making method. *Omega* 53: 49–57.
Rezaei, Jafar. 2016. Best-worst multi-criteria decision-making method: Some properties and a linear model. *Omega* 64: 126–130.
Rezaei, Jafar, Wilco S. van Roekel, and Lori Tavasszy. 2018. Measuring the relative importance of the logistics performance index indicators using best worst method. *Transport Policy* 68: 158–169.
Rocha, Álvaro. 2012. Framework for a global quality evaluation of a website. *Online Information Review* 36 (3): 374–382.
Sarabi, Elnaz Poormohammad, and Soroush Avakh Darestani. 2021. Developing a decision support system for logistics service provider selection employing fuzzy MULTIMOORA and BWM in mining equipment manufacturing. *Applied Soft Computing* 98: 106849.
Shaikh, Aijaz A., and Heikki Karjaluoto. 2015. Mobile banking adoption: A literature review. *Telematics and Informatics* 32 (1): 129–142.
Shankar, Amit, and Charles Jebarajakirthy. 2019. The influence of e-banking service quality on customer loyalty. *International Journal of Bank Marketing* 37 (5): 1119–1142.
Shankar, Amit, Biplab Datta, and Charles Jebarajakirthy. 2019. Are the generic scales enough to measure service quality of mobile banking? A comparative analysis of generic service quality measurement scales to mobile banking context. *Services Marketing Quarterly* 40 (3): 224–244.
Shankar, Amit et al. 2020. Exploring mobile banking service quality: A qualitative approach. *Services Marketing Quarterly* 41 (2): 182–204.
Sharma, Sujeet Kumar, and Manisha Sharma. 2019. Examining the role of trust and quality dimensions in the actual usage of mobile banking services: An empirical investigation. *International Journal of Information Management* 44: 65–75.
Sharma, Geeta, and Surendra Malviya. 2011. Exploring the dimensions of mobile banking service quality. *Review of Business and Technology Research* 4 (1): 187–196.
Sindwani, Rajiv, and M. Goel. 2014. Dimensions of technology based self-service banking service quality. *YMCAUST International Journal of Research* 2 (2): 17–25.
Sindwani, Rajiv, and Manisha Goel. 2015. The impact of technology based self-service banking service quality on customer loyalty. *International Journal of Marketing and Business Communication* 4 (3): 13–22.
Sindwani, Rajiv, and Manisha Goel. 2015. The impact of technology based self service banking dimensions on customer satisfaction. *International Journal of Business Information Systems Strategies* 4 (1/2): 1–13.
Sindwani, Rajiv, and Manisha Goel. 2016. The relationship between service quality dimensions, customer satisfaction and loyalty in technology based self service banking. *International Journal of E-Services and Mobile Applications* 8 (2): 54–70.
Taherdoost, Hamed. 2019. Electronic service quality measurement: Development of a survey instrument to measure the quality of e-service. *International Journal of Intelligent Engineering Informatics* 7 (6): 491–528.

Tan, Margaret et al. 2000. Factors influencing the adoption of internet banking. *Journal of the Association for Information Systems* 1 (1): 1–44.

Tong, Canon, Stanley Kam-Sing Wong, and Ken Pui-Hing Lui. 2012. The influences of service personalization, customer satisfaction and switching costs on e-loyalty. *International Journal of Economics and Finance* 4 (3).

Tsai, Ming Chun, Yu Ya Chien, and Ching Chan Cheng. 2018. Upgrading service quality of mobile banking. *International Journal of Mobile Communications* 16 (1): 82.

Wang, May, Stella Cho, and Trey Denton. 2017. The impact of personalization and compatibility with past experience on e-banking usage. *International Journal of Bank Marketing* 35 (1): 45–55.

Wilson, Alan, Valarie A. Zeithaml, Mary Jo Bitner, and Dwayne D. Gremler. 2012. Services marketing: Integrating customer focus across the firm.

Yadav, Santosh Kumar, and Rohit Kapoor. 2018. Financial performance ranking of automotive companies in India using TOPSIS method. *International Journal of Business Excellence* 16 (2): 149–161.

Zhou, Tao. 2013. An empirical examination of continuance intention of mobile payment services. *Decision Support Systems* 54 (2): 1085–1091.

Zhou, Qingji et al. 2021. A study on factors affecting service quality and loyalty intention in mobile banking. *Journal of Retailing and Consumer Services* 60: 102424.

Zoghlami, Amira Trabelsi, Karim Ben Yahia, and Sarra Berraies. 2018. From mobile service quality evaluation to e-word-of-mouth: What makes the users of mobile banking applications speak about the bank? *International Journal of E-Services and Mobile Applications* 10 (2)sss: 36–57.

A Study of Online Shopping Behaviour by Consumers During COVID-19 Pandemic

Bhuwandeep and Arvind Tripathy

1 Introduction

In December 2019, Covid19 started in Wuhan Province, China, and later spread like wildfire all over the world. It has created irreversible changes and has disrupted lives of people all over the globe. World Health Organization declared it as a pandemic in early 2020.

Despite leading to a huge health crisis, the COVID-19 outbreak has also affected societies and economies all over the world in varied ways. This has also further widened the gap between the underdeveloped and developing world. It has severely impacted the economy by significantly slowing the growth process triggering negative growth. The world trade and commerce, education and other activities have been severely disrupted as result of Covid19. To cope with the worsened scenario, precautionary measures were initiated the governments.

The drastic change triggered due to Covid19 forced consumers to adopt alternate mechanisms of survival. Shopping of staples like grocery, medicines and sanitizers took priority in the shopping list. Non-utilitarian goods purchases were procrastinated to a later date.

Covid19 pandemic has forced a change in the rate of adoption of online shopping behaviour. This study aims to identify the factors that influence the shopping behaviour in an online ecosystem and more specially the disruption in shopping behaviour during Covid19 conditions.

In this study, consumers mostly drawn from eastern belt of India (Odisha, Jharkhand, West Bengal and Chhattisgarh), feel and adopt the online format. Efforts are made in the study to explore the factors some generic and some exclusive impact of their behaviour.

Bhuwandeep (✉) · A. Tripathy
KIIT School of Management, Bhubaneswar, Odisha, India
e-mail: bhuwandeep@ksom.ac.in

R. N. Subudhi et al. (eds.), *Future of Work and Business in Covid-19 Era*,
Springer Proceedings in Business and Economics,
https://doi.org/10.1007/978-981-19-0357-1_13

2 Literature Review

2.1 Online Shopping During COVID-19

World Health Organization (WHO) in early 2020 announced Covid19 as a pandemic. Due to the restrictions imposed by governments across the world, 52% consumers adhered to the social distancing norms by wearing masks to prevent any infection spread by the virus in the communities (Andrienko 2020). Many consumers shifted to e-commerce platforms for purchases instead of physically visiting the retail stores. Needless to add, this pandemic completely created serious dismantling of existing industry demand pushing every company to disrupting their product lines. Most of the organizations have adopted e-commerce facilities to reach out to the consumers. This proactive response has seen major gains for the companies.

It is interesting to note that lockdown has given an opportunity to e-commerce players to widen their area of services to cater to consumers demand (Giallonardo et al. 2020).

At the same time, there are people who do not maintain proper social distance nor follow the precautionary rules and guidelines during Covid19 lockdown (Busby 2020).

During the initial period of Covid19 pandemic, consumers were susceptible to hoarding habits and expenditure on bare necessities or household items increased significantly (Hobbs 2020). This can be attributed to anxiety among consumers emerging out of the situation which has resulted in panic buying. Panic buying as a trend has also become a universal phenomenon (Lufkin 2020).

Several research studies have focused on examining the behaviour of consumers during critical times like pandemic with respect to stocking of food, but there is hardly any study done to study the effect of online services on similar behaviours (Hori and Iwamoto 2014).

Online purchasing channels have helped to curb the panic buying behaviour by facilitating an effective way to buy without physically going to the store for their purchases. Such efforts by e-commerce players have been lauded for facilitating distribution of essential goods during Covid conditions (Hao et al. 2020). Another area to focus on would be the relative ease that online formats bring in carrying out the shopping process (y Monsuwé et al. 2004).

During any financial crisis, consumer becomes price sensitive and are attracted price-based offers while quality concerns take low priority (Sans et al. 2008). Whereas in a health-related crisis, the response gets reversed with increased priority on quality over price and offers (Theodoridou et al. 2019).

2.2 *Role of Gender on Online Shopping*

Gender-wise studies reveal interesting facts in the shopping behaviours. For few customer groups especially women, it is observed that shopping is a very enjoyable and pleasurable experience with a degree of involvement (Lubis 2018). They express their emotions through their social engagement channels (Rollero et al. 2019). In another study, it is found that younger females consider social networking, fun and enjoyment and entertaining activities to be the prime drivers while shopping for products and services (Haytko and Baker 2004).

However, in case of men the purpose of shopping as activity is logical and rational devoid of any emotions, exhibiting a highly focused approach in accomplishing their shopping objectives (Yet Mee et al. 2019). Further, their choice of stores and brands end up being extremely frequent and familiar (Khusaini et al. 2019).

When it comes to regular online shopping, men seem to be more involved in such shopping activities (Arora and Aggarwal 2018). They also perceive online mode to more effective mode of shopping than women and hence adopt such formats faster the women consumers (Stark and Meier 2001).

There is also a difference in their frequency of visits and amount of time spent in e-commerce sites (Baubonienė and Gulevičiūtė 2015). This has necessitated a need for retailers to motivate women to shop online more frequently. Many retailers adopted online platforms during the Covid19 pandemic to familiarize e-shopping among the people (Alfonso et al. 2021).

Since the COVID-19 outbreak, consumers have shown their willingness to pay more for quality assurance and safety standards that are verified. Hence for safety reasons, consumers purchased products that score high on health and hygiene aspects (Nguyen et al. 2020). Consumer sought quality assurances in their products such as expiry dates in pharma products (Yang et al. 2020).

3 Data Collection and Methodology

From the extensive literature review, we arrived at 18 questions to summarize the factors that explain the possible reason for e-shopping during the pandemic. The first set of questions in the survey delved into the demographic variable of the respondent, namely their age, occupation and gender. The second set of questions deals with the possible trigger/reasons for online shopping such as availability of branded products, assurance of quality product, available within budgetary constraints, great price vis-a-vis performance, low or negligible delivery charges, full-day availability, assurance of timely delivery, promise of shopper's security, secured transactions, promise of privacy on the website, being able to shop safely while quarantined, being able to follow WHO guidelines, etc. For example, the questions asked respondents to rate the statements such as—"I prefer e shopping because of presence of branded products; I prefer e shopping because of low price; I prefer e shopping because of safe and secured website etc." on a Likert scale of one to five with one denoting strongly disagree to and five denoting strongly agree.

The dependent variable is online shopping behaviour during the pandemic. The online simple random sampling yielded 120 (out of email sent to 200 participants, 120 responded correctly thus resulting in response rate of 60%) responses using the self-administered survey through the Google Form using convenience random sampling over a period of two months (1 December 2020–31January 2021). The data thus collected was analysed through various statistical tools such as factor analysis, chi square test of independence, reliability test and lastly test of correlation among independent variables using SPSS 24.0 software version.

4 Finding and Discussions

4.1 Principal Component Analysis

The survey used 15-factor scale to test the reasons for shopping. The factors were subjected to principal component analysis for finding out important underlying groups that led to e-shopping during the COVID 19 pandemic.

Bartlett's test of sphericity is used to test the hypothesis if the components are correlated. The value of chi square is 619.20 with 120 degrees of freedom. The value of Kaiser–Meyer measure of sampling adequacy is 0.748 which is more than the threshold level of 0.5, thus indicating that factor analysis may be considered an appropriate method for analysing the data. There is weak correlation among the factors showing a healthy model for factor analysis. Only one of the pairs has correlation coefficient factor greater than 0.500. Using the Varimax rotation for factor analysis, the data yielded a result with five major groups uncorrelated among themselves (the eigenvalue in the factoring analysis was kept above 1).

4.2 Five Factors Affecting Online Shopping

Each uncorrelated matrix is shown below. Along with uncorrelated matrix, we can divide the factors in to following groups.

(a) *Health Aspects of E-shopping* (following WHO guidelines, Social Distancing, Helps in Quarantining, Prevention of spread of virus)
(b) *Security during shopping* (assurance of safe and secure website, ensuring the shopper's security, trustworthiness of shopping experience, privacy of shoppers assured, availability of secured encrypted financial transactions),
(c) *Availability of products all day long* (24-h availability, all-day delivery),
(d) *Price conscious* (low price/huge discount, reasonable delivery cost),
(e) *Assurance of Quality product* (branded product, assurance on product quality)

Table 1 Chi square test result

	Value	*df*
Pearson chi square	7.217	8
Likelihood ratio	8.045	8
N of valid cases	120	

Source SPSS output table, compiled by author

The total variance explained by the five factors in component loading is 65%.

4.3 Does Gender Affect the Reasons for E-Shopping During Covid Pandemic?

Using the cross-tabulation method, chi square test of dependence is done. The significance value is more than 0.05, indicating we do not have sufficient evidence to reject the null hypothesis. Thus, there is not suffice evidence to show if there is significant interdependence between gender and the reasons for shopping during COVID-19 (Table 1).

5 Managerial Implications and Scope for Future Research

The e-commerce is a dynamic sector with fast-paced changes. The e-commerce sector competes with offline retail, and hence, the need for agility and adaptation is crucial for its survival. The research studies the reasons for the buying behaviour of consumers during the pandemic. The reasons were classified under the groups of product quality, place, price, security and safety from the pandemic while being able to shop. The safety and security emerged two very important reasons—why people preferred online shopping, hence if the company could strengthen the perceptions about both these aspects of shopping to potential customers, it could even add more value to the customers shopping online. Surprisingly, the research found no interdependence between the reasons for shopping and the gender of the shoppers. Hence, gender-based marketing communications will most likely not be effective.

The study was confined to eastern region of Indian Subcontinent. This study may further be extended on Pan India level for more robust study. Similarly, further demographic variables of respondent population may be included in the survey to gain further insights into the buying behaviour of the consumers during e-shopping.

References

Alfonso, Viviana, et al. 2021. E-commerce in the pandemic and beyond. *BIS Bulletin* 36.

Andrienko, O. 2020. *Ecommerce and Consumer Trends During Coronavirus.*

Arora, Nupur, and Aanchal Aggarwal. 2018. The role of perceived benefits in formation of online shopping attitude among women shoppers in India. *South Asian Journal of Business Studies* 7 (1): 91–110. https://doi.org/10.1108/SAJBS-04-2017-0048.

Baubonienė, Živilė, and Gintarė Gulevičiūtė. 2015. *E-Commerce Factors Influencing Consumers 'online Shopping Decision.*

Busby, Joshua W. 2020. Understanding the Anemic Global Response to COVID-19. *Journal of Health Politics, Policy and Law* 45 (6): 1013–21 (Duke University Press).

Giallonardo, Vincenzo, et al. 2020. The impact of quarantine and physical distancing following COVID-19 on mental health: Study protocol of a multicentric italian population trial. In *Frontiers in Psychiatry*, vol. 11. Frontiers Media SA.

Hao, Na, et al. 2020. The impact of online grocery shopping on stockpile behavior in Covid-19. In *China Agricultural Economic Review*. Emerald Publishing Limited.

Haytko, Diana L., and Julie Baker. 2004. It's all at the mall: Exploring adolescent girls' experiences. *Journal of Retailing* 80 (1): 67–83.

Hobbs, Jill E. 2020. Food supply chains during the COVID-19 pandemic. *Canadian Journal of Agricultural Economics/Revue Canadienne d'agroeconomie* 68(2): 171–76 (Wiley Online Library).

Hori, Masahiro, and Koichiro Iwamoto. 2014. The run on daily foods and goods after the 2011 Tohoku earthquake: A fact finding analysis based on homescan data. *The Japanese Political Economy* 40(1), 69–113 (Taylor & Francis).

Khusaini, Khusaini, et al. 2019. The influence of shopping and gender differences on online shopping. *Jurnal Pendidikan Ekonomi Dan Bisnis (JPEB)* 7(1): 22–30.

Lubis, Arlina Nurbaity. 2018. Evaluating the customer preferences of online shopping: Demographic factors and online shop application issue. *Academy of Strategic Management Journal* 17(2): 1–13 (Jordan Whitney Enterprises, Inc.).

Lufkin, B. 2020. *Amid the Coronavirus Outbreak, People Are Flocking to Supermarkets World-wide—But Are They Simply Preparing, or Irrationally Panicking? BBC.*

Nguyen, Hoang Viet, et al. 2020. Online book shopping in Vietnam: The impact of the COVID-19 pandemic situation. *Publishing Research Quarterly* 36: 437–45 (Springer).

Rollero, Chiara, et al. 2019. *Do Men Post and Women View? The Role of Gender, Personality and Emotions in Online Social Activity.*

Sans, Pierre, et al. 2008. Value-based labels for fresh beef: An overview of French consumer behaviour in a BSE crises context. *International Journal of Consumer Studies* 32(5): 407–13 (Wiley Online Library).

Stark, Jerrold, and Robert Meier. 2001. A longitudinal study of usage and satisfaction levels of internet shopping by college students. *Journal of Computer Information Systems* 41(4): 65–68 (Taylor & Francis).

Theodoridou, Glykeria, et al. 2019. The impact of the economic crisis on Greek consumer behaviour towards food consumption. *International Journal on Food System Dynamics* 10(3): 298–314.

y Monsuwé, Toñita Perea, et al. 2004. What drives consumers to shop online? A literature review. In *International Journal of Service Industry Management* (Emerald Group Publishing Limited).

Yang, Kiseol, et al. 2020. Effects of retailers' service quality and legitimacy on behavioral intention: The role of emotions during COVID-19. *The Service Industries Journal* 1–23 (Taylor & Francis).

Yet Mee, Lim, et al. 2019. Gender differences in perceptions and attitudes toward online shopping: A study of Malaysian consumers. Lim, Y.M., B.L. Cheng, T.H. Cham, C.K.Y. Ng, and J.X. Tan (2019). *Gender Differences in Perceptions and Attitudes Toward Online Shopping: A Study of Malaysian Consumers. Journal of Marketing Advances and Practices*, vol. 1, no. 2, pp. 11–24.

The Influential Role of Trust in Understanding Online Product Recommendation System

Priyadarsini Patnaik and Biswajeet Patnaik

1 Introduction

The development of technology has enriched every aspect of people's day-to-day lives. "*Online recommendation system has developed on the basis of individual preferences on product attributes to support consumer's buying decisions*" (Ghasemaghaei et al. 2019). People opt to interact with recommendation agents because of their human-like interfaces (Benbasat et al. 2020). Online Product recommendation [hereinafter, it is called OPRs] on any shopping sites are the suggestions made based on user's interests (Bathla et al. 2020). These recommendation systems use many techniques such as content-based, collaborative filtering and trust-based recommender systems. The collaborative filtering technique is the most commonly used recommendation systems because they do not need any previous knowledge about users or items, rather they make recommendations based on interactions between them (Nassar et al. 2020). Based on the information about the customer's most recent purchase, frequency of purchase and the value of past purchase, OPRs predict the likelihood of further or future purchasing and can offer a personalized recommendation to the customers.

Customers often buy the same things and follow some repeated patterns and behave in a similar way. Recommender system driven by artificial intelligence can monitor human buying behaviour to identify the next buyer by mining internet data, i.e. by observing who is searching for a given product or service, learn the buyer's

P. Patnaik (✉)
Birla School of Management, Birla Global University, Bhubaneswar, India
e-mail: ppattnaik.scholar18@bgu.ac.in

B. Patnaik
Marketing Management, School of Management, KIIT University, Bhubaneswar, India
e-mail: biswajeet.patnaik@ksom.ac.in

R. N. Subudhi et al. (eds.), *Future of Work and Business in Covid-19 Era*,
Springer Proceedings in Business and Economics,
https://doi.org/10.1007/978-981-19-0357-1_14

pattern and identify the next buyer! Due to the predictive ability of the recommendation system, marketers can predict what customers will intend to buy (Davenport et al. 2020). Based on predictive accuracy, firms can change their business models to reach out to the customers. As both price and promotions are two important aspects in marketing, the recommender system is much expected to play a crucial role in predicting customer's next purchase with what price and promotions to be offered (Zhao et al. 2015). With the help of a recommender system, online retailers can predict and forecast customers want with accuracy. Retailers can identify customers preference by personalization and can ship items to them which indeed can transform the business model of retailers. Accordingly, items can be shipped to customers with having an option to return (Agarwal et al. 2018; Gans 2017), and the negative effects associated with product returns can be avoided. Nowadays, many business houses are using this OPRs model and can predict their customers want.

1.1 Purpose of the Study

Nowadays, many companies are using OPRs to deliver more personalized experiences to their customers to anticipate what they want or need and can predict potential customers who will buy the product. This prediction is based on customer taste, browsing history, personal preferences, spending patterns, and recommend more relevant suggestions to their customers which makes personalized marketing a step further. So, eventually, OPRs are adopted by the company will only continue to rise.

Though online product recommender systems have gained much more attention in both industry and academia, the adoption of it by the consumers has been slow. The purpose of this study was to investigate consumers' perception towards acceptance of recommender system with reference to trust. Also, this study examines how trust influences attitude and consumer decision process. This paper used the theory technology acceptance model (TAM) to understand consumers' adoption behaviour towards online product recommender system. As adoption of OPR is a determinant of consumers' purchase intention, few studies have incorporated construct trust to increase the hypothetical power of the model (Venkatesh et al. 2003).

1.2 Objectives of the Study

This study approaches the knowledge of consumer acceptance of OPR in online retail by examining the influential role of trust. The objectives of the study are:

1. To develop a concept regarding the technology acceptance model in the context of OPR uses

2. To identify the constructs related to the trust, attitude and behavioural intention towards the use of OPR technology by consumers
3. To analyse the causal relationship between the constructs.

2 Literature Review and Theory

2.1 OPR: Online Product Recommender System

As purchase habits of customers shift from traditional offline shopping to shopping online, online product recommendations have gained much significance, Tsagkias et al. (2021) and E-commerce recommendation have been used to help online shoppers in terms of increasing product awareness, reduce information overload and narrow down their product consideration set, Jingjun (David) Xu et al. (2020). So, online product recommendations influence the purchasing behaviours for the recommended products (Zhang and Bockstedt (2020). These product recommendations not only guide customers to explore a massive product catalogue but also assist them to find the right products from a huge number of options, Guo et al. (2021). Online recommendations create trust among online buyers and develop a favourable attitude towards online shopping, Chetioui et al. (2020). On this basis, we can hypothesize that

H1: OPR creates trust and a favourable attitude in online shopping.

2.2 Trust

Gambetta, the famous Sociologist opines that "*trust is a particular level of the subjective probability of one agent to assess another agent or a group of agents who will perform a particular action*" (Gambetta 1988). "*In online social networks, trust is an effective mechanism in all human interactions. It exerts an enormous impact on decisions whether to believe or disbelieve the information asserted by others*" (Chen 1994; Lu and Yuan 2018). Gefen et al. (2003) define "*trust has multiple features including subjectivity, uncertainty, context-dependence and summarized trust: as a set of specific beliefs dealing with the integrity, benevolence, and ability of another party,*" "*as a general belief that another party can be trusted or the willingness of a party to be vulnerable to the actions of another,*" *and* "*as an effect reflected in feelings of confidence and security in caring response of the other party.*" Pavlou and Fygenson (2006) found, trust can predict consumers' attitudes towards e-commerce in the context of a theory of planned behaviour and affects consumer behaviour and determines the success of technology adoption, Holsapple and Sasidharan (2005).

2.3 Trust and Online Product Recommender System

In the context of the online product recommender system, "Ashraf et al. (2019) *depict trust as a combination of competence, integrity, and benevolence which drives user's intention and a positive relationship between recommendation quality and trust*", (Abumalloh et al. 2020). "*It is considered as one of the important factors in e-commerce* (Hoffman et al. 1999; Nöteberg et al. 1999), *and influence customers' intention to purchase products online*", Kim et al. (2008).

2.4 Attitude

In the year 1975, Fishbein and Ajzen defined "*attitude as an individual's degree of evaluative effect towards the target behaviour (p. 216) which is composed of cognitive, emotional, and behavioural elements and are assumed to have internal consistency with each other*" (İnceoğlu 2010). Attitude further can be termed as a psychological construct which can influence individuals' behaviour. Regarding acceptance of technology, "*individual's intention to perform a given behaviour is the immediate causal determinant of his or her overt performance of that behaviour*" (Davis 1985) and "*it is the strongest factor to influence the intention to use technology*" (Chua and Hu 2002; Cheung and Vogel 2013; Davis 1993; Hussein 2015; Liu et al. 2009; Louho et al. 2006; Wu and Chen 2017). "*Attitude is a predictor of future intention as revealed by the theory of reasoned action and the TPB*" (Ajzen and Fishbein 1980; Ajzen 1991). Again, attitude towards the behaviour defines the intention (Dishaw et al. 2002). *Moreover in online shopping,* "*consumer attitude is determined by the trust whereas higher trust leads to a more favourable attitude of consumers toward online shopping*" (Hassanein and Head 2007; Lin 2011).

2.5 Trust, Attitude and OPR

"*Trust is a determining factor towards the attitude of an individual as well as the purchase intention*" (Hassanein and Head2007; Lin 2011; Hsu et al. 2013; Ashraf et al. 2014) whereas *(Chetioui et al. in the year 2020,* depicts online product recommendation (OPR) creates *trust among customers to form a more positive attitude* ***towards online shopping whereas trust influence customers' intention to use OPRs'*** *through the usefulness of OPRs,* Ashraf et al. (2020)." But lack of direct interaction results in higher risk for consumers during Online shopping (Pavlou et al. 2007) which signifies "***buyers' attitude gets influenced by trust***" (Van Heijden et al. 2003). Since trust and social networks are closely related to each other, researchers concentrate more on trust to increase and enhance the quality of recommendations (Parvin et al. 2019).

In this study, trust is defined as the extent to which an individual believes using OPR is secure. Once consumers develop trust for product recommendations, their purchase intention towards the recommended product gets stimulated as a result they may end up with buying the product from that website (Gordon 2007). On this basis, this study can postulate the hypothesis as

H2: Attitude to use OPR is affected by trust while online shopping.

2.6 *Purchase Intention*

"*Purchase intention refers to the combination of consumers' interest in a brand or a product and the possibility of purchasing these items*" (Lloyd and Luk 2010). It *represents three statements, the consumer willingness to consider the act of buying, the buying intention in the future and the repurchase intention*". *It is a process which actually determines the purchase behaviour* (De Magistris and Gracia 2008).

Purchase intention is highly dependent on users trust (Kang and Johnson 2013) and influence their purchase in the online environment, Everard and Galletta (2005). The more trust users exhibit on e-commerce platform has the greater chance to purchase them (Kim and Park 2013). Again attitude and purchase intention are closely related to each other, and it has a positive effect on behavioural intention to purchase (Lodorfos et al. 2006; Sreen et al. 2018), and it demands a higher purchase (Jun and Jaafar 2011). So, the study can postulate the hypothesis as

H3: Positive effect of attitude leads to a favourable purchase intention.

2.7 *Technology Acceptance Model*

The Technology Acceptance Model (TAM) was developed by Davis in the year 1989 to predict individual users perception towards adoption of new information technology and further explained by the beliefs perceived usefulness towards using the technology and perceived ease of use to use the technology. These two beliefs can achieve the desired outcomes and reflect the technology usages. Again in 1992, Davis et al. Introduced perceived enjoyment in the context of hedonic aspects of technology usage. In TAM, these three beliefs predict the attitude to use the technology. In the context of this study, only perceived ease of use (PEOU) and perceived usefulness (PU) have taken into consideration along with trust. Since the behavioural intention of an individual is affected by attitude and perceived usefulness; this study found the suitability of TAM to describe users behavioural intention towards technology use (Legris et al. 2003) also this study utilized this theory to adopt and use OPR.

On the ground of the above context, the hypothesis was made as mentioned below.

H4: PU positively affects the attitude towards using OPR.

H5: PEOU favourably affects attitude to use OPR.

H6: PU affects behavioural intention positively to use OPR.

2.8 Research Gap

Though it has been observed that consumers perceive trust as an important factor towards the adoption of OPR uses, Ashraf et al. (2020), research says e-commerce players generate only a certain percentage of sales from OPRs, which indicates that customers have yet to develop trust towards OPR because of the relatively low usage rates. We draw upon TAM theory to verify customers' acceptance of recommendations. Though recommender systems have gained much more attention in both industry and academia, but how to improve consumers' trust level is yet to be focused on. This study examines how trust influences OPR usages and the consumer decision process.

2.9 Proposed Research Model

Based on the proposed hypothesis and literature review, the research proposed a model with six propositions such as perceived usefulness, perceived ease of use, online product recommendation, trust in product recommendation, attitude to use product recommendation and intention to use product recommendation, which recommends, perceived usefulness, ease of use and trust drives the attitude to use OPR. This model explores fundamental preconditions for behavioural intention towards making use of OPR by addressing users' disposition to accept and adopt "technology". Here technology refers to the online product recommendation which is driven by artificial intelligence. Since perceived usefulness and perceived ease of use are the critical determinants of defining attitude and behaviour towards intention to adopt recommended products, this model has considered these two constructs. In Perceived usefulness, a person tends to perceive their specific needs, wants or interest to be in relation to the recommended product while considering the product attributes. It is associated with the benefits the person gets after purchasing the recommended product. Similarly, in the context of perceived ease of use, a person perceives how effortless and easy it is to use the technology. Here the technology signifies online product recommendations. Two additional constructs "trust" and "online product recommendation" have considered as part of this conceptual model because trust is an integral part of this model and users' perceive trust as their beliefs in OPR's competency (ability and expertise to perform), compassion (acts as users' interest) and integrity (maintaining honesty). So, Trust develops a favourable attitude among users to adopt OPR as OPR adoption is possible when users have trust in them. Again, online product recommendation (OPR) recommends as per the past purchase history and browsing history of the users, and users perceive the credibility of OPR as it recommends as per the choice of the users. When users engage in online shopping with the assistance of OPR. It assists them in shopping decision-making as it does the initial screening, narrows down the available choices and provides the most recommended promising alternatives. It reduces the effort exerted during the preliminary

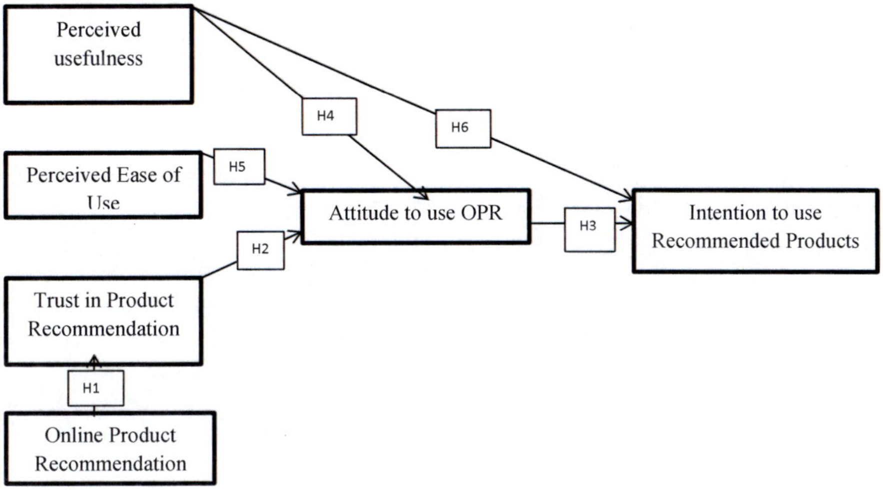

Fig. 1 Proposed model *Source* Own conceptualization by author

stage of shopping, i.e. at arriving at a product choice, reduces the decision effort and decision time at the same time helps in product evaluation while indicating the preferences. So it creates trust among users to intend for OPR adoption. Again a person's attitude is an expression of their inner feelings towards their past experiences if any, concerns and information which influences the person's behaviour (Fishbein and Ajzen 1975), and it reflects the favourable or unfavourable predisposal to an object. The object may be a brand, a service or can be a retail establishment. Previous studies suggest that a positive attitude of an individual towards a certain product positively influence their purchase intention (behaviour). As attitude which leads to (behavioural intention) purchase intention, the faster online product recommendation (OPR) assists a user in finding the right product; higher are the chances of getting user conversion and adoption. Hence, trust and attitude become important factors to get users' need for better product discovery, customer experience and behavioural intention to adopt online product recommendation. Hence, this proposed model aimed at consumers' perception towards OPR adoption while doing their online shopping. In order to accomplish this, the above propositions have taken into consideration with the application of technology acceptance model (TAM) (Fig. 1).

3 Research Design/Research Methodology

To conduct the survey, both secondary and primary data were gathered followed by a critical review of existing literature in the form of secondary data. Further relationships between the variables are identified which paved the way to formulate hypotheses and analyse the primary data results. Subsequently, the proposed conceptual model bloomed to an operational level. To accomplish this transition, an online survey has been conducted with the help of a questionnaire. The questionnaire assessed: (1) respondents' consumption and buying behaviour, (2) their preferences and inherent intention to adopt and purchase along with their demographic characteristics.

An online survey was conducted to test the proposed hypotheses. A total of 293 valid and useable responses were received. Few responses were discarded because of mismatching the screening criteria and for the monotonous response. In the survey questionnaire, one screening question was included to check whether the respondent has used OPRs to purchase any product in the last six months and the survey considered only those valid responses that matched the screening criteria and included those responses in data analysis. A web-based survey was distributed to Indian consumers who had experience with online store experiences. A confirmatory factor analysis was applied. A survey instrument was used to collect data using a seven-point Likert scale. A sample test of the questionnaire survey was done to eliminate probable problems in this study.

3.1 Scale Development

From the prior studies, all the items were adopted. An expert panel view was considered to validate the construct and survey instrument. A seven-point Likert scale with "strongly disagree" to "strongly agree" was used for the construct items perceived usefulness, ease of use are modified from Davis (1989), Taylor and Todd (1995) Behavioural intention to use was accessed by three items modified from Pavlou (2003). Items pertaining to attitude towards OPR modified from Yu et al. (2005). Trust is measured by considering the modified items from Luarn and Lin (2005), Cho (2006).

3.2 Data Collection

See Table 1.

3.3 Data Analysis

The data were analysed using SPSS. Scale validity is examined by using Confirmatory Factor Analysis (CFA). Then proposed hypothesis was tested. Measurement reliability and validity were accessed using CFA to check correct loading of the items. The data were collected from 293 respondents residing in Eastern India in the month of November–December 2020, and hypothesis was tested on them.

Table 1 Demographic profile of the respondent

Category	Variable	Frequency	Percentage
Gender	Male	140	47.8
	Female	153	52.2
Age	15–20	25	8.6
	21–26	48	16.4
	27–32	133	45.3
	33–38	87	29.7
Monthly expenditure	3000 and below	34	11.6
	3001–4000	76	26
	4001–5000	115	39.2
	5001 and above	68	23.2
Qualification enrolled	UG	78	26.7
	PG	188	64.1
	Ph.D.	27	9.2
User experience (online buying)	Novice	25	8.5
	Beginner	38	12.9
	Competent	178	60.8
	Expert	52	17.8

Source Primary data, collected by authors

3.4 Research Methodology and Measurements

See Table 2.

3.5 Convergent Validity

The items under defined construct share a high variance and the value range lies in between 0 and 1. Standardized factor loadings are greater than 0.70 which confirms convergent validity.

3.6 Analysis of Measurement Model

This study conducts CFA to test the validity of the scale, whereas AVE can be used to assess the convergent validity of the scale. Since, Cronbach's alpha is an indicator of the consistency of the items in the scale, the internal consistency reliability of the scale is assessed through the composite score of Cronbach's alpha.

Table 2 Factor loading of construct items

Construct items	Standardized factor loadings	Sources
Trust (TR)		
It is easy for me to trust technology	0.819	
My tendency to trust technology is high	0.833	Luarn and Lin (2005), Cho (2006)
I tend to trust technology even if I have little knowledge about it	0.847	
Attitude towards online shopping AT		
Using OPR to shop is a good idea for me	0.847	Yu et al (2005)
I have a positive opinion of OPR	0.83	
Purchasing product by OPR seems an intelligent idea to me	0.808	
Purchase intention PI		
I opt OPR to purchase the product	0.86	Pavlou (2003)
In future, I expect to purchase through OPR	0.856	
In future, I will purchase through OPR	0.818	
Perceived usefulness PU		
OPR will allow to shop easily	0.835	
OPR will allow me to shop more quickly	0.821	Davis (1989)
OPR would be useful to do my shopping	0.890	
Perceived ease of use PEOU		
Learning OPR to purchase a product is easy for me	0.836	
Using OPR to purchase a product would be easy for me	0.828	Taylor and Todd (1995)
OPR is easy to do my shopping	0.89	

Source Primary data, collected by authors

Cronbach's alpha for the construct trust, attitude, purchase intention, perceived use, perceived ease of use towards online product recommendation are 0.810, 0.710, 0.852, 0.860 and 0.962 (Table 3). All Cronbach's alpha (CA) values were found above 0.70 indicating the constructs reliabilities are acceptable (Nunnally 1994). AVE and the composite reliability (CR) method (Fornell and Larcker 1981) were applied to check the properties of the instruments. Since the values of AVEs for the constructs are above 0.5 and the CRs are above 0.7, this model supports convergent validity.

Table 3 Measurement model results (factor loadings, item reliability and convergent validity)

Constructs	Items	Loadings	CA	AVE	CR
Trust (TR)	TR1	0.883	0.810	0.722	0.886
	TR2	0.882			
	TR3	0.781			
Attitude (AT)	AT1	0.895	0.710	0.610	0.812
	AT2	0.742			
	AT3	0.913			
Purchase intention (PI)	PI1	0.849	0.852	0.693	0.900
	PI2	0.781			
	PI3	0.821			
	PI4	0.878			
Perceived usefulness (PU)	PU1	0.918	0.860	0.782	0.915
	PU2	0.829			
	PU3	0.903			
Perceived ease of use (PEOU)	PEOU1	0.983	0.962	0.930	0.976
	PEOU2	0.926			
	PEOU3	0.983			

Source SPSS output table, compiled by author
CA = Cronbach's Alpha; AVE = Average Variance Extracted; CR = Composite Reliability

In this study, CFA was conducted to validate the research whereas composite reliability (CR) and Cronbach's alpha (CA) were used to determine the construct reliability. To test the convergent validity of the construct the average variance extracted (AVE) was used. The five constructs of this study, "trust," "attitude ", "purchase intention", "perceived use " and "perceived ease of use "had CR scores between 0.812 and 0.976, which is more than 0.70 and signifies the construct reliability is good for the variables. Again the lowest value of CA (Cronbach's alpha) found 0.710, which is more than 0.70. At the same time, all item loadings have found larger than 0.70. Using exploratory factor analysis, item reduction conducted to determine which items out of all items represent best in each category, and the weakest value which was less than 0.70 was removed. For AVE, the scales values are found above 0.50 which signifies higher reliability of the constructs. Higher values of Cronbach's alpha indicate strong internal reliability of each construct (Hair et al. 2006). Since all the items related to each individual construct loadings exceed 0.70 and loadings for all individual items for the respected construct exceeds 0.780, and AVE values for all constructs exceed 0.50, the measurement model including reliability and convergent validity found satisfactory.

Internal consistency of the items has been checked by reliability test which shows good result as mentioned in Table 4. Four of them are F2, F3, F4 and F5 are identified as constructs with the same characteristics of TAM model. But F1 can be considered as the external variables having a direct effect on F2 and F3.

Table 4 Reliability analysis of five factors identified in case of OPR uses

S. no.	Factors	Cronbach's Alpha
F1	Trust	0.810
F2	Attitude	0.710
F3	Purchase intention	0.852
F4	Perceived usefulness	0.860
F5	Perceived ease of use	0.962

Source SPSS output table, compiled by author

3.7 Findings

The purpose of this study was to find out the role of trust in adopting online product recommendation empirically by applying the TAM to explain how perceived ease of use and perceived usefulness affect attitude and behavioural intention to adopt OPR, at the same time this study outlined how trust is associated with consumer's attitude and how attitude drives towards adoption of OPR. This study also identified online product recommendation (OPR) creates trust among users by its prediction accuracy, whereas Perceived Ease of Use (PEOU) and Perceived Usefulness (PU) predict a favourable attitude towards the adoption of OPR or a willingness to adopt OPR. Further, this study conducted a CFA, to validate the scale and to check the internal reliability of each measurement by evaluating the values of Cronbach's *alpha.* It found C.alpha values were above 0.70, which confirmed strong internal consistency of measures. Also, composite reliability (CR) values for all variables were calculated as per Fornell and Larcker (1981). As presented in Table 3, the CR values were higher than the recommended value which is 0.70 indicating good reliable measure of the constructs. Also, the study calculated the average variance extracted (AVE) values which were all above 0.5 and confirmed convergent validity of the constructs (Hair et al. 1998)

Since the objective of this study was to identify the causal relationship among the constructs, from the literature review it is evident that the construct trust has a positive association with attitude and attitude has a favourable association with intention. Again, online product recommendation affects trust positively. So, This study outlines the role of trust in using and accepting online product recommendations and found trust has an important role in driving consumers' intentions to purchase the recommended product and can influence decisions to buy from recommended products. Also, this study outlines that the OPR uses by the customer is influenced by attitude and the perceived usefulness to use OPR. Again both perceived usefulness and perceived ease of use are the determinant of attitude and intention to adopt online product recommendation, as it is evident from the survey that users' feel that OPR allow them to shop easily and quickly, and they intend to purchase in the future by the help of recommended product by OPR which signifies that both the constructs PEOU and PU are the determinant of attitude and intention to adopt OPR. Also, the hypothesis developed in this study holds good that OPR creates trust among users to do online shopping by providing relevant available options which further helps in decision-making. Again attitude to use OPR is influenced by trust as users' cannot adopt OPR if they cannot build trust on it. Since a positive attitude favouring things natural and in a positive way, and it is a result of direct experience with the product (here product signifies online product recommendation) as well as the information received from the product, it reflects that a positive attitude is the result of developed trust on online product recommendation (OPR). So from the survey conducted, it can be conclusion can be drawn as trust influence the users to adopt online product recommendation.

3.8 Limitations, Further Scope of the Research

This study had several limitations which need to be addressed. Such as, this study focused on consumers' intentions to use OPR rather than the actual buying behaviour towards using online product recommendations which could be investigated further. Second, the study highlighted the influential effect of trust on product recommendations, whereas there are many other factors that can be considered as consumers' intention to purchase the recommended products. Such as transaction cost, security of data, quality of recommendations and so on. Our research participants were young consumers and they may not be representative of all consumers. The study is limited to Eastern India only. The study was limited to the young consumers only as in this age group the tendency towards technology adoption is much higher other than the other age group. This study can be done by adding different age groups in different geographical regions in order to elude selection biases.

4 Conclusion

Online Product Recommender systems (OPRs) are an essential component of e-commerce marketplaces; assisting consumers to access inventory as per their choice, need or love. But consumers' have yet to develop trust in OPRs. The study outlines a lack of trust in OPR acceptance and validates TAM model. Though OPRs are convenient and useful for consumers' but they should be trustworthy for continuous usage. The study concludes trust is a significant factor in the acceptance of OPR. Trust in OPR's can increase because of Prediction Accuracy. Perceived Usefulness (PU) and Perceived Ease of Use (PEOU) also creates a favourable attitude towards the adoption of OPR. Future studies on various constructs like perceived risk and continuous usage could deepen the understanding of use of OPR and its impact on OPR acceptance. Also, this study helps marketers and practitioners gain a better understanding of designing multiple sources of recommendations. Marketers should strategize to strengthen consumers' trust in OPR's for improving overall OPR acceptability.

References

Abumalloh, Rabab Ali, Othman Ibrahim, and Mehrbakhsh Nilashi. 2020. Loyalty of young female Arabic customers towards recommendation agents: A new model for B2C E-commerce. *Technology in Society* 61: 101253.

Agarwal, Pankaj, Sreekanth Vempati, and Sumit Borar. 2018. *Personalizing Similar Product Recommendations in Fashion E-commerce.* arXiv preprint arXiv:1806.11371 (2018).

Ajzen, Icek. 1991. The theory of planned behaviour. *Organizational Behaviour and Human Decision Processes* 50 (2): 179–211.

Ashraf, Abdul R., Narongsak Thongpapanl, and Seigyoung Auh. 2014. The application of the technology acceptance model under different cultural contexts: The case of online shopping adoption. *Journal of International Marketing* 22 (3): 68–93.

Ashraf, Muhammad, Noor Ismawati Jaafar, and Ainin Sulaiman. 2019. System-vs. consumer-generated recommendations: affective and social-psychological effects on purchase intention. *Behaviour & Information Technology* 38(12): 1259–1272.

Ashraf, Muhammad, et al. 2020. The role of continuous trust in usage of online product recommendations. *Online Information Review* 44(4): 745–766.

Azjen, Icek. 1980. *Understanding Attitudes and Predicting Social Behaviour.* Englewood Cliffs.

Bathla, Gourav, Himanshu Aggarwal, and Rinkle Rani. 2020. A graph-based model to improve social trust and influence for social recommendation. *The Journal of Supercomputing* 76 (6): 4057–4075.

Benbasat, Izak, et al. 2020. The role of demographic similarity in people's decision to interact with online anthropomorphic recommendation agents: evidence from a functional magnetic resonance imaging (fMRI) study. *International Journal of Human-Computer Studies* 133: 56–70.

Chen, Wai-kai. 1994. *Linear Networks and Systems: Algorithms and Computer-Aided Implementations: Problems and Solutions.* World Scientific.

Chetioui, Youssef, Hind Lebdaoui, and Hajar Chetioui. 2020. Factors influencing consumer attitudes toward online shopping: the mediating effect of trust. *EuroMed Journal of Business.*

Cheung, Ronnie, and Doug Vogel. 2013. Predicting user acceptance of collaborative technologies: An extension of the technology acceptance model for e-learning. *Computers & Education* 63: 160–175.

Cho, Jinsook. 2006. The mechanism of trust and distrust formation and their relational outcomes. *Journal of Retailing* 82 (1): 25–35.

Chua, P.Y.K., and P.J.H. Hu. 2002. Investigating healthcare professionals' decision to accept telemedicine technology: An empirical test of competing theories. *Information and Management* 39 (4): 297–311.

Davenport, Thomas, et al. 2020. How artificial intelligence will change the future of marketing. *Journal of the Academy of Marketing Science* 48(1): 24–42.

Davis, Fred D. 1985. *A Technology Acceptance Model for Empirically Testing New End-User Information Systems: Theory and Results.* Diss. Massachusetts Institute of Technology.

Davis, Fred D. 1989. Perceived usefulness, perceived ease of use, and user acceptance of information technology. *MIS Quarterly*, pp. 319–340.

Davis, Fred D. 1993. User acceptance of information technology: System characteristics, user perceptions and behavioural impacts. *International Journal of Man-Machine Studies* 38 (3): 475–487.

De Magistris, Tiziana, and Azucena Gracia. 2008. The decision to buy organic food products in Southern Italy. *British Food Journal.*

Dishaw, Mark, Diane Strong, and D. Brent Bandy. 2002. Extending the task-technology fit model with self-efficacy constructs. In *AMCIS 2002 Proceedings*, p. 143.

Everard, Andrea, and Dennis F. Galletta. 2005. How presentation flaws affect perceived site quality, trust, and intention to purchase from an online store. *Journal of Management Information Systems* 22 (3): 56–95.

Fishbein, M., and T. Ajzen 1975. *Belief, Attitude, Intention and Behaviour: An Introduction to Theory and Research.* Reading: Addison-Wesley.

Fornell, Claes, and David F. Larcker. 1981. *Structural Equation Models with Unobservable Variables and Measurement Error: Algebra and Statistics*, pp. 382–388.

Gambetta, Diego. 1988. *Trust: Making and Breaking Cooperative Relations.*

Gans, Herbert J. 2017. The participant-observer as a human being: Observations on the personal aspects of field work. In *Institutions and the Person*, 300–138. Routledge.

Gefen, David, Elena Karahanna, and Detmar W. Straub. 2003. Trust and TAM in online shopping: An integrated model. *MIS Quarterly*, pp. 51–90.

Ghasemaghaei, Maryam, Khaled Hassanein, and Izak Benbasat. 2019. Assessing the design choices for online recommendation agents for older adults: Older does not always mean simpler information technology. *Mis Quarterly* 43 (1): 329–346.

Gordon, K.T. 2007. *Looking for Ways to get People Talking About Your Products? The New Social Shopping Trend can help you Build Buzz*, vol. 1, 2007. Retrieved July.

Guo, Mingming, et al. 2021. *Deep Learning-based Online Alternative Product Recommendations at Scale.* arXiv preprint arXiv:2104.07572.

Hair, J. F., Jr., R. E. Anderson, R. L. Tatham, and W. C. Black. 1998. *Multivariate data analysis*, 5th ed. Upper Saddle River: Prentice Hall.

Hair, J.F., Jr., W.C. Black, B.J. Babin, R. Anderson, and R. Tathum. 2006. *Multivariate Data Analysis*, 6th ed. Upper Saddle River: Prentice Hall.

Hassanein, Khaled, and Milena Head. 2007. Manipulating perceived social presence through the web interface and its impact on attitude towards online shopping. *International Journal of Human-Computer Studies* 65 (8): 689–708.

Hoffman, Donna L., Thomas P. Novak, and Marcos Peralta. 1999. Building consumer trust online. *Communications of the ACM* 42 (4): 80–85.

Holsapple, Clyde W., and Sharath Sasidharan. 2005. The dynamics of trust in B2C e-commerce: A research model and agenda. *Information Systems and e-Business Management* 3 (4): 377–403.

Hsu, Chin-Lung., Judy Chuan-Chuan. Lin, and Hsiu-Sen. Chiang. 2013. The effects of blogger recommendations on customers' online shopping intentions. *Internet Research* 23 (1): 69–88.

Hussein, Z. 2015. Explicating students' behaviours of E-learning: A viewpoint of the extended technology acceptance. *International Journal of Management and Applied Science* 1 (10): 68–73.

İnceoğlu, Metin. 2010. *Tutum, algı ve iletişim.* İstanbul: Beykent Üniversitesi Yayınları.

Jun, Guo, and Noor Ismawati Jaafar. 2011. A study on consumers' attitude towards online shopping in China. *International Journal of Business and Social Science* 2(22): 122–132.

Kang, Ju-Young M., and Kim KP Johnson. 2013. How does social commerce work for apparel shopping? Apparel social e-shopping with social network storefronts. *Journal of Customer Behaviour* 12(1): 53–72.

Kim, Dan J., Donald L. Ferrin, and H. Raghav Rao. 2008. A trust-based consumer decision-making model in electronic commerce: The role of trust, perceived risk, and their antecedents. *Decision Support Systems* 44(2): 544–564.

Kim, Sanghyun, and Hyunsun Park. 2013. Effects of various characteristics of social commerce (s-commerce) on consumers' trust and trust performance. *International Journal of Information Management* 33 (2): 318–332.

Legris, Paul, John Ingham, and Pierre Collerette. 2003. Why do people use information technology? A critical review of the technology acceptance model. *Information & Management* 40 (3): 191–204.

Lin, Hsiu-Fen. 2011. An empirical investigation of mobile banking adoption: The effect of innovation attributes and knowledge-based trust. *International Journal of Information Management* 31 (3): 252–260.

Liu, Su-Houn, Hsiu-Li Liao, and Jean A. Pratt. 2009. Impact of media richness and flow on e-learning technology acceptance. *Computers & Education* 52(3): 599–607.

Lloyd, Alison E., and Sherriff TK Luk. 2010. The Devil Wears Prada or Zara. *JGAMS* 1: 129–141.

Lodorfos, George N., Tom A. Trosterud, and Chris Whitworth. 2006. E-consumers' attitude and behaviour in the online commodities market. *Innovative Marketing* 2 (3): 77–96.
Louho, Riki, Mika Kallioja, and Pirkko Oittinen. 2006. Factors affecting the use of hybrid media applications. *Graphic Arts in Finland* 35 (3): 11–21.
Lu, Lilei, and Yuyu Yuan. 2018. A novel TOPSIS evaluation scheme for cloud service trustworthiness combining objective and subjective aspects. *Journal of Systems and Software* 143: 71–86.
Luarn, Pin, and Hsin-Hui. Lin. 2005. Toward an understanding of the behavioural intention to use mobile banking. *Computers in Human Behaviour* 21 (6): 873–891.
Nassar, Nour, Assef Jafar, and Yasser Rahhal. 2020. A novel deep multi-criteria collaborative filtering model for recommendation system. *Knowledge-Based Systems* 187: 104811.
Nöteberg, Anna, Ellen Christiaanse, and Philip Wallage. 1999. The role of trust and assurance services in electronic channels: An exploratory study. In *ICIS 1999 Proceedings*, 49.
Nunnally, Jum C. 1994. *Psychometric Theory 3E*. Tata McGraw-hill education.
Parvin, Hashem, Parham Moradi, and Shahrokh Esmaeili. 2019. TCFACO: Trust-aware collaborative filtering method based on ant colony optimization. *Expert Systems with Applications* 118: 152–168.
Pavlou, Paul A. 2003. Consumer acceptance of electronic commerce: Integrating trust and risk with the technology acceptance model. *International Journal of Electronic Commerce* 7 (3): 101–134.
Pavlou, Paul A., and Mendel Fygenson. 2006. Understanding and predicting electronic commerce adoption: An extension of the theory of planned behaviour. *MIS Quarterly* 30 (1): 115–143.
Pavlou, Paul A., Huigang Liang, and Yajiong Xue. 2007. Understanding and mitigating uncertainty in online exchange relationships: A principal-agent perspective. *MIS Quarterly*, pp. 105–136.
Sreen, Naman, Shankar Purbey, and Pradip Sadarangani. 2018. Impact of culture, behaviour and gender on green purchase intention. *Journal of Retailing and Consumer Services* 41: 177–189.
Taylor, Shirley, and Peter Todd. 1995. Decomposition and crossover effects in the theory of planned behaviour: A study of consumer adoption intentions. *International Journal of Research in Marketing* 12 (2): 137–155.
Tsagkias, Manos, et al. 2021. Challenges and research opportunities in ecommerce search and recommendations. In *ACM SIGIR Forum*, vol. 54, no. 1. New York, NY, USA: ACM.
Van der Heijden, Hans, Tibert Verhagen, and Marcel Creemers. 2003. Understanding online purchase intentions: contributions from technology and trust perspectives. *European Journal of Information Systems* 12(1): 41–48.
Venkatesh, Viswanath, et al. 2003. User acceptance of information technology: Toward a unified view. *MIS Quarterly*, pp. 425–478.
Wu, Bing, and Xiaohui Chen. 2017. Continuance intention to use MOOCs: Integrating the technology acceptance model (TAM) and task technology fit (TTF) model. *Computers in Human Behaviour* 67: 221–232.
Xu, Jingjun, Izak Benbasat, and Ronald T. Cenfetelli. 2020. The relative effect of the convergence of product recommendations from various online sources. *Journal of Management Information Systems* 37 (3): 788–819.
Yu, Jieun, et al. 2005. Extending the TAM for a t-commerce. *Information & Management* 42(7): 965–976.
Zhang, Mingyue, and Jesse Bockstedt. 2020. Complements and substitutes in online product recommendations: The differential effects on consumers' willingness to pay. *Information & Management* 57(6): 103341.
Zhao, Qi, et al. 2015. E-commerce recommendation with personalized promotion. In *Proceedings of the 9th ACM Conference on Recommender Systems*.

Learning Continuity in the Realm of Education 4.0: Higher Education Sector in the Post-pandemic of COVID-19

Debarshi Mukherjee and Khandakar Kamrul Hasan

1 Introduction

The National Education Policy (NEP) 2020 highlights the government's focus on developing India as a world knowledge hub (Forbes 2020) thereby capturing the government's intent of exploiting 'digital intervention' in primary, secondary, and tertiary education which is befitting the requirement of alternate educational infrastructure in the post-COVID-19 era. When the teaching–learning process across institutions came to a sudden halt in late March 2020, the academic fraternity worldwide rebounded with a digital intervention that allowed continued academic endeavors. Educators realized the need for a technology backbone and the evolution of a new pedagogic order. Over the last few years, academic luminaries have consistently clamored for attention from different quarters of interest to highlight that there is an inverse relationship between the output of educational institutes and the employability quotient. Specifically, in the case of professional education, the absence of the skills demanded in the industry has caused mass unemployment and hindered large-scale innovation. The pillar of this relationship is the basic architecture of the Indian education system that is expected to deliver the desired outcomes with assistance from various stakeholders, including the administrative sector, teachers, and most importantly the students at the bottom of the pyramid. When many Indian states are struggling to increase the gross enrollment ratio (GER) at the primary level, the subsequent propagation of the same set of students at the secondary and tertiary levels may be a huge challenge. Looking at the challenges of both engagement and learning, a series of theories and models has evolved from academia, which has tried

D. Mukherjee
Business Management, Tripura University (A Central University), Agartala, India
e-mail: debarshimukherjee@tripurauniv.ac.in

K. K. Hasan (✉)
Department of Business Management, Tripura University (A Central University), Agartala, India

R. N. Subudhi et al. (eds.), *Future of Work and Business in Covid-19 Era*,
Springer Proceedings in Business and Economics,
https://doi.org/10.1007/978-981-19-0357-1_15

to find a solution to ensure higher learning gain. Herein, learning gain may be identified as the enhancement of a learner's ability to execute a specific task following a planned training module (Evans et al. 2018). In line with the Government's Skill India or Startup India movements, a framework needs to be built that goes beyond classroom evaluation. Proponents of constructivist theory have suggested that at the tertiary level, peer-group learning, which calls for maturity among learners, both within and outside the classroom is an important component to disseminate knowledge (Dewey 1986). On the other hand, the media richness theory (Draft and Lengel 1986) has advocated for technology intervention in knowledge sharing, as richer media would ensure higher learning. However, recent studies have found a triad of erst while expeditious learning, which encompasses some key factors of easy delivery, enriched content, and experiential learning, which have become a learning triangle consisting of factors based on choice, context, and a networked learning system. In the absence of a 'perfect solution to ensure higher learning gains, policymakers have adopted some of these aspects and introduced strategic learning interventions. Courses ranging from choice-based credit systems (CBCS) to massive open online courses (MOOCs) are offered today from different platforms like Swayam, Swayam Prabha, NPTEL dedicated to tertiary education. These platforms bridge the digital divide that exists at various levels of educational institutions. Herein, it is worth mentioning that even pedagogic styles have contributed significantly to reducing the overall learning aim. In the higher education sector, for instance, pedagogic overtures have failed to capture students' requirements, and andragogy, which has higher self-learning and self-paced learning components, has been adopted.

It is here that blended learning establishes its identity; essentially, it incorporates various ways of learning, teaching models, and behavioral styles, which take place in a realistic learning environment by interactive means. Blended learning courses integrate learning experiences online and in a classroom, leveraging tools to maximize student learning outcomes, while resolving major structural concerns (Garrison and Kanuka 2004). Largely, it can be described as an innovative combination of well-chosen and supportive approaches to face-to-face as well as online learning (Graham 2018). The rapidly developing technological world, including the intensive production of new data and communications, is routinely adopted by businesses running on a technology backbone. Higher education institutions form an integral part of the market, for which introducing new technologies in the fields of both teaching and learning help to improve the quality of education while fulfilling young people's expectations, in terms of knowledge and skills to be mastered during their studies. Blended learning concepts have been seen from a variety of perspectives; they are:

1.1 Holistic Outlook

This refers to the incorporation of digital media into a classroom or remote learning environment. Students learn through a media-independent combination of instructional support using synchronous and/or asynchronous modes of learning.

1.2 Educational Outlook

Blended learning from an educational point of view alludes to online hybrid training courses designed with a pedagogical format and where a certain degree of traditional face-to-face contact is involved. This approach to learning converges mainly on two different paradigms, that is, synchronous physical classroom and asynchronous online classroom.

1.3 Pragmatic Future

Classes are taught in the classroom and online, incorporating multiple pedagogic strategies, which include.

- Blending various pedagogical methods, including constructivism, behavior, and cognitive learning, with or without training technologies, to achieve the best results from teaching.
- Combining all forms of instruction, such as DVDs, videos, online training, and face-to-face programs.
- Blending or integrating training technologies with real work activities to create harmonious learning and work results.

1.4 Enterprise Training Viewpoint

This involves the use of many educational tools, such as online learning content, pre-reading, lectures, and role-playing activities.

1.5 Chief Learning Officer (CLO) Perspective

It is important to develop a learning approach that combines several modes (synchronous and asynchronous) that offer the target group the best possible solution.

This paper proposes the idea of an integrated learning ecosystem, supporting the growing global trend to use blended learning to efficiently deliver higher educational content. This approach may involve one or multiple forms in which social media workshops, problem-solving gaming, video chats, role-playing games, virtual apprenticeship programs, immersive online quizzing, or competitions, and various simulations are accessible online (Hamilton and Tee 2010).

While extensive work has been carried out into e-learning and blended learning experiences with its various global models, there is sufficient scope for additional research. This research discusses this gap and examines educators' views on the future of blended learning in India.

Research Gap

The literary evaluation shows that the ideal education system is a system of education that can lead to a higher human civilization. Naturally, to do this, a leader needs to be able to do this. We know that today's global education development (online learning during the COVID-19 pandemic) cannot be separated from that of today's industrial revolution (Education 4.0) because other studies also demonstrate that indirect changes in economic order change also the education system in a country (Burke 1985; Manz and Sims 2001; Fairholm 2013).

2 Literature Review

2.1 Background

Almost every country globally still has instability due to the spread of coronavirus disease (COVID-19). Though activities are progressing slowly, in daily life, a lot has changed. The government continues to make efforts to address the COVID-19 virus. In carrying out a plan to prevent the spreading of this outbreak, the community is required to be controlled. Education is an unending process and building fundamental skills, both in intellectual strength and emotional feelings aimed at human nature. Therefore, the learning process is essential for educational success, such that the quality of education demands good management of service (Dewey 1986). During the learning process, an educational ecosystem enables thinking, character, innovation, independence, comfort, and student competence to grow and flourish. Therefore, freedom to study has the impact of producing superior or high-quality resources in the Industrial 4.0 era to create a nation and a state in general (Yamin and Syahrir 2020).

Student involvement is described here as students who are involved and engaged in the classroom have an impact on curriculum design and have a sense of belonging to a community. Kahu (2013) has stated that student participation has an essential impact on higher education attainment and learning. This represents the attributes of student life in a university and is a strong measure of a student's academic performance and institutional efficiency (Coates 2005; Robinson and Hullinger 2008). Student engagement (Coates 2005) explains the interaction between students and their learning experiences with the resources they have at hand for effective learning. Today, the word 'participation' is used to describe constructions such as the level of effort and engagement with learning activities. Although all students usually benefit from good educational activities, the more extreme effects are conditional and rarely compensatory. Most educators and schools provide tremendous opportunities to introduce students to new ways of learning while harnessing the growth of learning technology. When used properly, technology encourages student participation and thereby improves students' success and satisfaction (Revere and Kovach 2011); Hsu and Hsieh 2011; Johnson et al. 2008). Technique-mediated classes, such as e-learning courses or blended courses, provide students with the versatility to engage in their own space, pace, and time (Holsapple and Lee-Post 2006) and thus facilitate traditional classroom interaction, which otherwise is not feasible. Students' engagement in learning technologies is undeniable; however, these well-meaning advances can also pose a major risk to students (Holley and Oliver 2010). Learning through technology does not adequately deal with multiple student issues (Johnson et al. 2008) and may adversely impact different student populations (Chen et al. 2010). Holley and Oliver conclude that students' success in an online learning environment primarily depends on previous experiences, attitudes, and personal circumstances of the students, and it can pose barriers to students' participation and learning. The understanding of students regarding their output following digital teaching also tends to affect their success (Venkatesh et al. 2014; Wu et al. 2010).

Hu and Hui (2012) further observed that technical learning may disadvantage students with low computer skills, as they prefer less online work than those with high computer skills. Institutions are, therefore, trying to incorporate varying techniques to equitably include students from a range of cultures, attitudes, and abilities in the contemporary classroom. Efficiencies of learner technologies are measured across many factors (Young and Bruce 2011), inclusive of student features and expectations (Holley and Oliver 2010). E-learning has been growing, and students today can interact with both their peers and teachers in course content online (Johnson et al. 2008). The interaction is reinforced by the student's sense of social identity, along with a shared space for learning, which instills a sense of belonging to a learning group (Johnson et al. 2008; Young and Bruce 2011). The awareness and availability of help for a common group promote social interaction, and the lack of social interaction between people dissipates the feeling of isolation in online learning (Muilenburg and Berge 2005). Online networks have also argued that actual in-class presence and casual contact are never substituted (Chen et al. 2010; Sanders 2006). While modern education progresses, students still want the human touch (Holsapple and Lee-Post 2006). Therefore, the task of university education is to use technological transformation to recognize and shape learning opportunities without losing human contact (Holsapple and Lee-Post 2006). Blended learning offers a format, which combines the strengths of learning that seem to be appealing in responding to this challenge. In particular, blended learning aims to enhance engagement, communication, self-reliance, and self-awareness of students, as well as facilitating both interaction and collaboration not only with their teachers but also with their peers and the course materials, leading thereby to a more productive and holistic student experience. Blended learning can be done by introducing state-of-the-art technology and tools to improve learning activities to offer courses that are already comfortable for many students of this digital age to better participate and cooperate with others in those practices that promote constructivism (Hoic-Bozic et al. 2015; Cummings et al. 2017).

However, for these advantages, it is necessary to consider blended learning as part of the learner's experience that can in turn be used to build a more comprehensive and practical approach to meet the educational needs of the student community at large (Kim 2012). Research by Wu et al. (2010) postulated that students had success in a mixed learning environment. Nevertheless, others have indicated that the interactions between teachers and peers are reduced in a blended learning environment (Kim 2012). Learning materials are an essential component of blended learning. However, blended learning may isolate some students if teachers struggle to encourage social and group networking (Donnelly 2010), which in turn can result in decreased enthusiasm for learning together (Osguthorpe and Graham 2003). A recent meta-analysis (Castro 2019) of different studies found that a set office factors makes or precludes incentives for blended learning—obstacles, drivers, results, challenges, and particular resources or technologies—that influence learning practices in the classroom. The efficient use of teacher's tools [computers, electronics, and software for learning management system (LMS)] and their skills play a part in how they handle blended learning.

2.2 Evolution of Blended Learning

The young generation that has grown up in the digital age learn differently, because they are techno-literate, fast techno-learners, and have the exploratory learning skills obtained from video games for instance. The essence of learning technologies and how they are to be used are expected to transform the future of global education. Graham (2018) stated, 'while technology continues to develop, finding a successful balance between creativity and development will be a constant challenge for those who build blended learning systems.' Web 1.0 and Web 2.0 are the blended learning online portal instruments currently in use. In Web 1.0, the information is provided to users in a read-only environment, while in Web 2.0, users create and edit information in a reading and writing environment that supports social activities. Examples of common Web 2.0 resources include forums, Wikis, Twitter, YouTube, Facebook, and Flickr. Globally, Web 2.0 users have increased dramatically. The result for 'E-learning 1.0' represents Web 1.0 that 'was correlated with communication or relational learning style in an atmosphere that typically promotes the idea of constructivist learning as the preferred approach' (Robertson 2008). E-learning 2.0 (Web 2.0) permits knowledge-building collaborations almost simultaneously. Rapid advances in e-learning are encouraging research about the effect such developments have on blended learning. Recently, work has begun investigating the blended learning features using Web 2.0. For example, Motteram and Sharma (2009) discussed the role that Web 2.0 could play in improving the production of language learning within a blended learning context. They stressed the development of suitable initiatives to meet the needs of students to help them understand the language. We believe that the use of technology improves our capacity to understand language teaching. Continuous development of various implementations of online apps and interactive 3D environments, such as second life, called E-learning 3.0 (see Fig. 1), using artificial intelligence (AI) takes us into the realm of augmented and virtual reality which in turn leaves a positive impact of learner's ability to synchronize with the subject. Future technological advancements must change the modes of distribution and performance, along with the modern educational landscape.

While linking employability, affordability, relevance, and choice together, it can be observed that only a small portion of students obtain education, while a significant portion of the population is left behind (Mukherjee 2014) (Fig. 2).

The philosophy of mass production needs an immediate conversion to mass customization for learning, and prudence is required to acknowledge the appropriate blend of theory and practice in the courseware at the design stage. It has been observed that both pure forms of e-learning and the traditional chalk-n-talk method are not effective, and that challenge can only be overcome through blended learning. However, the appropriate blend in terms of content digitization and classroom training or experience vis-a-vis theory is highly subject-specific.

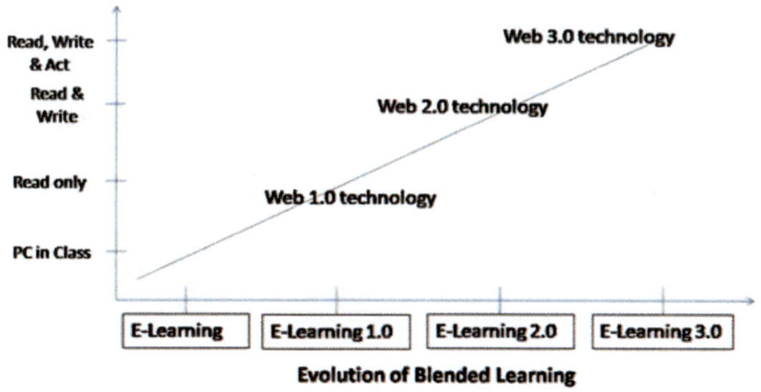

Fig. 1 Evolution of blended learning. *Source* Mukherjee and Hasan (2020a; b)

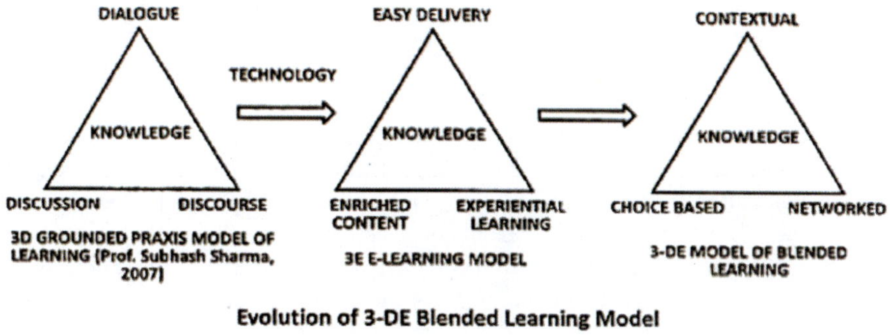

Fig. 2 Evolution of 3-DE blended learning. *Source* Mukhopadhyay (2011)

2.3 Benefits of Blended Learning

Higher education institutions are now more and more likely to offer courses through multimedia platforms, in particular using the blended learning process. This method of education has many benefits, including unrestricted access to course materials, improved time productivity during classes, smoother and more effective communication between teachers and students, considerably more attention to the needs of the students, and additional help in the problem-solving content of the course. Researchers Eisenbradt (2005) and Owston et al. (2013, pp.38–46) confirmed these advantages as follows:

- Access to educational content is facilitated
- Better focus occurs during lectures
- Comfortable and better contact with the lecturer, which leads to faster and more effective monitoring, both during and just before exams of the vital content.

2.4 Theoretical Underpinning

The interpretive paradigm, which seems ideally suitable for recognizing and interpreting the aspirations of both students and teachers in a new learning environment, inspired this study. According to Mason (2002), an interpretive study 'tries to achieve an interpretation of the universe and what it means for the research participants.' The emphasis is on knowing people 'without deliberately generating research-related situations' (Punch and Oancea 2014, p. 17). A combination of a constructivist and a theoretical context of social construction supports this study. The constructivist factor would enable us to view and learn from the perspective of the individual about the nature of social reality. Within this sense, the importance of what the human mind can do vis-a-vis the personal experiences of each one of us is explained (Galbin 2014). Constructivists regard people as constructive agents, who see the concept of interest (meaning or knowledge) as being generated rather than as being received passively from others who control what they have seen, experienced, and valued (Spivey 1996). Social constructionism, on the other hand, assumes that learning is a collective activity. Our diverse cultures play a crucial role in influencing our social attitudes and experiences, and researchers focus on collectively generating and communicating meaning. Social developers view the human experience as being represented culturally and traditionally through ever-changing social practices (Burr 2015). Therefore, the principle of social constructionism is followed in this analysis because of the role of the socio-cultural context in constructing the interactions of the teacher and the student. A thematic review of the academic literature was performed to determine the extent of the current knowledge of this phenomenon. Only peer-reviewed original research papers were included to determine validity and trust. The papers were then re-reviewed, and the main topics were ascertained. Notably, the study offers a summary of the extant literature on the future of blended learning, the importance of which has been illustrated under different learning contexts by numerous previous researchers.

Methodology

As a strategic imperative, digital and non-digital content needs to be apportioned within a course structure at the policy level and consistently implemented with periodic assessments to track the progress of the course under the new environment so that course correction can be made if needed during the program or later for the whole program. The Internet is just a vehicle for knowledge transmission, and educators must concentrate on learning mechanisms rather than content delivery to strike a bond with the students, which in turn may yield higher learning gains for students in the long run. By considering course-specific subjectivity, the percentage of blending could be mapped for each course. Since the objective of this action should be to measure the effectiveness of blended learning over traditional modes in tertiary education, the research could well be directed toward measuring the learning gain through various structured instruments over a period (Mukherjee 2014), (Fig. 3).

Once the entire population is trained to assimilate technology interventions in regular education programs, the academic progress of the pupils can be monitored through the pre-diagnosis, learning prescription, and post-diagnosis (PLP) method. A battery of periodic tests should be conducted under a homogeneous sample size,

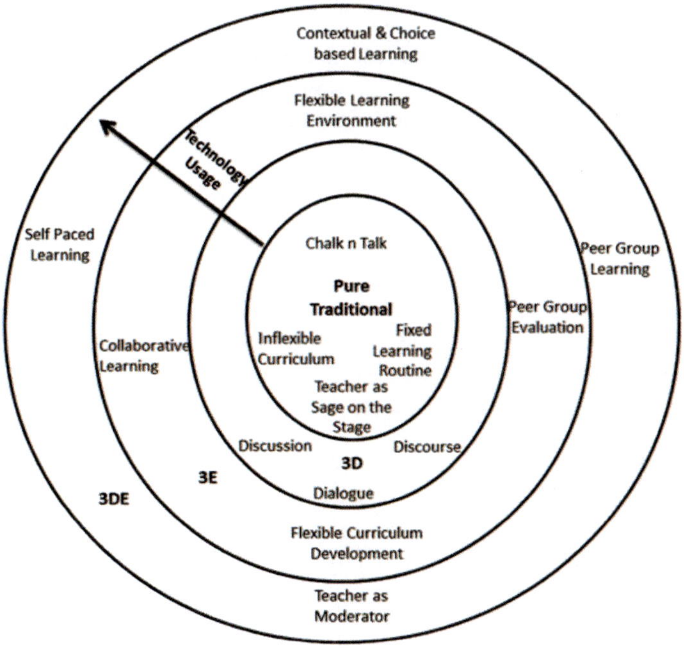

Figure3 Evolution of blended learning. *Source* Mukherjee (2014)

where the difference between groups and within groups could be measured, indicating if there is any growth in academic performance compared to past performance. Secondly, these scores could be compared with the scores of pupils studying in colleges who have either no or limited technology access, to ascertain if there has been any impact of information and communications technology use in tertiary education. Since the constructivist theory demands a pupil's maturity, another aspect of applicability would come to light in terms of its appropriateness at the undergraduate or postgraduate level. These analyses could well be managed using a structured instrument for data capture along with various second and third-generation statistical tools to extract the influencing variable(s), which in turn could further be evaluated to reduce any kind of ambiguity. Andragogic systems would work as a mediating variable where the influence of blended learning tools could be measured on tertiary students. Technology deployment is required to be implemented across all of the tertiary sectors in Tripura with the scope being limited to professional courses only. Over a while, the same model could be replicated on a pan-India basis for a comparative analysis between states, aiming to derive a national-level summary. After some time, a planned evaluation could use the open-source Moodle application.

3 Components of Blended Learning

A model may be a device or a phenomenon definition that shows its known or suspected features and can be used for further examination of its features. A blended learning model can also be used as a framework for evaluating and integrating various elements that contribute to the knowledge-imparting educational system. Figure 4 shows the blended learning components.

3.1 Learning Environment Component

Synchronous and asynchronous learning technologies, used for the interactions among students and teachers, encourage greater commitment and improve learning

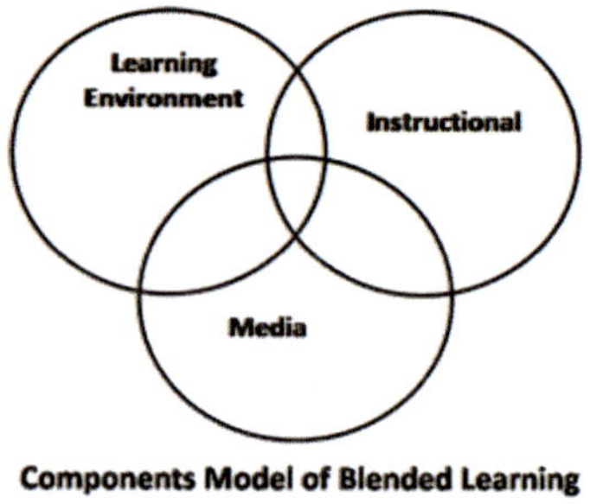

Fig. 4 Model of blended learning components. *Source* Authors

outcomes. The goal of blended learning is to use every community's positive aspects to ensure that the available resources are used in the best possible way to achieve the goal of education.

3.2 The Part Played by Media

Media refers only to vehicles that provide the learning material. The synchronous or asynchronous learning environment may be used in certain interactive media, but none is better than the other. Although it is not possible to influence the desired content by choosing a specific media, it can influence how the content is built using unique characteristics of the media. However, learning results should not be influenced if the most appropriate media is chosen.

3.3 Part of the Instruction

Instructional approaches are the result of learning goals and help to protect learning goals and encourage information communication. Maintaining an education quality is important when developing blended learning. Therefore, learning priorities should not be undermined when designing a blended learning program.

4 Discussion

4.1 The Grand Purpose

It has been observed in the past that the entire gamut of programs in secondary and tertiary education has suffered due to the intermittent and inappropriate use of technology. To foster an enabling self-learning environment, a policy framework with definite guidelines to exploit knowledge through effective networking across partner institutions to deliver online learning capsules needs to be developed. The major cause behind the digital divide has not been the goodwill to use it, but the unavailability of technology infrastructure at desired locations (Mukherjee 2012). In the absence of a networked academic knowledge repository, students mostly rely upon the content available on social media or from search engine offerings, which are mostly free, and thereby students become vulnerable to spurious and erroneous content that affects learning.

However, a policy level change is needed wherein affirmative action is required to assess the learning gain among tertiary students, particularly in geographically disadvantaged states like Tripura. The state of Tripura with a population of around

3.7 million bordered by Bangladesh on three sides comprises almost 85% of its border area. Its land-locked nature has hit, among other issues, the education system severely. After high school, students can take admission to one of the sixty-plus colleges, and after college, there are about four postgraduate institutions available in the state. The situation is even worse in the tribal-dominated areas, which contribute to approximately 31% of the state's population. Infrastructure development and training of the teachers are two major challenges facing policymakers before they can foster a sustainable blended learning environment. The digital divide due to poor or non-accessibility to Internet infrastructure has jeopardized the prospect of blended learning in India as a vehicle for mass education across the primary, secondary, and tertiary sectors; in fact, there has also been stiff resistance to blended learning from a certain section of society.

4.2 *Embracing the New Normal*

It is important now to envisage the pioneering work in institutions of higher learning in India, which are expected to deliver a critical analysis of the education policy and to suggest the ideal mix of learning components in a professional tertiary course. Institutes located in geographically disadvantaged places suffer in many ways on the development front, for example, lack of skilled resources, teaching aids, and infrastructure, among others. This effort would establish effective learning content over a digital platform, which could bridge the digital divide and bring equality and unity to the learning space. This paper understands the fact and aims to propagate universal learning content, which would permeate a feeling of equality and reduce social conflict. Besides other social issues, lack of education has been one of the major reasons behind society conflict, and this proposition of deploying a blended learning approach in tertiary education will help manage students' learning aspirations and thereby will help resolve the crisis partially if not completely. The strategic intervention of educational technologies (EdTech) has seen the rise of a new paradigm in tertiary education, that is, Education 4.0 where students exhibit maturity and enjoy self-paced learning and intend to succeed beyond the boundaries of a formal setup.

4.3 *Novelty*

The two major programs add zest to the blended learning model. Firstly, the measurement of skill gaps using a blend of technology and physical interaction with students will help to realize the importance of computing devices in knowledge dissemination. Secondly, a study will reveal if there is any correlation between the type of delivery and the learning gain and measure the impact of online learning. Further, as a mixed-mode learning strategy is being adopted to deliver the courses, formal induction of online content delivery has already commenced in classroom settings.

As there is currently inadequate infrastructure, this practice will improve the efficacy of blended learning once online learning is available to more students.

The blended learning model adopted by institutions across the world has revealed a framework for including technology in regular classroom teaching and highlighted the fact that the quantum of blending accepted by pupils does have a positive correlation with their learning gain. The aspects of learning continuity essentially highlight the intervention of technology to prevent learning disruptions. Since March 2020, it has been observed that academic institutions worldwide have redesigned their andragogic strategies and evolved with different methodologies to meet the learning challenges (Mukherjee and Hasan 2020a; b).

5 Conclusion

This study argues that blended learning in higher education can deliver an outstanding and rewarding learning experience. Students consider the use of technology in blended learning as an educational advancement. To provide decision-makers with input, it is essential to consider the potential of blended learning. As learning technologies are the vehicle of resource sharing in the blended learning environment (BLE), the maturity of the learners and their independent learning skills need to be trusted. However, the programs or courses can always be designed and structured to suit individual learning cohorts depending on the underlying learning objectives with a focus on overall learning gain. Now is the time for policymakers to formulate definite strategic interventions for the augmentation of the blended learning approach in institutions across India to harness the positive results of learning continuity. Although face-to-face learning offers a psychological assurance to the learners in a physical classroom setting, using blended learning can fill the void of iterative and self-paced learning, which instills confidence even among slow learners.

Acknowledgements The authors are grateful to all national and international authors whose published work was used in our study and made the study possible.

References

Burke, W. Warner. 1985. "Leaders: The strategies for taking charge", by Warren Bennis and Burt Nanus (Book Review). *Human Resource Management* 24(4): 503.

Burr, Vivien. 2015. *Social constructionism*. Routledge.

Castro, Robin. 2019. Blended learning in higher education: Trends and capabilities. *Education and Information Technologies* 24 (4): 2523–2546.

Chen, Pu-Shih Daniel, Amber D. Lambert, and Kevin R. Guidry. 2010. Engaging online learners: The impact of Web-based learning technology on college student engagement. *Computers & Education* 54(4): 1222–1232.

Coates, Hamish. 2005.The value of student engagement for higher education quality assurance. *Quality in Higher Education* 11(1): 25–36.
Cummings, Cynthia, et al. 2017. Active learning strategies for online and blended learning environments. In *Flipped Instruction: Breakthroughs in Research and Practice*, 88–114. IGI Global.
Daft, Richard L., and Robert H. Lengel. 1986. Organizational information requirements, media richness and structural design. *Management Science* 32(5): 554–571.
Dewey, John. 1986. Experience and education. In *The Educational Forum,* vol. 50, no. 3. Taylor & Francis Group.
Donnelly, Roisin. 2010. Harmonizing technology with interaction in blended problem-based learning. *Computers & Education* 54 (2): 350–359.
Eisenbardt, Tomasz. 2005. Wykorzystaniemetody blended-learning w ciągłymprocesiekształcenia. *PraceNaukowe/AkademiaEkonomiczna w Katowicach,* 177–184.
Evans, C., C. Kandiko Howson, and A. Forsythe. 2018. Making sense of learning gain in higher education. *Higher Education Pedagogies* 3(1): 1–45.
Fairholm, Matthew R. 2013. *Putting Your Values to Work: Becoming the Leader Others Want to Follow*. ABC-CLIO.
Forbes India. 2020. 'We Are Doubling Our E-Learning Efforts': HRD Minister Ramesh Pokhriyal. *Forbes India*, 22 June 2020. www.forbesindia.com/article/coronavirus/we-are-doubling-our-elearning-efforts-hrd-minister-ramesh-pokhriyal/60263/1.
Galbin, Alexandra. 2014. An introduction to social constructionism. *Social Research Reports* 6 (26): 82–92.
Garrison, D. Randy, and Heather Kanuka. 2004. Blended learning: Uncovering its transformative potential in higher education. *The Internet and Higher Education* 7(2): 95–105.
Graham, Charles R. 2018. Current research in blended learning. In *Handbook of Distance Education*, 173–188.
Hamilton, J., & Tee, S. (2010). Smart utilization of tertiary instructional modes. *Computers & Education, 54*(4), 1036-1053.
Hoic-Bozic, Natasa, Martina HolenkoDlab, and VedranMornar. 2015. Recommender system and web 2.0 tools to enhance a blended learning model. *IEEE Transactions on Education* 59(1): 39–44.
Holley, Debbie, and Martin Oliver. 2010. Student engagement and blended learning: Portraits of risk. *Computers & Education* 54 (3): 693–700.
Holsapple, Clyde W., and Anita Lee-Post. 2006. Defining, assessing, and promoting e-learning success: An information systems perspective. *Decision Sciences Journal of Innovative Education* 4 (1): 67–85.
Hsu, Li-Ling, and Suh-Ing Hsieh. 2011. Effects of a blended learning module on self-reported learning performances in baccalaureate nursing students. *Journal of Advanced Nursing* 67(11): 2435–2444.
Hu, Paul Jen-Hwa, and Wendy Hui. 2012. Examining the role of learning engagement in technology-mediated learning and its effects on learning effectiveness and satisfaction. *Decision Support Systems* 53(4): 782–792.
Johnson, Richard D., Steven Hornik, and Eduardo Salas. 2008. An empirical examination of factors contributing to the creation of successful e-learning environments. *International Journal of Human-Computer Studies* 66(5): 356–369.
Kahu, Ella R. 2013. Framing student engagement in higher education. *Studies in Higher Education* 38(5): 758–773.
Kim, Jin-Young. 2012. A study on learners' perceptional typology and relationships among the learner's types, characteristics, and academic achievement in a blended e-Education environment. *Computers & Education* 59(2): 304–315.
Kuh, George D. 2009. The national survey of student engagement: Conceptual and empirical foundations. *New Directions for Institutional Research* 2009 (141): 5–20.

Manz, Charles C., and Henry P. Sims. 2001. *The New Superleadership: Leading Others to Lead Themselves*. Berrett-Koehler Publishers.

Mason, John. 2002. *Researching Your Own Practice: The Discipline of Noticing*. Routledge.

Motteram, Gary, and Pete Sharma. 2009. Blending learning in a web 2.0 world. *International Journal of Emerging Technologies and Society* 7(2): 83.

Muilenburg, Lin Y., and Zane L. Berge. 2005. Student barriers to online learning: A factor analytic study. *Distance Education* 26 (1): 29–48.

Mukherjee, Debarshi. 2012. Role of communication medium in web based instructional environment in Indian management education. *Indian Journal of Open Learning* 21 (1): 41–59.

Mukherjee, Debarshi. 2014. Factors of management education in India as perceived by learners and providers: An empirical study. *Vision* 18 (2): 73–80.https://doi.org/10.1177/0972262914527872

Mukherjee, Debarshi, and Khandakar Kamrul Hasan. 2020a. Metaliteracy: A comprehensive learning framework for new age students. In *Purvottaran—The Rise of North East: Paradigms of Development in the VUCA World*, by Debarshi Mukherjee and Mahasweta Saha, 393–410. Bloomsbury.

Mukherjee, Debarshi, and Khandakar Kamrul Hasan. 2020b. Challenges in learning continuity during the COVID-19 pandemic: A methodological and thematic review. *South Asian Journal of Management* 27(3).

Mukhopadhyay, Debarshi. 2011. *A Strategic Blended Model for Indian Management Education: Using Multimedia Instructional System*, 1st ed., 208. LAP LAMBERT Academic Publishing.

Osguthorpe, Russell T., and Charles R. Graham. 2003. Blended learning environments: Definitions and directions. *Quarterly Review of Distance Education* 4(3): 227–233.

Owston, Ron, Dennis York, and Susan Murtha. 2013. Student perceptions and achievement in a university blended learning strategic initiative. *The Internet and Higher Education* 18: 38–46.

Punch, Keith F., and Alis Oancea. 2014. *Introduction to research methods in education.*

Revere, Lee, and Jamison V. Kovach. 2011. Online technologies for engaged learning a meaningful synthesis for educators. *Quarterly Review of Distance Education* 12(2).

Robertson, Ian. 2008. 'Learners' attitudes to wiki technology in problem based, blended learning for vocational teacher education. *Australasian Journal of Educational Technology* 24(4).

Robinson, Chin Choo, and Hallett Hullinger. 2008. New benchmarks in higher education: Student engagement in online learning. *Journal of Education for Business* 84(2): 101–109.

Sanders, Robert. 2006. The "imponderable bloom": Reconsidering the role of technology in education. *Innovate: Journal of Online Education* 2(6).

Spivey, Nancy Nelson. 1996. *The Constructivist Metaphor: Reading, Writing and the Making of Meaning*. Brill.

Venkatesh, Vivek, Anne-Marie Croteau, and Jihan Rabah. 2014. Perceptions of effectiveness of instructional uses of technology in higher education in an era of Web 2.0. In *2014 47th Hawaii International Conference on System Sciences*. IEEE.

Wu, Jen-Her., Robert D. Tennyson, and Tzyh-Lih. Hsia. 2010. A study of student satisfaction in a blended e-learning system environment. *Computers & Education* 55 (1): 155–164.

Yamin, Muhammad, and Syahrir Syahrir. 2020. Pembangunan pendidikanmerdekabelajar (telaahmetodepembelajaran). *JurnalIlmiah Mandala Education* 6(1).

Young, Suzanne, and Mary Alice Bruce. 2011. Classroom community and student engagement in online courses. *Journal of Online Learning and Teaching* 7(2): 219–230.

Debarshi Mukherjee is a Professor and Head of the Department of Business Management, Tripura University (A Central University) actively engaged in management and social science research over the last two decades. He has executed many sponsored research projects and has published over 70 research papers.

Khandakar Kamrul Hasan is an International Research Scholar from Bangladesh in the Department of Business Management, Tripura University (A Central University).

Sustainable Development and Rights of Prisoners During Pandemic: An Appraisal

Deblina Majumder

1 Introduction

The year 2020 has etched a strong impression in the lives of most people across the world. During lockdown, people were left restless under societal prisons. While the fortunate ones have spent quality time with family working from home, exploring culinary skills and showcasing their talents, the pandemic has enormously affected the criminal justice system in general and prison administration in particular. Most people spent time looking after their mental health; life of prisoners was devastating. Prison life is deliberately planned to provide compulsory isolation, i.e. social segregation. The condition of prisoners behind physical bars was precarious. Mass incarceration, poor hygiene, and lack of infrastructure are common issues among prisoners. The only moment of joy in their lives is meeting their families which was at stake. The Sustainable Development Goals (SDGs) have specifically emphasized on setting global goals to establish fair, sustainable and holistic wellbeing of all, but this pandemic escalated anxiety, depression and stress in the prisoners. Physical distancing is essential, but mental health issues arising out of prolonged separation cannot be ignored.

2 Conceptualizing Sustainable Development and Rights of Prisoners

The concept of sustainable development has gained momentum in the present scenario (Kurian 2012). The United Nations has particularized sustainable development as "encompassing the achievement of three interconnected objectives, i.e.,

D. Majumder (✉)
School of Law, KIIT University Bhubaneswar, Bhubaneswar, India

R. N. Subudhi et al. (eds.), *Future of Work and Business in Covid-19 Era*,
Springer Proceedings in Business and Economics,
https://doi.org/10.1007/978-981-19-0357-1_16

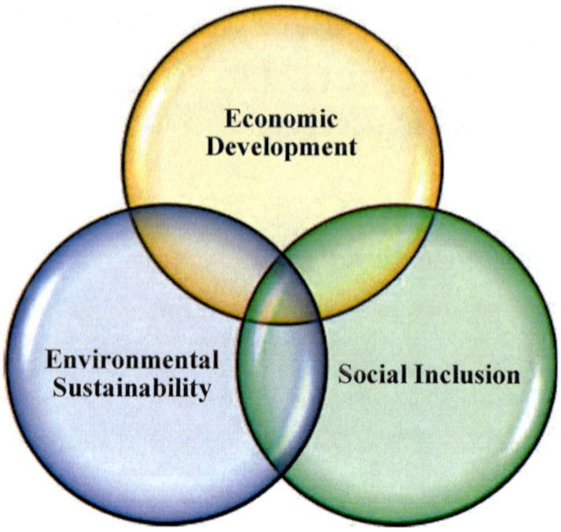

Fig. 1 Sustainable development as interconnected concept. *Source* Prepared by Researcher

economic development, social inclusion, and environmental sustainability which are necessary for the well-being of individuals and societies." (United Nations 2013). Improving the economy, shielding natural resources, and warranting social justice are not contradictory but interwoven and complementary (Victor 2006) (Fig. 1).

Prisoner is a person who is found guilty or is awaiting his trial. Prisoners can be categorized into "under trial prisoner, convicted criminal, or civil prisoner". There are no codified rights of prisoners. Often the judiciary has reiterated what rights the prisoners have. It is an accepted fact that precedent is more powerful law than legislation and is binding on all courts in India (Malik 2011).

The researcher has attempted to draw a link between which goals of the SDGs correspond to the rights of prisoners available in India. Various Jail Reforms Committees and judiciary have taken initiative in upholding *economic development* of prisoners like: equal and adequate wages for the prisoners; *social inclusion* initiatives like offering opportunity to meet family and close kins, scope for parole and probation so that the prisoners can maintain the social ties; and lastly *environment sustainability*: the researcher is conceptualizing this environment as the physical environment within the prison: How conducive the physical environment of the prisons. To uphold sustainable development among prisoners most of the rights as upheld by the judiciary and incorporated in the Jail Reforms Committees are a set of benefits. These include: remission of punishment for good conduct, payment of rightful wages, facilities like canteen, and permitting privileges to write letters and meet family members and close friends.

3 Research Methodology of the Study and the Objectives

This research paper is a humble attempt to undertake content analysis of newspaper articles. The primary data has been collected from government reports and secondary data have been retrieved from books, articles, journals, and newspaper articles. The paper aims to explore the rights which prisoners have during incarceration towards their fair, sustainable and holistic wellbeing, and to evaluate the impediments faced during the pandemic.

4 Sustainable Developmental Goals (SDGs) and Criminal Justice System

The SDGs undoubtedly offer a determined and extensive range of global vision for a sustainable future (Jose et al. 2017). As stated earlier, it is an amalgamation of "economic development, social inclusion, and environmental sustainability". This is obligatory for the wellbeing of people at large. It is a matter of fact that the Millennium Development Goals are narrower than the Sustainable Developmental Goals (Halle, 2016). Health has been prioritized at international arena for more than 20 years. Health is a right and, also a means to achieve holistic development (Singh 2016). Sustainable development of the prisoners does not only mean the physical health, it also includes the mental health of the prisoners. Development must be holistic.

According to the United Nations (2015), "the Agenda 2030 with its 17 Sustainable Development Goals (SDGs) provides the framework that all 193 United Nations (UN) member states have pledged to achieve."(Kroll et al. 2019) (Fig. 2).

Among the 17 goals of Sustainable Development, the following goals can be addressed as crucial for Criminal Justice System:

- Majority of the prisoners are from lower socio-economic strata of the society. For most of them, their social, economic, and psychological circumstances have cornered them to commit offences. Law enforcement officers also frequently use

Fig. 2 The seventeen Sustainable Developmental Goals . *Source* Official Website of United Nations

"poverty, homelessness or disadvantage as an indicator of criminality". Poverty is one of the hindrances why there are large number of under trial prisoners who cannot afford bail. (Goal 1)

- Despite formation of several committees at national and state levels, the food provided to the prisoners need to meet the basic nutritional level. Prisoners who are unwell, elderly, women in general and mothers (or to-be) and their children must be provided with special diet. (Goal 2)
- Prisoners lead very conditional yet unhealthy lifestyle which is obviously owing to their poverty. So proper health services must be catered to them. (Goal 3)
- Prisoners too have right to be educated. Ignorant minds trigger criminality. The authorities must ensure that the all the categories of prisoners are given education. (Goal 4)
- Men and women prisoners must have equal access to all the benefits inside the prison. (Goal 5)
- The prison authorities must ensure that prisoners have hygienic environment, proper sanitation, and clean water to drink. (Goal 6)
- The prisoners, both men and women, must be given adequate wages. (Goal 8)
- The rule of law must be upheld in the prison premises. The authorities must ensure that prison violence must reduce, overcrowding needs to be addressed. Food, water, and medical care must be given priority. (Goal 16)

The prisoners are human beings living in controlled environment. One cannot seize to be a human being within the prison premises. In this pandemic situation, Goals 2, 3, 4, 6, and 16 are very essential to ensure sustainable development of the prisoners.

5 Rights of Prisoners in General

5.1 The Following Are the Rights Which the Prisoners Have Which Ultimately Leads Them Towards Their Fair, Sustainable, and Holistic Wellbeing

The prisoners have been guaranteed certain rights under the Constitution of India, the law of the land; the Code of Criminal Procedure, 1973, and the Prisons Act, 1894 (Fig. 3).

As and when problems have been faced by prisoners, different rights have been secured. The majority of the rights of the prisoners are fundamental rights per se or have derived their source from the fundamental rights as enshrined under the Constitution of India. These rights fulfil the holistic development of the prisoners in normal circumstances.

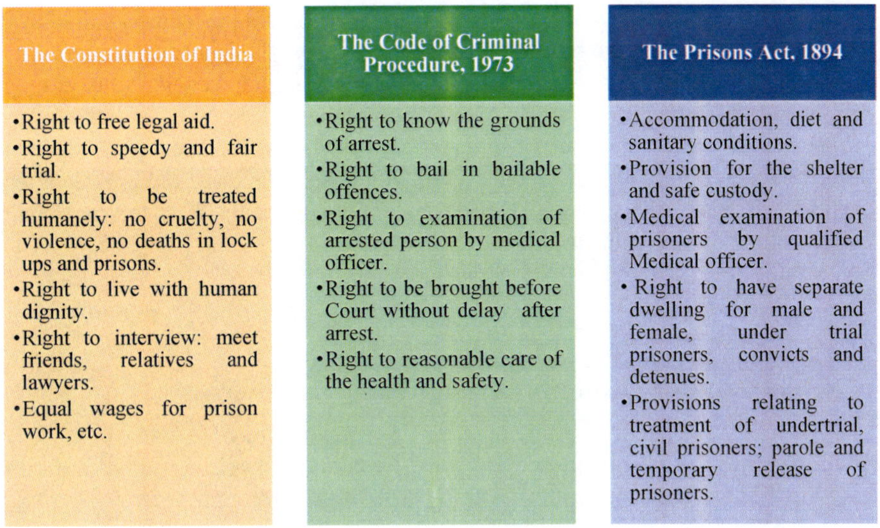

Fig. 3 Following chart is prepared by the researcher to showcase the rights of prisoners guaranteed by different laws in India. *Source* Prepared by Researcher

5.2 *Rights of Prisoners During Pandemic and the Impediments Faced by Correctional Services*

There are number of rights which were compromised during the pandemic, i.e. the new normal. This research paper has highlighted how the sustainable developmental goals have been observed during "new normal" phase. With the onset of the contagious COVID19 in India, life has become *topsy turvy*. Life was not how it used to be for people in the society let alone the ones in the prisons.

The constant issue with the Correctional Services in India has been overcrowding of prisons. Lack of infrastructure leads to overcrowding which further gives rise to unequal distribution of services. One cannot expect the prison system to provide holistic developmental ambience with these shortcomings. The Prison Statistics gives a glaring example of the condition of prisoners in India.

Table 1 shows that the jails in India are overcrowded with inmates with a constant

Table 1 Prison occupancy

Year	No. of prisons	Actual capacity of prisons	No. of prisoners at the end of the year	Occupancy rate at the end of the year (%)
2017	1361	3,91,574	4,50,696	115.1
2018	1339	3,96,223	4,66,084	117.6
2019	1350	4,03,739	4,78,600	118.5

Source Prison Statistics India–2019

increase in the occupancy rate every year. This gives the impression that the Indian Judiciary is keen to rely on intramural sentencing despite having several alternatives like probation, parole, and community sentencing. The judiciary has always opted *expressed* punishment over *reformation* of the convict.

The Hon'ble Supreme Court of India on 23rd of March, 2020 passed a judgement ordering the State governments and prison authorities to release the prisoners who are fit for parole. This was a welcome step. This ignited the idea to strategically tackle with the contagion. In this way, the Goal 16 (upholding rule of law) of the Sustainable Development was implemented.

6 Situation of Prison and Prisoners

The researcher has attempted to highlight the condition of prisons across India and how the prison authorities have dealt with it by going through several newspaper articles, both online and offline:

6.1 **Maharashtra State Government** was proactive in dealing with the menace. They have given a strong fight against this contagious disease during the first wave. In *the Hindustan Times,* it was reported that there were **36,000 inmates** in the state prisons at all levels: central, district and subjails. As on 11th November, 2020, there were 60 number of active cases out of the total 28,590 inmates across 43 prisons in the state. Till then only 6 prisons had succumbed to the disease. Overcrowding was combatted by **releasing** people who had committed non-serious offences; the ones who were already on **bail** were asked not to return till the lockdown was lifted. There were a few prisoners released on **emergency parole** earlier, they were instructed to stay at home till the Epidemic Act and Disaster Management Act were revoked. So the state government had to deal with 28,590 inmates (Yadav 2020). By doing so 20% of the total prison population could be reduced. Each group of staff was given **roaster duty** for a month. In that month, they were not allowed to step out of the prison premises otherwise they would act as vectors. **14-day quarantine** was offered at temporary prisons for the new arrestees. A total of **26,740** COVID19 tests were conducted across the state. Even **homeopathy** oral dose of *Camphora* was given to the prisoners.

6.2 **Kerala State Government** had 6000 inmates occupying 54 jails at the three different levels. The following steps were taken to secure the rights: In *the Hindustan Times,* it was reported that they had **prepared isolated cells** for suspected coronavirus-infected inmates. This segregation had stopped the disease from spreading further (Asian News International 2020). The case of Poojappura Central Prison was reported in *The Hindu* that the prison was ravaged by COVID19. It reported its first casualty after an aged prisoner succumbed to the illness. In total 462 inmates and staff had tested positive

(George 2020). On 2nd November, 2020, as reported by of India in *the Business Standards*, the government ordered that these **elderly** were to be released on **parole** for more than a month. Hence, special care was taken of the elderly prisoners over 65 **years** of age. Special **parole** and **remission** orders were also passed (Anonymous 2020).

6.3 **Karnataka Government** took the following steps: There were about **10,000 prisoners** in 9 central jails; 3500 prisoners in 21 district jails and 900 prisoners in 26 subjails. Bengaluru central jail has been the most **congested** prison with 4881 prisoners including 3585 under trial prisoners. On 16 April 2020, it was reported in *The Indian Express* that 1112 prisoners were released on **bail** and **parole**. As reflected in *The Hindu*, a petition was filed by Amol Kale before the High Court. As a consequence, the state government was asked to submit what measures they have taken to look after the **health and safety** of the prisoners, as it is a matter of right (Special Correspondent, 2020). The authorities were asked to set up **isolation centres** and provide immunity boosting vitamin tablets to all the inmates. Meanwhile, over 1379 prisoners were released on **parole**. A total of 636 under trial prisoners were **granted bail**. A welcome step taken by the prison authorities was introducing **video calling** for the inmates. The families of the prisoner had to register at e-prison website with their AADHAAR and other identification details to book a meeting with their loved ones who were behind the bars.

6.4 **Delhi** prisons are immensely overcrowded. The government took the following measures: As reported by Acharya in *the Business Standards*, "In the national capital's three prison complexes–Tihar, Mandoli and Rohini–175 of 240 confirmed COVID19 cases (72.9%) by August 30 were among jail staff and the rest (65 or 27.1%) were among inmates. Cases among inmates increased by 22.6% while those among staff increased by 108.3% in 58 days to August 30," said DG Prisons, Delhi, Mr. S. Goel (Acharya 2020). As per *the Wire*, over 6700 prisoners were released on **interim bail** or **parole**. Prisoners who surrendered and tested negative for coronavirus were quarantined for 15 days, and those who tested positive were admitted to a hospital or a COVID19 care centre (Pillay 2020). The prison population was around **16,000** in October, 2020, the jail authorities said. *The Hindustan Times* reported that after months the Central allowed "**virtual interview time**" for prisoners to meet their family and friends on the prison premises. This was carried out respecting COVID19 guidelines (Lama 2020).

6.6 According to *the News18 India*, **West Bengal** Government has released as many **as 3000 inmates** on bail or parole in order to decongest correctional homes since the outbreak of COVID19. It is pertinent to note that the total number of inmates registered is 20, 802 including 1637 females (Press Trust of India 2020d).

6.7 In the case of **Gujarat** as reported by *The Business Standards*, as many as **2500** prisoners have been released from 28 jails across the state so far since the coronavirus outbreak. There were **14,000** prisoners confined in various prisoners across the state (Press Trust of India 2020c). To mention a few instances of positive cases information retrieved from *The Deccan Herald and The Print*: 23 prisoners in Rajkot Central jail (Press Trust of India 2020b, Aug 16) and 64 in Vadodara jails (Gerewal and Jain 2020) had tested positive.

6.8 In **Assam**, as stated by *Mint*, 576 prisoners were tested positive, state government decided to release as many as 300 prisoners in order to decongest jails. Later 111 prisoners were released from Guwahati jail. A 200-bedded COVID19 care facility had been set up in Guwahati Jail (Anonymous 2020).

7 Suggestions and Concluding Remarks

The following table is an attempt to relate the rights of prisoners with the sustainable developmental goals, and how these rights were being implemented prior to and post the pandemic. It also includes what strategies were undertaken to overcome the impediments.

Table 2 shows that, on perusing news articles, the state government through prison administration has attempted to implement the rights of prisoners in tune with sustainable development goals. During pandemic, certain SDGs were at risk. The prison administration has distributed masks, implemented special screening and quarantining new entrants: prisoners, conducted periodical check-ups of inmates and staff, maintained social distancing. There were petitions made by inmates to provide them with immunity boosting vitamins, and temporary quarantine centres and COVID19 health centres were set up. The judiciary in India has been instrumental in decongesting prisons by releasing the prisoners on parole, interim bail or such period have been extended or remission of sentence and lately encouraged house arrest. The crucial aspect of rights of the prisoners is to meet their family members is of mental health issue of the prisoners. The idea of total segregation could lead to anxiety, depression, and frustration finally paving way to prison violence. So such impediments were overcome by introducing video calling or *e-mulakaat* concepts, if not by all the prisons in India but by m ost. Physical meeting resumed after almost ten months in a few containment zones.

When the entire nation was marching towards fulfilling the SDGs. This pandemic became a speed breaker. The prison administration in India has considered rights of prisoners important. Genuine attempts have been made to attune these rights with a holistic development, i.e. setting global goals to establish fair, sustainable and holistic wellbeing of all, but this pandemic escalated anxiety, depression and stress in the prisoners.

One never knows if we are hit by another pandemic. One must always make tactical plans to avoid impediments faced this time. The government must increase infrastructure and also make vaccines available for staff and prisoners. The prison authorities must include special classes on "Yoga and meditation for Prisoners". The judiciary must opt extra mural sentencing. Sustainable development for prisoners means providing a peaceful, safe, and hygienic environment in prisons.

Table 2 Rights of prisoners and sustainable development goals

Sl.	Right of prisoners	Goal of SDG	Status: prior pandemic	Status: during pandemic	Strategy to bridge the gap:
1	Right to free legal aid	Goal 16	Yes	Yes	–
2	Right to speedy and fair trial	Goal 16	Yes	No	Introducing e-hearing at courts
3	Right to be treated humanely: no cruelty, no violence, no deaths in lock ups and prisons	Goal 3 & Goal 16	Yes	Yes	–
4	Right to interview: meet friends, relatives and lawyers	Goal 16	Yes	No	Introducing e-mulakaat/ e-prisons concept
5	Right to know the grounds of arrest	Goal 16	Yes	Yes	–
6	Right to bail in bailable offences	Goal 16	Yes	Yes	–
7	Right to examination of arrested person by medical officer	Goal 16	Yes	Yes-additionally COVID19 test	–
8	Right to be brought before Court without delay after arrest	Goal 16	Yes	Yes	–
9	Right to reasonable care of the health and safety	Goal 3	Yes	Yes	–
10	Right to proper accommodation	Goal 3	Yes	No	Overcrowding reduced by releasing prisoners on parole, remission, etc.
11	Shelter and safety	Goal 3 and Goal 6	Yes	Yes	Distribution of masks,COVID19 testing, quarantining

Source Prepared by researcher

References

Acharya, Preety. 2020. A 75% spike: How Covid spread faster among Delhi prison staff than inmates. *The Business Standards*, October 1, 2020, www.business-standard.com/article/current-affairs/a-75-spike-how-covid-spread-faster-among-delhi-prison-staff-than-inmates-120100100362_1.html.

Anonymous. 2020. COVID-19: Assam to release 376 prisoners to decongest jails. *Mint*, July 23, 2020, www.livemint.com/news/india/covid-19-assam-to-release-376-prisoners-to-decongest-jails-11595512662306.html.

Asian News International. 2020. Kerala jails to set up isolation cells for suspected coronavirus-infected inmates. *The Hindustan Times*, March 11, 2020, www.hindustantimes.com/india-news/kerala-jails-to-set-up-isolation-cells-for-suspected-coronavirus-infected-inmates/story-eEq7jSYZBBzzVokEpfma0K.html.

George, Sarath Babu. 2020. Kerala prisoner succumbs to COVID-19. *The Hindu*, August 16, 2020, www.thehindu.com/news/national/kerala/kerala-prisoner-succumbs-to-covid-19/article32366558.ece.

Gerewal, Kairvy and Jain, Praveen. 2020. 64 Covid-positive Vadodara jail inmates moved to guest house, many fear there could be more. *The Print*, August 3, 2020, www.theprint.in/india/64-covid-positive-vadodara-jail-inmates-moved-to-guest-house-many-fear-there-could-be-more/473129/.

Halle, Mark et al. 2016. Sustainable development goals IISD perspectives on the 2030 agenda for sustainable development. *The International Institute for Sustainable Development*.

Jones, Peter, Martin George Wynn, David Hillier, and Daphne Comfort. 2017. The sustainable development goals and information and communication technologies. *Indonesian Journal of Sustainability Accounting and Management* 1 (1): 1–15.

Kroll, Christian, Warchold, Anne., and Pradhan, Prajal. 2019. Sustainable development goals (SDGs): are we successful in turning trade-offs into synergies? *Palgrave Communications*. https://doi.org/10.1057/s41599-019-0335-5.

Kurian, Anju Lis. 2012. Sustainable development in the energy sector. *The Indian Journal of Political Science* 73(4). JSTOR. www.jstor.org/stable/41858875.

Lama, Prawesh. 2020. In the time of Covid-19, Tihar allows virtual meetings between prisoners, families. *The Hindustan Times*, August 22, 2020, www.hindustantimes.com/india-news/in-the-time-of-covid-19-tihar-allows-virtual-meetings-between-prisoners-families/story-IRlB7nQzJQcJII0GI4vJnN.html.

Malik, Krishna Pal. 2011. *Penology, Victimology & Correctional Administration in India*. Allahabad Law Agency.

Pillay, Anjali. 2020. Over 6,700 Prisoners released on bail amid covid-19 to surrender in a phased manner. *The Wire*, October 29, 2020. www.thewire.in/law/prisoners-released-on-bail-covid-surrender.

Press Trust of India. 2020d. Covid-19: 3,000 inmates released from West Bengal Jails. *The News18 India*, May 17, 2020, www.news18.com/news/india/covid-19-3000-inmates-released-from-west-bengal-jails-2624127.html.

Press Trust of India. 2020a. 1,112 prisoners released on bail, parole from Karnataka prisons due to COVID-19. *The Indian Express*, April 16, 2020, www.newindianexpress.com/states/karnataka/2020/apr/16/1112-prisoners-released-on-bail-parole-from-karnataka-prisons-due-to-covid-19-2130985.html.

Press Trust of India. 2020b. 23 prisoners of Rajkot Central jail test positive for Covid-19. *The Deccan Herald*, August 16, 2020, www.deccanherald.com/national/west/23-prisoners-of-rajkot-central-jail-test-positive-for-covid-19-873948.html.

Press Trust of India. 2020c. COVID-19 outbreak: 2,500 prisoners released from Gujarat jails. *The Business Standards*, May 17, 2020, www.businessinsider.in/india/news/covid-19-outbreak-2500-prisoners-released-from-gujarat-jails/articleshow/75787060.cms.

Press Trust of India. 2020e. Kerala govt extends parole of aged prisoners in the wake of COVID-19 spike. *Yahoo News*, Nov 2, 2020, https://in.news.yahoo.com/kerala-govt-extends-parole-aged-124609149.html.

Singh, Zile. 2016. Sustainable development goals: Challenges and opportunities. *Indian Journal of Public Health* 60: 247–248.

Special Correspondent. 2020. How many prison inmates have tested positive for COVID-19, asks Karnataka HC. *The Hindu,* September 3, 2020, www.thehindu.com/news/national/karnataka/how-many-prison-inmates-have-tested-positive-for-covid-19-asks-karnataka-hc/article32518069.ece.

United Nations General Assembly Report of the Secretary General 26th July, 2013. www.un.org/en/ga/search/view_doc.asp?symbol=S/2013/444. Also Singh Z. 2016. Sustainable development goals: Challenges and opportunities. *Indian Journal of Public Health* 60.

Victor, David G. 2006. Recovering sustainable development. *Foreign Affairs* **85**(1). 91–103. www.jstor.org/stable/20031845.

Yadav, Vijay Kumar. 2020. How Maharashtra's jails stayed free of Covid-19. *The Hindustan Times*, November 2020, www.hindustantimes.com/mumbai-news/how-maharashtra-s-jails-stayed-free-of-covid-19/story-bFqlWFA3OhX5RjgU31jZIN.html.

Impact of COVID-19 on Ecotourism in India and Egypt: A Comparative Analysis

Deepanjali Mishra, Hassan Refaet, and Rabi Narayan Subudhi

1 Introduction

Taylor defines culture by talking about its complexity and further arguing that they are more concerned with knowledge, beliefs, rituals, etc. which is received by any individual from his/her parents and ancestors. In the same way, it is defined as 'culture is the deeper level of basic assumptions and beliefs that are shared by members of an organization that operate unconsciously and define in a basic 'taken for granted' fashion an organization's view of its self and its environment' by Edgar Schein. It is considered to be one of the most important, sensitive aspects of a human being for it is the beliefs or the mind-set that exists in a person's heart. As per one's beliefs, he or she follows the rituals or customs. Culture can be either high conditioned, moderately conditioned or low conditioned. People across the globe loved to visit other places either in their country or in another for pleasure, visiting holy shrines or to sea beaches. This leads to the development of tourism, but gradually, it became an industry with a varied range of activities getting involved in it.

Tourism is basically the temporary movement made by the people from their home to another location whether it is a place in their state or country or beyond for a short period of time with an objective of pleasure or visit to any religious place or a hill station or even a market. Tourism has emerged as one of the fastest growing industries in the world contributing major source of income generation for a country. This is one of the reasons why countries spend huge revenue in this industry. However, it is not every time that tourism has proved to be money spinner for a nation. There have

D. Mishra (✉)
School of Humanities, KIIT University Bhubaneswar, Bhubaneswar, India

H. Refaet
Luxor University, Luxor, Egypt

R. N. Subudhi
School of Management, KIIT Bhubaneswar, Bhubaneswar, India

R. N. Subudhi et al. (eds.), *Future of Work and Business in Covid-19 Era*,
Springer Proceedings in Business and Economics,
https://doi.org/10.1007/978-981-19-0357-1_17

been so many events in the past like pandemics, epidemics, terrorist attacks which have proved to be decisive, for example, 9/11 terrorist attack, swine flu, Ebola virus. COVID-19 is the most recent pandemic which has made a huge impact on the world. It was originated in a laboratory in Wuhan Province of China. When the first case was reported in China, it did not have any clue about the hazardous effect it was going to have in the entire world. Apart from tourism industry, it was almost all the major sectors that were effected due to COVID-19. It was through railway stations, airports the virus got spread as it was too early to detect or even understand anything about the virus. However after getting to understand about it, many countries like India, USA, European countries cancelled all flights that were traveling to and from the country, and tourists were not allowed to go to their home country. Educational institutions and the government had to cancel all the conferences, seminars till an indefinite period due to which there would be a decline in the number of tourists both nationwide and internationally 1–3% compared to 3 to 4% growth in the year 2019.

2 Impact of Covid-19 on Tourism

COVID-19 has caused huge impact across the world. It would not be wrong to say that economy was worst affected due to this pandemic. Looking into the safety of the people, nationwide lockdown was imposed. People were not allowed to travel outside their homes except for few hours in the morning just to purchase daily needs. All the shopping malls, general stores and commercial organizations except banks stopped functioning. This led to huge loss to the economy. It is really very unfortunate that there would be a huge loss on Indian economy by approximately 32,000 crore on a daily basis. This is expected to continue during the first twenty-one days from the day lockdown was declared due to which not even 2.8 trillion amount of money movement was functional. Out of all the sectors, tourism was the most affected sector that made major impact of the economy. Tourism industry cannot be easily defined because it does not give clear figures that it contributes to the world economy. There are so many factors that are responsible for tourism sector like hotels, means of transportation, spots related to attractions, travel agencies. As per the definition in a wider sense, tourism means when people of one place visit another nationally or internationally for less than a year with an objective of staying for business or pleasure like sight-seeing or for health. This would make them feel the change in environment as they would be away from home. In 2019, just before the COVID-19 effect, globally, the contribution to GDP through tourism sector was approximately 2.9 trillion USD. The countries which earned maximum revenue from travel and tourism were the USA which amounted to a huge 580.7 billion US dollars. At the same time, the city which contributed maximum GDP to the world economy from travel and tourism was Macao. However, with the advent of COVID-19, it not only effected the tourism and travel, but the people were afraid to come out of their houses because of the fear that it would infect them.

3 Status of Tourism During (Peak 4, 5 months) of COVID-19 Pandemic in India

As per the latest 2020 reports that were published by FICCI, there are a total number of 3961 heritage sites that are protected by the central government centrally protected sites which directly come under UNESCO or the Archeological Survey of India abbreviated as (ASI). As per the reports, historical monuments, like the Taj Mahal of Agra that is situated in Uttar Pradesh, are considered to be the highest revenue generators for India which is as high as INR 77 crore, on an annual basis. After this comes the Agra Fort and Qutub Minar which generate 34 crore and 26 crore on annual basis. Tourism does not only generate revenues for the national and state government but also for so many people who are entirely dependent on them. For example, nearly 1.75 lakh daily earners, tourist guides, taxi drivers, auto and rickshaw drivers, site camera people, etc. who now do not have any source of income left. It is even more unfortunate that those tourist guides who have their license are not permitted to look out for alternate arrangement to earn money even during this pandemic.

Stringent travel restrictions were imposed by not only the Indian government, but also all the governments across the world were forced to do so. Many academicians, researchers had booked their tickets for visiting various places in the home country as well as in other countries too as a part of their academic or business or leisure trips. In India, summer season is mostly preferred for leisure trips because of the holidays and people prefer to go to various beaches or hill station. Therefore, as per the data, approximately 40–50% of tickets that were booked for Kerala, Goa, etc. has been canceled resulting in a huge impact on India tourism. As a precautionary measure, the Government of India did not want to take any risk or make any careless move. Therefore, it imposed a four-phase lockdown which started from March 17, 2019. It was probably because it wanted to ensure the safety of the Indians. It was among the first countries to impose the lockdown. The people were not allowed go out of their homes or let anyone to visit their homes. It was a very dreadful atmosphere. In this case, therefore, tourism was one of the worst hit industries among all others. India too had to face this critical situation of the tourism decline and faced a considerable decline in the number of tourists visiting India in 2020. India is also among those countries of the world who depend on tourism to earn foreign exchange.

Similarly, there were many other countries around the world who earned major source of revenue through tourism is Egypt. It is famous for its Spinx and other tourist sites.

4 Current Scenario of Tourism in Egypt

Egypt is considered one of the richest destinations in terms of cultural heritage from prehistoric to modern times. So, when it comes to tourism, the mental image that has been taken about Egypt is that it is a country for heritage tourism (Ragab et al.

2019). Despite this fact, Egypt also has very unique pristine environmental resources as it has very unique and diversified ecosystem zones including desert, coastal, riverbanks and wetland. Comprising the Red Sea, River Nile and vast eastern and western deserts with its unique oasis, marvelous mountains and valleys (Egyptian Ministry of Environment 2016). Also, it has to be mentioned that Egypt has 30 protected areas covering 15% of the terrestrial area, while over 9% of the coastal and near shore environment is protected (Allam 2012). These protected areas include a representative range of habitats and physiographic regions, along with other sites of importance such as biodiversity hotspots, cultural heritage sites, geological formations and landscapes of outstanding natural beauty. The protected areas are of varying size, from the largest, Elba, at about 35,000 km to Saluga and Ghazal Islands, at 0.5 km (Egyptian Ministry of state for Environmental affairs 2006). These protected areas have been established to conserve representative examples of the nation's natural habitats and physiographic regions, as well as to help maintain the nation's biological diversity and also to help maintain the nation's ecological viability (Egyptian Ministry of state for Environmental affairs 2006).

These natural resources have endowed Egypt with a great competitive advantage to be a well-known nature-based tourism destination the matter which will help in the optimization of economic and social return from the nation's natural systems in a manner that insures the long-term sustainable development in terms of generating foreign currency and new job opportunities raising the sense of pride and identity of the local communities which will lead to the preservation of these natural resources. Despite all what I have mentioned above, according to the statistics of the Egyptian Ministry of Tourism, approximately 94% out of the inbound tourism to Egypt is for leisure tourism, and the remaining 6% is divided among other types of tourism including sports tourism, golf tourism, safari tourism, ecotourism, festivals tourism and heritage tourism which account for less than 2% of the total inbound tourism to Egypt (Egyptian Ministry of Tourism 2018).

These figures show that Egypt did not manage to make full use of its environmental resources in promoting ecotourism, and this is because mass tourism has become the main target as the government seeks a higher share of the world tourism market. With coronavirus pandemic, this business model has to be changed, as this alarming situation has grabbed the attention of the National Tourism Organization, investors, employees and other stakeholders that this tourism model will never workout during and post –COVID-19 revival phase, as the present social distance measures and travel restrictions have driven mass tourism that has forced all the destinations to substitute this tourism style with what so called alternative tourism (Samarathunga 2021) which can play a pivotal role to utilize our tourism resources and to protect the tourism stakeholders in the short run. Or, in another meaning, this situation has urged the tourism destinations all over the world to search for higher-quality tourists, who have the economic capacity to spend more and stay longer at the tourism destination rather than targeting big numbers of price sensitive tourists (The tourism industry in the face of COVID-19: an unprecedented impact 2020). The alternative tourism takes the tourists away from their comfort zones and gives them an exotic experience which is close to the nature, culture, history or even the religion of the country that they visited.

The forms of alternative tourism are: 'health and wellness tourism,' 'rural tourism,' 'agro-tourism,' 'ecotourism,' 'back-packing tourism,' 'community-based tourism,' 'pro-poor tourism,' 'volunteer tourism,' 'spiritual tourism,' etc. (Samarathunga and Gamage 2020, p. 3).

In addition to what is mentioned, the Egyptian Ministry of Tourism in (2019) has adopted what so called tourism reform program which outlined a new tourism strategy which covers a number of objectives including diversification of the tourism products, diversification of revenue streams and increases the sector's resilience by tapping new international source markets (Ministry of Tourism 2018). According to what is mentioned above, it shows that Egypt has a great opportunity to make full use of the current situation by rising up ecotourism as a sustainable tourism form rather than promoting unsustainable forms of tourism.

5 Impact of Ecotourism as a Strategy to Boost Tourism During the Ongoing Pandemic

Therefore, to overcome this huge loss, people began to think of alternatives to overcome the boredom, dullness and depression they had received due to the lockdown. Even the government started to explore opportunities to earn revenue. It was then they wanted to explore ecotourism and the impact it may cause on the tourists. Ecotourism could mean 'a responsible travel to natural areas that conserves the environment, sustains the well-being of the local people and involves interpretation and education.' Education is one of the options by which people could understand the importance of ecotourism. Ecotourism is a means of sustainable tourism which emphasizes on conservation and sustainable travel. It is a means to implement the policies of ecotourism and participate in all the activities that lead to sustainable tourism. Some of the policies could be implemented to propagate ecotourism in a state or any country which are as follows:

Social, mental and physical impacts due to lockdown should be avoided during lockdown.

Awareness of cultural and environmental aspects should be developed.

It should be capable to provide a positive ambience to the tourists.

Direct financial benefits should be given for the conservation of wildlife and forests.

It should be capable of generating employment and other benefits to the local people.

The tourists should carry memorable experiences from these visits so that when they return, they could help their country to teach conservation and create awareness about the climate changes. The spiritual beliefs and the religious practices of the local tribal inhabitants should be understood and empathized and should be collaborated in order to be empowered.

The basic concepts on which ecotourism works on are environment-friendly, educational, and economic and social sustainability. Within these components, both benefits and costs exist, and in some circumstances, there is disequilibrium toward greater costs. Fundamentally, ecotourism could merit wider credibility, but only when the different actors involved avoid over marketing and control the overuse of its products by consumers. In the light of these pitfalls, this paper focuses on the three components of ecotourism and includes a review of ecotourism's definitions followed by an examination of its natural-based, sustainability and educational components. It concludes with the future state of ecotourism research in the light of the changes in trends in the tourism industry.

6 Survey of the Tourists of India and Egypt

A survey was conducted keeping in mind various attributes related to the profession, social status and age group. This section discusses the results of investigating to which extent can ecotourism be the best approach for the Egyptian tourism industry to overcome the current COVID-19 crisis?

In order to answer this question, five semi-structured interviews were conducted, with five persons, including three Egyptian tour operators, one official from the Egyptian tourism board and a professor at faculty of tourism and hotels specialized in tourism marketing.

The discussion with the interviewees has shown that ecotourism is an effective solution for the Egyptian tourism industry to overcome this crisis for many reasons:

(i) **The limited number of Egyptian tourism attractions and products**: Despite the fact that Egypt has very unique and diversified cultural and natural resources that cover approximately the whole country and represent unique selling points for the tourism industry, the actual tourism destinations which are being offered to the customers are limited in number including Hurgada, Sharm Al Shiekh, Cairo, Luxor and Aswan. As the government has given these destinations, the ultimate priority when it comes to tourism development, so the tourism development projects has been concentrated on these destinations including infrastructure projects and other facilities development projects that have been carried out in cooperation with public and private entities.

A Participant 1 added 'this limited number of tourism destinations has created a negative impact on both cultural and natural resources at these destinations, as well as the economic benefits of tourism sector in Egypt have become available only for limited numbers of local communities.' Promoting ecotourism will enable the Egyptian tourism sector to expand its geographical scope and increase the numbers of the local communities who can benefit from the tourism sector. Participant 2 added, 'the Egyptian protected areas which are considered the key areas for promoting ecotourism are scattered all over the country the matter which will help in expanding the geographical area of Egyptian tourism,' in addition most of these protected areas are located in the Eastern and Western Egyptian deserts which means that ecotourism will be a very effective tool to promote the less-known destinations in Egypt and benefit greater numbers of local communities.

(ii) **Diversifying Visitors profile**:
The business model of Egyptian tourism has given too much attention to leisure tourism the matter that has resulted in 94% out of the inbound tourism to Egypt is leisure tourism (beach tourism) which means that leisure tourism is dominating the scene. Respondent 3 added 'leisure tourists are generally the most price-sensitive and budget-constrained and therefore consume the least amount of domestic services; their large volume has a negative impact on the natural and cultural resources of the country, and consequently, it has a negative impact on sustainable tourism development.' The Ministry of Tourism is working to further improve the profile of targeted customers by attracting higher-quality customers who can benefit the economy and at the same time keep and maintain the cultural and natural resources of the local communities. Respondent 4 added 'ecotourism tourists tend to be higher income and consume more domestic services as they must often use multiple hotels, tour guides, more domestic transport, etc., they also appreciate and respect the natural resources and cultural diversity of local communities.'

(iii) **Meeting the tourists behavioral changes**:
The behavior of tourists is the most important indicator which can be used as a predictor of the future of tourism industry. The manifestations of tourist behavior are diverse and, in principle, take place in several phases including pre-, during and post-holiday phases; each phase contains the processes of planning, decision-making and purchase (Juvan 2018). Respondent 5 added 'the COVID-19 pandemic is expected to cause major changes in the way the customers behave, as the customer will search for more sustainable forms of tourism like ecotourism rather than mass tourism forms, there is a growing demand to save and protect the environment and limit the damage caused by mass tourism.' It is very essential for the tourism operators to offer the customers the tourism products that make them feel the safety and security.

Respondent no. (1) mentioned that 'the key words now and in the post-coronavirus phase are safety and security, as the customer will never compromise his/her safety and security by being part of one of mass tourism forms; ecotourism forms offering itineraries in safer, low-risk environments with smaller groups the matter which will make the customers able to keep social distancing.' Respondent no. (2) added 'being lockdown in homes for a long period of time, this created a great desire from the customers side to tour and experience the environment and practice ecotourism activities like walking, hiking, bird watching, ..., especially that these activities are much safer where the risk (the virus infection in the case of COVID-19) is very minimal.'

(iv) **Sustainable form of tourism**:
Ecotourism is one of the tourism forms that define sustainability as a priority, as it takes into consideration to improve the management of limited natural resources such as water, coral reefs, forests, mangroves, coastlines and encourage the resilience of hazards both in urban and natural habitats by

minimizing the environmental effects of tourism activities (How tourism can recover responsibly from COVID-19 2020). This beside that it also tries to addressing the needs of visitors, the industry and host communities, the matter which makes it a very effective tourism form for achieving sustainable development of tourism destinations (Zacarias and Loyola 2017, p. 142). Respondent no. (3) mentioned that 'the Egyptian 2030 Vision focuses on activating the principals of sustainability in all the economic sectors including tourism to benefit the local communities through providing them with job opportunities and sustainable sources of livelihood, and at the same time, the Egyptian government tries to keep and protect the cultural and natural resources to gain visitor appreciation and satisfaction, and ecotourism has been proven to be a very effective tool for all the objectives.' Respondent no. (4) said that 'sustainable tourism is they key model to reassure the customers and enhance their desire to choose a certain destination to visit'; when the customer knows that a certain destination applies the principals of sustainability, this will make the customer feel the credibility of the destination and increases its competitiveness especially at post-coronavirus phase.

(v) **Different activities diversified experiences**:
It is expected that there will be a fierce competition between all the tourism destinations all over the world during the recovery phase of the coronavirus, and one of the tools that could increase the competitiveness of the destination is the diversified experiences being offered. Respondent no. (5) said that 'The post-Covid tourist will search for safety and the destination that can offer him different experience as well,' while Respondent no. (1) adds 'ecotourism offers a wide range of activities that can provide the customers with different experiences including; diving, snorkeling, bird watching, hiking, Mountains climbing, swimming, trekking, camping and walking,' while Respondent no. (2) said 'the activities of ecotourism are mainly carried out in open spaces where the customers can enjoy the healthy open air atmosphere and at the same time they can keep social distancing.'

7 Case Study of India

Similarly in case of India, same questionnaire was prepared, and responses were collected from the same number of people. Five semi-structured interviews were conducted with five persons including three Indian tour operators, one official from the Odisha tourism board and one professor at faculty of tourism and hotels specialized in tourism marketing.

First participant who was a regular tourist opined that he has not been able to move out because of lockdown but would certainly prefer to visit the eco-retreat spots in the future for safety reasons. Second respondent was enthusiastic about the ecotourism spots but was not able to identify all the spots. She too answered that ecotourism could bring in more tourist if they are publicized by the state government.

(i) **Behavioral Changes of a tourist due to the Pandemic**
When contacted the people who were frequently traveling either in India or abroad, they opined that lockdown has caused serious change in their behavior. Earlier when used to travel, they felt more refreshed and energized, but now, they were confined to their office or homes. This led to an aggressive behavior which could not be avoided.

(ii) **Different activities diversified experiences**
When contacted the tourists what were the activities they were involved in during the pandemic, there were varied responses. Some of them said that they spent time with their family at home, and some said they visited their friends and relatives whose visit was due. Some academicians said they went to the field to pursue their research. Some visited the botanical and zoological parks.

(iii) **Sustainable form of tourism**
When the respondents were contacted to know if they were aware about the concept of ecotourism, they agreed and said that ecotourism could emerge as a source of sustainable tourism. They also opined that due to restrictions on beaches, temples, etc., ecotourism can be used for entertainment or pass time. Apart from that, it uses the flora and fauna which is indeed safe for the tourists during this pandemic.

(iv) **Diverse Profile of the tourists**
The tourists had varied profiles which were completely different than the other. In fact, they were poles apart. Some traveled as a part of their business and corporate trips, while some were academicians who visited places to participate in conference and seminars. Apart from that, there were also some visitors who went abroad as a part of pleasure trips or on pilgrimage. So, they did not have much ideas about the concept of ecotourism.

8 Conclusion

Therefore, it could be concluded that ecotourism is considered effective solution for both the Indian and Egyptian tourism industries in order to overcome this COVID-19 crisis as it will help in widening the geographical scope of the Egyptian tourism by adding many less known destination to Egyptian tourism map which will help in reducing the pressure on traditional tourist destinations as well as benefiting more local communities. Ecotourism will also play a major role in diversifying the tourism products which are being offered to the customers with variety of activities walking, hiking, bird watching, diving and snorkeling, these multiple activities that can provide the customers with different experiences which constitute a competitive advantage for a tourist destination. Ecotourism can meet the behavioral change of the customer caused by COVID-19 as the activities of ecotourism are mainly carried out in open spaces which means that the customers can enjoy the healthy open air atmosphere, and at the same time, they can keep social distancing especially that the customer will search for less crowded destinations and activities.

9 Suggestions, recommendations

The scope of ecotourism could be explored at a larger scale to bring about a change in the conventional mode of tourism. For example, Odisha has started at least six major ecotourist spots that would provide scope to the tourists to visit them and get maximum benefit from these spots. Some of them are Similipal Tiger Reserve, Bhitarkanika National Park, Nandan Kanan, Satkosia Tiger Reserve, etc. Also, ecotourism will help in diversifying the profile of the traditional inbound tourists to the Egyptian destinations through attracting quality tourists who can benefit the economy and at the same time keep and maintain the cultural and natural resources of the local communities rather than attracting low-quality mass tourism. It can open various avenues of earning source for not only the government but also for the people who are dependent on tourism like the taxi drivers, tourist guides, the hotels and restaurants. Since tourism industry has been the worst sufferers due to COVID-19, and it is already a year that has passed, but travel restrictions are still on; therefore, the Government of India should take maximum measures to revive it.

References

Allam, K. 2012. *Action Plan for Implementing the Convention of Biological Diversity's Program of Work on Protected Areas*. Ministry of state for environmental Affairs. https://www.cbd.int/doc/world/eg/eg-nbsap-powpa-en.pdf.

Egyptian Ministry of Environment. 2016. *Egyptian Biodiversity Strategy and Action Plan (2015–2030)*. https://www.cbd.int/doc/world/eg/eg-nbsap-v2-en.pdf.

Egyptian Ministry of state for Environmental affairs. 2006. *Protected Areas of Egypt: Towards the Future*. https://www.cbd.int/doc/world/eg/eg-nr-ripa-en.pdf.

How tourism can recover responsibly from COVID-19. 2020. Retrieved from https://www.oneplanetnetwork.org/sustainable-tourism/covid-19-how-tourism-can-recover-responsibly#_ftn6.

Juvan, E. 2018. *Tourist Behaviour: An Overview of Models to Date*.

Ministry of Tourism. 2018. *Egypt—Tourism Reform Program*. Available from: http://egypt.travel/media/2338/egypt-tourism-reform-program.pdf.

Ragab, H., A.A. Mahrous, and A. Ghoneim. 2019. Egypt's perceived destination image and its impact on tourist's future behavioural intentions. *International Journal of Tourism Cities* 6 (2): 449–466. https://doi.org/10.1108/ijtc-12-2018-0105.

Samarathunga, W.H.M.S, and D. Gamage. 2020. *Alternative Tourism as an Alternate to Mass Tourism during the Post-COVID-19 Recovery Phase: the Case of Sri Lanka*. SageSubmissions. Preprint. https://doi.org/10.31124/advance.12361301.v1. https://www.researchgate.net/publication/341811933_Alternative_Tourism_as_an_Alternate_to_Mass_Tourism_during_the_Post-COVID-19_Recovery_Phase_the_Case_of_Sri_Lanka. Accessed February 9, 2021.

Samarathunga, W. 2021. *Restructuring Tourism Economies to face the 'New Normal': COVID-19 and Alternative Tourism.* SSRN. Retrieved from https://papers.ssrn.com/sol3/papers.cfm?abstract_id=3771760.

The tourism industry in the face of COVID-19: an unprecedented impact. 2020. Retrieved from https://www.caixabankresearch.com/en/sector-analysis/tourism/tourism-industry-face-covid-19-unprecedented-impact.

Zacarias, D., and R. Loyola. (2017). How ecotourism affects human communities. In *Ecotourism's Promise and Peril*, 133–151. https://doi.org/10.1007/978-3-319-58331-0_9

Pedagogical Shift in Education Sector: A Necessity in Light of COVID-19 Pandemic

Nafis Mahmud Khan and Khushboo Kuddus

1 Introduction

COVID-19, a highly infectious disease caused by severe acute respiratory syndrome coronavirus 2 (SARS-Cov-2), originated in Wuhan city, China (Remuzzi and Remuzzi 2020), has carried out significant changes along with benefits and challenges in the whole education system throughout the world. Besides, dolorous consequences in the world economy, the pandemic has caused great havoc to global education including schools, colleges, universities, and other academic institutions which has consequently led to a sudden shift from face-to-face education to online education.

There has been a paradigm shift in the teaching and learning pedagogy witnessing a lot of innovative experimentation of approaches and methodologies in education accompanied with challenges and opportunities. New pedagogical modifications have been embraced to keep teaching and learning ongoing in the education sector. Though COVID-19 comes with, particularly, addressing many challenges in the education sector, measures and steps to overcome the challenges are still under process.

The COVID-19 outbreak has made the situation of children and adolescents worst. UNESCO, 2020 reports that more than 1.5 billion learners of different ages around the world are affected due to school and university closures owing to the COVID-19 (Bozkurt and Sharma 2020).

In this circumstance, a ray of hope has emerged when online education has been introduced in schools, colleges, and higher education across the world. Although, e-learning has been considered as one of the popular forms of non-formal education,

N. M. Khan
Division of Research, Daffodil International University, Dhaka, Bangladesh

K. Kuddus (✉)
School of Humanities (English), KIIT Deemed to be University, Bhubaneswar, Odisha, India

R. N. Subudhi et al. (eds.), *Future of Work and Business in Covid-19 Era*,
Springer Proceedings in Business and Economics,
https://doi.org/10.1007/978-981-19-0357-1_18

in recent times, it becomes the formal and only option left to keep the education system going on during COVID-19 for continuing academic-related activities.

The impact of the remarkable advancement in information and communication technology (ICT) can be observed in almost all aspects of our lives. No one can refute the growth in its popularity and usage in the education sector in the form of educational technologies. Though, it was less utilized earlier, it has come to the rescue of all during this pandemic. Several studies have observed that easy access to online resources enhances the awareness of learners and provides exposure to authentic content. It makes the learning autonomous, flexible, active, and interesting and at the same time helps the learners to develop critical analysis and creativity skills (Kuddus and Khan 2020; Dash and Kuddus 2020).

Many popular online communication platforms like start.me, Neo, Classtime, Classwize, Ted-Ed, Coursera, we video, Google classroom, Bakpax, Pronto, Skillsshare, ClassDojo, Edmodo, Blackboard Learn, Parlay, Docebo, Feedback Fruits, Udemy, WizIQ, Flipgrid, Codeacademy, Gynzy, Adobe Captivate, Seesaw, Edx GoGuardian, Elucodat, Kami, Pluralsight, G Suit, Otus, Articulate 360, Floop, Future Learn, Hapara, Shift, Lectora Inspire, Kialo Edu, Buncee, LanSchool, and many others can be used properly in this COVID situation that could contribute to the change of the destination and direction of the total education system across the world after post-COVID circumstances (Mishra et al. 2020).

The present paper attempts to explore the challenges that academicians, students, and authorities are facing, suggestions to mitigate the pitfalls, and to assess the benefits of online learning during the COVID-19 pandemic. An in-depth review from reliable quality information sources has been done so far with careful consideration to make the research unique and appropriate to the argument.

2 Challenges of Online Education

Literature indicates that during COVID-19, teachers, students, and parents of school-level students have encountered numerous challenges. Atmojo and Nugroho (2020) conducted a study where 16 English as a Foreign Language (EFL) teachers participated on online EFL learning and delineated the challenges they have experienced. Researchers found a number of problems emerging from teachers, students, and parents' side. Students from Indonesia find it difficult to afford smartphones and face the challenges like unstable Internet connection, especially for the students from remote and rural areas and the inability to afford the data package of the Internet. The research also finds students with difficulties in using applications and platforms for online learning. Low response is another predominant challenge of online teaching and learning.

Teachers are experiencing problems in creating materials for online classes due to their lack of knowledge and experience and unavailability of high technology applications. Giving personal feedback and engaging students who are reluctant to online learning are major problems that the teachers face in online teaching and learning settings.

Apart from describing the difficulties faced by the students and teachers, the researchers also analyzed some other issues faced by the students' parents. It is expected that parents must monitor their children during online learning at home. But in most cases, the research found that the parents are carefree towards monitoring their children; instead, they remain engaged in their works and business (Atmojo and Nugroho 2020).

Asanov et al. (2020) conducted a study on time duration and the status of mental health of Ecuadorian high-school students during the COVID-19 quarantine and found that the only problem faced by the students is social isolation. The study reveals that the majority of the participants are mostly happy but 16% of students had mental health issues.

Abuhammad (2020) conducted a qualitative study in Jordan on parents' perceptions of the challenges their children are facing. Parents' perception shared on Facebook has been thematized into four threads as: (a) personal barriers, (b) technical barriers, (c) logistical barriers, and (d) financial barriers. The personal barriers include lack of training and support, lack of technical expertise, inadequate communications with professionals, and lack of qualification to handle the technology properly; thus, they are not able to assist their children in their studies. Some technical challenges such as lack of time management, insufficient investment, and poor Internet connection lead the parents to show a negative attitude towards online teaching and learning setting. Apart from these, some logistical barrier issues include difficulties in distance learning and lack of student preparation due to the unavailability of logistical support, dissatisfaction in distance learning as it has started suddenly with short notice and the unpreparedness of the children in using distance learning as the medium of instruction. Some parents raised the issue of financial barriers with the inability to buy technical aids and pay for Internet service.

A study conducted on medical students during the COVID-19 pandemic at the college of medicine of Alfaisal University in Riyadh, Saudi Arabia, reveals the challenges that students are experiencing, such as online assessment, rare access to computer hardware and software, lack of experience in using online education tools, pandemic-related anxiety, and the fear of using a computer. Despite being exposed to many challenges, the majority of the respondents confessed the enhancement of confidence in the effectiveness of online teaching and learning (Rajab et al. 2020).

Another study done by Akhter (2020) in Saudi Arabia on the challenges faced by college students comes with the similar result including, limited experience in technology, poor past experience, de-motivation, personal poor cognition, insufficient support, and technical issues as they do not have strong Internet connection required for online learning.

Mondol and Mohiuddin (2020) conducted a study on the paradigm shift in teaching and learning during COVID-19. The study aimed to assess the attitude of both faculty and students about online education and the challenges they experienced in online teaching and learning during the pandemic. Some of the common issues highlighted are Internet connection disruption and interruption of electricity supply, lack of experience, and unpreparedness. To mitigate the challenges, faculty had expectations of training facilities on online teaching and learning, which would help them to handle the whole online class settings.

The shift to online classes not only brings challenges at the institutional level but also creates a digital division—a long existed socio-economic inequality and discrimination between the poor and the rich. As a consequence of it, students from poor socio-economic backgrounds started feeling vulnerable, which led them to depression.

Another study done by Cassum et al. (2020) in Aga Khan University, Karachi, Pakistan, on 'Challenges in Teaching Palliative Care Module Virtually during COVID-19 Era comes with the challenges faced by the participants and facilitator during online classes from home. It reveals that both the participants and facilitator, in online classes, suffer a lot due to the poor Internet connectivity, discontinuation of proper electricity flow in some parts of the city. The study also comes with the most crucial issue—unfair means adopted by the students, where maintaining quality assurance becomes the vital question.

3 Recommendations

Though the pandemic has caused great destruction to every sector, it also brought great opportunities and innovations for survival. It has provided opportunities to get expertise in using virtual classroom, having patience, empathy, care for students, proper handling of the available teaching–learning tools (Mishra et al. 2020).

According to Atmojo and Nugroho (2020), good planning and preparation before online class and more time investment for online learning than face-to-face learning should be ensured. Integration of technology in language teaching and learning should be incorporated in upcoming teachers training programs. Side by side, students should be made acquainted with online teaching–learning system and make their understanding clear about online learning. Parents also should monitor and ensure their children's participation in their online classes.

In dealing with the future challenges of COVID-19, especially in higher education in Philippines, Toquero (2020) offers several ways to mitigate the vulnerability caused due to the pandemic. As initiatives, the researchers encourage the authority to integrate environment and health courses in the curriculum, strengthening environmental policies and hygiene practice, emphasizing on online mental health and services, introducing training facilities on online education to a great extent, focusing on research work, data monitoring, proper documentation.

Bao (2020), in his research, introduces six instructional strategies to improve students' engagement in online teaching and learning platforms effectively in Peking University, China. Firstly, the researcher suggested to always keep alternatives to deal with unexpected situations, if necessary, to ensure students' total concentration in study. Secondly, the researcher advocates to break the topic into several subtopics.

Thirdly, it is more important to emphasize on voice rather than body language, and facial expressions of the faculty in online teaching, as the researcher recommends. The study also reveals the fact that most of the faculty are likely unskilled in technology. Fourthly, the researcher suggests the faculty to communicate with teaching assistants in order to get maximum online support from them. Simultaneously, strengthening and ensuring students' active participation in learning inside and outside the class and different methods should be adopted by the faculty members. Lastly, in order to make online learning effective, the researcher emphasizes on the combination of online learning and offline self-learning activities.

4 Conclusion

The unprecedented pandemic COVID-19 is a big challenge to the entire world including the education system. It led to a sudden shift in the education system from the traditional face-to-face teaching and learning to the virtual mode or online classes. It is not that the students, academicians, and institutions were unaware of the virtual mode of teaching and learning as it existed for the last many years before the pandemic. However, it had several challenges which inhibit its integration in the educational system in a full-fledged manner. As discussed in the study, there are several inhibiting factors like infrastructure, poor network connectivity, unequal socio-economic background, lack of training and experience, and several other challenges as highlighted in the study.

Moreover, in order to overcome the emerging challenges during online classes, several measures have also been suggested. The study reflects on the measures to mitigate the challenges faced by the teachers and students during the implementation of the newly developed pedagogy which mostly focuses on the active participation of learners by creating friendly environment, enhancing students' engagement in the online classes by creating interesting teaching learning materials and designing the lesson plans properly.

References

Abuhammad, Sawsan. 2020. Barriers to distance learning during the COVID-19 outbreak: A qualitative review from parents' perspective. *Heliyon* 6 (11): 1–5.

Akhter, Tawhida. 2020. Problems and challenges faced by EFL students of Saudi Arabia during COVID-19 pandemic. *Rupkatha Journal on Interdisciplinary Studies in Humanities* 12 (5): 1–7.

Asanov, Igor, et al. 2020. Remote-learning, time-use, and mental health of Ecuadorian high-school students during the COVID-19 quarantine. In *Policy Research Working Paper*, No 9252. https://openknowledge.worldbank.org/handle/10986/33799 License: CC BY 3.0 IGO.

Atmojo, Arief E.P. and Arif Nugroho. 2020. EFL classes must go online! Teaching activities and challenges during COVID-19 pandemic in Indonesia. *Register Journal* 13(1): 49–76.

Bao, Wei. 2020. COVID-19 and online teaching in higher education: A case study of Peking University. *Human Behavior and Emerging Technologies* 2 (2): 113–115.

Bozkurt, Aras, and Ramesh C. Sharma. 2020. Emergency remote teaching in a time of global crisis due to CoronaVirus pandemic. *Asian Journal of Distance Education* 15(1): i–vi.

Cassum, Shanaz et al. 2020. Challenges in teaching palliative care module virtually during COVID-19 Era. *Asia-Pacific Journal of Oncology Nursing* 7(4): 301–304.

Dash, Arun, and Khushboo Kuddus. 2020. Leveraging the benefits of ICT usage in teaching of english language and literature. In *Smart Intelligent Computing and Applications. Smart Innovation, Systems and Technologies*, ed. Satapathy S., V. Bhateja, J. Mohanty, and S. Udgata, vol 160, 225–232. Springer. https://doi.org/10.1007/978-981-32-9690-9_22.

Kuddus, Khushboo, and Nafis M. Khan. 2020. Attitude of the international students towards integrating ICT in foreign language learning: A case study. In *ICT Systems and Sustainability. Advances in Intelligent Systems and Computing*, ed. by Tuba M., S. Akashe, and A. Joshi, vol 1270, 685–695. Springer. https://doi.org/10.1007/978-981-15-8289-9_66.

Mishra, Loknath, Tushar Gupta, and Abha Shree. 2020. Online teaching-learning in higher education during lockdown period of COVID-19 pandemic. *International Journal of Educational Research Open*, 1: 100012.

Mondol, Md S., and Mohammad Golam Mohiuddin. 2020. Confronting Covid-19 with a paradigm shift in teaching and learning: A study on online classes. *International Journal of Social, Political and Economic Research,* 7(2): 231–247.

Rajab, Mohammad H., Abdalla M. Gazal., and Khaled, Alkattan. 2020. Challenges to online medical education during the COVID-19 pandemic. *Cureus* 12(7): 1–11. https://doi.org/10.7759/cureus.8966

Remuzzi, Andrea, and Giuseppe Remuzzi. 2020. COVID-19 and Italy: What next?. *The Lancet* 395(10231): 1225–1228.

Toquero, Cathy Mae. 2020. Challenges and opportunities for higher education amid the COVID-19 pandemic: The Philippine context. *Pedagogical Research* 5(4): 1–5, em0063. https://doi.org/10.29333/pr/7947.

Emerging Role of Social Enterprises During COVID-19 Pandemic

Nirmal Kumar Mandal and Rabi N. Subudhi

1 Introduction

After it was first reported in Wuhan, China in 2019, the Corona virus (COVID-19) has wreaked havoc on socioeconomic norms (Rowan and Laffey 2020). Many countries are witnessing second or subsequent waves of COVID-19 infection, rendering the pandemic difficult to foresee. COVID-19 will eventually have a negative effect on people and the economy; however, both will recover over time, and new opportunities will arise.

The COVID-19 pandemic has wreaked havoc on the social sector, exacerbating the very issues that social purpose organisations are attempting to fix. The primary distinction between social and commercial entrepreneurship is how social entrepreneurs seek to contribute to society by pooling social utility (Alvord et al., 2004). This means that rather than concentrating on stakeholder importance, the emphasis is on contribution to the community. The United Nations (UN) Sustainability Goals programme defines social enterprises as a fundamental tool for attaining sustainability (SDGs, United Nations, 2020). These enterprises are businesses that prioritise the creation of social benefit while adhering to business standards (Shaw and Carter 2007; Estrin et al. 2016).

Benefits or profits generated by Social enterprises are often centred on social enhancement or alleviation of a social problem, and are generally reinvested into the firm rather than dispersed as profits to stakeholder or shareholders, which distinguishes Social enterprises from other enterprises. Social enterprises are defined as organisations that use "entrepreneurial behaviour for social ends rather than economic aims, or conversely, earnings gained from market activity are utilised for the benefit of a certain disadvantaged group" (Holdsworth et al. 2020).

N. K. Mandal (✉) · R. N. Subudhi
KIIT Deemed to be University, Bhubaneswar, India
e-mail: nirmal@ksrm.ac.in

R. N. Subudhi et al. (eds.), *Future of Work and Business in Covid-19 Era*,
Springer Proceedings in Business and Economics,
https://doi.org/10.1007/978-981-19-0357-1_19

Although there are many types of social enterprises in operation, the two most popular are non-profit organisations and for-profit socially oriented enterprises. The COVID-19 pandemic has caused a worldwide humanitarian crisis, placing lives and livelihoods in jeopardy. In the early stages of the pandemic, social enterprises were particularly active and stepped up to provide relief, especially in situations where the state machinery was caught off guard or lacked capacity, or both. During the COVID-19 pandemic, the activity of social entrepreneurs is crucial because they reach individuals who the market and governments are unable to cater (World Economic Forum 2020). As the pandemic continues to spread, these social enterprises will become increasingly relevant, with recovery likely to be a lengthy process.

2 Research Objective

As the world grapples with a major social and economic crisis as a result of the COVID-19 pandemic, the aim of this research is to learn about the reactions and how social enterprises are serving as a support mechanism during the pandemic. This paper explores the emerging role of social enterprises during COVID-19 outbreaks.

3 Methodology

The study involved the review of existing literature on social enterprises during pandemic and analysis of secondary data of social enterprises in India collected from newspaper, online articles, other publications, and websites. It also involved the telephonic interview of key officials of few major social enterprises in India in order to understand their perspective.

4 Social Enterprises During Pandemic in India

Increasing numbers of social enterprises all over the world are using businesses to help tackle social problems. In a study, Ratten (2020a; b) suggests that in order to bring about sustainable change; social entrepreneurship can be used to mitigate the problems created by COVID-19.

According to research from the Thompson Reuters Foundation, India ranks as the 20th best country to be a social entrepreneur (Thompson Reuter Foundation poll 2019). Many social enterprises in India have jumped into action in response to the pandemic and have been actively involved in actively reacting to the pandemic. According to an online study conducted by the "Jasani Centre of Social Entrepreneurship & Sustainability Management, NMIMS" for 30 non-profit and for-profit social enterprises operating in Maharashtra, India, more than 90% of social enterprises have acted quickly to address new and diverse needs of local communities. Approximately 67 per cent of organisations were able to organise and mobilise resources in order to provide relief. Here are a few examples of social enterprises that are fighting to save lives in India during this crisis.

4.1 *Food Security*

Goonj, an Indian social enterprise has already worked with over 400 partner organisations to expand its reach in both rural and urban regions during the crisis. It has supplied over 8800 tonnes of food and other essentials, served over 362,000 meals, obtained 2,25,000 kg of vegetables from farmers, and reached out to over 380,000 families (about 1.5 million people). Similarly "Akshaya Patra Foundation" provided 70 million servings, with around half of those being dry rations and the rest being cooked meals.

4.2 *Health Care and Sanitation*

A number of Social enterprises were engaged in providing essential hygiene items such as soaps, masks, and sanitizer to the community. Glocal Healthcare, for example, has launched a free telemedicine consultation for COVID-19 testing for the people living in remote and under-served areas. The goal is to avoid panic, provide proper screening, triage, and treatment before conditions worsen, and keep the health system from failing.

4.3 *Online Training to Medical Staff to Manage COVID Cases*

"Tata Trusts" has partnered with two medical institutions to provide online training to help some of their healthcare professionals develop their critical care skills in COVID-19 management. For this project, this organisation has teamed up with Christian Medical College (CMC) in Vellore and Care Institute of Health Sciences (CIHS) in Hyderabad, as well as the Tata Group. A 22-h free online training programme for medical professionals on COVID-19 critical care has been curated as part of the programme, and it is intended for unique personnel selected by specified hospitals.

4.4 Online Education

"e-Vidyaloka", an Indian educational social enterprise, used technology to link enthusiastic individuals from all over the world as volunteer teachers with Government schools in remote and rural villages across India. It is built for children aged 10 to 14 (5th to 8th grade), and it offers live interactive classes in the local language.

4.5 Supply of Essential Commodities (Milk)

During pandemic, "Amul", a social enterprise with their pan India presence ensured steady supplies of milk to consumers at regular price. When the commercial dairy enterprises stooped procuring milk from farmers, it took extra initiatives to procure milk from the farmers, thereby preventing the loss of livelihood of farmers. It procured 15–17% more milk from dairy farmers during pandemic.

4.6 Moving Towards Circular Economy Through Recycling

"Cloth Box Foundation" donated clean clothes to those in need using social media in a transparent manner. They obtained discarded clothing from volunteers for those in need.

4.7 Developing Innovative Product and Process

Social entrepreneurs are getting creative to help communities hit hard by the pandemic. For instance, Maker's Asylum (a creative group space) created one million eco-friendly face shields for front-line workers using OHP sheets. It was a solution with collective effort of over 300 individuals/groups who had never met before but came together for a common cause. These low-cost face shields were mass-produced across the country quickly and were intended for front-line healthcare staff.

4.8 Impact Investing

One of WIPRO's social enterprises, the Azim Premji Foundation, has pledged Rs. 1,000 crore to all pandemic-affected communities. This fund was set up to assist with humanitarian relief and healthcare capacity building in the aftermath of the COVID-19 outbreak.

4.9 *Virtual Hackathons*

It encouraged people to embrace creativity, innovation, and collaboration in order to develop and implement solutions. Global Hack held a global hackathon of over 12,000 participants from over 100 countries. During COVID-19, they worked on 500 life-changing initiatives ranging from mental health to the climate to remote education solutions. Affordable Solar-powered hand disinfection solutions were one of the solutions.

4.10 *Awareness Though Behaviour Change Communication (BCC)*

A major in-school awareness campaign was organised by 17,000 ft Foundation, a social enterprise in India's mountainous region in Ladakh. They could reach out to every remote village to raise awareness about the COVID-19 epidemic among young students, provide advice about how to remain safe and healthy, and ensure that the villagers have all of the requisite health and hygiene supplies to fight the disease. They trained facilitators to perform health and hygiene workshops with students, teachers, and Village Education Committee representatives using audio-visuals, discussions, and plays to raise awareness about COVID-19, health, and hygiene practices.

4.11 *Raising Donations*

"Give India" via its online donation platform, aims to mobilise financial support to not-for-profit social enterprises across India. They are raising money to provide food packets to daily wage earners and hygiene kits to those who live in high-risk areas.

5 Cross Sector Collaboration

As used in this study, cross-sector partnerships refer to the official and informal contacts, networks, and alliances that social entrepreneurs develop with companies, government, and civil society organisations from multiple sectors of the economy (Koschmann et al. 2012).

Previous research shows social enterprises struggle with scaling up their organisations (Pinch and Sunley 2019). The need for institutional partnerships is one of the obstacles that social enterprises face. Collaborations and partnership with organisations have long been relevant for social entrepreneurs, and they may be even more so now (Weaver 2020). COVID-19 being a significant health crisis with consequences for significant social problems such as housing and hunger call for a re-evaluation of the function of social entrepreneurs and a shift in their position—from individual agents of change to community resource orchestrators (Bacq and Lumpkin 2020). Cross-sector collaboration among Social enterprises, government, and corporate is important during crisis such as COVID-19 pandemic. Despite the major challenges surrounding COVID-19, the crisis presents many opportunities for social entrepreneurs to mobilise multi-partner initiatives to create creative strategies that can be replicated and meet the challenge in the localised context (Lumpkin and Bacq 2019).

Tello-Rozas et al. (2015) proposed that large-scale socially motivated collaborations can both scale up social value creation and lead to more focused collective action. Collaborations between purpose-driven organisations and social enterprises via co-innovation, joint go-to-market projects, and service delivery, can exponentially increase the impact of both parties. To promote behaviour change communications and relief initiatives, governments may partner with a number of organisations, including social enterprises. For instance, The NITI Aayog, think tank of Government of India enlisted the support of social enterprises to help the government recognise COVID-19 hotspots and provide services to vulnerable section of the society Social enterprises across India stepped in to support the government's efforts by transferring their primary focus from their primary activities to relief efforts. To cite another example, Mann Deshi Foundation collaborated with a district administration to create a 300-bed COVID-19 hospital by renovating an existing, underutilised rural hospital and converting it into a free COVID-19 hospital.

As a result of the COVID-19 pandemic, India's corporate social responsibility laws have changed. According to the Indian government's directive, now all spending on COVID-19-related operations will be counted as CSR spending, As a result, many businesses that spend money on CSR will engage more social enterprises to carry out their ventures. As a result, collaboration opportunities will grow.

At the global level, the COVID Response Alliance for Social Entrepreneurs has been launched by the World Economic Forum's Alliance for Social Entrepreneurs, which brings together 40 leading global organisations that support over 15,000 social entrepreneurs. The goal is to share knowledge, experience, and resources in order to better coordinate and amplify the response of social entrepreneurs to COVID-19.

6 Challenges Faced

Despite social entrepreneurs' recognised role in alleviating social problems exacerbated by the pandemic (Bacq and Lumpkin 2020), keeping afloat is usually the most difficult task (Doherty and Pulido 2016). When it comes to addressing the socioeconomic problems generated by the epidemic, social enterprises struggle to thrive and confront numerous hurdles (World Economic Forum, 2020). Due to a lack of resources and know-how, the transition to digital for social enterprises has been gradual. However, these enterprises are coping with this new way of working (Amadi-Echendu and Thopil 2020).

One of the major challenges, according to an online study conducted by the "Jasani Centre of Social Entrepreneurship & Sustainability Management, NMIMS" on the "Impact of COVID-19 on NGOs and Social Enterprises", was financial. More than a third of executives said that controlling operating expenses, paying workers salaries are just a few of the many challenges that social enterprises face. According to new research, the most significant impact of the COVID-19 pandemic on entrepreneurship has been financial (Weaver 2020). Today, there are a number of avenues for social organisations to raise support. Grants, fellowships, crowdfunding and online networks, angels and venture capitalists, and loan providers are listed as per the study by Lyons and Kickul (2013). However this may be a more challenging task for social enterprises than for commercial enterprises, because their dual mission makes some investors wary of investing in them (Mair, et al., 2012).

According to Brown, Rocha, and Cowling (2020), seed-stage financial prospects have decreased considerably since the epidemic. Furthermore, equity investments have declined considerably, according to Brown and Rocha. While these studies show limited investment prospects, Kuckertz et al. (2020) also indicates that despite having constant costs, entrepreneurs saw severe decrease in revenue.

The country-wide lockdown and gradual unlock process has slowed economic growth significantly. Due to which, the net earnings of corporate will diminish. The sum of corporate social responsibility (CSR) fund would decrease proportionately as net earnings and net profits decline. This decreases the amount of capital available to social entrepreneurs who use CSR funds.

Finding and retaining talented employees is the second most difficult task. Unlike other difficulties that social enterprises face, such as funding, logistics, or regulatory compliance, finding the proper skill becomes more difficult as they grow. According to the opinion of a few social enterprises in India, talent is scarce and thus expensive. Employees find it difficult to resist the status, pay, and job security offered by large firms. Social enterprises cannot compete on that basis, even if they are adequately funded.

A final challenge that social enterprises may confront is balancing their social and financial goals. Financial capital is positively associated to innovativeness and partnerships (Meyskens et al. 2010), hence social enterprises with strong financial capital will do well.

When social enterprises become too focused on their financial objectives, they lose sight of their social mission. While social mission is the "heart and soul of the business" as social entrepreneurs reported (Weaver 2017), this unpredictable period necessitates a focus on creating economic value that will sustain organisations during the epidemic and beyond.

7 New Opportunities

The COVID-19 pandemic is a burden for humankind, but it may turn out to be a blessing in the end because of its profound impact on our attitudes towards sustainable development and on the economic activities that industry must continue and adapt. Entrepreneurs are not just victims of the crisis; they are also playing a key part in dealing with the societal ramifications of COVID-19, as society and the economy grapple with a "rising of new, urgent and overwhelming requirements" (Bacq and Lumpkin 2020).

This has forced entrepreneurs to modify and adapt swiftly for their businesses to survive (Thorgren and Williams 2020). This crisis also presents business opportunities, particularly for social innovation that is driven by social demands and evolves in response to pressing social issues (Krlev et al. 2018). As a result, a crisis like COVID-19 may offer up new entrepreneurial opportunities that traditional market or government actions cannot meet Gümüsay and Harrison (2020). According to a study by Raten (2020), the COVID-19 crisis has many positive effects in terms of social entrepreneurship.

Therefore, the COVID-19 pandemic's socioeconomic impact on societies around the world presents a range of opportunities for social innovation and entrepreneurship. Companies and government agencies should collaborate to promote innovation and entrepreneurship, not just to combat the virus, but also to develop new and sustainable lifestyles (Li-Ying et al. 2020).

COVID-19 has the potential to develop disruptive technologies in agri-food, health, the environment, and information technology. It has the potential to drastically revolutionise and disrupt food safety and quality, food waste management, and recycling, authenticity and traceability in the context of food disruption (Rowan et al. 2020). The growing demand for more safe and nutritious meals to feed rising populations, which reflects dynamic changes in eating patterns and attitudes towards climate change, will affect disruptive technologies in the agri-food sector. Foods that improve the immune system and overall well-being are likely to become more popular as COVID-19 spreads (Galanakis 2020). Residents who have been confined to their homes as a result of the COVID-19 pandemic have realised that being able to see greenery from their homes, or even having the option of growing plants in their homes, can improve their well-being and health (Daniela et al. 2020). Accordingly, green living social enterprises will be in high demand. Terrace gardening, bottle greens, and micro greens will be popular among city dwellers.

Supply chain disruptions are increasing at an alarming rate as a result of government-mandated lockdowns and tight travel restrictions. Corona virus related supply chain interruptions have been reported in 94 per cent of Fortune 1000 organisations (Kilpatrick and Barter 2020). As a result, it is vital for the business environment to explore novel techniques to secure a sustainable supply chain against future global disruptions (Remko 2020). E-commerce is on the rise. Similarly the growing awareness of sustainable products among consumers has increased the demand on businesses to embrace sustainable practices.

Many of the opportunities presented by COVID-19 particularly because of the physical separation it produced allow for social innovation in response to unfulfilled basic human needs (Van Wijk et al. 2019). This physical separation has resulted into the demand for digital brokering and digitised online services. For instances, modified social needs in the workplace have resulted in opportunities such as online hiring, online internships, and online mentorship. Similarly, entrepreneurial opportunities arose to digitise social interactions.

One positive outcome of the pandemic is that far more people are now conscious of others' sufferings and are eager to help in whatever way they can. The awareness level has gone up. In India, the traffic to the crowd funding platforms has increased by three times during COVID-19. This has resulted in a positive impact for the fundraising. This positive trend is also evident in current times, with a slew of philanthropic programmes –whether it's assisting migrant workers, raising funds for disaster victims, or supplying food for the poor and hungry. As a result of this trend, the government is likely to support social innovators and entrepreneurs who will function as system change agents. More new development institutions and programmes for social entrepreneurship will be established.

8 Conclusion and Suggestions

Social enterprise are playing a vital role in communities that have suffered during the current pandemic. The economic crisis, on the other hand, is expected to restrict both donor and investor capacity and availability. To mobilise financial resources and make a long-term impact, social enterprises will need to reinvent and update their business models. Collaborations and partnerships with institutions have long been important for social entrepreneurs, and they may be even more so during the crisis. Both short and long-term resilience and crisis management methods should be implemented by social enterprises.

In India, the social enterprises play a unique and significant role in providing social assistance during and after COVID-19. They are well positioned to operate swiftly, measurable, and long-term, and can supplement the government's efforts in making a good impact during crises like the COVID-19 pandemic, as well as contribute positively to achieving the 17 Sustainable Development Goals by 2030.

In the growth of these social enterprises, the government should play a critical role. Accordingly, the government must consider providing impetus to the impact investment and come out with a policy specific for social entrepreneurship. Social enterprises will become increasingly important in the post-COVID-19 environment.

More social entrepreneurship institutes should be supported by the government, and it should be included in school and college curricula. Corporations' CSR funds may be used to finance incubators for social enterprise start-ups. Similarly, pooling funds from various government grants could cover a large portion of a worthy social enterprise start-up's needs. In the same way that the government supports technology business incubators, the government should encourage social enterprise incubators with a social incubator fund.

The government may provide a legal form for social enterprises that want to put their profits to good use and make it easier for them to be recognised for tax purposes. Similarly, loans to social enterprises that generate social capital and extend the social economy's base can be organised. It is also recommended that an institutional framework be formed to sustain social enterprises.

References

Alvord, Sarah H., L. David Brown, and Christine W. Letts. 2004. Social entrepreneurship and societal transformation: An exploratory study. *The Journal of Applied Behavioral Science* 40(3): 260–282.

Amadi-Echendu, Joe, and George Alex Thopil. 2020. Resilience is paramount for managing socio-technological systems during and post-covid-19. *IEEE Engineering Management Review* 48(3): 118–128.

Anheier, Helmut, Gorgi Krlev, and Georg Mildenberger. 2018. *Social Innovation [Open Access]: Comparative Perspectives*. Routledge.

Bacq, Sophie, and G. T. Lumpkin. 2020. Social entrepreneurship and COVID-19. *Journal of Management Studies*

Brown, Ross, Augusto Rocha, and Marc Cowling. 2020. Financing entrepreneurship in times of crisis: Exploring the impact of COVID-19 on the market for entrepreneurial finance in the United Kingdom. *International Small Business Journal* 38 (5): 380–390.

Daniela, D'Alessandro, et al. 2020. *COVID-19 and Living Spaces challenge. Well-being and Public Health recommendations for a healthy, safe, and sustainable housing*, 1–15.

Doherty, R., and A. Pulido. 2016. *3 ways social entrepreneurs can solve their talent problem*. https://hbr.org/2016/06/3-ways-social-entrepreneurs-can-solve-their-talent-problem. Accessed on 23rd May 2021

Estrin, Saul, Tomasz Mickiewicz, and Ute Stephan. 2016. Human capital in social and commercial entrepreneurship. *Journal of Business Venturing* 31 (4): 449–467.

Shaw, Eleanor, and Sara Carter. 2007. Social entrepreneurship: Theoretical antecedents and empirical analysis of entrepreneurial processes and outcomes. *Journal of Small Business and Enterprise Development*.

Galanakis, Charis M. 2020. The food systems in the era of the coronavirus (COVID-19) pandemic crisis. *Foods* 9(4): 523.

Gümüsay, Ali Aslan, and Pegram Harrison. 2020. 'Never let a crisis go to waste': entrepreneurship in the age of coronavirus. *LSE Business Review*.

Holdsworth, Carol, et al. 2020. The role of social enterprises in post covid recovery in Africa. *Studii Europene*, p. 73.

Kilpatrick, Jim, and Lee Barter. 2020. *COVID-19: Managing Supply Chain Risk and Disruption*. Deloitte: Toronto, ON, Canada.

Koschmann, Matthew A., Timothy R. Kuhn, and Michael D. Pfarrer. 2012. A communicative framework of value in cross-sector partnerships. *Academy of Management Review* 37 (3): 332–354.

Kuckertz, Andreas, et al. 2020. Startups in times of crisis—a rapid response to the COVID-19 pandemic. *Journal of Business Venturing Insights* 13: e00169.

Li-Ying, Jason, and Phillip Nell. 2020. Navigating opportunities for innovation and entrepreneurship under COVID-19. *California Management Review*.

Lumpkin, G. T., and Sophie Bacq. 2019. Civic wealth creation: A new view of stakeholder engagement and societal impact. *Academy of Management Perspectives* 33(4): 383–404.

Lyons, Thomas S., and Jill R. Kickul. 2013. The social enterprise financing landscape: The lay of the land and new research on the horizon. *Entrepreneurship Research Journal* 3 (2): 147–159.

Mair, Johanna, Julie Battilana, and Julian Cardenas. 2012. Organizing for society: A typology of social entrepreneuring models. *Journal of Business Ethics* 111 (3): 353–373.

Meyskens, Moriah, et al. 2010. Social ventures from a resource–based perspective: An exploratory study assessing global Ashoka fellows. *Entrepreneurship Theory and Practice* 34(4): 661–680.

Pinch, Steven, and Peter Sunley. 2019. Social enterprise. In *The Wiley Blackwell Encyclopedia of Urban and Regional Studies*, 1–4.

Ratten, Vanessa. 2020. Coronavirus (covid-19) and entrepreneurship: Changing life and work landscape. *Journal of Small Business & Entrepreneurship* 32 (5): 503–516.

Ratten, Vanessa. 2020a. Coronavirus (covid-19) and social value co-creation. *International Journal of Sociology and Social Policy*.

Remko, Van Hoek. 2020. Research opportunities for a more resilient post-COVID-19 supply chain–closing the gap between research findings and industry practice. *International Journal of Operations & Production Management*.

Rowan, Neil J., and Charis M. Galanakis. 2020. Unlocking challenges and opportunities presented by COVID-19 pandemic for cross-cutting disruption in agri-food and green deal innovations: Quo Vadis?. *Science of the Total Environment*, p. 141362.

Rowan, Neil J., and John G. Laffey. 2020. Challenges and solutions for addressing critical shortage of supply chain for personal and protective equipment (PPE) arising from Coronavirus disease (COVID19) pandemic–Case study from the Republic of Ireland. *Science ofThe Total Environment* 725:: 138532.

Tello-Rozas, Sonia, Marlei Pozzebon, and Chantale Mailhot. 2015. Uncovering Micro-practices and pathways of engagement that scale up social-driven collaborations: A practice view of power. *Journal of Management Studies* 52 (8): 1064–1096.

The Sustainable Development Goals Report. 2020. https://unstats.un.org/sdgs/report/2020. Accessed on 24th May 2021.

Thompson Reuter Foundation poll. 2019. *The Best Countries to be a Social Entrepreneur*. https://poll2019.trust.org/. Accessed on 24 May 2021.

Thorgren, Sara, and Trenton Alma Williams. 2020. Staying alive during an unfolding crisis: How SMEs ward off impending disaster. *Journal of Business Venturing Insights* 14: e00187.

Weaver, Rasheda. 2020. Social enterprise and the capability approach: Exploring how social enterprises are humanizing business. *Journal of Nonprofit & Public Sector Marketing* 32 (5): 427–452.

Weaver, Rasheda L. 2017. *Social enterprise and the capability approach: examining the quest to humanize business*. Diss. Rutgers University-Camden Graduate School.

Van Wijk, Jakomijn, et al. 2019. Social innovation: Integrating micro, meso, and macro level insights from institutional theory. *Business & Society* 58(5): 887–918.

World Economic Forum. 2020. *Why Social Entrepreneurs are Critical to Our Response to and Recovery from the COVID-19 Crisis*. https://www.weforum.org/agenda/2020/05/schwab-foundation-covid-response-alliance-social-entrepreneurs-coronavirus-recovery-response/. Accessed on 24 May 2021.

An Exploration of Socio-Economic Factors and Post-COVID-19 Impact on Children in Conflict with Law: A Study in Odisha, India

Pragnya Das and Arpita Mitra

1 Introduction

This ongoing pandemic has affected everybody in every aspect of life; to this, even crime is also no exception. The current lockdown measures taken by the government has actually activated the reduction of crime to a certain extent. The concept of juvenile delinquency is the most complex and challenging issue faced across the global wide. The commission of crimes by the children is attributed by various sociological as well as economic factors. These factors play a very dominant role in the development of delinquent behaviour among children. This paper focuses on the socio-economic factors which led a child alleged to be in conflict with law and the COVID-19, pandemic effect on the children in conflict with law. According to many sociologists, social conditions become social problems through a process of social constructionism. From this perspective, societal reactions are central to the process through which a social condition is redefined as a social problem. Societal reactions can come from many sources. In spite of this global health crisis and the risk factors involved, many facilities, especially those managed by the private sectors, have been not willing to share their knowledge on this deadly virus. It is necessary to consider the impact of such pandemic on the entire juvenile justice system, as contagious disease. In the state, there are two kinds of target groups found. The first one concerns with the children living in a problematical situation. It can be stated in which the physical integrity, moral, intellectual aspect as well as social development of the child are at risk due to conflict in relationships or the surrounding in which he or she lives. The second concern is with the children who are alleged to be in conflict

P. Das (✉) · A. Mitra
School of Law, Kalinga Institute of Industrial Technology Deemed to be University, Bhubaneswar, Odisha, India

A. Mitra
e-mail: arpitamitra@kls.ac.in

R. N. Subudhi et al. (eds.), *Future of Work and Business in Covid-19 Era*,
Springer Proceedings in Business and Economics,
https://doi.org/10.1007/978-981-19-0357-1_20

with law. Children behave in proper manner and maintain a discipline life when the factors such as socio-economic conditions, environment, psychological conditions, family interpersonal relationships are stable around them. As the consequences of the COVID-19 pandemic are the most challenging in the matter of youth in rural areas of the state is seen indulging in criminal activities as a matter of restrictions at home, closure of schools, college and other vital learning institution, while in urban areas there has been reduction in the crime rate due to the change in the routine activities of each and every individual. During this pandemic, the juvenile justice system of Odisha has continuously monitored the situation and taken necessary measures to safeguard the safety of the children from the spread of the noble virus.

2 Conceptualisation

(a) **Children in Conflict with law**: "Child in conflict with law" has been defined under section 2(13) of the Juvenile Justice (Care & Protection of Children) Act, 2015 as a child who is alleged or found to have committed an offence and has not completed eighteen years of age on the date of commission of such offence (The Juvenile Justice (Care & Protection of Children) Act 2015).

(b) **COVID-19**: This is a contagious disease in the form of virus transmitted through air droplets. This virus affected not only a particular state or nation but the worldwide nations globally.

(c) **Juvenile**: "Juvenile" means a child below the age of eighteen years (The Juvenile Justice (Care & Protection of Children) Act 2015).

(d) **Juvenile Delinquency**: Crime committed by children and adolescents under the age of 18 years is known as delinquency. The maximum age limit and also the meaning of delinquency vary from country to country. But it is always below 18 years of age which is the statutory age for delinquency.

3 Review of Literature

The delinquent behaviour among the children not only manifests issues like social disorganization but also the characteristics of social breakdown. The nature of the problem varies from culture to culture, state to state and nation to nation. Edwin H. Sutherland discovered certain social aspect of characteristics prevalent in homes "from which delinquent behaviour come most frequently". Such factors are conflict within family members, separation or divorce, defective discipline due to ignorance and so on the part of parents, rigorous or severe treatment of minors in the name of discipline and the most crucial factor poverty. Albert K. Cohen found youth generally adopt illegitimate means rather than accepting the value and morality of the society to achieve their goals. It is observed the middle class youth get exposed to negative attitudes (Kobrin 1951). The size of the family is also a contributing factor towards juvenile delinquency. It was observed that the socio-economic status impact on the students academic that family income did not bring anything new to the students achievement. It was the education level of families that affect the most, so it was considered that every family should be accessible towards the education factor and should encourage their children for getting the education facilities. The socio-economic policies shall be formulated to encourage the students belonging from lower income background to high level of income in order to avoid inequalities among children (Gobena 2018).

4 Objective

To analyse the measures taken by the state government for children in conflict with law to mitigate the risk factor from prevention of virus.

To determine the crime rate by children in conflict with law.

5 Methodology

The data regarding this article have been collected from both the primary as well as secondary sources. The primary sources include legislation, interview via video call. The data from secondary sources have been collected by books, journals, newspaper reports and various Websites.

6 Impact of Socio-Economic Factors on Children in Conflict with Law

The process of shaping a child begins at home itself. From this, it is understood family is the most dominant and vital aspect in the lives of the children. The important factors that are mainly responsible for the causation of children being alleged to be in conflict with law are the economic factors, social factors and surrounding factors.

(a) Family Background: Family is the first foremost root to the overall development of the child. It is the family members who spread bond of love, care, cooperation, harmony, brotherhood and the feeling of positive energy with the child. The family dealings with the child explain why and how the child get carried away from the right path and entered into the world of crime. There are several factors observed which have adverse impact on the children found in conflict with law. The first factor is time; it is proven that parents spending much more time with their children make them to understand their child more regarding all aspects starting from their likes, dislikes to their strength and weakness. When parents does not spend much time with the children, then children also start to find different medium to spend their time especially the digital world is the current medium. Thus, parents tend to fill the pockets of child to compensate the time mismanagement and the needs which are not fulfilled by them. A family share both emotional and intense bond with their children. So, the bonding with the family can turn the table both in positive and in negative ways provided the way it is with the children. The second factor is parenting; when issues arise with respect to parenting, parents tend to abuse while taking the responsibility of children and this creates a negative impact on the child. There is a saying every child is and will remain a child in the eyes of their respective parents. Due to such reason of being subordinate to the elders; parents, siblings and other relatives take the children for granted and usually make them to do such work which are not suitable for them to do Beckett (2007).

The other factors such as lack of intimacy cause breaking up within family members, and it is through the broken families, the juvenile delinquency arises. The characteristics, features and personality of a child are influenced by the conduct and behaviour of the parents at home as well as in the society. The insecurity among children develops when they see disregard on the part of the parents which creates complexity in the young minds. Apart from this, a child's personality also depends on the attributes of his or her brother or sister's personality. This influencing part is mostly found among girls as they are not much exposed to outer world rather than boys. It is evident that if the elder ones get indulge into criminal activities, then obviously the younger ones will be influenced invariably by them (Sandhu (1977), p.23).

(b) Institutional Environment: After the parenting factor, the second most important factor which plays a vital role in the lives of children is school or any learning institution. After home, a child spent most of his time at schools, so the environment of school has major impact on the children. When violence gets started in the learning institutions, then the delinquent behaviour among children and adolescents starts to get develop. Although school violence can take many forms, bullying and its causes and consequences have by far received the most attention from researchers. It is identified the form of bullying among the peers, which involves students coercing their classmates into committing dangerous acts in order to fulfil an obligation imposed by a group of organization. Due to the bullying factor, delinquent characteristics starts to develop in the way of absconding from the school premises, indulging into crime such as theft, gambling, gaining membership into criminal gangs, etc. (Cohen (1951), p. 121).

(c) Area Factor: There are certain regions or areas which is considered to be not suitable for children as well as adolescents to live. The neighbourhood or the surrounding does matters a lot for nurturing a child. It is observed children and youths staying in localities with more abundance in criminals are at high risk to get indulged into committing crimes; in this manner, the locality also affects the young minds.

(d) Bad Crowd: The criminal characteristics is mostly grasped by the inter-relationships within the peer groups. Children's exposure to interpersonal violence is one form of criteria giving rise to delinquent acts. The delinquent behaviour arises within the friend circle in the form of jealousy, aggression, low self-esteem and anxiety, when one cannot achieve something while the other one had achieved. A child as well as adolescent being present in a bad company tends to progress his step towards the crime world, and they are found to be in conflict with law. In order to make children to accept the values and morals of the society, a healthy environment has to be formed which shall include prevention programmes targeting the behaviour management and skills training approaches including anger management and developmental empathy (Flanagan and Battaglia 2010).

(e) Economic Factors: The economic factor is considered to be extreme poverty. Crime and poverty is always seen to be interlinked with each other. At times the human needs get converted into its greed. It is found the greater risk among single parents is not a function of raising children alone but rather a function of high rates of poverty and stress in such families. It is evident that the families having lower income capital share more burden on the shoulders of the children to make him or her earn rather than focusing on their education aspect. While such children have many unfulfilled desires and so on by committing property crimes, they find it as an easy way to fulfil their want. Researchers have found spur of criminal tendencies is more within employed youths than unemployed ones due to the exposure with the outer world. The environment aspect has a check on the activities of the children. So, if the environment is healthy, then the children will also lead their way in a positive path.

The above data show the crime rate in the state of Odisha is not stable in nature. During the year of 2018, the crime rate decreased to 1.2%, while it increased in the year of 2019, and during the period of pandemic, it decreased due to the lockdown. But traditional forms of crime did not take place instead of that crime took place in digital form, for example cybercrime (State Crime Records Bureau, 2020).

During the beginning of pandemic, many lost their jobs and spend most of the time at home, and this period showed significant drop of crime rate in the mid of April 2020. As when the outbreak of COVID-19 had begun, the crime rate was controlled due to imposition of restriction in the form of lockdown and night curfew. But such drop of crime rate was only for a period of few months. Gradually, when the situation became better, the pandemic impact on the youngsters as well as adults

Table 1 Crime rate report of children in conflict with law of Odisha 2017–2020 (*Source* Crime in India, (2019, 2020))

Sl. no.	Year	Crime rate
1	2017	7.9
2	2018	7.7
3	2019	8.3
4	2020	7.6

got more worsened. In this emergency time, the incidence of property crimes such as theft, robbery and burglary has been reduced. The reduction in crime rate is observed during the beginning of lockdown, but later when the business and other employment sectors were shut down, the unemployment rate increased to an extreme level. When the complete lockdown was imposed all over the globe, during the first period of six months the crime rate went down drastically. While contrary to the property crime, domestic violation increased to a maximum level. This process of unemployment and loss of income made way for increasing the rate of crime. The COVID-19 pandemic has reduced the transitional crime and increased other forms of crimes such as cybercrime, domestic violence. The cybercrime, especially phishing, increased because 90% of the population spend their time on online. This global crisis affected the vulnerable groups and worldwide global economic. The education sector has been affected much more beginning from the primary level to tertiary level of education due to which most of the students spend their leisure time on cell phones, video games and so on.

7 Measures Taken by the State Government to Combat with COVID-19

The government played the most crucial role in taking the preventive measures to combat with this global pandemic. Many important decisions have been taken for the prevention from the virus for the children alleged to be in conflict with law at observation homes and special homes in the state of Odisha. Any outsiders were not allowed to enter the premises of the observation homes and special homes. The number of children apprehended during the time of the pandemic was first informed to the juvenile justice board, and then, the COVID test of the certain individuals has been conducted, and thereafter, the children having negative test report was admitted to the main ward of the concerned homes. The another important measure taken was formation of COVID homes within the premises of the observation and special homes. In the rehabilitation centres, a separate hall was taken for newly admitted children alleged to be in conflict with law. In the concerned hall, the children will stay for a period of fourteen days and after the completion of fourteen days they will be shifted to the main ward according to their age, and also for the entertainment, television was provided. There were distribution of masks and sanitizers to each and every children social distancing was maintained. The screening of all children prior to transportation was done. While conducting the proceedings of the alleged children, video conferencing system was adopted.

The Supreme Court issued guidelines for conducting special online or video sessions for taking preventive measures to combat with the spread of virus, as physical appearance was not possible. Formation of online help desks system for resolving the queries at the state level. The apex court ensured the counselling services are provided through electronic virtual medium for all the children present in observation homes.

The Health Ministry created a new National Helpline number, that is childline 1098, to clarify any matter regarding COVID-19 (In Re: Contagion of Covid Virus v. N. Raghupathy (2020). The Juvenile Justice Board has to ensure the other basic necessities for the girls; especially, hygienic needs has been provided. It was also ensured no child is subjected to any form of stigmatizing words or actions due to sneezing and coughing. The necessary steps to be taken to release the children alleged to be in conflict with law on furnishing of bail with proper and valid reasons. Though the inmates at observation and special homes live in proximity under the same roof, the risk level of transmission is also high, still then daily preventive measures have been taken for the welfare of the children.

8 Concluding Remarks

The deviance among children is still largely tackled through informal means of social control; however, the socio-economic transition resulting in large-scale migration from rural to urban areas, mostly in search of gainful vocations, tends to disrupt and undermine the stability of the institution of family. The conflict within the interpersonal relationships and change of social attitudes towards sex and morality can be seen as some of the factors contributing to the rise of children being in conflict with law. The juvenile justice system in India reflects many of the social characteristics of the Indian society. The children alleged to be in conflict with law in families, schools and in justice institutions are still handled harshly for their deviant and illegal misconduct. The guideline issued by the Apex Court was based on observing the scenario of the pandemic and looking into the best interest of the children. The Juvenile Justice Committees of every High Courts ensured the concerned guidelines has been complied with every child care institutions present in the state. It is the responsibility of each and every child care institution to make feel the children staying over there that they are at home away from home. However, during this pandemic, the measures such as lockdown and social distancing have acted as deterrence to crime. It is observed that the regions with stricter lockdown have greater the reduction of the crime.

References

Albert, K. Cohen. 1951. *Delinquency and Opportunity*. New York: Free Press.

Beckett, C. 2007. *Child Protection: An Introduction*. California, US: SAGE Publications Ltd.

Crime in India. 2017. National crime record Bureau. *Juveniles in Conflict with Law*.

Crime in India. 2018. National crime record Bureau. *Juveniles in Conflict with Law*.

Crime in India. 2019. National crime record Bureau. *Juveniles in Conflict with Law*.

Crime in Odisha. 2020. State crime records Bureau. *Children in Conflict with Law*.

Flanagan, K., and Battaglia, K. 2010. *Preventing and treating bullying and victimization*. New York: Oxford University Press.

Gobena, G.A. 2018. Family socio-economic status effect on students academic achievement at college of education and behavioral sciences, Haramaya University, Eastern Ethiopia. *Journal of Teacher Education and Educators* 7: 2017–2222.

Hagan, F.E. 2017. *Introduction to Criminology*. California, US: SAGE Publications Ltd.

https://www.open.edu/openlearn/ocw/mod/oucontent/view.php?id=4498&printable=1

Juvenile Justice (Care & Protection of Children) Act. 2015.

Kobrin, S. 1951. The conflict of values in delinquency areas. *American Sociological Review* 16: 653–661.

Sandhu, H.S. 1977. *Juvenile Delinquency: Causes Control and Prevention*. New York: McGraw-Hills.

Supreme Court of India. 2020. *In Re Contagion of Covid 19 virus in Children Protection Homes*.

Changing Gender Roles at Homes: Impact of Corona Pandemic

Binita Behera, Pratikhya Priyadarshini, and Amarendra Pattnaik

1 Introduction

Human beings are social animals, and many of their behaviours are influenced by societal expectations. We witness behaviours of others in the society and inculcate those almost like a habit. It all starts when we are babies. The toys that our parents give depend on our gender. Boys get toys that are masculine like cars, bikes, guns, cricket bats and balls, etc. On the other hand, girls are given barbie dolls, teddy bears, kitchen sets, fancy items, etc. After a certain age, boys and girls realize the gender difference and play with kids of same gender. As we grow up, we witness what all our mothers and sisters do. We also see what all our fathers and brothers do. There is a clear demarcation of their responsibilities. With time we also inherit and perpetuate such role differentiation. In many homes, girls follow the footsteps of their mothers and sons toe the line of their fathers. Adoption of such roles and transfer of such roles from one generation to another is so seamless and smooth that we even don't realize when and how we get into that kind of roles. We just fall in line. Whenever we try to tread into opposite gender roles, it is promptly noted by others. We get to see or listen to their reactions and correct ourselves. Most of us choose the easy way. We toe the tradition. To challenge the tradition is tough. We adjust ourselves to our gender roles as we have witnessed at our homes and society.

Sometimes circumstances force us to get into gender roles opposite to ours. Men cook and clean when he stays alone and no help is available. In ancient times, it was an acceptable norm that 'Men hunt and Women take care of Home'. But times have changed. Large number of women have joined 'work' outside their home and are supplementing the income of the household. In some cases, they are the only income earner of the family. Women have entered into activities traditionally meant for men

B. Behera · P. Priyadarshini (✉) · A. Pattnaik
School of Law, Kalinga Institute of Industrial Technology, Bhubaneswar, India
e-mail: pratikshya.priyadarshini@kls.ac.in

R. N. Subudhi et al. (eds.), *Future of Work and Business in Covid-19 Era*,
Springer Proceedings in Business and Economics,
https://doi.org/10.1007/978-981-19-0357-1_21

and are shining in those new roles. They have even joined defence forces and are in roles which are physically demanding. But they have proved themselves in all these new roles. Everyone has now accepted that there is nothing that women can't do. In short, both men and women are capable of doing things beyond their socially determined gender roles.

While women have treaded into new roles, their responsibility at home has remained static. Not many men have taken over the roles of women at home. Cooking, cleaning and caring still remain the singular responsibility of women. Men shy away from such work. Many consider themselves inadequate to do those jobs. But a big section also considers it small job and feels embarrassed to undertake them at home. Of course, many times women themselves perpetuate this legacy and don't allow the male counterpart to undertake household chores or works that women normally do at home.

During the corona pandemic, all remained limited in their homes—men, women and children. Work from home became a new normal. House helps were asked not to come and burden of housework became even bigger for the women at home. But we witnessed welcome change in gender roles at homes. In many homes, men joined the women in house work. They cooked and cleaned. Even children joined their parents in housework. Time will tell whether these change is episodic or permanent. But the fact that men did not shy away from doing works traditionally done by women is a pleasant development.

There are some advantages of gender division of roles but to remain hostage to the tradition and to limit women to homes is not correct. The stress of 'double burden' is not easy to handle, and it is known to result in health problems that women may have to bear. Like men, women have many dreams and aspirations. It is also this double burden which many a times may compel women to leave the formal workforce or may be an obstruction in their vertical mobility in the career. Men have to be an equal partner of women in the management of the household. She should also have ample time for rest and to pursue her interests. In one article in Times of India, journalist Sagarika Ghosh said 'Marriage is a partnership between men and women, where men have limited liability'. She meant, after marriage the responsibility of women increases manifold but the men remains as free as before. His responsibilities changes very little. This situation is not limited to uneducated lower class of the society. It is prevalent across social class and caste. It is very deep rooted and it is difficult for women to break-away from such shackles. The burden of sacrifice and dedication befalls on women and they silently accept the same. This situation must change as we look forward to become a progressive and developed society. Women have to be equal partner in economic activities and men must share some of her roles at home. By that both men and women can grow together. Women don't have to stay back for men to step forward. They can walk together, grow together and lead a happy life together, and this can have tremendous dividends for the society at large.

2 Review of Literature

Work from home has become a familiar phrase to us especially in the times of the pandemic COVID 19. From a time when the concept was first used in few of the developed Western countries (Bonacini et al. 2021) who kept the option of 'tele commuting' or 'working remotely' as an alternate mode of working available to the employees in order to accommodate some people who have the commensurate skills but due to certain disability or domestic responsibilities are unable to enrol for a job wherein they have to come to the physical office set up. If we were to look at the studies done so far, we see that in the turn of the present century there were some broad-based country-wise analyses wherein the researchers and scholars studied the consequences of this trend both for the employees as well as the employers were analysing nationally based work-related survey data, e.g. European Working Conditions Survey, 2015; Italian Survey of Professions (ICP) for the year 2013 (Bonacini et al. 2021), Survey on Labour Participation and Unemployment (INAPP-PLUS) for the year 2018 (Bonacini et al. 2021) and some utilized time use data, e.g. Australian Time use Survey, 2006 (Powell and Craig 2015). There were also some qualitative studies done which primarily were done to have an in depth understanding of the dynamics of working remotely and its impact both on the home front and the employers (Powell and Craig 2015). Some studies focus delineating only the work responsibilities and the household responsibilities. Whereas some do mention a third category of which they refer to as 'leisure time and recreation', but it is Powell and Craig (2015) which in fact frame the classification to include a third category 'recreation' which includes time for sleep, leisure, self-care and socializing (Powell and Craig 2015). There are two ways that researchers have looked at the 'work from home' (WFH) option being an option and availed by employees. Studies have either tried to analyse the issues that workers face due to this WFH option in balancing the work life or how it mars their performance and the other is how it places the benefits of flexi working where persons can attain work–life balance. Studies show that there are varying outcomes of either kind, and the fact that the benefits accruing from it are highly variable and are markedly gendered (Chung and Lippe 2020). The cause for such gendered outcomes as established in these studies is due to the existing traditional gender norms and role expectations of doing works such as chores and care giving at home. Hence, these studies show that men tend to use flexible working for performance enhancement purposes increasing their work intensity. On the other hand, women increase their working hours more towards the accomplishment of family responsibilities (Chung and Lippe 2020). In case of either, there is increase of work family conflict and whereas men are rewarded with income premiums, women are not. Flexible working also has a gendered impact on the labour market (Chung and Lippe 2020). Some studies show that flexible working has potential advantages to the employees. Therefore, employers also have a vested interest in flexible working as part of a high-involvement system. Flexible working has been linked to individuals working longer hours which increases performance outcomes for companies and career progression/income for workers (Chung and Horst 2018). Simplistically put, many studies maintain a clear-cut connect between work from home and more time and better coordination of household responsibilities such as child care (Chung and Lippe 2020); other studies have looked at continuity of services for women workers after maternity period in the sense work from home is providing for the continuity of service and also to maintain the working hours (Chung and Horst 2018). The blurring of the temporal and spatial dimension in the sense of the amount and the flexibility in scheduling work may have adverse impact or beneficial in keeping work–life balance. However, the studies also reiterate that it is essential to critically analyse the forms of flexible working because it is directly linked to lessening or increasing of work family conflicts and at the same time its impact on stress levels experienced by the employees which essentially impact the wellbeing of the employees (Chung and Horst 2018). It is also very important to operationalize flexible working because there are various types of flexible schedules available and finding place in the employer's policy regarding this. So which is the kind of flexible working or telecommuting that is available to the individuals is very significant to be enumerated in any study WFH phenomenon (Powell and Craig). Therefore, it is essential to critically analyse and classify the varied forms of flexible working because it is directly related in the studies to lessening of work family conflicts which essentially results in wellbeing of the persons (Powell and Craig 2015). Studies show that in fact work from home on the contrary may result in increased work family conflicts (Chung and Lippe 2020). So we can say empirically the cause and effect relation cannot be put in a straightforward manner between flexible working and lessening of work family conflict. The gender-related assumptions are mostly based on qualitative studies. As yet no quantitative studies have been undertaken to prove or disprove this clearly. How the society, the individual and his or her inner circle looks at the gender roles performance whether of home or work it results in how they are going to use this flexibility of work. Each category of tale-commuting or flexible timing may not be very favourable to and resulting in the attainment of work–life balance. It also depends on the type of occupation and one's level in the company. There are different types of flexible arrangements, and each can have very different outcomes on the person himself or herself. The other important factors to be considered relating to this field of study are the different levels of parent–child interactions and household structures within the family which may determine the benefits of flexible working. These factors are income level, marital status and social class of the persons who are working (Clawson and Gerstel 2014). There are various modes of telecommuting or remote working. Some companies include this in their policy and for some accessibility to this is allowed as per the country's national legislation on it such as in the UK. Whatever it might be, the sudden situation of the pandemic and its alarmingly fast spread were enough to pressurize the corporate to adhere to a national practice by all employers in different countries abruptly almost overnight. One of the key factors for telecommuting being adopted by employers is that the employees are representing the millennial (young crowd) who have grown up surfing, and it is second nature for them to be online. Digital defines if not anything else, the ease of working for these persons who are fast thronging the workforce of today (Chung and Lippe 2020). Considering the fact that mostly women take up telecommuting in order to cope with their domestic responsibilities, it can have a negative impact on their careers. For instance in case of the liberal welfare regime in UK, many women typically avail the WFH option and eventually it leads to a part-time mode of working which entails a down-slide in their wages and hence their occupational status. So that results a considerable gender gap in earning (Chung and Horst 2018). Many women in the UK, moving to a part-time job, entails a drop in their occupational status as well as wage levels. Whereas this picture seems intact for the western countries wherein flexible working is accepted in the mainstream corporate sector, one may say that there are very few studies of developing countries in this regard. Few of the studies undertaken in South Asia show that contrary to the Western studies, adoption of telecommuting does not reduce employees intention to leave and a clear-cut picture is emerging in Asia that WFH does not reduce the employees intention to leave if they face a negative work home interface (Ahmad et al. 2016). This is notwithstanding the fact that no clear-cut policy of the government in this regard has been framed. Very few employers in the private sector have undertaken it in countries such as Malaysia, and there are concerns about associated negative perceptions which might affect their career progression may diminish their uptake. Strangely, it has not kept pace with the technological transformation in the countries. Only the government sector is making this option available to its employees till the year 2015–1 (Ahmad et al. 2016).

Study-based exclusively on the IT and ITeS of India (Pandu et al. 2013) shows that there is very strong correlation between work–life balance or lack of it with variables such as family defendants, feelings about work and absence from work. The authors speaking about the first set of variable 'family dependent' means family responsibilities which are diverse such as taking care of not just children, but elderly, siblings, sibling's children, etc. The second set of variable 'feelings about work' which is also crucially influencing the work–life balance denotes affective organizational commitments, turnover intentions and intrinsic job satisfaction. The third set of variable 'absence from work' basically refers to keeping away from work and availing facilities such as annual leave, maternity leave, medical and earned leaves can also lessen the work fatigue and burn outs due to stress. (Pandu et al. 2013). As per the study, the employees who work in larger organizations experience a work–life imbalance to a larger degree in comparison to the medium and small organizations. The 2017 study undertaken to explore the present-day India-based corporate policies and practices to enable employees to attain work–life balance, what the employees desire with regard to these and to understand the gap between the two (Bansal and Agarwal 2017). It is a qualitative study wherein flexible arrangements are referred as one of the methods adopted amidst an array of many other facilities. The authors refer to two kinds of flexible arrangements, i.e. flexible working hours and work from home (Bansal and Agarwal 2017). This is amidst other facilities given for better work–life balance such as work autonomy, child care facilities, recreational activities at workplace, organizational culture, working conditions (Bansal and Agarwal 2017).

Having looked at the work from home literature, the authors also analysed articles that were sociological (Lyonette and Crompton 2015) to try and probe into the distribution of work in the domestic site. They look at how negotiations happens between the spouses at an interaction level. They find that where wife is the senior partner in terms of her earning, men contribute in housework to a large extent. The situation does differ along different class demarcations, and in spite of men sharing the housework, it in all cases is the prime responsibility accorded to women and so they end up being more burdened and for longer hours. In the paper by Kurowska (2020), explores gendered impact of home-based work (HBW) on the capability to balance work with non-work in double-earner families with dependent children in two countries with distinct models of division of labour: Poland and Sweden. The two countries are taken because one caters to the 'male bread earner model' and the latter is a classic example of supported universal bread earner model'. The author uses the capability approach wherein some of the important findings of the study are namely that men in both countries have higher capabilities to balance work with non-work than women, but the difference between the two genders is smaller in Sweden. She also found that HBW is related to lower capability to balance work with non-work for mothers in both countries and for fathers in Sweden only (Kurowska 2020). The results of the study that in a relatively gender equal society such as Sweden, the negative impact of home-based work on the capability to balance work with non-work affects both genders. On the contrary, in a more traditional society such as Poland, men are able to 'escape' the trap of double burden of paid and unpaid work when working from home while women do not (Kurowska 2020).

3 Research Gaps

Based on the review of literature, the common findings of various studies are listed below:

(i) Covid-19 pandemic has made work from home a necessity, and employees of many sectors of the economy have adopted and adapted the new way.
(ii) One of the ways to keep domestic conflicts at bay is through sharing of responsibilities beyond the gender roles.
(iii) Employers should have gender-neutral flexitime and WFH policy allowing their employees to take care of their responsibilities at home.
(iv) Role modelling by learning and unlearning the established traditional gender roles will help the next generation to take up work beyond their traditional gender roles.
(v) Government policies should encourage and facilitate WFH. This will prompt more employees to go for such options.

From the above list, the authors noticed that there is not much study that has been done around the shift in gender roles during Covid-19 pandemic. Therefore, they tried to delve into that subject.

4 Research Objectives

The primary objective of this research is to find out if during the corona pandemic male members of the family participated in the household work normally done by women.

Other objectives of the research are (i) to find out the common opinion on the matter of men sharing household work with women, (ii) to find out the common opinion on the matter of children helping parents in such work and (iii) to find out the reasons why men don't participate in the household work in normal times.

Research Questions

1. Did men share house work with women during corona pandemic or not?
2. Household work is a shared responsibility of men and women or not?
3. What are the main reasons for which men do not share house work with women?
4. What is the opinion about children helping parents in the household work?

5 Research Methodology

Descriptive quantitative research method is followed in this research work. Variables like gender, age, education and marital status were taken into account to find out the opinions across these variables. Questionnaire was used to collect data from 226 respondents. There are 121 female respondents and 105 male respondents. In the questionnaire, we tried to find out what is the opinion of people with respect to the responsibility of housework—whether only the women is supposed to do the house work or it is a joint responsibility of both men and women. We also tried to find out what is the opinion about the girl child doing some household chores vis-a-vis sons doing similar work at home.

Simple random sampling was used to select the respondents. Percentage table and cross-tables were used for data analysis.

The demographic profiling of the respondents is shown at Table 1.

6 Data Analyses and Findings

Finding-1: Tables 2 and 3 were used to find the answer to Research question-1. The authors tried to find out what percentage of respondents either agree or strongly agree to the three assertions and also checked if there is a gender-based variation to such response. On data analysis, we found that male members in general have shared house work with women during corona pandemic.

79% of respondents affirmed that husbands did share responsibility of household chores during the pandemic. Also, 74% of the respondents said that sons helped their

Table 1 Demographic profile of respondents

Gender	Marital status	Education	Grand total
Female	Married	Doctorate	5
		Graduate	4
		Post-graduate	8
	Married total		17
	Unmarried	Graduate	2
		Post-graduate	6
		Undergraduate	96
	Unmarried total		104
Female total			121
Male	Married	Doctorate	4
		Graduate	7
		Post-graduate	22
	Married total		33
	Unmarried	Graduate	3
		Post-graduate	3
		Undergraduate	66
	Unmarried total		72
Male total			105
Grand total			226

Source Primary data, collected by authors

Table 2 Sharing of housework by males

Response	During pandemic in most homes husbands helped their wife in cooking, cleaning and other household chores		During pandemic, sons helped their parents in cooking, cleaning and other household chores		During pandemic, male members helped in cooking, cleaning and other household chores	
Agree	113	50%	122	54%	126	56%
Disagree	23	10%	24	11%	19	8%
Indifferent	24	11%	34	15%	31	14%
Strongly agree	65	29%	45	20%	31	14%
Strongly disagree	1	0%	1	0%	19	8%
Grand total	226	100%	226	100%	226	100%

Source Primary data, collected by authors

Table 3 Gender-based opinion about men sharing housework during pandemic

Gender	During pandemic in most homes husbands helped their wife in cooking, cleaning and other household chores	During pandemic, sons helped their parents in cooking, cleaning and other household chore	During pandemic, male members helped in cooking, cleaning and other household chores
Male	91	82	79
Female	87	85	78
Total	178	167	157
% (Male)	51	49	50
% (Female)	49	51	50

Source Primary data, collected by authors

parents in the household chores. Similarly, 70% of the respondents said that male members shared household chores during the pandemic.

When we look at the gender profile of the respondents who agreed/strongly agreed to the assertions, we find there is no significant variation based on gender.

Finding-2: More than 90% of the respondents agreed that household work is a shared responsibility. In this context also, the authors tried to find out the opinion of the respondents regarding sons doing house work. A male child who participates in household work grows up to become a man with similar habits and outlook. Children develop habits and learn by observing their parents in action. Therefore, parents have a great influence in inducting children into such work without any gender bias.

Table 4 indicates that 93% of the female respondents and 92% of the male respondents either agree or strongly agree that sons should also share house work. Therefore, there is a uniform kind of view on the subject without much of a variation based on

Table 4 Opinion about sons doing household work

Gender	Sons should help parents in household work	Count	%
Female	Agree	38	31
	Disagree	4	3
	Indifferent	4	3
	Strongly agree	75	62
Female total		121	100
Male	Agree	39	37
	Disagree	3	3
	Indifferent	5	5
	Strongly agree	58	55
Male total		105	100
Grand total		226	100

Source Primary data, collected by authors

Table 5 Gender-based expectation about sharing of housework by men

Gender	How frequently men should help women in housework?	Grand Total	%
Female	Everyday	97	80
	Need based	17	14
	Occasionally	2	2
	Weekends	5	4
Female total		121	
Male	Everyday	69	66
	Need based	25	24
	Occasionally	1	1
	Weekends	10	10
Male total		105	

Source Primary data, collected by authors

the gender of the respondent. It is also noticed that there is no respondent who has a strong view that sons should not do any house work.

The authors also tried to find out the level of expectation about men doing housework from all the respondents to check if there is a variation based on gender. As can be seen in Table 5, Female respondents expect males to share household responsibility more frequently compared to what males consider right thing to do.

Finding-3: Table 6 shows the top two reasons as to why men do not do household work are—(1) They have never done that in their childhood and (2) they feel embarrassed to do such work (Fig. 1).

Finding-4: It is found from Table 7 that 93% of women and 92% of men consider that sons should help parents in household work. On the other hand, 95% of women and 90% of men consider that daughters should help parents in household work. There are two positives from this observation—(1) Large majority of people expect their children to undertake household work, and (2) there is not much of discrimination between boy child and girl child in terms of such expectation.

7 Limitations of the Study

(i) We could not include social class as a variable to find out how the opinions vary with social class. It is commonly held that people become more progressive in their thought as they move high in their social hierarchy. They feel less shame in doing jobs of other gender.

(ii) We have not checked how the opinions vary with respect to marital status and education. We have looked at only one variable, namely gender.

(iii) We didn't check whether the sharing of household work by men is episodic and limited to the pandemic period or it had been consolidated.

Table 6 Reasons of men not participating in housework in normal times

In normal time, what is the prime reason of men not sharing any household work	Gender	Grand Total	%
Men are busy in other work	Female	18	8
	Male	36	16
Men are busy in other work Total		54	**24**
Men feel embarrassed to do such work	Female	38	17
	Male	18	8
Men feel embarrassed to do such work Total		56	**25**
They have never done it in their childhood	Female	45	20
	Male	31	14
They have never done it in their childhood Total		76	**34**
Women are better suited for household work	Female	14	6
	Male	6	3
Women are better suited for household work Total		20	**9**
Women don't expect men to do such work	Female	6	3
	Male	14	6
Women don't expect men to do such work Total		20	**9**
Grand total		226	

Source Primary data, collected by authors

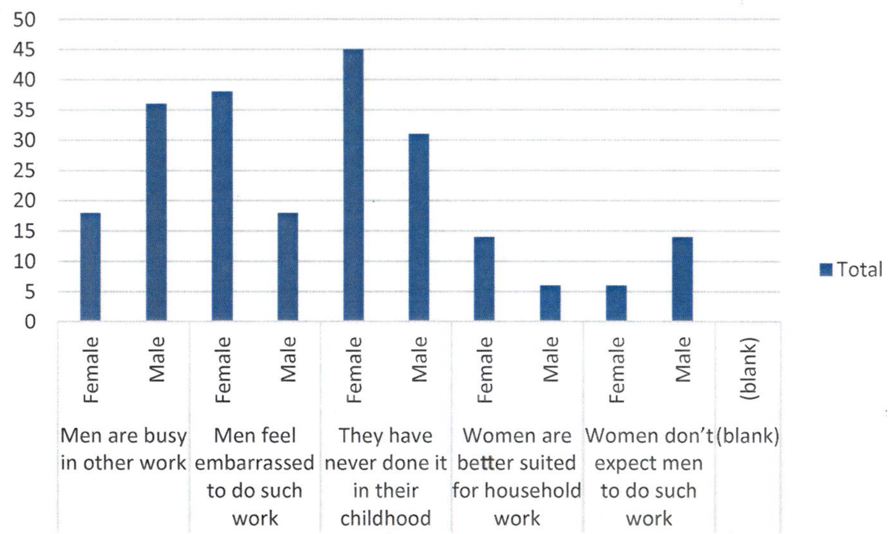

Fig. 1 Reasons of men not participating in housework in normal times *Source* SPSS output based on authors own compilation of primary data

Table 7 Opinion about children helping parents in household work

Gender	Response	Sons should help parents in household work	Daughters should help parents in household work
Female	Agree	38	50
	Strongly agree	75	65
	Overall %	93%	95%
Female total		121	121
Male	Agree	39	46
	Strongly agree	58	49
	Overall %	92%	90%
Male total		105	105

Source Primary data, collected by authors

(iv) We did not check if the opinions vary based on the 'occupation'/profession or a particular sector.

(v) We did not check if the opinions vary based on 'wife's earning' and 'her position in her job'.

8 Conclusion

Majority of men did share household work with women during corona. One of the reasons could be that servants were not available during the pandemic. The other reason may be most men were working from home or were staying at home without any work to do. This is a welcome change as in normal times women bear full responsibility of the household work.

Children not learning and doing household work during childhood is one of the reasons why they shy away from such work during later stage of their life. Parents have a responsibility in this regard. Even in schools, students should learn some life skills like cooking, cleaning, caring, etc. They must be sensitized that housework is gender-neutral and all should share.

Only when housework is shared, women can really participate in the economic activity in large numbers. Work from home has created opportunities for women who have limited themselves to housework only. They can work remotely not only to add to the income of the family but also to fulfil her personal dreams and aspirations.

References

Ahmad, Azlinzuraini, Nicky E. Shaw, Nicola J. Bown, Jean Gardiner and Khatijah Omar. 2016. Impact of negative work home interface on intention to leave and the role of flexible working arrangements in Malaysia. *The Journal of Developing Areas* 50 (5): 507–515. Special Issue on the Kuala Lumpur Conference, November 23–24, 2015.

Bansal, Nidhi, and Upasana A. Agarwal. 2017. The gap between availability and expectations of work life practices. *Indian Journal of Industrial Relations* 52 (3): 528–542.

Bonacini, Luca, Giovani Gallo, and Sergio Scicchitano. 2021. Working from home and income inequality: Risks of a 'New Normal' with Covid 19. *Journal of Population Economics* 34: 303–360.

Chung, Heejung, and Mariska van der Horst. 2018. Women's employment patterns after childbirth and the perceived access to and use of flexitime and teleworking *Human Relations* 7 (1): 47–72.

Chung, Heejung, and Tanja van der Lippe. 2020. Flexible working, work life balance and gender equality. *Social Indicators Research* 151.

Clawson, D., and N. Gerstel. 2014. *Unequal Time: Gender, Class and Family in Employment Schedules*. New York: Russel Sage Foundation.

Kurowska, Anna. 2020. Gendered effects of home-based work on parents' capability to balance work with non-work: two countries with different models of division of labour compared. *Social Indicators Research* 151: 405–425.

Lyonette, Clare, and Rosemary Crompton. 2015. Sharing the load? Partners' relative earning and the division of domestic labour. *Women, Employment and Society* 29 (1): 23–40.

Pandu, A., A. Balu, and K. Poorani. 2013. Assessing work-life balance among IT & ITeS women professionals. *Indian Journal of Industrial Relations* 48 (4): 611–620.

Powell, Abigail, and Lyn Craig. 2015. Gender differences in working at home and time use patterns. *Work, Employment and Society* 29 (4): 571–589.

Educational Technology: A Last Resort to Academia Amid Pandemic

Arun Dash and Khushboo Kuddus

1 Introduction

The world has changed, drastically and more importantly, hastily, over the past few months. The impact of COVID-19 on humans and their lifestyle has been so disturbing that the United Nations states, "The coronavirus COVID-19 pandemic is the defining global health crisis of our time and the greatest challenge we have faced since World War Two" (UNDP 2020). At the time of writing this paper, on 30 January 2021, the WHO Coronavirus Disease (COVID-19) Dashboard shows, "there have been 101,406,059 confirmed cases of COVID-19, including 2,191,898 deaths", across the globe (WHO COVID Dashboard 2021). A highly contagious disease has left Homo Sapiens, the best of the species, hapless and helpless. Now society does not seem to thrive on close human bonding; social distancing has become the new norm. So far, social distancing seems to have proven to be the best and only way to prevent the spread of this deadly virus. Hence, across the world, public facilities like transport, shopping malls, food joints, cinemas, tourist places, and train services have been suspended forcing a total lockdown. The offices and the schools have been closed.

Some countries have gone past the worst of COVID-19 and hence they are slowly opening to sustain their falling economy. Some have experienced the second wave of COVID-19 too. Unfortunately, India by now has been in the second place among all the countries in the world on the basis of the number of people affected by this disease. Among all things that have been worse affected by the impact of COVID-19-triggered lockdown is the education of the school children. As per the research data made available by the United Nations, "School closures kept 90% of all students out of school reversing years of progress on education" (UN 2020). "Quality education" being one of the sustainable development goals set by the United Nations to

A. Dash (✉) · K. Kuddus
School of Humanities, KIIT University, Bhubaneswar, Odisha, India

R. N. Subudhi et al. (eds.), *Future of Work and Business in Covid-19 Era*,
Springer Proceedings in Business and Economics,
https://doi.org/10.1007/978-981-19-0357-1_22

"transform our world", such unpredicted interruption to the academic progress of the children has made the concerned authorities to think and act decisively. Neither the teachers nor the students were prepared to handle the sudden shift in the teaching pedagogy from the traditional face-to-face mode to complete online mode.

Therefore, the present study aims to assess the preparedness of students, teachers and institutions for adopting online teaching and learning method in home-bound situation enforced by a pandemic like COVID-19 and to evaluate the factors that shall impact the education of the children in the days ahead, especially in the preparedness for tackling a COVID-19 like situation. It further enlists and suggests effective usages of educational technologies that can facilitate comprehensive learning among the students studying at home due to lockdown.

Objectives of the Study

The study focuses on the following objectives:

- To assess the usefulness of educational technology for the academia as an effective alternative to continue education in India amidst the pandemic COVID-19.
- To evaluate the readiness of all the stakeholders of education for adopted online teaching and learning during a pandemic like COVID-19.
- To understand the challenges the academia faces in India to continue education amidst COVID-19 pandemic.
- To highlight some effective measures to continue education during a pandemic like COVID-19.

2 Research Methodology

To meet the objectives of the study, data was collected from empirical research published in books, peer-reviewed journals, conference proceedings and book chapters in order to assess the integration of technology in education as the only effective alternative amidst the pandemic. Websites of various world organizations and Indian national government, reports prepared by national and international agencies of COVID-19 and statistics organizers were also referred. The keywords used for data collection were; COVID-19, Pandemic, Educational Technology, Online Teaching, Education, Advantages and Challenges, Google Scholar, Research Gate, Educational Resources Information Center (ERIC), JSTOR, and Proceedings were among the databases used to collect data.

3 Review of Literature

The statistics published by the United Nations claims that "In 2020, as the COVID-19 pandemic spread across the globe, a majority of countries announced the temporary closure of schools, impacting more than 91 per cent of students worldwide. By April

2020, close to 1.6 billion children and youth were out of school" (UN 2020). COVID-19 may not be the deadliest of all the pandemics that had gone by. But in terms of the expanse of the regions it has spread into and the number of people infected, it certainly has enough to scare the posterity too.

From the Antonine Plague of 165-180 AD until this COVID-19, pandemics have been constant companions to humanity from time to time. The Antonine Plague that swept through Rome in the late Second Century caused nearly five million deaths. It "was so deadly that today it is thought to contribute to the eventual fall of the Roman Empire" (Carpenter 2020). The Spanish flu of 1918 "was a direct killer, resulting in the deaths of at least 50 million people" (Garrett 2005). It is estimated that almost one-third of the global population at that time were infected by this flu. The Black Death that swept through Asia and Europe between 1347 and 1351 can be considered to be the deadliest of all the pandemics that history has witnessed. It spread very fast across the regions and took nearly 200 million lives. Many other pandemics such as HIV/AIDS in the Sub-Saharan Africa and Cholera in India and Indonesia had caused the dance of death in the human history.

But due to the tectonic changes in social bonding of modern beings and their ultra-social lifestyle, COVID-19 seems to have impacted the world quite dangerously. The uncertain delay in developing a vaccine that can potentially fight the deadly virus added to the woes of rising deaths across the globe. The deadly spread of COVID-19 has impacted almost all the sectors including the academics. "To mitigate and slow the spread of COVID-19, many countries have adopted unprecedented physical distancing policies" (Jin et al. 1970). As a direct consequence, the schools have been closed by government order. This decision taken to ensure public safety and prevent loss of human life has hampered the kids' education. According to statistics provided by UNESCO, "With an increasing number of states, provinces and even whole countries closing institutions of learning as a response to the COVID-19 pandemic, 363 million learners worldwide are being impacted" (UNESCO 2020).

With the schools closed, the progress of the studies for the academic year was hindered. Not only that, the co-curricular activities that kids used to get involved in, at school, had to stop. The scheduled examinations were rescheduled. The physical copy correction by the teachers did not happen anymore. The social skills that are taught in school outside the classroom have been shelved. "How can we ensure that valuable time is not lost and our learners at all levels continue to learn wherever they are?" (COL 2020) As the situation was unforeseen, neither the teaching community nor the administrators were prepared to handle such a challenge with no buffer time to prepare.

Mishra et al. observe in their study, approximately 264 million children and adolescents are not in school (Mishra et al. 2020), and this pandemic made this situation further worst. They did highlight that in the aftermath of COVID-19 crisis, online education has witnessed a pedagogical shift from traditional method to the modern approach of teaching–learning from classroom to Zoom, from personal to virtual and from seminars to webinars (Mishra et al. 2020).

Temitayo Deborah Oyedotun of the University of Guyana did a research study to provide rapid assessment of the benefits of the online mode and the challenges that accompany the dynamics of this pedagogy. This sudden transition to online pedagogy education as a result of COVID-19 in developing countries has exposed some inequalities and challenges as well as provided some benefits (Oyedotun 2020). The study by Patricia Aguilera-Hermida explored the perception of college students about the use, adoption, and acceptance of emergency online learning during the stay-at-home orders due to COVID-19. The quantitative and qualitative results of this study discovered that the students prefer face-to-face instruction over online education (Patricia Aguilera-Hermida 2020). Similarly, a recent study by Sawsan Abuhammad on the perceptions of the parents in Jordan establishes that they had to deal with personal, logistical, financial and technical barriers while supporting distance learning among their children during COVID-19. Efforts must be taken to remove these barriers (Abuhammad 2020).

According to a UNESCO report, 50% (826 million) of pupils globally do not have access to a computer and 43% (706 million) do not have access to the internet at home. Furthermore, about 56 million students are unable to use mobile phones due to a lack of coverage by mobile networks. Around 89% (216 million), 82% (199 million), and 11% (26 million) of students in Sub-Saharan Africa countries do not have a computer, home internet access, or are not covered by mobile networks, respectively. Furthermore, over 56 million students in Sub-Saharan Africa do not have access to mobile networks (UNESCO 2020). Zhang reiterates the same by stating that access to computers and internet is essential for successful remote teaching. However, in developing countries, this is not guaranteed for all the students (Zhang 2020).

The PM e-Vidya Programme was recently launched by the Union Government to unify all efforts related to digital/online/on-air education in order to enable equitable multi-mode access to education. This is expected to benefit nearly 25 crore school-aged children across the country (MHRD 2020). The following are the major interventions included in this programme: *Swayam Prabha*, *Diksha* Portal, the National Knowledge Network, *Bharat Padhe* Online campaign, *VidyaDaan* 2.0 and the National Mission on Education through Information and Communication Technology (NME-ICT). The Indian government is also using All India Radio and Doordarshan to continue teaching (MHRD 2020; Kundu 2020).

Although the Indian government and various stakeholders of education have explored the possibility of Open and Distance Learning (ODL) by implementing various digital technologies to address the current COVID-19 crisis, India is not fully equipped to make education accessible to all corners of the country via digital platforms (Jena 2020). In addition, there is a significant difference between rural and urban India. Only 4.4% of rural Indian households have a computer, compared to 23.4% in urban India; only 15% of rural Indian households have access to the internet, compared to 42% in urban India (MOSPI 2019).

4 Academics Amidst the Fight Against COVID-19

In the context of continuing education, this uncertain situation has brought in some opportunities for those who have been blessed to have the resources and the zeal to fight the menace and surge ahead. On the other hand, it has left many struggling against the humungous challenges that has befallen before them due to lack of resources and infrastructure to continue their education.

4.1 Opportunities

The physical and social distancing forced by the Centre and the State governments to avoid spread of COVID-19 infection has left people safe but stranded at home. The uncertain long period when life would be normal has therefore compelled all to resume their office and the schools for their kids using educational and internet technologies at disposal. While the people working in the corporate sector, especially Information Technology companies, mostly have a smooth transition due to their prior experience and exposure, people from various other sectors are finding it tough to get the infrastructure ready. At times, it is observed that even when they can successfully get their IT infrastructure at home ready, they still would have to struggle to get used to these new ways of working. Many employees who never used a personal computer in their job are being forced to report their presence in virtual office via online video conferencing. Besides the salaried individuals, the students are the next lot who require to study online sitting at home. The excitement of the students to experience the exposure to new learning environment has brought in new opportunities for them, of course, amidst the many infrastructural bottlenecks for some.

Researchers involved in a UNESCO project observe that even though the pandemic has brought before us opportunities to explore newer and better way to continue education, this is easier said than done in a society that is still not fully inclusive and equitable. They view that "innovation will not happen if societal inequity issues are not addressed. We are seeing that the capacity for innovation in education is limited by wealth and access; those who have privilege, technologies, devices and safe homes are advantaged. What we need now are innovations that give educators the platform to enhance learning for a truly inclusive and equitable education for all" (Doucet et al. 2020).

Mobile Learning

Smartphones (or smart mobile phones) so far used as a luxury for entertainment purposes like photography, music, movies and games are seen as the best tool to be used for online classes. The parents, usually reluctant to hand over their smartphones to their children, are now changing their mindset to adapt to the time and needs by assisting their children to become experts in handling their smartphones, so they do not face any technical glitches while attending online classes. People of older generations are looking at awe how technology has partially won against a disease that had the ability to stop all.

COVID-19 has forced the teachers and the students to fully switch over to online teaching modes. Smartphones are quite handy due to their designs and ease of use. So, most of the students and their teachers are using smartphones to connect to an integrated online platform where they all can join as a group and continue their LIVE conversation using both video and audio modes. Some schools have been proactive in developing a dedicated comprehensive online platform with their own customizations to ease the facilitation of teaching. They have even got their own mobile apps catering to both Android and Apple Operating Systems.

Social Media Apps

These are boom days for the social media. Increasing use of social media in every walk of life has left many worried for a good reason. But in these home-bound days, social media has come to the rescue of those who are fond of socializing with their friends and relatives. The best thing about a social media tool, WhatsApp, has been that it has all that is required to facilitate online teaching and learning. Integration of its mobile app with the camera of the smartphone helps in live streaming of the video and thus enables video calling and video conference too. With subscription to a stable mobile network, the messages can be sent and received on the go. Exchanging media files, Microsoft Word documents, PDFs and images in various formats is also easier in WhatsApp. Recording and sending a voice message to the recipient has been perhaps the easiest thing to do in this app.

All these features are being exploited very well by the teachers and the students. One of the key advantages of WhatsApp has been its easy adaption. It has been years for most of the smartphone users to have started using this app for socializing among their distant friends and relatives. Most of them have mastered the use of this app much before this COVID-19-enforced lockdown. "High infiltration of Smartphones has initiated growing use of WhatsApp for groups of teachers and their students to support the learning process by allowing direct access to lots of online resources. Combination of medium like videos, pictures and voice notes along with constant availability of facilitator and learning anytime anywhere, has made WhatsApp a new and convenient tool for teaching–learning activity" (Gon and Rawekar 2017).

4.2 Challenges

The major difficulties with e-learning include availability, moderateness, adaptability, learning instructional method, deep rooted learning and instructive arrangement (Murgatrotd 2020). The infrastructure that has provided opportunities for some has posed as a major challenge in its absence. The students in the rural area with poorly developed infrastructure are deprived of all resources essential for continuing online education, such as smartphone, mobile network, internet connection, dedicated space or room, power outage. The government initiatives are in place to fill these gaps, but with COVID-19 restrictions at place, the challenges seem to aggravate further.

Many teachers are also struggling to manage with the infrastructural challenges. According to a survey conducted by ASSOCHAM and Primus Partners, only 17% of teachers in government schools were trained to conduct online classes, while 43.8 per cent of teachers in private schools were (Kundu 2020). Conducting online classes in itself is a major challenge for the teachers most of whom are not trained in working with the new technologies. Communication between parents and teachers gets broken many a time. The school diary of the kid that used to help the parents in keeping abreast of their kids' learning progress is missed so badly. WhatsApp messages sometimes are not being delivered promptly due to poor mobile network or data bandwidth.

Co-curricular activities take a back seat. As most of the co-curricular activities require socializing and physical proximity, ensuring the same enthusiasm among the students over a video session becomes challenging. Even though teachers may be thoroughly attentive and take all measures to attend to each of the participants online, the virtual atmosphere may not bring the same result as a real-life scenario. "All the elements of technological infrastructure, including the administrative support and the elements of production cycle and learning material presentation, must correspond to the state standards. This infrastructure is of strategic importance, as teaching materials are being converted into high-quality distance learning data. There are two problem areas in this perspective: writing the learning materials in accordance with the standards and in the appropriate form; converting the prepared material into a form that will allow the students to learn at any time and take advantage of learnt material in any situation" (Leontyeva 2018).

5 Educational Technologies as a Saviour During COVID-19

Educational Technologies utilized earlier, due to various factors, have come to the rescue of all during this pandemic. It has been observed that easy access to online resources on subjects enhances the awareness of learners. It also inspires them further to adopt different e-learning strategies and "helps them to build higher order thinking and creativity skills while constructing knowledge" (Kuddus and Khan 2020). Digital technologies enhance the engagement of students and promote active learning, build learner autonomy and a love for learning which becomes apparent while assessing their accomplishments. Technology promotes collaborative learning, development of critical thinking and interpersonal skills of students, enables friendly competition and creates a lively classroom dynamic" (Jaiswal 2020).

Even in India, Ministry of Human Resource Development (MHRD) and the apex body of Higher education University Grant Commission (UGC) ensured that students got academic support through online learning and shared several ICT initiatives of various organizations in the form of digital platforms for teaching–learning during this pandemic period (UGC Order dated 25-03-2020). A recent research has found out that smartphones have come out as the most used gadget to access online learning. It says, "The most utilized gadget was the cell phone (51.0%) trailed by PC (32.8%) and tablet (9.6%), while the most un-utilized gadget was the PC (6.6%)" (Kumar 2021). Among the platforms or tools that smartphones use to facilitate digital learning, video conferencing applications are the most popular and widely used.

5.1 Video Conferencing Applications

These applications when installed or accessed on smartphones, PCs or other handheld devices, make up for the absence of a physical classroom, to a large extent. "Video conferencing is a technology that allows real-time transmission and reception of audio and video data over a network between users who can be at any distance from each other. A solution that can ensure that people living in different locations can hold face-to-face meetings without having to do so in physical space" (Kristóf 2020).

Zoom

Zoom is a collaborative, cloud-based videoconferencing service offering features including online meetings, group messaging services, and secure recording of sessions (Zoom Video Communications Inc. 2016). Widely used for video conference calls, Zoom offers a number of sought-after features like ability to securely record and store sessions with no need of third-party software and the role-based user security. Role-based user security offers a comprehensive control to the host of the meeting, which is quite useful for the teachers to get a hold on the students. Some of these features are –expel a participant or all the participants, mute/unmute a participant or all participants, enable/disable a participant or all participants to record the session, share the screen of the presenter to all attendees. What comes as a blessing to the teachers handling an unruly class is the option to mute/unmute a participant or all participants. The integrated chat feature further helps the users and enables them to chat privately with the host or as a group. "Zoom has become an indispensable tool for the way we work, teach and learn together" (Sutterlin 2018).

Skype

With Skype, you can have meetings and create great things with your workgroup, share a story or celebrate a birthday with friends and family, and learn a new skill or hobby with a teacher. It's free to use Skype—to send messages and have audio and video calls with groups of up to 50 people! (Skype 2020) Some of the features Skype offers are call recording and live subtitles, audio and HD video calling and screen sharing.

Google Meet

"(Google) Meet is a secure and reliable video conferencing solution that's trusted by schools, governments and enterprises. Anyone with an email address can sign up for Meet and enjoy many of the same features available to our business and education users, such as simple scheduling and screen sharing, real-time captions and layouts that adapt to your preferences, including an expanded tiled view" (Google 2020). The advantage of Google Meet is that it is a Google product and most of the people in India prefer their personal email system to be on Gmail. It becomes far easier to set up meetings through Google Meet when it is enabled to sync with Google calendar. Google Meet offers most of the features offered by other video conferencing tools, such as up to 100 members as participant, screen sharing option, encrypted calls between all users, and live subtitles. However, all participants must have a Google account to use Google Meet.

Microsoft Teams

"Microsoft Teams is a digital hub that brings conversations, meetings, files, and apps together in one place. Because it's built on Office 365, schools benefit from integration with their familiar Office apps and services. It delivers enterprise grade security and compliance that is extensible and customizable to fit the needs of every school" (Microsoft 2020).

Peter Tsai's predicted earlier that by the end of 2020, 41 per cent of the organizations worldwide may have chosen to use Microsoft Teams (Tsai 2018). Close on his predictions, "The number of daily active users of Microsoft Teams have more than doubled in recent months, increasing from 32 million users in March 12. 2019 to 75 million as of April 30. 2020" (Liu 2020).

5.2 Conducting Tests Online

One of the essential proofs of the complete learning is the assessments and examination to know how the teachings have been grasped by the students. So, teaching–learning process will be incomplete without a proper assessment at the end of the classes. To facilitate proper assessments in online teaching, there are multiple educational technologies that are used. Google Forms, Moodle, OMR sheets and various online survey tools are some of these platforms that help evaluating the students' learning. They offer better learner-centred environment to the students.

Moodle

"Moodle is the world's open source learning platform that allows educators to create a private space online and easily build courses and activities with flexible software tools for collaborative online learning" (Moodle 2020). Moodle offers many customizations that willing teachers can use to get the best learning outcome. It "uses different plugins that teachers can choose to install, depending on their needs. In case of a writing course, for example, they may want to install a module detecting plagiarism. Assignment submission, portfolio, and other plugins will help the teachers to tailor the system to their needs and preferences" (Szirmai 2020).

Google Forms

Google Forms proves to be a handy tool to conduct online surveys and gather specific feedback from the students. Subsequently, the responses can be used to benefit the learning process. Conducting assessment of students' learning becomes easier through Google Forms as the students can be allowed to know their scores immediately after they submit their responses into these online forms. At a time like this when online teaching seems to be the only viable alternative, Google Forms can be used "to improve students' participation, engage them in their learning, and evaluate their learning" (Nguyen et al. 2018).

5.3 *Other Platforms and Tools*

Besides the specific tools and applications discussed above, there are several other online platforms, tools and mobile apps that can be exploited to foster effective collaborative learning among the participants. For example, the teachers can also run their own YouTube channels where they can upload the recordings of their classes taken during those Zoom or Skype sessions. They can organize webinars for the students to clarify their doubts. After re-evaluating the myriad ways available for imparting teaching online during compelling circumstances, it is observed that "this learning mode has many advantages than the traditional mode, as it provides the students with the ability to learn at their own pace and in their own space" (Thoms and Eryilmaz 2014; Dash and Kuddus 2020; Khan and Kuddus 2020).

6 The Way Forward for Academics in Post-COVID-19 Era

While preparing to face a post-COVID-19 era, there is an urgent need to address the major issues that may need immediate attention. One among them certainly is the infrastructural readiness to switch fully to ICT-enabled education that relies heavily on Internet technologies. The New Education Policy 2020, brought in by the Ministry of Human Resource Development (MHRD), Government of India after 34 years, proposes ambitious plans to exploit Machine Learning and Artificial Intelligence towards the comprehensive understanding of the New Generation kids:

- "An autonomous body, the National Educational Technology Forum (NETF), will be created to provide a platform for the free exchange of ideas on the use of technology to enhance learning, assessment, planning, administration, and so on, both for school and higher education" (NEP 2020).
- "A rich variety of educational software, for all the above purposes, will be developed and made available for students and teachers at all levels. All such software will be available in all major Indian languages and will be accessible to a wide

range of users including students in remote areas and Divyang students" (NEP 2020).

Further, the NEP 2020 has taken cognizance of challenges faced for continuing education during a pandemic like COVID-19. "It calls for carefully designed and appropriately scaled pilot studies to determine how the benefits of online/digital education can be reaped while addressing or mitigating the downsides. In the meantime, the existing digital platforms and ongoing ICT-based educational initiatives must be optimized and expanded to meet the current and future challenges in providing quality education for all" (NEP 2020).

However, the implementation of the ambitious proposals included in the NPE, 2020 looks challenging, especially due to the infrastructural bottlenecks prevailing now in a country as diverse as India. "With over 560 million internet users, India is the second largest online market in the world, ranked only behind China. It was estimated that by 2023, there would be over 650 million internet users the country. Despite the large base of internet users, the internet penetration rate in the country stood at around 50 per cent in 2020. This meant that around half of the 1.37 billion Indians had access to internet that year" (Keelery 2020). Unless all parts of India are connected through a robust fibre broadband network, the facilitation of educational technology can never be successful in the scale it is proposed in the National Education Policy 2020.

The present study conducted to evaluate the factors that shall impact the education of the children in the days ahead, especially in the preparedness for tackling a COVID-19 like situation if ever, has the following findings:

- The mobile phone network must be made better by augmenting the supporting infrastructure so that people in the remote places can use smartphones as a cost-effective solution to take up online education for their children.
- The MHRD must take steps to manufacture high-performance tablets preloaded with a uniform software that can contain the e-copies of the textbooks of a prescribed syllabus and mandate its use by the students. To ensure its affordability, the government may provide these devices at a subsidized rate for all the students.
- Connecting all city and rural schools to a shared Internet would pave the way for safeguarding the future. The gaps in the digital divide must have to be fixed.
- Comprehensive teacher orientation programmes must be designed to prepare them to adapt to the new technologies within a specified time frame. With the fast-changing technological developments across the world, slow pace or half-hearted approach to prepare ourselves may hinder our progress.
- Subsidized tablets preloaded with all textbooks with multiple language support, so the mother tongue is not neglected.

7 Conclusion

Extreme situations require extreme measures. Life after COVID-19 may return to normalcy, sooner or later. But none can rule out the possibility of another pandemic of this scale or higher in the coming days. So, preparedness to deal with such unforeseen calamities should be the best approach, especially for educational needs. Next to the basic necessities and public health, education provides a means to human life. To ensure that the teaching and learning process becomes place and space independent and it is continuous, unaffected by anything, we must adapt to the evolving educational technologies and make them more efficient with time. Revamping the digital infrastructure, encouraging a fair blend of online learning and physical classroom learning wherever possible, and equipping the teachers with proper training and tools—these initiatives must be taken up now so that the stage is set for educational technologies to flourish in the Indian education field. Active interest and willingness to explore and utilize technological innovations like Artificial Intelligence and Machine Learning in the teaching and learning process hold the key to brighter academic pursuits in the days ahead.

References

About Moodle—Our Mission and Values. 2020. *Moodle*, (27 Apr. 2020), moodle.com/about/.

About Skype: Contact: What Is Skype. *Contact|What Is Skype*, www.skype.com/en/about/.

Abuhammad, Sawsan. 2020. Barriers to distance learning during the COVID-19 outbreak: A qualitative review from parents' perspective. *Heliyon* 6 (11): 1–5.

Carpenter, Dan. 2020. 10 deadliest pandemics in history were much worse than coronavirus. *The Federalist*, (17 Apr. 2020), thefederalist.com/2020/04/18/10-deadliest-pandemics-in-history-were-much-worse-than-coronavirus-so-far/.

Coronavirus Disease COVID-19 Pandemic. 2020. *UNDP*, (7 July 2020), www.undp.org/content/undp/en/home/covid-19-pandemic-response.html.

Dash, Arun. and Khushboo Kuddus, "Leveraging the Benefits of ICT Usage in Teaching of English Language and Literature", In: Satapathy S., V., Bhateja, J, Mohanty, and S., Udgata (eds.). *Smart Intelligent Computing and Applications. Smart Innovation, Systems and Technologies*, 160, 225–232. Springer. https://doi.org/10.1007/978-981-32-9690-9_22.

Doucet, Armand., Deborah Netolicky, Koen Timmers, and Francis Jim Tuscano. 2020. *Thinking about Pedagogy in an Unfolding Pandemic* (An Independent Report on Approaches to Distance Learning during COVID-19 School Closure). Work of Education International and UNESCO.

Education—United Nations Sustainable Development. 2020. *United Nations*. www.un.org/sustainabledevelopment/education/.

Garrett, Laurie. 2005. The next pandemic? *Foreign Affairs* 84 (4): 3. https://doi.org/10.2307/20034417.

Gon, Sonia, and Alka Rawekar. 2017. Effectivity of E-learning through Whatsapp as a teaching learning tool. *MVP Journal of Medical Sciences* 4 (1): 19. https://doi.org/10.18311/mvpjms/0/v0/i0/8454.

Jaiswal, Preeti. 2020. Integrating educational technologies to augment learners' academic achievements. *International Journal of Emerging Technologies in Learning (IJET)* 15 (02): 145. https://doi.org/10.3991/ijet.v15i02.11809.

Jena, Pravat K. 2020. Impact of pandemic Covid-19 on education in India. *International Journal of Current Research* 12 (7): 12582–12586.

Jin, Y.H., and L. Cai et al. 1970. Quantifying the impact of physical distance measures on the transmission of COVID-19 in the UK. *BMC Medicine*, BioMed Central, (1 Jan. 1970), https://doi.org/10.1186/s12916-020-01597-8.

Keelery, Sandhya. 2020. Topic: Internet Usage in India. Statista, (7 July 2020). www.statista.com/topics/2157/internet-usage-in-india/.

Keeping the Doors of Learning Open COVID-19. *COL*, (13 Mar. 2020). www.col.org/resources/keeping-doors-learning-open-covid-19.

Khan, Nafis M., and Khushboo Kuddus. 2020. Integrating ICT in English Language teaching in Bangladesh: Teachers' perception and challenges. *Rupkatha Journal on Interdisciplinary Studies in Humanities* 12 (5); 1–10. (Special conference Issue).

Kuddus, Khushboo, and Nafis M. Khan. 2020. Attitude of the international students towards integrating ICT in Foreign language learning: A case study. In Tuba M., S., Akashe, A., Joshi (eds.). ICT systems and sustainability. *Advances in Intelligent Systems and Computing*, 1270, 685–695. Springer. https://doi.org/10.1007/978-981-15-8289-9_66.

Kumar, Pradeep. 2021. Online learning and its effects on academic performance of secondary school students during COVID-19 pandemic. *Pramana Research Journal* 11 (5): 49–58.

Kundu, Protiva. 2020. Indian education can't go online—only 8% of homes with young members have computer with net link. The Scroll, (5th May 2020). https://scroll.in/article/960939/indian-education-cant-go-online-only-8-of-homes-with-school-children-have-computer-with-net-link.

Kristóf, Zsolt. 2020. International trends of remote teaching ordered in light of the coronavirus (COVID-19) and its most popular video conferencing applications That implement communication. *Central European Journal of Educational Research* 2 (2): 84–92. https://doi.org/10.37441/cejer/2020/2/2/7917.

Leontyeva, Irina A. 2018. Modern distance learning technologies in higher education: Introduction problems. *EURASIA Journal of Mathematics, Science and Technology Education* 14 (10). https://doi.org/10.29333/ejmste/92284.

Liu, Shanhong. 2020. Microsoft teams daily active users worldwide 2019–2020. *Statista*, (8 June 2020). www.statista.com/statistics/1033742/worldwide-microsoft-teams-daily-and-monthly-users/.

Ministry of Human Resource Development (MHRD). (2020). India Report Digital Education. https://mhrd.gov.in/sites/upload_les/mhrd/les/India_Report_Digital_Education_0.pdf.

Mishra, Loknath., Tushar Gupta, and Abha Shree. 2020. Online teaching-learning in higher education during lockdown period of COVID-19 pandemic. *International Journal of Educational Research Open* 1; 100012. https://doi.org/10.1016/j.ijedro.2020.100012.

Ministry of Statistics and Programme Implementation (MOSPI). 2019. Key Indicators of Household Social Consumption on Education in India 2017-18. NSS 75th Round. http://www.mospi.gov.in/sites/default/files/NSS75252E/KI_Education_75th_Final.pdf.

Murgatrotd, Stephen. 2020. COVID-19 and online learning, Alberta. *Canada*. https://doi.org/10.13140/RG.2.2.31132.85120.

National Education Policy 2020. 2020. *Ministry of Human Resource Development*, Government of India. www.mhrd.gov.in/sites/upload_files/mhrd/files/NEP_Final_English_0.pdf.

Nguyen, Ha, et al. 2018. Using google forms to inform teaching practices. In *Proceedings of the Interdisciplinary STEM Teaching and Learning Conference*, (2018), digitalcommons.georgiasouthern.edu/stem_proceedings/vol2/iss1/10/?utm_source=digitalcommons.georgiasouthern.edu%2Fstem_proceedings%2Fvol2%2Fiss1%2F10.

Oyedotun, Temitayo Deborah. 2020. Sudden change of pedagogy in education driven by COVID-19: Perspectives and evaluation from a developing country. *Research in Globalization* 2; 100029. https://doi.org/10.1016/j.resglo.2020.100029.

Patricia Aguilera-Hermida, A. 2020. College students' use and acceptance of emergency online learning due to COVID-19. *International Journal of Educational Research Open* 1. https://doi.org/10.1016/j.ijedro.2020.100011.

Quick Start—Microsoft Teams for Education Admins—Microsoft Teams. *Microsoft Teams|Microsoft Docs*, docs.microsoft.com/en-us/microsoftteams/teams-quick-start-edu.
Sutterlin, Jane. 2018. Learning is social with zoom video conferencing in your classroom. *ELearn Magazine, an ACM Publication*, (Dec. 2018), elearnmag.acm.org/archive.cfm?aid=3236697.
Szirmai, Monika. 2020. Moodle: The ubiquitous teacher. *Electronic Journal of Foreign Language Teaching* 17 (1); 190–204. Suppl. 1.
Thoms, Brian, and Evren Eryilmaz. 2014. How media choice affects learner interactions in distance learning classes. *Computers & Education* 75: 112–126. https://doi.org/10.1016/j.compedu.2014.02.002.
Tsai, Peter. 2018. Business Chat Apps in 2018: Top players and adoption plans. *The Spiceworks Community*, (10 Dec. 2018), community.spiceworks.com/blog/3157-business-chat-apps-in-2018-top-players-and-adoption-plans.
UN. 2020. *Education—United Nations Sustainable Development*. United Nations. http://www.un.org/sustainabledevelopment/education/
UNESCO. 2020. *UNESCO Rallies International Organizations, Civil Society and Private Sector Partners in a Broad Coalition to Ensure #LearningNeverStops*. (2020), UNESCO. https://en.unesco.org/news/unesco-rallies-international-organizations-civil-society-and-private-sector-partners-broad.
"Welcome to the United Nations, It's Your World. 2020. *United Nations*. www.un.org/.
What's New in Google Meet. *Google Meet Help*, Google, support.google.com/meet/answer/9545619?hl=en-GB.
WHO Coronavirus Disease (COVID-19) Dashboard.
World Health Organization. (2021). covid19.who.int/.
Zhang, X. 2020. Thoughts on large-scale long-distance web-based teaching in colleges and universities under novel coronavirus pneumonia epidemic: A case of Chengdu University. In *Proceedings of the 4th International Conference on Culture, Education and Economic Development of Modern Society (ICCESE 2020)*, 1222–1225. Atlantis Press, Amsterdam. https://doi.org/10.2991/assehr.k.200316.266.

Impact of COVID-19 on Indian Education System: Practice and Applications of Intelligent Technologies

Saumendra Das, Janmenjoy Nayak, and Bighnaraj Naik

1 Introduction

Novel COVID-19 (SARS-COV-2) has emerged as one of the most hazardous pandemics across the globe. Till now, the pandemic has resulted in around 106,377,991 confirmed, 2,321,376 death cases (https://www.worldometers.info/coronavirus/) and threatened economic crisis. Governmental policies like social distancing, lockdown, self-isolation and travel restrictions have reduced the work-force and redundant employment in several sectors. Different important sectors such as oil refinery, aviation, education, banking, civil service, markets, religious sectors and sports are hugely affected due to the massive cancellation of international flights. Further, the shutdown of schools or universities, work from home, 14 days home quarantine, closure of food market, ban order of religious places and cancellation of all sports events have made the economy spill over (Ozili 2020). In addition to the massive loss of life, the global pandemic has the changed scenario of the economy, society, technology and policy. Due to the first, second, and third phases of lock-down, the primary, secondary and tertiary sectors in India transformed their business strategies from physical to online. A progressive change in digitalization took place particularly in the education sector where an indefinite shut down of schools and universities occurred as 1.716 billion students affected on 8 April 2020. Distance

S. Das (✉)
Department of MBA, Aditya Institute of Technology and Management (AITAM), Tekkali 532201, India

J. Nayak
Department of Computer Science, Maharaja Sriram Chandra Bhanja Deo (MSCB) University, Baripada, Odisha 757003, India

B. Naik
Department of Computer Applications, Veer SurendraSai University of Technology, Burla, Odisha 768018, India

R. N. Subudhi et al. (eds.), *Future of Work and Business in Covid-19 Era*,
Springer Proceedings in Business and Economics,
https://doi.org/10.1007/978-981-19-0357-1_23

learning, virtual education and intelligent solutions in the education sector became the new solution to prevent the disease, but some of the stakeholders could not resist the sudden change (Kumar et al. 2020).

Among all the sectors, the impact on the education industry is one of the major global concerns. Due to the spread of this virus, there was a forcible postponement of physical education. This moved the whole education system into a fringe condition for uncertainty and no hope for further progress. Though few countries have opted for online education, a country like India is partially succeeded. COVID-19 is one of the biggest challenges in front of the education sector ever seen in the history of the education system. In this regard, a strategic decision was taken by most of the government to cease the face-to-face educational instruction to the students overnight and ordered them to continue the education through online or virtual mode. The new form of virtual education forced us to prepare the guideline for teachers, heads of the institutions and state officials on curriculum design, assessments and test to reassure the students and parents to study at home. This has given tremendous insight into the students who could learn virtually to avoid viral infections (Daniel 2020). Globally, the crisis forced to close the school and universities permanently for several months in 2020. But it represented an opportunity to rethink the global education system. To extend the continuous learning, some of the questions evolved on "what", "where" and "how" aspects of learning (Zhao 2020). Rethinking and redesign to bring back this turmoil condition of the education system could only possible through community development. Iyengar (2020) suggested that the post-COVID-19 education systems should differentiate community-driven support systems from technology to transform digital device learning and centre on SDG 4.7 and climate change environment.

The crisis in the education sector was not only the opportunity for higher education but it had a tough challenge before all stakeholders which had a tremendous impact on the education and mental health of student and academic staff (Crawford et al. 2020; Burns 2020). It had also a reciprocal impact on children education where the digital divide transforms the education possibilities for the younger generation. As children are surrounded by all kinds of digital technologies since their birth, they need a bright future (Iivari et al. 2020). Children education has a greater impact in this crisis as the schools are locked for an indefinite time. Moreover, the children are not able to attend the physical class and they are forced to adopt the online and ICT mode of teaching, which was a matter of great concern (Kim 2020). As the student community is vulnerable, the initial teacher education (ITE) was a bitter hard task in this crisis. They supposed to prepare the study material online instead of face-to-face education (la Velle et al. 2020). In this volatility, uncertainty, complex and ambiguous (VUCA) world, the teachers' education is becoming very critical for the preparation and delivery of the lecture. They have to prepare the academic regulation and course intent for the students to avoid the face-to-face learning (Mutton 2020).

In this crisis period, most of the educational disciplines are affected where the teachers and student forced to adopt online education to complete their curriculum. The disciplines such as entrepreneurship, management research, medical, rheumatology, nursing, dental, accounting, social science education have created massive attention among the student in the different discipline. These need a holistic approach towards entrepreneurship education which could improve the courage among the entrepreneurs for future growth and survival (Ratten and Paul 2020). The pandemic has strained many educational organizations to endure significant transformation, rethinking key elements of their business processes and usage of technology for maintaining the operations while adhering to a changing landscape of rules and new measures where the information management education could replace the uncertainties (Beech and Frederik 2020). COVID-19 has changed the situation of face-to-face teaching in medical education also. The use of online learning became an emergency measure that has affected the stakeholders like students, faculty, support staff and administrators. It became a challenge for the academician and medical graduates to adopt the virtual platform. Most of them are hesitant as the method included in clinical practice not possible online. The old practices of physical observation of the patient in rheumatology have shifted to a virtual transaction. The shift termed as a challenge for rheumatology specialist (Gaur et al. 2020; Hammond et al. 2020; Rafi et al. 2020). A faculty of nursing should be innovative, flexible, dexterous and agile, but there have been many challenges in this crisis. All the physical contact changed online, made the nursing faculty critical (Morin 2020). In this emergency, oral cares like dental education were not away from online and prevent themselves from discontinuity (Iyer et al. 2020). Accounting education in this pandemic should make a holistic environment in managing the 4-phases of the COVID-19 crisis such as recovery, redesign, crisis response and stabilization (Sangster et al. 2020).

The urgent demand for online classes in school and university of India had partial influence like other countries. Lockdown, social distancing and restrictions paved the system universally unique. However, the perception of the students should be examined thoroughly to understand the effect of the online class. In their article, Muthuprasad et al. (2021) examined the perception of students regarding the online class. In that study, majority of the responses favoured online class to adjust with the curriculum due to lockdown where the technical proficiency of the teacher was very important. In India, the education sector completely closed for nearly 10 months. In this regard, the government of India had taken initiatives to provide education through the Internet and television. Different schemes such as e-Pathshala, Diksha portal and National Repository of Open Educational Resources (NROER) are provided for secondary education. For higher education, Swayam, Swayam Prabha and e-PG Pathsala are also provided (Jena 2020a, 2020b).

Online education transformed the position of a teacher into an administrator. The teacher insights the information through media like the internet or a device and the student receives it at his ease. The entire system is very dynamic, where the role of a teacher is planning and organizing the curricula design and transmitting the education to the mass of student. The COVID-19 has changed the education system where artificial intelligence and robotics can automate the expedition of administrative duties for teachers and academic institutions. AI could prepare the grading sheet, experimental classifications and upload and downloading reading materials.

2 Global Scenario of Education System During COVID-19

No administrative plan, no teaching instruction, no arguments on hi-tech policies or politics, no opinion about the advantages and disadvantages just we should accomplish it. The use of technology in all educational domain becomes emergent in many countries. Particularly, a country like Germany who is specialized in technology with all aspects also suffered from inadequate technical infrastructure (Kerres 2020). The crisis also affected in Philippines (Toquero 2020). The closure of physical education created both opportunities and challenges before the world in the education sector. Around 188 countries suffered due to this epidemic. The Teachers' education system changed in Israel, Portugal, Sultan Qaboos, England, China, Vietnam, India and Sweden. It became the supernova in this crisis. Table 1 analyses the measures adopted by different country authorities to tackle the education system in the pandemic.

3 Fruitfulness of Online Education System Over Offline System

COVID-19 has forced us to accept the digital device to offer online education. The digital platform provided the reading soft copy, collaborative work, virtual meetings, sharing of information and also enhanced digital literacy. Online education has more advantages over physical education in few cases, where the physical education system could not provide all kinds of facilities for remote education.

4 Developments of Various Online Applications (Apps)

While all the countries are at various points in the infection rates of COVID-19, there are more than 1.3 billion children across the world affected by sudden shut- down of schools, colleges and universities because of the pandemic. Due to this, education has altered vividly with the typical growth of e-learning, and thus, teaching is carried out remotely through digital platforms. With the rise in online learning applications, the visibility of progression in technology is very obvious and emerging at a rapid pace. The schools, as well as tutors, are executing these technologies in their course to present the students with amazing learning knowledge through upgrades and overwhelming features in the online learning setting. Various digital initiatives such as UG/PG MOOCs, SWAYAM online courses, e-PG Pathshala, e-Content courseware in UG subjects, SWAYAMPRABHA, CEC-UGC YouTube channel, National Digital Library, Shodhganga, e-Shodh Sindhu, Vidwan are being offered by the Ministry of Human Resource Development (MHRD) and University Grants Commission (UGC)

Table 1 Steps taken by different countries in COVID-19 guidelines for education

Country	Steps taken by the Government
Australia	Social isolation for both international and domestic students; building cleaning; supplemented online recordings/offerings; and continuous progressions towards online learning without suspension
China	All schools closed up to 31 January 2021; 26 January announced to postpone the spring semester; several examinations like GRE, GMAT, IELTS and TOEFL cancelled; and several universities started online class from February 2020
Egypt	The government encouraged the e-learning system through Moodle, Microsoft Class Notes and Microsoft Teams software
Germany	Independent decision taken by 424 higher educational institutions; from 12 March face-to-face teaching completely suspended; university staff were allowed to work from home, university libraries were closed, oral examinations conducted through Skype, face time or other digital media, university building closed from 24 March to 19 April 2020, meetings and committee work allowed online, all students instructed to vacate the hostels and campus from 22 March 2020
Hong Kong	From 27 January 2020, the Hong Kong government suspended all kindergarten, primary and secondary schools; the Chinese New Year holiday extended for two weeks in early February and announced for online learning; online teaching training provided to staff and students; videos and teaching specially prepared for universities and schools
India	The state governments announced the school closure from March 2020; Schools in Delhi closed from 13 March where Maharashtra government declared closure from 16 March; All university examinations are postponed; University Grants Commission (UGC) advised to postpone all examinations until the end of March
Indonesia	The government ordered to continue the education online and closed all the educational institution for prevention control
Italy	From 2 March 2020, the government announced online lessons; thermal scanners were compulsory; medical and other health-related internships and trips were suspended; shutdown of all schools and universities from 4th March 2020
Jordan	The government converted many courses to online
Malaysia	The online study became mandatory for school and universities

(continued)

Table 1 (continued)

Country	Steps taken by the Government
Republic of Ireland	All examinations cancelled; virtual education initiated by the ministry of education
Nigeria	All school and colleges are closed
Republic of Ireland	Innovative technologies adopted for online classes
Republic of Korea (South Korea)	Video conferencing classes initiated and training provided to the teachers
Singapore	The government announced partial lockdown, where educational institute permitted to continue through online; physical transactions closed and all activities conducted online
South Africa	Digital delivery methods encouraged
South America (Chile and Brazil)	Potential strategies initiated on online education
United Kingdom	Work from home adopted by higher education and schools continued in online mode
United Arab Emirates	All universities of UAE instructed to attend training on effective online delivery
United States of America	Remote education, social distancing, restricted Chinese students

Source Own compilation by authors

of India during the lockdown (Jena 2020a, 2020b). Also, some free external repositories of online learning include Brookings, Commonwealth of Learning, Education Nation, EdSurge, Global Business Coalition for Education, etc., were classified based on remote learning requirements. There are numerous live-video contact platforms presented on the Web, but a few open-access online platforms such as Zoom, Google Meet, Skype, Facebook Live, YouTube Live, UberConference, FreeConference is DingTalk, Lark, Teams, TrueConf Online, Slack Video Calls, Lifesize Go, etc., were used by the learners of all category. So, e-learning policies assisted teachers to educate their students tenuously, and speak with them over live video calls. Several educational apps were used by the students during pandemic from the overall world to acquire uninterrupted education. Google Classroom, edX, BYJU's, UMANG Application, Duolingo, Classdojo, EkStep, abXchange, Unacademy, Vedantu, Toppr, Doubtnut, Alison, Harvard University mobile app, etc., are also frequently used by the students during pandemic.

There are various apps evolved to provide effective online education to all level of students.

- Online learning application like BYJU's is universally subscribed by several students. It offered free access to the learners till the end of lockdown. BYJU's provide all kind of study materials to the students also.
- The Indian government has offered a UMANG application for school going students to collect more than one crore programmed materials, important courses

and various study books for essential learning. During this pandemic, the UMANG app permitted students to obtain NCERT's E-Pathshala from the respective app. It acquires incredible determination and practice to study novel dialects as well as languages.

- On the other hand, the Duolingo app has made learning a language an easy task.
- Another online app known as Classdojo is a liberated educational app that allows teachers, students as well as parents to communicate online. It permits teachers to generate an implicit classroom in which they can easily share pictures and videos.
- *EkStep* is a significant platform that permits educators to generate, share and allocate free community resourced learning content for grade 1 to class 12 students, respectively. This app was completely loaded with numerous educational videos where learners can easily access and learn in a self-paced way during the lockdown.
- *LabXchange* is a free online podium that fetches top featured content together from varied resources, including assessments, videos, as well as simulations.
- The Unacademy included several courses from UPSC to SSC, JEE, NEET and Bank exams, among other things. The app assisted to recognize concepts with everyday live classes, practice, review and live mock tests. Similar to BYJU's, the Unacademy app is also paid, but during a pandemic, there are few free courses made available for the sake of students.
- Doubtnet app became more useful during the pandemic for students to make clear their doubts.
- Vedantu and Toppr also include free and live classes for the preparation of NEET, NDA and JEE exams. These apps were primarily concentrated on live classes, coding for kids and school students.
- Google Classroom or Google Meet is mostly an effective classroom of varieties; however, we can use it for constantly sending announcements, forming classes, continuous chats, presenting and analysing tasks, appealing remarks as well as replies, distributing education articles and many more.

Al-Maroof et al. (2020) has introduced a study on the usage of Google Meet as a learning medium in various educational establishments. The authors have utilized the methods of machine learning (ML) and partial least squares structural equation modelling (PLS-SEM) to analyse the acquired data. The major supposition of their research was associated with the consequence of COVID-19 on the approval of Google Meet due to the increase of various fears in COVID-19 such as "fear because of study failure", "fear of dropping", "family lockdown circumstances" and "social relationships" kinds of risks that may be faced by the students as well as teachers. The outcomes exposed that both data investigation methods have productively offered to support all the assumed relationships of the research technique. The J48 classifier was found to have better performance compared to other classifiers in forecasting the reliant variable in the majority of cases. Meanwhile, Tencent's classroom has been utilized extensively since the mid of February, after the Government of China instruction about full-time students for restarting their studies through digital platforms. This resulted in the major digital movement of education with roughly 81%

of school students, listening classes through the Tencent online schools. Likewise, many studies have described the effects and results of online learning during the pandemic. Dong et al (2020) have made a study on the Chinese parent's opinions regarding their children's online learning during the pandemic. The authors have reviewed 3275 Chinese parents' opinions as well as attitudes regarding their children's digital mode of learning. The authors found that most of the parents have a negative opinion about online learning and preferred conventional learning due to the reasons such as the inadequacy of learning methods, deficiency of time as well as professional facts in supporting young children's online education. The results recommended that the execution of online learning throughout the pandemic has been difficult and demanding for families. Mishra et al (2020) have surveyed to identify the impact of online learning in higher education institutions during a pandemic. The main purpose of their study is to tackle the needed fundamentals of online teaching–learning in education and how can obtainable sources of learning institutions efficiently alter formal learning into online learning with the assistance of practical classes and additional essential digital methods in this repeatedly changing learning landscape. The authors have utilized both qualitative and quantitative advances to examine the teachers' and students' perception of online learning.

5 Role of Intelligent Computing Approaches in Education System

From the various literatures, it is proved that the technological developments as well as innovations, computers and the computer-connected tools, and additional innovations have persuaded the growth of intelligent computing methods, which has pervaded different sectors of society and will have a primary impact on the several industries. The educational sector is one of these fields in which intelligent techniques have been widely used. Intelligent computing techniques provide artificial intelligence, embedded systems like robots, and facilities with human-related capabilities such as learning, adaptability, decision making and cognition, respectively. Various intelligent techniques can be used in the educational field to provide several advantages to students such as educational software can be modified to the requirement of students, it can summit out places where courses require developing, students could get extra support from intelligent trainers, intelligent technical driven courses can provide students and teachers cooperative feedback and many more. Different technical applications like artificial intelligence (AI), machine learning, learning analytics (LA) and data mining (DM), Internet of Things (IoT), etc., are associated with the education system in this modern age (Chen et al. 2020).

5.1 Artificial Intelligence Approach

AI develops as a brain of a supercomputer, a processor with huge processing abilities, including adaptive performance like insertion of sensors and extra abilities that allow all kind of human-related functional and cognition abilities and certainly advances the interaction of supercomputers with humans. Undeniably, unusual motion pictures have been done to showcase the capabilities of artificial intelligence, such as in smart buildings which include the ability to deal with air eminence in a building and temperatures which depend on the logical mood of the residents of the space. Particularly in the field of education, a massive application of AI found that is above the traditional concept of artificial intelligence as a mainframe to incorporate embedded computer models. Artificial intelligence can computerize basic actions in education like grading. It is possible for teachers to computerize grading for almost all types of multiple choices and an automatic score of student script may not be distant behind. During a pandemic, apart from grading, AI has been used and showcased its efficiency more on digital or online teaching and learning, respectively.

5.2 Machine Learning Approach

The central part of ML is the data discovery method; the parsing procedure relied on sampling information known as training data, producing meaningful prototypes and controlled knowledge. Machine learning acts as a gateway for students to generate suggestions. It controls all kinds of achievements information, objectives and preferences of scholars. Also, it helps the tutors to perceive the ideas of the students (Kučak et al. 2018). In specific, for student evaluation, image detection, as well as a forecast of ML, can be utilized for grading student assignments and exams. Further, the sub-field of ML, deep learning draws much interest among the students. This application is extensively used in decision tree learning method, clustering, inductive logic programming, reinforcement learning (RL), and Bayesian networks. Khattar et al. (2020) studied the effects of the catastrophic pandemic on learning styles, actions and mental well-being of Young Indian scholars by using an ML approach. The major aim of the study was to understand the lockdown effect on the mental health of young students of classes 11th and 12th who were registered in colleges as well as universities in undergraduate and postgraduate courses respectively. The outcomes of the proposed study have confirmed that the learners feel that online learning education can enhance classroom education but it cannot replace classroom surroundings and the face-to-face communications.

5.3 Learning Analytics Framework

Learning analytics is a knowledge domain model which concentrates on features and data objects from the learner. It is a novel idea of technology as ML being useful to a non-scientific world of education. The main reason behind adopting this technique is only for the individual learner's requirement and capability, i.e., overruling with students at threat or presenting feedback and instructional substance (Tsai and Dragan 2017). Mostly, it utilizes ML related methods like data image, study sciences and semantics. The next idea of learning analytics is to elevate the difficulties faced by arts, literature, interpersonal skills and others domain. However, it requires an exact form of learning applicable to all kinds of courses. During the pandemic, learning analytics has majorly utilized and incorporated advanced methods to support learning for tutors, learners, institutions and administrators.

5.4 Data Mining Approach

Educational data mining (EDM) used for methodical and automatic responses from students. AI-based EDM aspires for increasing intrinsic association policies and presenting data objects to learners to convene their private requirements. For example, grading and demographic feature data of students' can be examined through a small number of written assignments (https://www2.deloitte.com). It can also be attained by an ML regression technique which can be utilized to forecast the upcoming performance of students. Besides, DM is considered as a commanding tool to progress the learning procedure and information mastery, directing to an enhanced perceptive of the learning condition and students. DM can be observed as pattern detection and prognostic modelling employed in extorting unknown knowledge, which permits teachers to make alterations to progress curriculum growth in the educational method.

5.5 Integration of Internet of Things and Machine Learning

Despite the global physical shutting of educational establishments due to this pandemic, the process of learning was not disturbed. Learning management models and online tools for digital association guaranteed a secure distance and stability of learning actions. On the other hand, the fast transition to isolated learning in electronic surroundings has produced various challenges in higher education. Ilieva and Yankova (2020) have proposed a novel model for remote learning in advanced education based on the IoT method. The model gathered detailed data, assists the option of the most suitable learning materials, and is also able to remove the corruption during examinations. The benefits of projected IoT framework for the distance learning in electronic surroundings such as the capacity of students' behavioural signs are acquired from a distance; teachers immediately collected data regarding every student and their group and taken rapid decisions; assembled information is practised immediately and may be evaluated further from cloud records. Freitas et al. (2020) has presented an IoT model on forecasting dropout with ML techniques such as support vector machine (SVM), decision tree (DT), logistic regression (LR), K-nearest neighbours (KNN), multilayer perceptron (MLP) and deep learning (DL) based on socioeconomic information. The authors have introduced the computerized prediction procedure by a technique capable of attaining data that would be complex and time overriding for individuals to attain, adding to a new precise prediction. With the initiation of IoT, it is probable to make a highly competent and flexible device for developing management related concerns, which can provide a forecast of dropout of new learners entering into higher education, permitting modified follow-up to learners to overturn a possible failure.

6 Critical Analysis

This section is dedicated to critically analysing some of the important factors such as the statistics of pros and cons of the effect on the online education, number of educational institute adopted the online education, the impact of intelligent approaches to deal such scenario and adverse effects of online education.

6.1 Statistics of Benefited and not Benefited Students in Covid-19

The spread of pandemic has directed to the closure of educational sectors all over the globe. This hardened the awareness of institutions of higher education to contract with a disaster that requires the assistance of superior methodologies comprising software as well as hardware to allow efficient online learning. Such closure fastens the growth of online education so that learning won't be interrupted. Most of the institutions have become attracted to how to teach course content digitally, connect learners and carry out assessments. Therefore, pandemic while being a risk to people has developed institutions to spend in online learning. Online learning models are web-related software for dispensing, training and organization lessons over the Internet (Mukhtar et al. 2020). It engages the execution of innovations in technology to lead, plan and distribute the learning content and to aid mutual communication amid students as well as faculty. They enclose features like polls, quizzes, whiteboards, chat rooms, surveys and discussion forums that permit tutors and students to talk online and share training materials and contents. These can present creative and suitable ways to attain learning goals. Faculty believed that online learning facilitated guarantee remote learning, and it was convenient, and students could expediently access tutors and learning materials. It also condensed the use of travelling sources and additional costs. It relieved administrative assignments such as footage of lectures and marking presence. Both the students as well as teachers had an outlook that the modalities of online learning had encouraged learner centeredness during the pandemic situation. Even though most individuals still consider conventional universities as the greatest way to attain knowledge, online learning confirms to be a great substitute. Students can learn in their time and particularly for free. It signifies an immense way to learn many areas and to improve the stage of self-motivation. Online learning is so efficient since students can complete their work quickly, and there is additional time left for discovering a job. The online stage might be the only method to reach students during a pandemic, but the digital medium approaches with its individual confront. Few students and teachers existing in distant areas are facing complexity due to low internet and slow connectivity issues.

Remote areas were badly hit due to online learning during a pandemic. Highlighting India's online divide, deprived connectivity, and deficiency of smart tools is confirming an annoyance for many students. Major respondents from remote areas do not have sources that support online classes. A few more challenges faced by students due to online learning's includes: incapability to concentrate on screens, technical issues like poor Internet connection, sense of isolation where there will be no live interaction with their students, peers, as well as teachers, no proper teaching training, management of screen time which became one of the huge considerations of online learning's, server issues and many more. According to the students as well as tutors, online learning is an efficient source of guiding and learning since the majority of them decided upon the detail that this aids in remote learning with simple management and convenience along with less use of source and time. Despite the time limit, students can effortlessly access the learning objects. Both the teachers and students observed incompetence to educate psychomotor skills, source intensiveness, and mishandled modesty in sessions as restrictions of online learning. According to the survey in (https://www.qs.com), several steps and measures are taken to manage the educational curriculum in higher education institutions (Fig. 1). The outcome of this survey indicates that many respondents are willing to switch over their course to online mode.

By considering the professors as respondents in an online survey (https://unibuc.ro), more than 60% of respondents expressed that they got technical help to give lectures in online mode during the coronavirus pandemic in Romania. However, nearly 25% of the respondents didn't get any support for online instruction as illustrated in Fig. 2.

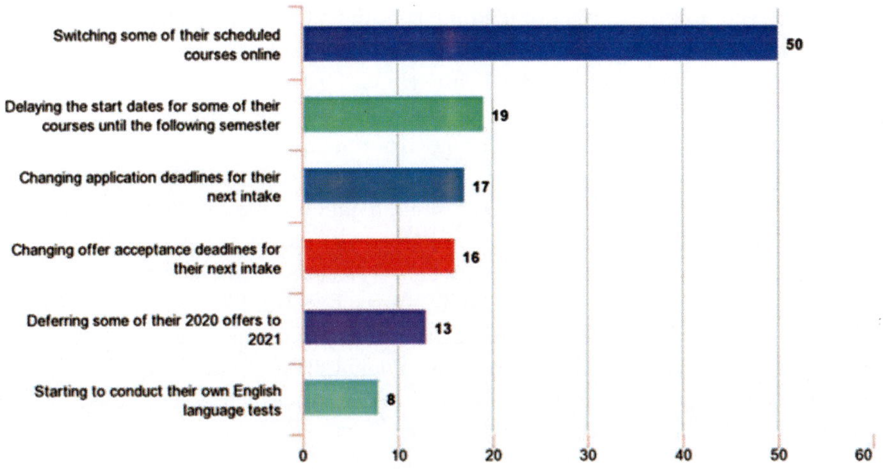

Fig. 1 Changing of different schedules during COVID- 19 *Source* SPSS output, compiled by authors, using secondary data, from Crawford, Joseph, et al. 2020

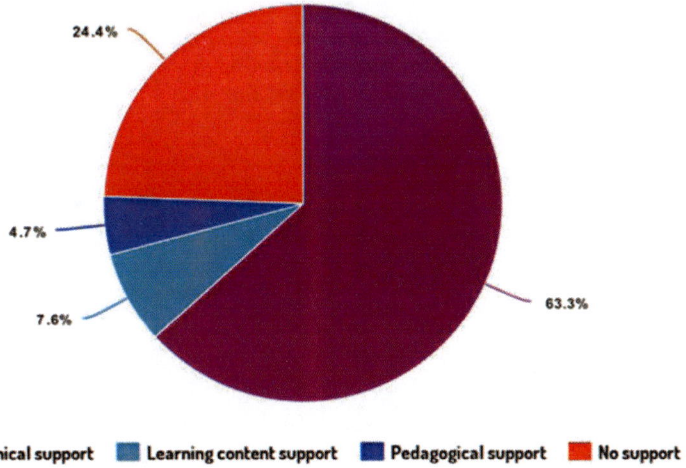

Fig. 2 Support received by professors for online education in Romania *Source* SPSS graphical output, compiled on secondary data, by authors

6.2 *Percentage of Educational Institute Adopted Online Method*

Schools, colleges, institutes, private tutors are faced with confront of upholding the stability of learning as the risk of educational institutes shutting extensions was imminent. The simple and instant solution is to perform online education for educational institutes remotely by utilizing various digital resources. Online learning appeared as a secure and feasible option for learning continuity as pandemic twisted worlds of personal as well as professional into ups and downs. Worldwide online learning was showed huge growth during the pandemic (Imed 2020). USA, India, China, South Korea and the UK have been recognized to spend most in E-learning and the market share of the majority of E-learning arrives from the content linked digital learning products. According to a survey, more than 50% of graduate scholars in the US got their online college stage learning to present an enhanced learning experience than offline education. Learning experience platforms continued to play a vital role in presenting adapted online learning experience. According to another survey in the USA, it was found having more than 60% of students utilized mobile gadgets to complete all the course-related activities. Besides, higher education has also had a drastic effect on the pandemic. It was estimated that the pandemic's result will cause 6 months to 5 years of interruption. It is forecasted that there will be around 25% chances to reject in enrolment of higher educations.

Kantar Media (2021) surveyed education issues in G7 countries due to COVID-19 in March 2020, where around 4595 people participated. Almost 30% of the participants are from different countries like France, Canada, Great Britain, Germany, Italy, Japan and the USA, who are very much concerned about their education (Fig. 3).

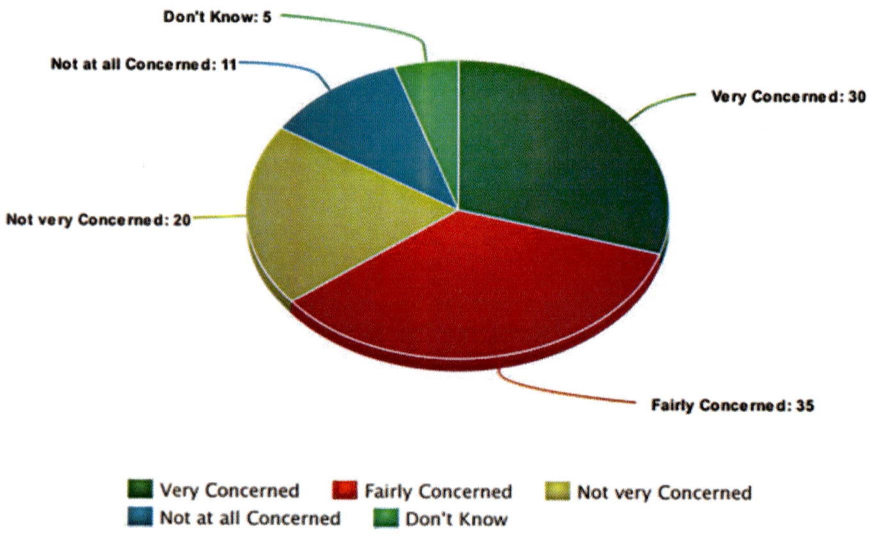

Fig. 3 View and concern of various respondents on education *Source* SPSS graphical output, compiled on secondary data, by authors

6.3 Role of Intelligent Computing Approaches in Developing Online Learning Models

School walls around the globe have been shut for some months to hold the spread of the COVID-19 epidemic. Throughout this disaster, we have observed an absurd quantity of large-scale efforts to utilize technology in carrying of distance learning. At a similar time, this disaster has uncovered confronts for tools in education, with many imbalances starting at the deficiency of access to computers as well as the Internet. Due to this far-reaching effect, the COVID-19 has provided us enormous imminent into how the function of technology can thoroughly transfer to achieve 1.6 billion learners and how to adjust education procedures in difficult times. Digital innovation in education allows us to discover new solutions not only to what the public learns but also to know when, how and where they study. Besides, digital technology can assist improve the teacher's role. Accessible digital learning methods can move extreme ahead of mere teaching. Authorized by intelligent computing techniques, these models can also scrutinize how students learn. Also, they can determine what type of tasks and thoughts interests them mainly, and what type of issues they find dull or hard. These methods can then acclimatize the learning procedure to hold the learning styles of individual students.

From the intelligent computing techniques, IoT is a novel model designed to augment connectivity among computer methods, quickly assembling its approach into classrooms in ways nowhere before anticipated. IoT developed the system of education and takes a complete lot of additional value to the physical education surroundings and controlled learning. Smart schools have services that function smoothly with extremely modified learning techniques. The physical methodology that strengthens this can make utilization of networks as well as Wi-Fi to send and receive information, directions and learning materials. One of the major ways that the teaching method is altering today is with the interaction of IoT learning models. Learning is not merely restricted to old textbooks. Most of the course books that we currently utilize are online and instructors can connect students in the classroom surroundings by offering a series of extra materials, reviews, videos and assorted interactive knowledge experiences with brilliant IoT software. During the pandemic time, the technology of IoT was used creatively and allowed students as well as tutors to present videos, enhanced quality images, communicative whiteboard style sources and many additional learning materials. Students were capable of taking notes digitally without losing them. So, eBooks played a vital role during online classes. Students complete their works on the same device. Similarly, many advanced technologies have showcased their effectiveness while earning online. Due to intelligent techniques, numerous types of management types of equipment were utilized to create new resources for student learning. One of the finest usages of IoT is that it can present learning where it is required at any time it is desired. Advanced knowledge enables tutors to observe the exact growth of any of the learners in the classroom. Some of the schools made pre-recorded live statements for various disaster situations. IoT has a deep impact on the educational sector, especially during a pandemic, with optimistic alterations for the upcoming future. Not only is studying faster but also became more expedient with improved consumption of resources. We are now belonging to an even extra protected world.

6.4 Adverse Effect of Online Education Method

As it is quite obvious that the pandemic has drastically disturbed the overall educational sector with the sudden imposing of shutting schools, so, the major claim was already losing its significance. Online learning is persuasive because of some reasons during a pandemic. One can obtain information staying at home and can preserve social hostility. The spread of COVID-19 can be minimized. It offers highly efficient learning surroundings. It offers to balance interactive support that permits students to study. It offers favourable scheduling. It is obtainable in any place, student can attend easily anywhere with an Internet connection. Even though online education methods have played a crucial role in education sectors like enhancement of Child's interaction with their parents to talk about their future, proper communication with parent and teachers as well, giving access to a huge library of digital resources like PDFs, test papers, digital manual books, etc., and provide entertainment by offering innovative techniques to play while they learn, endorse isolated learning, cost-effective, portability, sustainability, real-time performance report through E-learning procedures and live streaming lectures with current time doubt solving and many more. Besides these advantages, there are few major drawbacks to online learning, and these issues are frequently pushed away in online discussions.

Some of the issue of online learning includes limitation in the online student feedback, social isolation due to E-learning, need of strong motivation along with time controlling skills, deficiency of communication skill enhancement in online students, finding difficulty in preventing cheating while online exams conduct, online teachers directs to concentrate on theory than practical, lack of direct live communication (face-to-face interaction), online education was restricted to certain disciplines, not accessible to the computer illiterate population, and deficiency of quality as well as accreditation assurance in online education, etc. Besides, there are some demerits of online learning. Not every student has the essential knowledge, ability, and possessions to remain secure online. Spending additional time on effective platforms can depart students susceptible to online sexual exploitation. Students from low-income families are more possible to suffer throughout online learning as they might not pay for high pace Internet connection. It broadens space amid privileged as well as unprivileged learners. It may escort to idleness with some children's for being at their residence and may be short of self-discipline. The environment of a face-to-face gathering is mislaid. The safety of personal information may be negotiating as one can easily hack the digital gadgets with no newest software renewals and antivirus programmes, respectively.

7 Conclusion

COVID-19 has disrupted the face-to-face teaching method and created several problems in both teachings and learning. The adaptation of online learning as an alternative measure has adversely affected the students, faculty, support staff and administrators. It became a challenge for the academician and learner of every stage to adopt the virtual platform for gaining knowledge. The pandemic has created considerable challenges for higher education. The wide impacts of the virus have carried out and measured the dexterity of higher education across the globe, for the preparation of new curricula, rethinking the new age technologies and more so created an opportunity for virtual education. Even though we all reallocated to online education and the usage of digital materials, many tutors and students were not ready for this unexpected switch to complete online learning. Remote learning does not constantly permit teachers to create adjustments and hold students, as they would act in the class. As a consequence, students can get the online learning resources either too easy or too difficult, which could guide to disconnection and a lessening in learning results. Another difficulty refers to the reality that online classes cannot manage with thousands of students that try to connect discussions. Also, online learning can be hard, if it is destined for regulation that involves practice. It has been witnessed in various situations that, physical presence and appearance has been proved as the best way for teaching and learning. However, it is true that this pandemic has given us an alternative (yet advance) mode of teaching and learning.

References

Al-Maroof, Rana Saeed, et al. 2020. Fear from COVID-19 and technology adoption: the impact of Google Meet during Coronavirus pandemic. *Interactive Learning Environments*: 1–16. https://doi.org/10.1080/10494820.2020.1830121.

Beech, Nic, and Frederik Anseel. 2020. COVID-19 and its impact on management research and education: Threats, opportunities and a manifesto. *British Journal of Management* 31 (3): 447. 10.1111%2F1467-8551.12421.

Burns, Ryan. 2020. A COVID-19 panacea in digital technologies? Challenges for democracy and higher education. *Dialogues in Human Geography* 10 (2): 246–249. 10.1177%2F2043820620930832.

Chen, Lijia, Pingping Chen, and Zhijian Lin. Artificial intelligence in education: A review. *IEEE Access* 8. https://doi.org/10.1109/ACCESS.2020.2988510.

Crawford, Joseph, et al. 2020. COVID-19: 20 countries' higher education intra-period digital pedagogy responses. *Journal of Applied Learning & Teaching* 3 (1): 1–20. https://doi.org/10.37074/jalt.2020.3.1.7.

Daniel, John. 2020. Education and the COVID-19 pandemic. *Prospects* 49 (1): 91–96. https://doi.org/10.1007/s11125-020-09464-3.

Dong, Chuanmei, Simin Cao, and Hui Li. 2020. Young children's online learning during COVID-19 pandemic: Chinese parents' beliefs and attitudes. *Children and Youth Services Review* 118: 105440.https://doi.org/10.1016/j.childyouth.2020.105440.

Freitas, Francisco A. da S., et al. 2020. IoT system for school dropout prediction using machine learning techniques based on socioeconomic data. *Electronics* 9 (10): 1613. https://doi.org/10.3390/electronics9101613.

Gaur, Uma, et al. 2020. Challenges and opportunities of preclinical medical education: COVID-19 crisis and beyond. *SN Comprehensive Clinical Medicine*: 1–6. https://doi.org/10.1007/s42399-020-00528-1.

https://www2.deloitte.com/cn/en/pages/technology-media-and-telecommunications/articles /development-of-ai-based-education-in-china.html/accessed on 13th January 2021.

Hammond, David, et al. 2020. Undergraduate medical education and Covid-19: Engaged but abstract. *Medical Education Online 25* (1): 1781379. https://doi.org/10.1080/10872981.2020.1781379.

https://unibuc.ro/. Accessed on 13th January 2021.

https://www.kantarmedia.com/. Accessed on 25th January 2021.

https://www.qs.com/. Accessed on 3rd January 2021.

Iivari, Netta, Sumita Sharma, and Leena Ventä-Olkkonen. 2020. Digital transformation of everyday life–How COVID-19 pandemic transformed the basic education of the young generation and why information management research should care? *International Journal of Information Management* 55. https://doi.org/10.1016/j.ijinfomgt.2020.102183.

Ilieva, Galina, and Tania Yankova. 2020. IoT in distance learning during the COVID-19 pandemic. *TEM Journal* 9 (4): 1669–1674.

Imed Bouchrika. 2020. 50 online education statistics: 2020 data on higher learning & corporate training. guide2research.

Iyengar, Radhika. 2020. Education as the path to a sustainable recovery from COVID-19. *Prospects* 49 (1): 77–80. https://doi.org/10.1007/s11125-020-09488-9.

Iyer, Parvati, Kalid Aziz, and David M. Ojcius. 2020. Impact of COVID-19 on dental education in the United States. *Journal of Dental Education* 84 (6): 718–722. https://doi.org/10.1002/jdd.12163.

Jena, Pravat Kumar. 2020a. Impact of pandemic COVID-19 on education in India. *International Journal of Current Research (IJCR)* 12. https://doi.org/10.24941/ijcr.39209.07.2020.

Jena, Pravat Kumar. 2020b. Online learning during lockdown period for covid-19 in India. *International Journal of Multidisciplinary Educational Research (IJMER)* 9.

Kerres, Michael. 2020. Against all odds: Education in Germany coping with Covid-19. *Postdigital Science and Education* 2 (3): 690–694. https://doi.org/10.1007/s42438-020-00130-7.

Khattar, Anuradha, Priti Rai Jain, and S. M. K. Quadri. 2020. Effects of the disastrous pandemic COVID 19 on learning styles, activities and mental health of young Indian students-a machine learning approach. In *2020 4th International Conference on Intelligent Computing and Control Systems (ICICCS)*. IEEE. https://doi.org/10.1109/ICICCS48265.2020.9120955.

Kim, Jinyoung. 2020. Learning and teaching online during Covid-19: Experiences of student teachers in an early childhood education practicum. *International Journal of Early Childhood* 52 (2): 145–158. https://doi.org/10.1007/s13158-020-00272-6.

Kučak, Danijel, Vedran Juričić, and Goran Đambić. 2018. Machine learning in education-a survey of current research trends. *Annals of DAAAM & Proceedings* 29.

Kumar, Sandeep, et al. 2020. Social economic impact of COVID-19 outbreak in India. *International Journal of Pervasive Computing and Communications*. https://doi.org/10.1108/IJPCC-06-2020-0053.

la Velle, Linda, et al. 2020. Initial teacher education in England and the Covid-19 pandemic: challenges and opportunities. *Journal of Education for Teaching 46* (4): 596–608. https://doi.org/10.1080/02607476.2020.1803051.

Mishra, Lokanath, Tushar Gupta, and Abha Shree. 2020. Online teaching-learning in higher education during lockdown period of COVID-19 pandemic. *International Journal of Educational Research Open* 1: 100012.https://doi.org/10.1016/j.ijedro.2020.100012.

Morin, Karen H. 2020. Nursing education after COVID-19: Same or different?: 3117–3119. https://doi.org/10.1111/jocn.15322.

Mukhtar, Khadijah, et al. 2020. Advantages, limitations and recommendations for online learning during COVID-19 pandemic era. *Pakistan Journal of Medical Sciences 36 .COVID19-S4*: S27. 10.12669%2Fpjms.36.COVID19-S4.2785.

Muthuprasad, T., et al. 2021. Students' perception and preference for online education in India during COVID-19 pandemic. *Social Sciences & Humanities Open* 3 (1): 100101.https://doi.org/10.1016/j.ssaho.2020.100101.

Mutton, Trevor. 2020. Teacher education and Covid-19: Responses and opportunities for new pedagogical initiatives: 439–441. https://doi.org/10.1080/02607476.2020.1805189.

Ozili, Peterson K. 2020. Covid-19 pandemic and economic crisis: The Nigerian experience and structural causes. *Journal of Economic and Administrative Sciences*. https://doi.org/10.1108/JEAS-05-2020-0074.

Rafi, Aboobacker Mohammed, Pulikkottil Raphael Varghese, and Praveenlal Kuttichira. 2020. The pedagogical shift during COVID 19 pandemic: Online medical education, barriers and perceptions in central Kerala. *Journal of Medical Education and Curricular Development* 7: 2382120520951795. 10.1177%2F2382120520951795.

Ratten, Vanessa, and Paul Jones. 2020. Covid-19 and entrepreneurship education: Implications for advancing research and practice. *The International Journal of Management Education*: 100432. https://doi.org/10.1016/j.ijme.2020.100432.

Sangster, Alan, Greg Stoner, and Barbara Flood. 2020. Insights into accounting education in a COVID-19 world. *Accounting Education* 29 (5): 431–562. https://doi.org/10.1080/09639284.2020.1808487.

Toquero, Cathy Mae. 2020. Challenges and opportunities for higher education amid the COVID-19 pandemic: The Philippine context. *Pedagogical Research* 5 (4).

Tsai, Yi-Shan, and Dragan Gasevic. 2017. Learning analytics in higher education---challenges and policies: a review of eight learning analytics policies. In *Proceedings of the Seventh International Learning Analytics & Knowledge Conference*.

World o meter: https://www.worldometers.info/coronavirus/. Accessed on 3rd January 2021.

Zhao, Yong. 2020. COVID-19 as a catalyst for educational change. *Prospects* 49 (1): 29–33. https://doi.org/10.1007/s11125-020-09477-y.

Entrepreneurship Growth Studies at a Glance: A Meta-Analysis of 20 years' Ethiopian Firm Growth Studies

Mesaud Muhamed Hagos and Shikta Singh

1 Introduction

Growth of businesses is an important indicator growing economy Zhou and de Wit (2009, p. 3). Several researchers such as (Van Praag and Versloot 2007 and Audretschet al. 2006) strongly believed that economic growth of both developed and developing nations is droved by the establishment and growth of entrepreneurship in the countries. However, Baumol (1996) and Vivarelli, (2012) make a distinction between innovative and surviving firms' role. They argued that not all entrepreneurs contributed to an economy of developing countries. In such a case, innovative entrepreneurs who grow fast are presumed to contribute more in developing countries. Nevertheless, they also believe that survivalist firms can play a role of employment growth by hiring themselves and their family.

Consequently, the theme saying "firm growth drives the economy" has emerged as a leading idea among scholars and policymakers (Van Praag and Versloot 2007; Audretsch et al. 2006).

As a result, a large number entrepreneurial/firm growth studies have been and are emerging since the study by Gibrat's 1930s. Many researchers including such as Achtenhagen et al. (2010) considered study of firm growth as a way of providing

S. Singh
School of Management, KIIT Deemed to be University, Bhubaneswar, India

M. M. Hagos
School of Business and Economics, Department of Accounting and Finance, Semera University, Semera, Ethiopia

S. Singh (✉)
School of Management, Kalinga Institute of Industrial Technology, KIIT Deemed To Be University, Bhubaneswar, India
e-mail: shiktasingh@ksom.ac.in

R. N. Subudhi et al. (eds.), *Future of Work and Business in Covid-19 Era*,
Springer Proceedings in Business and Economics,
https://doi.org/10.1007/978-981-19-0357-1_24

all interested parties (policymakers, investors, and entrepreneurs) with required understanding of organization/business growth.

Different disciplines starting from the economics to finance from management to behavioral studies are among the major participants in the study of firm growth research (Zhou and de Wit 2009, p. 3).

Despite of the effort exerted by several researchers from various disciplines, firm growth study still remains inconclusive due to lack of comprehensive and integrated study (see Zhou and de Wit 2009) of firm growth determinants and variations in methodology difference, cultural, and environmental deviation of firms (Zhou and de Wit 2009).

Hence, the main objective of this review is to investigate major focus of firm growth studies in Ethiopia by studying Ethiopian firm growth studies over extended years.

2 Objectives

Generally, this review will try to evaluate firm growth studies in Ethiopia from the perspective of their focus of growth, their focus of size, and their coverage sample area. Thus, this review will try:

- To investigate focus area of Ethiopian firm growth measurement
- To identify the size, sector, and geographical area of Ethiopian firm growth studies and of firms
- To identify if any existing gap in Ethiopian firm growth for empirical research.

3 Review of Recent Studies in Ethiopia

In this subsection, we are going to discuss studies related to growth of firms in Ethiopia. Seyoum et al. (2016) investigated factors affect growth of micro- and small enterprises (MSEs) in Addis Ababa bole sub-city. The study has used a descriptive form of analysis, a chi-square test, and multivariate analysis. Result of his study depicts that trained owners, initial investment, being a service sector, being non-cooperative businesses have a positive impact on the growth of medium and large firms in Addis Ababa. However, the researchers try to measure growth of firms in terms of only employment growth. They did not see the effect of all the factors on other growth factors of firm's growth. Besides, the sample area is very limited which is only focused in one sub-city of the capital city. Another study by Bigsten and Gebreeyesus (2007) examines the relationships between firm growth and firm size, age, and labor productivity, in Ethiopia. The study used a panel data of manufacturing firms in Ethiopia. As a method of analysis, Bigsten and Gebreeyesus (2007) used linear regression to see the effect of size, age labor productivity, and other personality traits on the growth of firms similarly determined in terms of employment change like the study by Seyoum et al. (2016). The result shows that size of firms, age of firms, personal traits, and social aspect factors have a significant and negative effect on the employment measured growth of firms in Ethiopia. Only labor productivity was found a positive estimator of firms' growth according to the researchers.

A quantile regression Vs OLS regressions conducted on firms found in Addis Ababa by Garoma and Dijk (2015) regarding the determinants of success in small and micro-businesses shows that growth measured in terms of change in profit can be estimated by location of the firms, sector of the firm, social network of the firms, risk taking propensity of managers or owners of the firm, entrepreneurial orientation of the management. All these factors have been regressed against an alternative growth measured which is profit growth. The gap in this study is it is only focused on medium and large firms size-wise and on profit change growth measure-wise.

World Bank Enterprise Surveys of Ethiopia (2006 and 2011) and Kenya (2007 and 2013) by Lemi and Wright (2020) studied the significance of exports and foreign ownership in influencing firm-level efficiency. The study used a Cobb–Douglas production function of stochastic frontier analysis which is compared between the Ethiopian and Kenyan cases. Having exporting activity, having foreign ownership, and experience of managers were found positive determinants of firm-level efficiency in both countries. Among the variables employed to determine efficiency of firms, there have been few which specifically affect the efficiency of firms in one of the two countries. For instance, being smaller firms, having temporary employee for long time, and participating in innovation plaid a negative role in determining firm-level efficiency of Kenyan companies, whereas, experience of managers was negatively related with firm-level efficiency of firms in Ethiopia. This study focused on efficiency of firm rather than growth firms. On top of that, it did not see the social and behavioral aspects firm growth factors.

Another study by Nega and Desta (2014) tried to identify determinants of domestic private investment growth (measured in Capital and employment growth) in Mekele city. The data analysis has used a primary data using systematic random sampling, and an ordinary least square (OLS) regression model found that tax rate, incentives, finance, firm age, and firm size are negative determinants of investment growth. In contrast, interest rate, infrastructure, economic condition, and market access are significant and positive determinants of growth of firms measured in terms capital employed. The weakness of the study was its scope area which is Mekele city. The items were also only fourteen self-reported items. The study has not showed readers about the measures they take to tackle sector specific conditions.

Edjigu (2016) has conducted an investigation in to the determinants of growth and technical efficiency of Ethiopian manufacturing firms focusing on impact of finance and size of the firms. The study has used a panel data from 2000 to 2008 with system GMM method of analysis so that it can address endogeneity issues. The result from this study shows that small and young firms grow more rapidly than the old and big firms. Factors including leverage ratio, cash flow, internal finance, being smaller firms, ownership status, and legal status have been found positive indicators of growth and technical efficiency. On the other hand, leverage (borrowing), being a large firm, firm's asset value, labor quality, have been found a negative indicator of the service sectors' growth and technical efficiency. The gap in this study is it is merely focusing of the service sector and not trying to see the impact of social and behavioral factors in the model.

In an objective of identifying determinants of growth, investment, and innovation in the micro- and small enterprises, Tarfasa et al. (2016) conducted a survey of 300 firm-level data from Addis Ababa. From their ordinary least square (OLS), the researchers find that age of manager, being in the construction and manufacturing sectors, location (being in Yeka sub-city), having large number of skilled workers, being free from unregistered competitors, and having a business owned by association have found positive determinants of firm's growth. On the other hand, education level of managers, age of firms, start-up size, power outage, and access to finance have been found negative factors affecting growth firms in Addis Ababa. The limitation of the study was its focus merely on medium and large firms in the capital. Factors related to social and behavioral, environment, and firm-level variables have not been included in the study.

Abay et al. (2015) conducted a study examining owner-related factors affecting growth of MSEs. A semi-structured questionnaire of 160 random MSEs from a small city called Shire was distributed and collected as source of data. Using a binary logistic model, the researchers found that gender (being male owner) having education level above high school was found among the positive determinants of firm's growth. The study was focused on small business. The model was examined using only four factors. As a result, it fails to include different factors which are supposed major factors of firm growth. In a binary choice logit model by Tefera et al. (2013), a random of 178 MSEs from Mekele, a city in Northern Tigray, have been investigated to see the effect of four factors on the growth of the MSEs in the city. The result shows that employment size, start-up capital, gender (being male), initial investment, location, and sector of the firm have positive effect on the growth of small- and medium-size firms. The growth measure was only employment growth of small and medium firms. In addition to the luck of focus on large firms, the study focused only on Mekele area.

A multi-dimensional investigation studying success factors of micro-enterprise in the Addis Ababa's informal sector was conducted by Garoma and Van Dijk (2015) collecting a sample of 286 micro-enterprises from Addis Ababa city. Employing a quintile regression, the researchers found different success factors determining growth of firms. Internal locus of control, technical and managerial training, location of the firm, sector of the firm, social networks, demographic factors have been found positive indicators of firm's growth measured in terms of employment growth. As positive indicators, entrepreneurship orientation, and self-efficacy have been identified in the study. On the other hand, risk taking propensity, location of firms, sector of firms, entrepreneurship orientation, and social network size have been identified as indicators of profit growth. The attention of the study was only on the informal sector.

4 Methodology

We have reviewed 102 firm growth studies from 20 years' literature of Ethiopian business growth researches. To include a study in our analysis, we have used some selection criteria. The main criteria were finding the journal articles from at least scholastic research databases like Google scholar, EBESCC, ELISEVIER, WILLEY, JSTOR. Some words and phrases presumed most used in the business growth literature were also used in the searching stage of the review. The phrases were: firm growth in Ethiopia, entrepreneurship growth in Ethiopia, business growth in Ethiopian and enterprise growth in Ethiopia, organization growth in Ethiopia. And, the search was going until no more studies regarding Ethiopian firms' growth were extracted from the research databases.

5 Results

The result from the extensive search emerged with 102 articles in 20 years' study years. Above most of the journal articles were collected from Google scholar. Only few of them were retrieved from the other reputable journals. Nonetheless, since the objective was to examine how firm growth study in Ethiopia is going, any journal article concerning Ethiopia and its constituent parts focusing in the growth terminologies and phrases taken from the literature were included in the review.

The result from a systematic study of firm Ethiopian entrepreneurial growth studies shows that firm grow study in the country starts since 1998. That is, when Mengistae (1998) conducted a research on the effect of age and size on firm growth and productive efficiency. Except for Mengistae's panel data-based study, no published firm growth study, before the year 2000 (see Table 1), was found in the databases of Elsevier, JSTOR, EBESCO, Springe, and Google scholar journals. From the year 2001 up to 2012, there are 32 entrepreneurial growth studies which are about.

As we can see in Fig. 1 or Table 1, around 68% of entrepreneurial studies in Ethiopia have been conducted in the early years 2013 up to 2018. This shows that researchers in Ethiopia recently are getting extensively in to the entrepreneurial growth study issue of economic and business literature.

Table 1 Study distribution among range of years

Years range	No. of studies	Percent
Before 2000	1	1
2001–2012	32	31
2013–2018	69	68
Total	102	100

Source Own calculation in SPSS

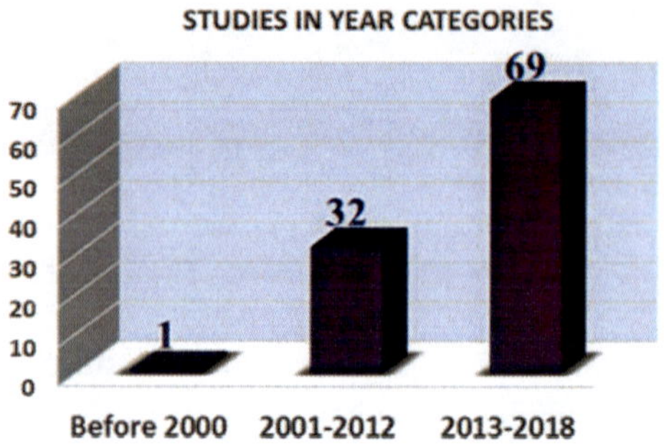

Fig. 1 Study distribution among range of years. *Source* Figure prepared in excel from SPSS result

Table 2 Growth measuring focus of the studies

Focus of studies	Frequency	Percent
Growth	25	25
Survival	8	8
Performance	29	28
Productivity	2	2
Efficiency	3	3
Others	35	34
Total	102	100

Source Own calculation on SPSS

Out of the total 102 studies, around 25% have focused on conventional growth measures, like: employment and sales growth. The rest are 8% on survival, 28% on performance, 2% on productivity, 3% on efficiency, and remaining on others group of entrepreneurial issues (see Table 2).

Figure 2 demonstrates the focus of entrepreneurial researchers in Ethiopian over 20 years starting little before the year 2000, in 1998 through the most of the recent studies in 2018. The front side bar graph with three columns (green columns) represents studies mainly focus on firm-level growth of business, whereas the back side

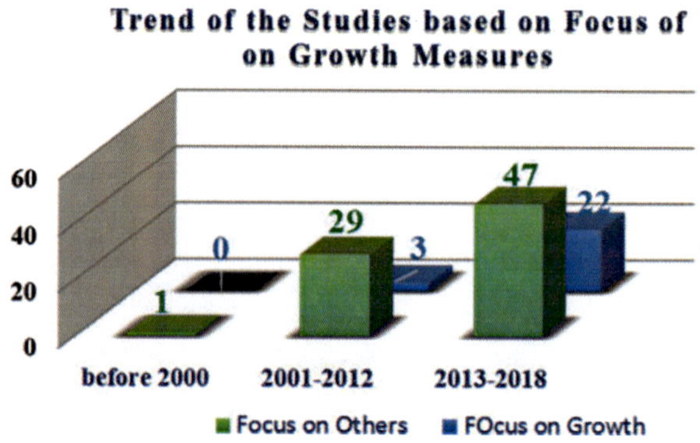

Fig. 2 Study distribution over years based on growth measure they used. *Source* Figure prepared in excel from SPSS result

of the bar graph represents studies which have focus on other entrepreneurial growth matters like performance and productivity (at micro-firm-level or macro-country level).

Accordingly, the focus of the first firm growth study in Ethiopia made in 1998 was analyzing panel data of manufacturing firms, focusing on performance measurement. In the years starting 2001 through 2012, out of 32 studies, only 3 have focused on growth, while the majority 29 studies have focused on other growth issues such as survival, performance, efficiency, productivity, and other measures other than the mostly used growth measures. Result of the review from the journal articles of early years, starting 2013–2018, shows that there are 22 and 47 entrepreneurial studies published focusing growth measures and other group measures, respectively.

Table 3 and Fig. 3 demonstrate about 73 out of hundred firm growth studies have been conducting their research on micro- and small enterprises (MSE). While 19% were focusing on small and medium enterprises (SME) only 7% of the studies have investigated about medium and large-scale enterprises (MLSE).

This indicates that except for 7%, the large part of entrepreneurship growth literature in Ethiopian focused on the micro- and small enterprises. The result supports the idea of Van Praag and Versloot (2007) which says 'researchers focus on entrepreneurship growth due to the believe that 'entrepreneurship derives economy'.'

Comparing the firm growth studies on MLSEs with that of the same studies on MSE and SME size of business, we tried to show the focus of researchers in what form of firm growth study they focus in. Consequently, as in Fig. 4 that is depicting

Table 3 Size focus of firm growth studies in Ethiopia

Firm size	No. of firms	Percent
MSE	73	73
SME	19	19
MLSE	7	7
All	1	1
Total	100	100

Source Own calculated in SPSS

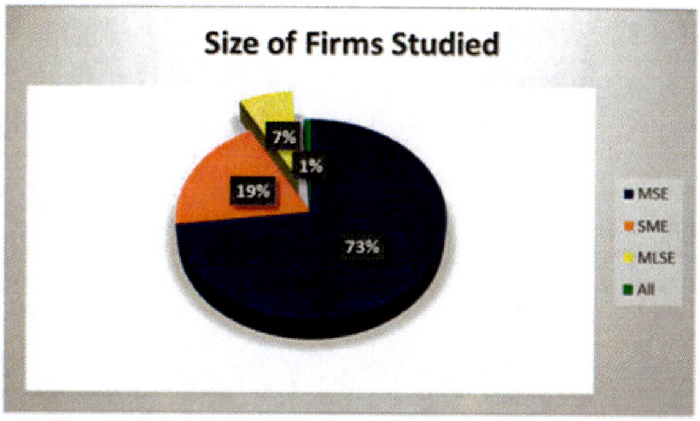

Fig. 3 Size focus of firm growth studies in Ethiopia. *Source* Figure prepared in Excel from SPSS result

Fig. 4 Study distribution based on focus of growth and firm size. *Source* Table from SPSS bar graph from excel

Ethiopian firm growth studies are more concentrated on non-MLSEs primarily, MSEs. Out of the seven studies focusing on MLSE size businesses, only one study has focused on growth rather than other growth-related (efficiency, productivity, performance….) studies.

The other major part of the studies (95 out 102) were conducted on non-MLSE. Of these, only 24 (see Fig. 4) have shown their interest in growth of the firms. Generally, large (77 out of 102) portion of firm growth studies in Ethiopia focused on non-growth aspects of connoisseurship growth studies.

We have also tried to investigate Ethiopian entrepreneurial growth studies based on their focus on sectors. The result demonstrated in Table 4 depicts that 76% of the studies have concentrated on manufacturing, 3% on merchandising, 7% on financial institution, and the remaining 14% have focused either on other group of sectors or not specified (Fig. 5).

As can be seen in Table 5, this review tried to look into the geographical coverage

Fig. 5 Sector distribution of studies. *Source* Figure prepared in Excel from SPSS result

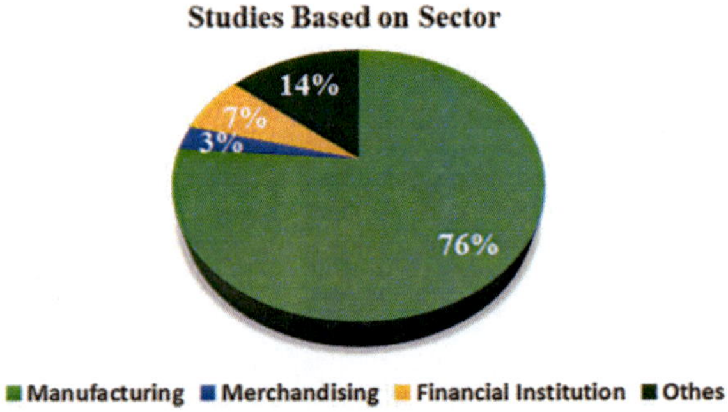

Table 4 Sector distribution of studies

Sector studied	No. of studies	Percent
Manufacturing	77	76
Merchandising	3	3
Financial institution	7	7
Others	14	14
Total	101	100

Source Own calculation in SPSS

Table 5 Geographical coverage of the studies

Geographical scope	Frequency	Percent
Ethiopian	15	15
Addis Ababa	13	13
Others cities and towns	74	73
	102	100

Source Own calculation in SPSS

of the firm growth studies in Ethiopia.

The result shows that 15% of the studies cover country-wise areas. Out of 102 studies in Ethiopia, 13% have targeted the capital city (Addis Ababa), while the majority 74% have focused on the regional and district-level cities and towns of the country. This indicates that little attention is given for firms' growth studies in Addis Ababa which hosts more than forty percent of Ethiopian business in number and more than seventy percent in value.

Selecting an eleven articles, presumed more comprehensive than the other 102 articles, we have tried also to compliment the review with somehow more detailed issues regarding the firm growth studies in Ethiopia. As can be seen in Table 6 the review is demonstrated by author, objectives investigated, methodology used, findings come up, gaps emerged from. The result from the additional review supports the result from the main review above. It shows that all the studies have limitations either in related to their focus (on growth measurement, firm size, firms' sector, study area coverage) or in conceptual and methodological limitations (like using panel data which can provide limited scope regarding variables). Consequently, these observed limitations lead to the generalization that firm growth studies in Ethiopia did not touch all issues of firm growth comprehensively and inclusively.

6 Conclusion and Recommendation

Generally, the review of Ethiopian entrepreneurial studies tried to analyze about five area focuses. Firstly, it tried to see how firm growth studies have been emerging over the last 20 years. The result shows that starting from 1998, the study of entrepreneurial growth is growing at a growing rate. This indicates that the research area is getting growing interest among researchers from time to time.

Secondly, this review analyzed focus area of the researches. Accordingly, the result shows that majority of the studies have focused on non-firm-level growth measures. Rather, they concentrated on performance, survival, efficiency, conductivity, and other macroeconomic contribution of entrepreneurship for country growth.

Thirdly, the review tried to evaluate size focus of entrepreneurship growth researchers in Ethiopia specifically comparing the size with focus of the on growth aspect of entrepreneurship growth. As a result, above 95% of the studies focus on enterprises below the size of medium enterprises of which 73% are micro- and small business. This shows that little focus was given to the large-scale business studies (only 7% of the reviewed journals).

The forth part we discussed in this study was about sector focus of the studies in Ethiopian entrepreneurship growth studies. Consequently, the result shows that majority (75%) of studies focus in manufacturing sector of firms in Ethiopia. This indicates that little attention is given to other sectors like trade, construction, and other service sectors.

Lastly, the review tried to analyze geographical coverage of the studies. And, it is found that most studies conducted on small districts and towns of Ethiopia represent small share of the business environment. Addis Ababa, a center of trade in Ethiopian, has got little attention by the entrepreneurship growth researchers.

Generally, even though entrepreneurship growth studies in the Ethiopia are emerging over the last 20 years increasingly, their comprehensiveness is in terms of growth measures, firms' size, firms' sectors, geographical scope. Hence, it could be concluded that firm growth studies in Ethiopia are progressing in terms of number, while it has forgotten the inclusiveness and comprehensiveness of the firm growth studies.

Thus, it will be beneficial for stakeholders if firm growth studies in the future in the Ethiopia try to make their concern about comprehensiveness and inclusiveness. Rather than conducting redundant studies only by changing geographical areas, it would be better if studies in the future try to make their target area coverage more wider, if the conduct comparative growth studies on different sectors and size of businesses and above all if they try to satisfy different interest of stakeholders. Trying to satisfy stakeholders in the firm growth study area is possible when firm growth studies can give each interested parties in the area, a comparable insight in to the growth measures and enable them to see different alternatives of growth with their most influencing factors. This will give the stakeholders more comprehensive view and wide choice for the informed decision.

References

Abay, Haftom Haile, Fisseha Girmay Temanu, and Araya Hagos Gebreegziabher. Owner factors affecting the growth of micro and small enterprises (Mses) in Ethiopia: A case study in shire Indaselassie Town, Tigray. *CLEAR International Journal of Research in Commerce & Management* 6 (5).

Achtenhagen, Leona, Lucia Naldi, and Leif Melin. 2010. "Business growth"—Do practitioners and scholars really talk about the same thing?. *Entrepreneurship theory and practice* 34 (2): 289–316.

Audretsch, David B., Max C. Keilbach, and Erik E. Lehmann. 2006. *Entrepreneurship and Economic Growth*. Oxford University Press.

Baumol, William J. 1996. Entrepreneurship: Productive, unproductive, and destructive. *Journal of Business Venturing* 11 (1): 3–22.

Bigsten, Arne, and Mulu Gebreeyesus. 2007. The small, the young, and the productive: Determinants of manufacturing firm growth in Ethiopia. *Economic Development and Cultural Change* 55 (4): 813–840.

Edjigu, Habtamu Tesfaye. 2016. Firm growth and technical efficiency in Ethiopia: The role of firm size and finance. *International Journal of Economics and Finance* 8 (10): 1–13.

Garoma, Belay File, and Meine Peter Van Dijk. 2015. Determinants of microenterprise success in the Addis Ababa's urban informal sector: a multidimensional analysis. In *International Interdisciplinary Business-Economics Advancement Conference*.

Lemi, Adugna, and Ian Wright. 2020. Exports, foreign ownership, and firm-level efficiency in Ethiopia and Kenya: An application of the stochastic frontier model. *Empirical Economics* 58 (2): 669–698.

Nega, Abraha Teklebirhan, and Tesfatsion Sahlu Desta. 2014. Determinants of domestic private investment firm growth in Ethiopia: A case study in Mekelle City, Tigray. *CLEAR International Journal of Research in Commerce & Management* 5 (6).

Seyoum, Arega, Muhammed Aragie, and Daniel Tadesse. 2016. Growth of micro and small enterprises in Addis Ababa City Administration: A study on selected micro and small enterprise in Bole Sub City.

Tarfasa, Solomon, et al. 2016. *Determinants of growth of micro and small enterprises (MSEs), Empirical evidence from Ethiopia*. R4D Working Paper 2016/3, 2016.

Tefera, Habtamu, Aregawi Gebremichael, and Nigus Abera. 2013. Growth determinants of micro and small enterprises: Evidence from Northern Ethiopia. *Journal of Economics and Sustainable Development* 4 (9).

Van Praag, C. Mirjam, and Peter H. Versloot. 2007. What is the value of entrepreneurship? A review of recent research. *Small Business Economics* 29 (4): 351–382.

Vivarelli, Marco. 2012. Entrepreneurship in advanced and developing countries: A microeconomic perspective.

Zhou, Haibo, and Gerrit De Wit. 2009. Determinants and dimensions of firm growth. *SCALES EIM Research Reports (H200903)*.

Sociological Imagination to Responsibility: COVID-19 Calls for Reshaping Future World Order

Bishnuprasad Mohapatra

1 Introduction

The outbreak of coronavirus (COVID-19) in China at the end of 2019 has created history itself, being the first biodisaster that has cut across geographies, communities, and cultures. Countries worldwide have already used every possible mechanism like lockdown, shutdown, quarantine, border seal, physical distancing, strengthening health infrastructure and healthcare system, started vaccination, and welfare provision, to minimize the spread of COVID-19. Before the implementations of all these mechanisms, COVID-19 has already contaminated thousands and thousands of people worldwide. The daily rise of COVID-19 cases reveals that the virus it never looked whether you are from any particular community, group, caste, class, religion, race, gender, or any other stratified part of society while infecting. For COVID-19, all are equal and negatively affected from its inception to all segments of society. It has halted and adversely affected individuals' everyday lives, livelihood, community activities, and institutional functions worldwide and created social and humanitarian crises in society. It has also acted as a magnifying glass that exposes various pros and cons of the present state our society. So, to understand the problem of COVID-19 on individuals and society across the world and for possible solutions mechanisms, its time to grasp the actual problems and causes behind which the present society is trapped. So, to find out real reasons behind any individual and society troubles, C. W. Mills once had proposed a solution to develop a new quality of mind, i.e., sociological imagination, through which we can understand and examine the larger

B. Mohapatra (✉)
Ph.D. Scholar, Department of Sociology and Fellow, Global Center for Rural Studies, Utkal University, Odisha 751004, India
e-mail: bishnuprasad.soc@utkaluniversity.ac.in

R. N. Subudhi et al. (eds.), *Future of Work and Business in Covid-19 Era*,
Springer Proceedings in Business and Economics,
https://doi.org/10.1007/978-981-19-0357-1_25

context of the individuals and society problems. In this context, his idea of sociological imaginations finds its relevance today. Before explaining the COVID-19 through the sociological imagination lens, let us have a brief idea of the Mills perspective.

The book 'Sociological Imagination' was published in 1959 by Mills after drawing the miserable pictures of the then society through his experience of experiencing two World Wars, the Great Depression, and the Civil Rights Movements. In describing the dismal images, he has highlighted the new developments of imperialism replacing colonialism, exclusion of peoples in the democratic process, development of bureaucratic forms limiting democracy, and rise of power, authority, and violence in bureaucratic scope and forms (Mills 1959 cited in Staubmann 2021). Mills considered these are the social circumstances, which created individuals' troubles in society and made them victims without being knowledge about the structural problem in which they are trapped. Individuals went through troubles and considered it their fates or destiny without understanding the actual causes behind it, which are the social issues (Staubmann 2021). For Mills, the social issues that victimized the individuals are the larger social structure and society institutions that try to constrain the individual lives. It gradually turned into a perspective providing a lens to see how macrothings create history and affect our personal lives. Simply speaking, it establishes a strong connection between biographies (individual context) and history (social and historical context where the individuals live). The Mills's perspective primary aim is to understand the private troubles of individuals as social issues. His perspective works between the 'individual troubles of the milieu' and 'public issues of social structure,' (Mills 1959: 8) and how they relate to each other in the social structure. Since his perspective came out, no one directly experienced or understood his perspective in day-to-day life, and COVID-19 did that. Now, COVID-19 is not more an individual or any single country problem; instead, it is a problem for individuals worldwide. So, it does not only remain trouble of individual or biography of COVID-19 patients but instead becomes a social issue associated with different historical and social contexts around the globe–which transformed COVID-19 to become pandemic. So, the individual issues of COVID-19 cannot be understood without taking the macroissues of COVID-19, nor COVID-19 can be understood fully without capturing the impacts it has on the individuals. Further, COVID-19 has evaporated the rising individualism that was enveloping the individuals. It has given a clarion call for collective action to fight against the disaster. This collective fight has emerged as the great 'responsibility' Mills talks about. This can empower humanity in due course to fight against the present and the forthcoming pandemics of this sort. In this context, sociological imagination finds its relevance in the present society.

2 Sociological Imagination and COVID-19

The COVID-19 pandemic can be seen from micro- and macroaspects. An individual infected by COVID-19 spreads to other individuals and its milieu through the epidemiological way (De Graaf et al. 2017), in a microaspect. In the process of virus transformation, it takes epidemic form in that milieu and society. In macroelements, it is more developmental than epidemiological. George (2020), MacIntyre (2020), and Wells et al. (2020), in their respective papers, argued that besides the epidemiological character of virus spread, the social, economic, political, and cultural aspects of the vulnerable population need to be considered while understanding the factors for the spread of the virus. This development character of the virus spread mostly related to how a virus transmitted and contaminated other cities, regions or countries. Country and territory infected by COVID-19 spread to other countries and territories through cross-country developmental activities (Mohapatra 2020). In this course of action, the spread of the virus to other regions and the rise of the infected population worldwide, the World Health Organization (WHO) declared COVID-19 a pandemic. In this way, one territory or country's problem becomes a worldwide social issue. Whether COVID-19 is an epidemiological or developmental character in virus transformation, but when it is transferred from one individual, group, society, and country to others becomes a public issue, it does not remain an individual problem. Mills rightly pointed out that individual trouble is occurred 'within the character of the individual and within his immediate relations with others,' and the public issues are occurred rise above these individual and immediate environment and related to 'organization of many such milieu into the institutions of an historical society as a whole.' Accordingly, a COVID-19 patient is a biological entity whose issues lie with its immediate social setting, whereas COVID-19 as a pandemic is a historically social entity and lies with the larger historical and social structure. Thus, to reveal how COVID-19 problem arises and becomes a public issue, we need to understand the origin of coronavirus and how it relates to individual actions in the broader social–historical context and social structure.

Social scientists, particularly sociologists, believe that social issues or problems are created and recreated in the social structure (Hironimus-Wendt and Wallace 2009). The social issues arise because of the dysfunctional arrangements in the society itself (Hironimus-Wendt and Wallace 2009). So, the social issues result from historical dysfunctional arrangements over functional arrangements in the social structure over the period. In this context, if we look into the origin of coronavirus in China in late December 2019, we will find two broad postulates or arguments among the media and experts—Bio-weapon (Nie 2020) and Zoonotic disease (Kukreti 2020a). The conspiracy theory of Bio-weapon over the origin of COVID-19 from Chains laboratory by China is to some extent found false, speculative, and without proper evidence. So, the paper sticks to only the arguments of the zoonotic origin of COVID-19.

The postulate of Zoonotic disease over the origin of COVID-19 is found to be logical and important by the experts. It is logical and important because of its historicity of different epidemics and pandemics that the world had already experienced from time to time. Whether it is Spanish Flu (1918–20), Asian Flu (1957–58), or Hong Kong Flu (1968–70), or Severe Acute Respiratory Syndrome (SARS-2003) or Swine Flu (2009–10), or Middle East Respiratory Syndrome (2012), all these epidemics and pandemics are related to zoonotic disease (Kukreti 2020a, b). The coronavirus belongs to the familiar virus that has been linked to previous pandemics.

Major sources of these viruses are found among animals and get transferred to humans with exposure to animals and raise pandemics. The study conducted by Beyer et al. (2021) also reveals that bats are the likely origin of coronavirus. Bat species' diversification and richness in the coronavirus origin regions happened because of climate change in these regions. So, the authors claim that climate change and the rise of the coronavirus may have been a strong correlation, and climate change may have a potential factor for the origin of the virus. It is happening because of the imperfect relationship of humans with other natural creatures like animals, which is against the balance of the human–environment nexus. So, in Mills perspective, the COVID-19 issues are a structural problem rather than merely individual patient issues. It is a structural problem because the historical exploitation and imperfect relationship of the individuals with the wild animals and the natural environment are the reason for such zoonotic diseases. Narain (2020a) argued that the outbreak of such viruses is due to a '*dystopian relationship with the natural world*.' For a long, the households that depend on cultivation to husbanding wild animals for domestic uses have been transformed to commercialization with population growth. The crop yield and production of animal foods have grown deistically in industrial farms with genetic modifications to meet the demand. The rise of toxins and chemicals in food items and the growth of industrial farms are significant sources of diseases and contagion in the world. These activities practiced growing more foods and their weight to create more profit against natural structural order. The study reveals by the NRC committee of US (2009) that the manmade ecosystem takes control over the natural ecosystem of production and reproduction and has a higher risk for diseases. So, it not only attached to the breaking of the boundaries between animal and humans habitats but also highlights the growth and mobility of population; the environmental changes like deforestation, habitat fragmentation, encroachment into wildlife habitat, climate change; urbanization; changes in agricultural practices; changes in human behavior and culture; changes in food habits in the planet; global food production and safety structure; illegal wildlife trade; and inadequate public health measures also responsible for the growth of such virus. These above factors somehow are part of our broader social and natural structure, and changes in the balance between different structural units lead to the rise of such risks in society. So, COVID-19 results from the long-standing violence over the different units of social and natural structure, which resulted in the rise of such zoonotic diseases and victimized individuals across the globe. Thus, it is the social circumstances that have created COVID-19 problem in society, and at the same time, it is the individuals and societies who are trapped in it. Hence, the problem COVID-19 is limited to individual troubles and social issues rather than a structural problem. Thus, COVID-19, as a structural problem, puts the questions why there is an imperfect relationship and imbalance in the different structural units in the present society. What are the real reasons behind this, and how can it be solved?

3 Why Did the Imperfect Relationship Happen?

COVID-19 as a social issue is rooted in the history of our dysfunctional and imperfect relationship with social structure and nature. So, the individual or country's endless choices of actions and activities determine the positive and negative results in society's function. Social scientists believe and argue that social issues are socially created through human agency (Wendt and Wallace 2009); it may be an individual, society or country system. These social problems can be socially solved through research and implementing social policies to tackle social issues (Wendt and Wallace 2009). But the problem here is that the current development and research model or debate or activities of different countries are more focused on 'concepts' and 'narrations' of development than engaging in actual problems. In implementing Mills' perspective, the abstract empiricism and grand theory held back to think about the real problem—personal troubles to social issues. Mills employed both the ideas to criticize the then academic and research activities in social science and sociology, particularly how these concepts hold the sphere, away from actual problem and research (Puga and Easthope 2017). Suppose we employ both the ideas in present development policies and practices of different countries. In that case, findings suggest that the countries are more focused on Corporatization, Economic Development and Growth, Export and Import, National Interest, Nation-State, Grand Institutions, New Policies and Regulations, Conferences, International Collaboration, Militarization, and other grand and abstract concepts. These issues are far away from the real issues of society. These meta aspects of grand and abstract entities have helped to shadow the real trouble in the actual world. So, we need to focus on more empirical and microelements of development and how to maintain the social relations in the society and nature, than moving around abstract empiricism and grand theories. From Mills perspective, we need to focus on the developments of people's life, well-being, self-sufficiency, village industries, to make a balanced relationship between nature and society, positive affects, bottom-up approach, community-based projects, empowerment of local institutions, local agency collaboration, and practical relevance, which can be measurable, verifiable and acted for the well-being of society. Thus, individuals and agencies need to solve the real and actual problems in society by discharging actual responsibilities to attain a well-balanced society. In discharging the responsibilities, agencies need to find out and focus on the real problems of society.

4 Towards Responsibility

To Mills, the individual troubles or social issues are attached to values, and these values are threatened by the problem, which we all consider essential. Hence, the values of the social or natural structure are against the dysfunctional and imperfect arrangements in society. To know, understand, and control the issues that affect values, we need to visit the history of social structure and its attached values, which are helping maintain order in society. For Mills, we must stick to our values for a positive change in our community lives (Mills 1959), and to keep that, we have to develop a sense of social responsibility (Wendt and Wallace 2009). Mills believes that there are three values—truth, freedom, and reason (which are keys to a traditional social scientist) (Mills 1959; Puga and Easthope 2017). These need to be maintained to avoid abstract empiricism and grand theories and find out real problems in society. These values help to remain in the actual social order of the world, and the individual trouble and social issues in the social structure need to be addressed through these values.

These three values find their relevance in the present crisis because of the COVID-19, which results from continuous dysfunctional and imperfect relationships with the long-standing values of social and natural structure. For the future world order and sustainability, we need to work on these three values as a responsibility and responsiveness to maintain a balance between values and social structure. Amid this pandemic, everyone thinking lots of questions in their imagination about what will be the future of human action, activities, and affairs in society? What will happen to the social order? Is everything will be normal as usual, or will something change? And when will society be normal, and who will take the responsibility to make it happen? Or we have to continue our work simultaneously with the pandemic, and so on.

The world is in the process of making free from COVID-19 through vaccination, but we do not have a vaccine for the violence of natural and social structure. The answer lies with individuals and their agencies, which breaks the values in making their choice within the history of social structure, particularly its responsibility. Both individuals and agencies need to change their way of living and act according to the values of social and natural structure. To make the future world order more sustainable, human agencies need to act upon the actual individual troubles that become social issues. Human agencies and their development models want to be empirical and practical, verifiably and measurable in maintaining social reality. Simultaneously, humans need to act according to the rules and regulations of agencies and values that are cherished for a sustainable social structure. Certain aspects of society, individuals, and institutions need to be revisited and restructured according to their original values in social and natural structure for better world order. Some of the significant aspects are democracy, decentralization, humanity and solidarity, collective action, transparency and accountability, cordial human-nature nexus, resource mobilization in important sectors (Health and Education), self-reliance, and self-sufficiency. These are the actual vaccine need to be implemented for restructuring and balance the world order. Both institutions and individual's responsibility are to implement these aspects in their thought and practices through key values—truth, reason, and freedom. The above concepts and ideas are the prime means to discharge the responsibility to attain a better structure of world order. The key means are discussed below, looking into the needs of its original value with certain examples and how these means are interrelated to maintain the balance between natural and social structures.

4.1 *Democracy and Decentralization Governance*

In addressing the issues, Mills discussed the idea of 'History Making,' which refers to the human potential to modify their collective destiny (Mills 1959). In modern society, history-making is being centralized and is in the hands of powerful elites in society. Mills states that to overcome this, we need to establish democracy, which is the opposite of elites' power. He means 'democracy as some kind of collective self-control over the structural mechanism of history' (Mills 1959). The new democratic rules and regulations are now self-controlled by the elite, politicians, and state for their benefits (Wolf 2009). The new governance system neither asks the common people nor addresses their troubles while implementing development programs. We have to fix the weakness or bottlenecks in the democratic value system by reaching the unreached and empowering the un-empowered society. More democracy will be achieved when power and freedom will equally be distributed and shared. Here, more democracy further needs to invest both in local and global communities simultaneously (Narain 2020a). Decentralized responsibility will be the better option for both institutions and individuals to get more freedom and power to common than self-control. When there is more democracy and transparency in society, accountability will be more (Filgueiras 2016). Because the system is collectively owned, any dysfunction marked will negatively affect both individual and whole. So, in this context, no one wants to be its enemy; thus, everyone has to maintain transparency and accountability in their policy and actions. The future world order lies in more democratic governance for the well-being of individuals and society. In this democratic governance, everyone has the right to know the information or knowledge; denial and delay in sharing knowledge are threats to democracy and solidarity. The present pandemic reveals the extreme power of the state or big state or government to control and exercise its authority over citizens (Ghose 2020a, b). Take the examples of India and its state power during the year 2020 across the country. India's lockdown was described as the world's largest and harshest during pandemic executed within short notice (Ghose 2020a, b). The lockdown was managed centrally without prior concerns of state and local preference (Ghose 2020a, b). It neither considers the importance of public or experts' opinion nor thought about its severe impact on people across the country. Lockdown was executed without any preparedness across the state. Police have been ruthless and threatened the public, migrants, and street vendors and forced them to act according to government instructed rules to restrict any activities in their provenance to control the spread (Mishra and Rath 2020; Ghose 2020a, b). Closure of workplace forced many migrants to take the street to reach out home far away from their workplace without any state support (Ghose 2020a, b). Further, the state has strictly controlled the third pillar, NEWS Agencies, during the period (Krishnan 2020). They are strictly instructed to disseminate that information that is provided by the government only. Any outsource information, media views, and citizen's perceptions have been strongly rejected, even summoned, and an arrest warrant has been issued to news agencies and citizens over their voices against state COVID-19 mismanagement (Wire 2020). The government has set up another example by establishing the PM Cares Fund to receive donations to utilize it for COVID-19 purposes. But unfortunately, it is outside of the RTI ambit (Jebaraj 2020), and a citizen does not have the right to know who the donors are or how much they have contributed. Though these state-instructed guidelines are placed to control and manage the pandemic situations, these activities are against the value system of democracy. At the same time, pass of farm bill 2020 without any consultancy, cancelation of the parliament winter session in the time of debate and discussion, and centralizing ruling through home minster across the country reveal the use of state power at the cost of individual freedom and liberty open-up the autocratic system of the state in India (Ghose 2020a, b).

The COVID management not only witnesses strong state power across the nation but also decentralization duty and responsibility. Decentralization of power has been a long-cherished goal of Indian democracy. It has been proposed to make citizens responsible and to steer participatory governance. On the one hand, the pandemic has shattered the nations, and on the other, it has enlarged roles and responsibilities to its stakeholders. But with a vast mass of population widely dispersed in various geographical locations, it was impossible to ensure these provisions. It led the government to resort to its decentralized governance system to manage. Decentralization of responsibility has transformed many dormant panchayat leaders, Anganwadi Workers, and ASHA Workers during the pandemic into active agents. Take the example of Odisha and its focus on the community-based pandemic management strategy through decentralizing its leadership and responsibility to Elected Heads, Bureaucrats, Aganwadi Workers, Accredited Social Health Activist (ASHA) Workers, Auxiliary Nurse Midwife (ANW) Workers, Self Help Groups (SHG's) Members both at rural and at urban spaces to combating against COVID-19 crisis. (Ghose 2020a, b; Sahu 2020). This political step has made them resilient risk managers. Participatory democracy has found a solid expression through this decentralization. The powers of local elected representatives have been enhanced, and their responsibilities have also witnessed a shift. They have exhibited real ownership in these few days, and they have gained the trust of the system of governance and the people. By looking the rural functionaries, they have nicely controlled the community spread of the virus. This is perhaps the best example they have set in the state for championing the cause of decentralization for the days to come. If state agencies successfully execute the values of democracy and decentralization of responsibility and power, it will ultimately bring equality and rights among citizens. So government and its agencies need to act and discharge their role effectively in a democratic way by implementing reason in the foreground while dealing with human affairs.

4.2 *Humanity and Solidarity*

The present situation stated if democratic governance to sustain, we need to overcome humanity and solidarity tests (Johannesen 2020) or structural violence. The pandemic as a magnifying glass opened up the structure of solidarity and humanity in present society and how both can be used to reshape the future world order. From a humanity perspective, COVID-19 has severely affected people living in a vulnerable situation, like people living in poverty, the elderly, and persons with a disability, unemployed youths, homeless people, migrants, and indigenous communities worldwide (Nicola et al. 2020). These vulnerable groups must be protected (Johannesen 2020) through government social welfare majors by providing adequate healthcare facilities, education, and social safety net during the pandemic and beyond. Our government, community, society, and people need to internalize humanitarian value that they are equal, not different. We have to reconstruct the present structure of violence by bringing back equality and rights within the structure. Solidarity can be discussed in various forms and spheres. Here an individual, a group, a community, a society, a nation, and an organization can all show their solidarity to make the world better, whether in mechanical form or organic form described by Durkheim. In the solidarity test, Johannesen (2020) mentioned that wealthy nations and people need to support financially less stable countries and people in both the short run and long run, who are hit harder due to lack of resources and access to good services. While examining Durkheim's concept of solidarity during the COVID-19 crisis, Mishra and Rath (2020) highlight that social solidarity plays an essential role in minimizing social distance and reducing health risks arising from the crisis by collective consciousness. It has the power to facilitate social order by the collective actions through its normative obligations in society (Mishra and Rath 2020). They further argued that the Mechanical Solidarity of Durkheim has the potentiality to bring solidarity in modern society, particularly in crises time. Here, individuals, communities, and institutions have a crucial role in bringing solidarity in society with the collective efforts both in the present crisis and shaping future order society. Besides this, solidarity can be built with global cooperation and act what is good for everyone in the World (Narain 2020b). International cooperation and collaboration across nations and regions can bring unitary actions in development and tackling social issues. The humanitarian and solidarity response among individuals, community, and corporate has been well observed during the pandemic lockdown period. Take the example of a donation to PM Cares Fund in India. Within a short period, individuals and corporations take their responsibilities and have voluntarily contributed enormously to the fund to fight against the COVID-19 resource crunch (Gupta 2020). India also witnessed community kitchen (Srivastava and Nagaraj 2020) and ration distribution free of cost by Self Help Groups, Wealthy Individually, and other voluntary organizations and associations for migrant workers and vulnerable communities across the nation (Mishra and Rath 2020). Another form of humanitarian action is also shown by wealthy individuals and few professional actors of the country. They have provided free transport to migrants and students, helping them reach out to their homes and also helps vulnerable people financially to re-establish their work in their hometowns (Pandey 2020; Zachariah 2020). With the government's help, corporate houses come forward in establishing COVID hospitals (IW 2020). These forms of humanitarian and solidarity actions by different individuals, corporations, and organizations with the help of government and their cooperation need to be continued through their practices to maintain a balance between equality and inequality and establish a sustainable society.

4.3 Cordial Human and Environment Nexus

The historical exploitation of natural environment structure in the name of development and economic growth changes the structure of the natural habitat of living species (Ascher and Healy 1990). The imperfect relationship between humans with wild animals and natural environment structure is why such zoonotic diseases rise (Kukreti 2020b). We can correlate between the increase of COVID-19 and the imperfect relationship between nature and human beings. Johannesen (2020) added that natural balance could be imagined and re-imagined if people change their choices over profit. To prevent such pandemics and epidemics in the coming future, we must stop the overexploitation of nature and wildlife and harmful wildlife trade. Besides COVID-19, other serious issues like climate change, pollution, forest degradation, soil erosion, water degradation, the rise of temperature, loss of vegetation, and other environmental concerns are attached with the imperfect relationship of human and environmental structure (Brauch 2005). Further, it goes with the daily rise of e-waste (Bhutta et al. 2011) and plastic (Vince and Hardesty 2017) worldwide. It is happing due to endless choices made by individuals and community members worldwide to fulfill their needs and greed, without thinking about the future generation. At the same time, the state failed to protect the natural structure of the environment because of bottlenecks in environmental laws' policies and practices. For the sustainability of the environment, we need to establish a cordial human-nature nexus where agencies can protect, facilitate, and regulate relations to maintain the world order. To achieve that, we need to put the environment, people, and society at the driving seat of development than profit. To protect the natural structure of the environment and outback of such diseases, we need to keep a boundary between human and animal habitats.

4.4 Collective Action and Cooperation

The pandemic has highlighted and unrevealed how we are interconnected and interrelated in the globalized world (Bapuji et al. 2020). It has underscored all the daily activities that are invisible in our everyday experience. We do not always feel, realize, notice, or acknowledge bringing equality through connectedness. Whether a person, region, system, corporation, state, or country, action has always affected its nearer fellow due to its interconnectedness. Though COVID-19 spread through this interconnectedness network, at the same time, we can use this network to bring equality through collective actions of various agents to combats the crisis at a different level. In this collective action, every agent will play their duty or role to earn collective welfare in society. While performing their task, every agent needs to stay within the rule of game or law or value, and they have to play the more significant responsibility while choosing their action throughout their duty. The collective action and cooperation can be executed in two forms; one is international, and the other is intra-national. In the pandemic or global crisis, the role of intra-national or global cooperation is much more essential to bring a fair and equitable agreement for the world's common interest. Here, key international and multinational agencies need to play a significant role in capitalizing the resources and services through a common action plan. At the inter-national or local level, agencies need to use their social networking tie to cooperate, which is the natural tendency of human beings for the greater societal good. We can take the examples of Sustainable Development Goals, Millennium Development Goals, Conference of Parties on Climate Change, and other international committed goals. International agencies, countries, and national and local voluntary organizations have contributed to achieving the targeted goals. Though there is a difference between the actual target achieved and the actual timeline, every stakeholder performs their duties in collective action to reach the goal. In this interconnected world and for its sustainability, a joint action plan between nations must be placed for every social issue because social issues are connected and interconnected across the globe. For its solution, we need a joint action plan and global cooperation for the common interest of the World (Narain 2020b). It will happen when there is a fair and proportionate agreement between nations.

4.5 Resource Mobilization

The pandemic has revealed that the greater the capacity or resources of a society, the more quick response to the social problem. So, the resources and their mobilization show the ability of a society or a country. Those who have greater capacity have greater resilience to risk adaptability. In this context, a country needs to capitalize on its necessary and needy resources to better off its community. As the pandemic opens up the present healthcare system worldwide (Walton 2020), it is time to increase investment in resource building in public health, education, environment, and research and development sectors to tackle such future pandemic. From infrastructure development, human resource engagement, capacity development to disseminating service and knowledge, every stakeholder has the key role in delivering their responsibility for every sector's smooth function. Like that, looking into the original structure of world order, agencies need to priorities the sectors of importance and investment through the value system. Then, the question arises, who will mobilize the resources of the priority sectors? In most cases, the state has to mobilize the resources for the better off of society. But, with the growing liberalization, privatization, and globalization, the state is in the process of withdrawing its responsibilities and handing over the welfare activities to the private player or corporate (Bairwa 2010). In the globalized era, both state and corporate individually or jointly need to internalize their responsibilities and mobilize their resources for greater public welfare through the public–private partnership model. Besides these two agencies, other voluntary and civil society organizations need to focus on their activities and projects in the line of need and priority of the community and society at large. In mobilizing resources, agencies need to decentralize the duty and responsibilities of its stakeholder for equal participation and inclusive growth of society. Take the example of the health sector, which is the fundamental right and need of every country's citizen to be healthy. During COVID time, our hospitals face a shortage of beds, human resources, ICU, ventilators, oxygen, infrastructure, lack of access to hospitals, and hospital staff on over duty (David et al. 2020). It shows the right to life and health of citizens is in danger. In this context, state priority should be to strengthen the countries health sector. To facilitate that state needs to devote more budgets to health sectors. The state needs to capitalize on its research and development, resource, infrastructure, equipment, and services in the health sector. The state needs to up-to-date with new technology and collaboration with various government, corporate, non-government, and international agencies for the said purpose. The state needs to decentralize its responsibilities and power to every health professional and practitioner across the country. Every health professionals need to be adequately trained to do their duty according to their assigned role and responsibility. Local or primary health centers need to be capitalized in every form. When we strengthen the needy and necessary sectors, we can revert with full potential to the problem in a time of crisis. Important and needy sectors should always be on the state's priority list as a value, but it should not be like discussing the priority sector after the crisis.

4.6 Self-reliant and Self-sufficient

The economy worldwide has been stagnated due to pandemics (McKibbin and Fernando 2020). The shutdown of borders and territories and lockdown across nations has further worsened the economy. It further aggravates the continuous closedown of the market and workplace, job loss, and lack of availability of work. It happens due to interconnectedness and interdependence among the stakeholders and market worldwide, which is powered by globalization (Mohanty 2020). Though this has a positive impact on economic development, at the same time, it has certain negative consequences on a society, which COVID-19 unfolds. Because no country or individual can self-sufficient or self-reliant on itself, they have to depend on each other while delivering a product or service in this globalized world. In this process, they go through the division of labor and that division of labor is organic, but COVID-19 once again revealed the importance of mechanical solidarity in society. Here, we are talking about the nation and its community as a whole. And to fulfill their basic needs in that society and community through division of labor within their space. It is not about addressing the requirements during the crisis, somewhat beyond that, where a community and nation can be self-sufficient and self-reliant on its own for basic needs and services, without depending on other countries. Take the example of Gandhi's ideas on a self-sufficient village economy, where every village will be the independent economic unit for basic needs (Gosalia 1979). He wants every village should be self-sufficient in every form, and every surplus of the village economy needs to devote to poor villagers. It will bring not only economic independence but also a self-reliant village. As India lives in the village, and if these units will be self-sufficient and self-reliant, the country will automatically be self-reliant and self-sufficient in their basic needs (Joshi 2002). We can also take the example of the Atama Nirbhar Bharat Abhiyan initiatives of the Government of India (PRS 2020). This campaign started to boost the Indian economy and revive the economic crisis because of pandemics. The initiative has been formed to become a self-reliant India, not become a self-centered system. It aims to establish a self-sustaining and self-generating India in every sphere of development and need. It is not the state's responsibility only; rather, corporate houses have a more prominent role in facilitating such things in their economic or business and social responsibility activities. Corporations need to lend their helping hand in other list priority and less developed sectors besides its core activities through resource mobilization. Take the example of Cadbury India advertisement during the lockdown period of COVID-19 (Cadbury 2020). The title of the ad highlights Cadbury Celebrations is not just a Cadbury advertisement. The ad shows how Cadbury goes beyond their daily business activities to promoting other small business activities and local stores across India during the pandemic. These small businesses and local stores are severely affected by continuous lockdown. As they struggle to stand with their feet and survive with no digital presence, Cadbury supported these local stores by advertising and locating their stores across India. However, whether it is the Gandhian ideology of self-sufficient or self-reliance village, or Atama Nirbhar Bharat or Cadbury India campaign, one thing is clear that to become self-sufficient, we need to capitalize our resources in needy and necessary sectors to become self-reliant so that it can lead to self-sustaining development.

5 Conclusion

The paper concludes that Mills perspective of sociological imagination finds its relevance and can be experienced in the present society like the COVID-19 pandemic. The paper further strengthens Mills's assumption that an individual's private trouble is a social issue, as COVID-19 is the problem of individuals and a social issue. These social issues are created and recreated in social structure by the endless and continuous choices made by individuals and agencies for their existence. The pandemic happened because of constant disturbance, violence, and imperfect relationship with our society's original structure. The postulates of zoonotic disease are related to an imperfect and dysfunctional relationship with the original structure. To re-establish the perfect and functional relationship with our social structure and for reshaping sustainable future world order, the paper suggests focusing on the real problems of society in the activities and actions of agencies, than abstract and meta-concepts. Looking into the activities and actions of agencies during COVID-19 and its beyond, the paper highlighted the need and importance of different form mediums like democracy and decentralized responsibility, transparency and accountability, collective action, humanity and solidarity, resource mobilization in priority sectors, cordial human and environmental relation, self-reliance and self-sufficient economy in delivering responsibilities to maintaining and ordering social structure. The agencies—individual, corporate, state, non-state actors, and other organizations—need to act according to their responsibilities without violating values while making their day-to-day choice within the social structure for sustainable world order.

Acknowledgements The author is thankful to the editors of the book for extending their continuous support in the publication process. The author is grateful to the anonymous reviewers for their valuable comments and suggestions in the original draft that helps in the quality improvement of the manuscript. The author also thanks Dr. Tanaya Mohanty and Prof. Navaneeta Rath of the Department of Sociology, Utkal University, for their constructive insights to improve the manuscript.

References

Ascher, W., and R.G. Healy. 1990. *Natural resource policymaking in developing countries: Environment, economic growth, and income distribution.* Duke University Press.

Bairwa, R.C. 2010. State in neo-liberal era of globalisation. In *A Marxist View,* State and Globalisation ed, ed. R S Bareth, and D Gupta, 205–246. Jaipur: Rawat Publication.

Bapuji, H., F.G.A. de Bakker, J.A. Brown, and C. Higgins. 2020. Business and society research in Times of the Corona Crisis. *Business and Society* 59 (6): 1067–1078.

Beyer, R.M., A. Manica, and C. Mora. 2021. Shifts in global bat diversity suggest a possible role of climate change in the emergence of SARS-CoV-1 and SARS-CoV-2. *Science of The Total Environment*, 145413.

Bhutta, M.K.S., A. Omar, and X. Yang. 2011. Electronic waste: A growing concern in today's environment. *Economics Research International.*

Brauch, H.G. 2005. Threats, challenges, vulnerabilities and risks in environmental and human security. *UNU-EHS.*

Cadbury. 2020. *Cadbury Celebration Not Just a Cadbury ad Campaign Video.* Published on 4th November 2020. https://www.youtube.com/watch?v=gBWLm6Sx1WI.

David, Blumenthal, E.J. Fowler, M. Abrams, and R. Collins. 2020. Covid-19—Implications for the Health Care System. *The New England Journal of Medicine* **383**, 1483–1488.

De Graaf, M., et al. 2017. Sustained fecal-oral human-to-human transmission following a zoonotic event. *Current Opinion in Virology* 22: 1–6.

Filgueiras, F. 2016. Transparency and accountability: Principles and rules for the construction of publicity. *Journal of Public Affairs* 16 (2): 192–202.

George, Mathew. 2020. Socio-cultural determinants of the spread of Covid-19. *Health and Primary Care*, 4.

Ghose, S. 2020a. *Year of Big State.* The Times of India. Bhubaneswar Edition. December 30, 2020.

Ghose, S. 2020b. *Leadership in Covid Times.* The Times of India, 18th June 2020.

Gosalia, S. 1979. The Gandhian model of self-reliance in the Indian economy. *Intereconomics* 14 (2): 80–83.

Gupta, M.D. 2020. *PM Cares gets Rs 6500 crore donation in a week, 3 times more than that PMNRF got in 2 yrs.* The Print. Published on 4th April 2020.

Hironimus-Wendt, R.J., and L.E. Wallace. 2009. The sociological imagination and social responsibility. *Teaching Sociology* 37 (1): 76–88.

IW. 2020. *Corporate Houses in Odisha to create their own COVID care facilities.* Indian Whispers: The Inside News.

Jeberaj, P. 2020. PM cares is not a public authority under RTI act: PMO. The Hindu. Published on 31st May 2020.

Johannesen, T. 2020. News from our societies—ICSW: COVID-19—Five tests we face. *International Social Work* 63 (3): 399–399.

Joshi, D. 2002. *Gandhiji on Villages.* Mani Bhavan Gandhi Sangrahalaya, Mumbai, 1.2002.

Krishnan, V. 2020. *Centre places restrictions on media in COVID press briefings; shifts focus to Tablighi Jamaat.* The Caravan. Publishes on 6th April 2020.

Kukreti, Ishan. 2020a. Bats Spread Viruses, so do humans. *Down To Earth,* 16 to 31 May, 2020a.

Kukreti, I. 2020b. Understanding zoonotic diseases: Global human interaction has eased transmission. *Down To Earth,* 7th May 2020.

MacIntyre, C.R. 2020. Global spread of COVID-19 and pandemic potential. *Global Biosecurity* 1 (3).

McKibbin, W., and R. Fernando. 2020. *The Economic Impact of COVID-19.* Economics in the Time of COVID-19, 45.

Mills, C.W. 1959. *The Sociological Imagination.* Oxford University Press.

Mishra, C., and N. Rath. 2020. Social solidarity during a pandemic: Through and beyond Durkheimian Lens. *Social Sciences & Humanities Open* 2 (1), 100079.

Mohanty, R. 2020. Macro level analysis of corona crisis: from world system perspective. *Odisha Sociological Imagination Series.* 2020.

Mohapatra, B. 2020. The development determinants of COVID-19: A cross country stocktaking. *Odisha Sociological Imagination Series.*

Narain, Sunita. 2020a. Contours of coronavirus. *Down to Earth.* 14th February 2020a.

Narain, Sunita. 2020b. Covid-19migrants: Future of work and production. *Down to Earth.* 17th May 2020b.

National Research Council (US). 2009. *Committee on Achieving Sustainable Global Capacity for Surveillance and Response to Emerging Diseases of Zoonotic Origin.* National Academies Press (US); 2009. Available from: https://www.ncbi.nlm.nih.gov/books/NBK215318/.

Nicola, M., Z. Alsafi, C. Sohrabi, A. Kerwan, A. Al-Jabir, C. Iosifidis, M. Agha, and R. Agha. 2020. The socio-economic implications of the coronavirus pandemic (COVID-19): A review. *International Journal of Surgery (london, England)* 78: 185–193.

Nie, Jing-Bao. 2020. In the shadow of biological warfare: conspiracy theories on the origins of COVID-19 and enhancing global governance of biosafety as a matter of urgency. *Journal of Bioethical Inquiry* 17 (4): 567–574.

Pandey, G. 2020. *India Coronavirus: Bollywood Actor Sonu Sood hailed for helping migrants.* BBC News. Published on 25th May 2020.

PRS. 2020. Summary of announcements: Aatma Nirbhar Bharat Abhiyaan. Published on 12th May 2020.

Puga, I., and R. Easthope. 2017. *An Analysis of C. Wright Mills's The Sociological Imagination.* CRC Press.

Sahu, S. 2020. *Put at the Centre of COVID Fight by Odisha CM, The Sarpanch Remains a Figurehead.* Outlook India. Accessed Date 25th June 2020.

Srivastava, R., and A. Nagaraj. 2020. *Covid-19: In India, Community Kitchens spring up across cities to feed stranded migrants.* Scroll. Published on 13th April, 2020.

Staubmann, H.C. 2021. Wright Mills' The sociological imagination and the construction of Talcott parsons as a conservative grand theorist. *Am Soc* 52: 178–193.

Vince, J., and B.D. Hardesty. 2017. Plastic pollution challenges in marine and coastal environments: From local to global governance. *Restoration Ecology* 25 (1): 123–128.

Walton, B. 2020. Healthcare facilities in developing countries a high risk for coronavirus transmission. Global Hand Washing. Accessed Date 16th June 2020.

Wells, C.R., P. Sah, S.M. Moghadas, A. Pandey, A. Shoukat, Y. Wang, et al. 2020. Impact of international travel and border control measures on the global spread of the novel 2019 coronavirus outbreak. *Proceedings of the National Academy of Sciences* 117 (13), 7504–7509.

Wendt, H.R.J., and L.E. Wallace. 2009. The sociological imagination and social responsibility. *Teaching Sociology* 37 (1): 76–88.

Wire. 2020. 55 *Indian Journalists Arrested, booked, threatened for reporting on COVID-19: report.* The Wire, Published on 16th June 2020.

Wolf, S. 2009. Subverting democracy: Elite rule and the limits to political participation in post-war El Salvador. *Journal of Latin American Studies*, 429–465.

Zachariah, S.S. 2020. *Celebrities Doing all they can to help the needy during lockdown.* The Better India. Published on 20th May 2020.

Social and Technological Renovation in Online Second Language Teaching: A Post-COVID-19 Study of Pedagogy and Its Implication

Barsarani Panigrahi

1 Introduction

The beginning of the twenty-first century marks the new age of technology, and the role technology played in everyday life is noticeable compared to the previous generation. As a result of the free access to knowledge through materials that are available as open sources, under creative commons and so on, it has consistently changed the human behaviour. For example the access to information is made easier over the internet platform where the data is available with a single click. Technology saves time and energy for the internet users in the process of procuring information. As information was available instantly, the technology has changed the very course of text production such as acronyms, emojis, digital texts. This novice text becomes a part of the communication, and the authenticity of it is often questioned. For example when a text is consumed based on the number of "likes" (a modern text) it gets from the users, there are chances that it might mislead the users. At this very juncture of text production, the users of internet take two different stand, one claims that the information available online is not reliable, and due to the novel text productions, the act of collaborative learning is changing drastically. None can deny the fact that there is growth in technological advancement, and at the same time, there is a social disconnection as well—having said that it is mandatory for the teachers, with respect to the new pedagogy, should be renovated with new norms in the education system.

B. Panigrahi (✉)
School of Humanities, KIIT Deemed to be University, Bhubaneswar, Odisha, India

R. N. Subudhi et al. (eds.), *Future of Work and Business in Covid-19 Era*,
Springer Proceedings in Business and Economics,
https://doi.org/10.1007/978-981-19-0357-1_26

1.1 Renovation in Online Teaching

Any renovation that is either technological or social should depart from the very basic of the user's necessity. Also, before proceeding with the renovation in teaching, let us try and understand if social and technological are interchangeable words. As we are transferring the social interactions in the classroom to the technological platforms, the following are some of the questions that we need to bear in mind, such as "can technology replace social networking? and how can one benefit from this change?" Nina Garrett in her article "Technology in the Service of Language Learning" says that, there is not much difference between technology and society. She further explains the above situation by presenting a series of questions on the possible role of technology and whether it replaces the social component; her queries are directed on how the social component such as teaching in a classroom can be compensated by technological interference. She asks.

(1) Should the technology be thought of as primarily assisting teaching. (2) what is the relationship between a theoretically and empirically based understanding of the language learning process. (3) should students work with pedagogically shaped materials or directly with authentic data? (4) should students' access to the material be directed or entirely under their own control. (5) what kinds of research does the use of technology for language learning demand or enable? (Garrett 1991).

She concludes her analysis as claimed in her article titled *"Technology in the Service of Language Learning: Trends and Issues"* that there is no "correct" answer. Since we are at the very early stage of exploiting the online platform for teaching, thereby the paper agrees with Garret's perspective. Though her research appears to be non-conclusive, this paper finds the article relevant even after two decades of her publishing. Furthermore, the article notes that when a technology establishes itself/accepted/adopted/used regularly, then eventually it becomes inevitable to ignore.

Teaching second language through online undergoes pretty much similar process of what Nina Garrett states as "testing and establishing the technology into the mainstream" teaching. Even though we adapted to the online platform due to COVID-19 pandemic, we should have all the learning tools to be tested in real time to make it more accessible to students. Also, we can provide sufficient technological support to meet the needs of the teachers. Even the content creators for the online classrooms are convenient to acquire in the present situation. Despite the readiness, the process of teaching and learning through online classroom can only happen if we can equip the teachers with modern technological tools.

2 Teachers Versus Society and Technology

Teachers play an inevitable role in delivering the lessons to the students, and they are integral part of a classroom both online and offline. The assumption is that even though the students have access to the modern gadgets such as smartphone, tablets, there is a fundamental problem in converting these into effective online media for learning. The possible reason behind this is the lack of effective pedagogy, there is no distinct pedagogy that is available for the teachers to follow in the online platform. Therefore, most of the online classrooms are ending up as a replication of traditional classroom environments (Barom et al. 2013). To assimilate technology and society into a single unit in the online platform, the teacher's experience on online platform and their changing roles should be taken into consideration to form a pedagogy that is novice. In other words, it is what the teacher teaches and how much he/she is technologically enabled will decide the innovative mind-set of the students to utilize the online platform. This way society, technology and the classroom will become single entity in establishing technology to its fullest.

2.1 Implementation of Technology

Following the teacher's role in the classroom both online and offline, parents and the society become equally important players in deciding the pedagogy and implementing appropriate technology. The implementation or the adaptation of technology can be evaluated in the following way: firstly, we must investigate, what is the expectation of the society? Does the society want students to learn every subject in detail or according to the prescribed syllabus? Secondly, is it necessary that we need to develop technology with exclusivity or do we need to make use of the existing one. And the thirdly, how effectively we can deliver the contents in the online classroom?

Although the renovation in technology changes the fundamentals of teaching, the society looks forward to all the changes that is taking place. But, difficulty in implementation arises when both the teachers and the society expect the attitude, belief, tradition, communication and interaction of the student and teacher like that of the face-to-face class environment. Evrim Baron in his article "Tracing Successful Online Teaching in Higher Education" observes that during the implementation of technology/pedagogy, there will be four important and major changes that the teacher must undergo: they are, (1) increasing structure and planning during course design, (2) increasing organization in course management, (3) increasing teacher presence for monitoring students' learning and (4) reconstructing student–teacher relationships. This suggests that the authoritative approach of the teachers and society must be relaxed, and they should become more of a facilitator in making the students explore subjects on their own. Further, the bond between the students and teachers stays eternal, and as discussed above, both compliment and facilitate each other but cannot be replaced.

3 The Changing Pedagogy

From the genesis of teacher-learner experience, the syllabus keeps changing according to the need of the students, and similarly, the pedagogy too is getting upgraded. In the earlier days of gurukul system, education was limited to an exclusive group of individuals, while after colonization, the English education system made education available for people from all social strata. In the former context, the pedagogy was customized according to the students need, while the latter introduced uniformity in education developing the pedagogy based on teacher-oriented learning, learners-oriented, subject/syllabus-oriented learning; in all the above said pedagogy, the process of teaching kept changing but kept the teacher-learners experience intact.

For an instance the introduction of modern technology into the classroom might increase the teacher's presence in the class, but it strives to maintain the teacher-learners experience more productive. While investigating about the changing pedagogy and the knowledge explosion on the online platform, we must be conscious about the feedback and interactions by the students. When both teacher and the students meet on online platform for the purpose of education, the feedback and interactions with them will provide us insight into using technology effectively. It might provide a vital answer to the often asked question; that is whether technology is a replacement for face-to-face class or an alternative tool for education? So far during the COVID-19, the online platform has been exploited for the benefit of the students in the classroom—and in such cases, online classes acted merely as an alternative and not as a replacement.

During COVID-19, Kerala government came up with a temporary solution to educate the students through technology. One such effort was utilizing television channel to take classes, and this happened due to the lack of facility in some part of Kerala. To reach out to majority of the students during lockdown, they chose television as a mode. Though television does not provide space to interact with students, the philosophy of the state that worked with the motive to reach majority of students was highly appreciated. Likewise, technology can be used reasonably as a tool with rationality in structuring the pedagogy.

Further, the Kerala education department had identified that there were over two lakh students, who lacked facilities for online classes and had suggested alternatives including television or internet facilities of neighbours, friends living nearby, libraries or Akshaya centres. Through sponsorships and making use of common facilities, the issue has been largely sorted out. Also, they achieved the monthly views of the YouTube channel www.youtube.com/itsvicters to 150 million, while the average daily viewership of classes in YouTube alone is 54 lakhs, which translates to a whopping 5 lakh hours a day. (NDTV-Education., 2020).

The above example of Kerala government does not quantify that television is future medium for education, but it is an alternative due to the pandemic situation. The socially renovative pedagogy that this paper refers to is every possibilities of technology that helps and reach out to a larger audience during pandemic situation.

The paper does not favour one medium over the other, but it would rather facilitate or simplifies the medium in the process of learning.

3.1 Ancient and the Modern Technologies

We often relate every invention or everything that involves technology has something to do with computers. But, technology is something that is as small as wristwatch to the huge satellites that are used in space. The question of what is new about computers takes us to the accessibility/variety and the vast information that it provides for its learners. Day-by-day the computers are becoming self-reliant and user-friendly. That is it guides the users by providing options based on the user behaviour in accessing it. For example the auto-correct option in the word document is provided whenever the user enters the spelling inputs incorrectly; the keywords in Google search engine automatically segregate information and provide to the user and learn the behaviour of the user through his search online. In other words, the computer employs a method called instructive commands to the users to fix the issue when occurred. It is this instructive facility available through technology that will be made use to teach second language through technology.

3.2 Second Language Learning and Technology

To learn English language—the traditional school system began with the use of bilingual method to teach English to the non-natives. And, the syllabus that has been designed at the earlier stage was grammar translation method. This system was followed for a very long time in Indian school system. Consistently, the pedagogy changed to other methods of teaching such as exercise-oriented teaching, activity-based teaching and computer-assisted language learning (CALL). Almost in all the above method, grammar played a major role in training the students. Now, taking technology into account, one can say that it follows a systematic method of delivering a subject. Further, English functions as the computing language, it follows a systematic command like that of the computers, such as the grammar structures. In this manner, teaching English using computers can become an integral part of language classroom.

During the pandemic, we did fail in some part of the country in offering alternative online classes to the students; not due to lack of experience by the teachers in the online platform but due to the lack of infrastructure. We find the unavailability of basic infrastructure for communication and technology establishment in many state-run schools and institutions in Odisha. There are schools and colleges which function highly depending on the textbooks. In fact, the reason for students joining in private institution is for the infrastructure, such as English laboratories, computer laboratories. It is only during the COVID-19 pandemic, students and teachers of state-run institutions realize the need of technological infrastructure for the education. Post-COVID-19, we may find the demand for such laboratory facilities.

The schools and colleges having the necessary laboratory facilities have already started to introduce different e-contents to the students for the purpose of training and exercise. In such scenario, the students become an autonomous body to apply all the theories and formulas that were taught in the class. For example the English phonetics and the transcriptions were practised time and again by the students depending on their interest in learning the accent and as per the requirement for examination. The number of hours allotted for students to spend in laboratory also varies for different schools. Further, along with language subjects like mathematics, science, social studies and mother language were taught using technologies in the private school of Puri District. (Ansuman Sar, 2014).

Ansuman Sar, in his research, found the importance of adopting ICT in school. Meanwhile, he also presented the challenges of implementation such as the infrastructural issues, structural transformation, teaching pedagogy and technology integration are some of the issues that he mentions and that we also have discussed on the same lines in this article. Thereby, the renovation should happen in the social and technological platform since *Sar* says that the pedagogies are well in place for integration.

3.3 Instructional Technology—Online Pedagogy

Studying the compelling growth in the pedagogy and the teacher being the chosen mediator of technology among the students. The paper favours the instructive technology as the future for the online education post-COVID-19 pedagogy. The future of the state and countries knowledge capital relies on the providing rich learning environment to the learners. The learner who is well trained and educated plays an important role not only to themselves and the family but also in the financial growth of the country. This could be the reason for the governments to invest or allot considerable budgets into educational institutions.

Educational institutions are the one that can provide a meaningful learning circumstance, while instructional designs will help to provide contents for the promotion of such learning. M.D Merrill writes that "the design phase includes activities aimed at developing a shared vision among stakeholders to create a balanced instructional mode that was tailored to the need of the students… developing assessment to evaluate the performance against their standards and creating aligned tools for reporting the results of the assessment". The process of learning will be made interesting through technology, and this will be achieved only when technology solves the real-life problem. Post-COVID-19 when the students are using the online platform, the interaction of the teacher-student shifts to student–student, student-content and student-environment. Though the technology can fill the gap of application of knowledge through multimedia tools and smart classroom, the social and technological renovation should happen so that it connects the students back to their teachers for the real-life problem-solving methods. Much research proves that the technology without the involvement of the teachers has not achieved its full potential in the process of developing students' knowledge and skill. Thereby, the pedagogy implies the growing need of integrating the teacher/mediator in the process of second language teaching through online platform, so that we will be technologically prepared to face any similar pandemic situation.

4 Conclusion

Using online learning environment for the purpose of teaching second language in school and colleges challenges the capacity of the teachers. It also enables them to explore a different type of pedagogy to the learners especially during the COVID-19 situation. For the teachers who have taught in the traditional face-to-face class might find it difficult to adapt to the modern system; but eventually, they can unlearn the outdated methodologies and can shift to the new ones. Online platform decentralizes the hierarchy between student and teachers through the collaborative learning, instructional learning and so on. The ICT will make the students autonomous in choosing their own curriculum. This will offer the teachers the new role of a "facilitator". And, through this article, we find that the online platform is suitable for second language teaching as well as other subjects and concludes by promoting the wide scope of language teaching through online.

References

Ansuman Sar, Satya Narayan Misra. 2008. A study on policies and implementation of information and communication technology (ICT) in educational systems, 1–12. Print.

Evrim Barom, Ana-Paula Correia, Ann D. Thompsom. 2013. Tracing successful online teaching in higher education: Voices of exemplary online teachers. *Teachers College Record*, 01–14. Print.

Garrett, Nina. 1991. Technology in the service of language learning: Trends and issues. *Modern Language Journal* 75: 74–101. Print.

McLuhan, Marshal. 1994. *Understanding Media*. The MIT Press. Print.

Merrill, M.D. 2007. First principles of instruction: A synthesis. *Trends and Issues in Instructional Design and Technology* 2: 62–71. Print.

NDTV-Education. 2020. https://www.ndtv.com/education/online-classes-in-kerala-cross-1,000-mark. May 2020. Electronic, April 24: 2021

Nina Garrett, James S. Noblitt and Frank Dominguez. 1989. Computers in foreign language teaching and research: A "new humanism". Computing Across the Curriculum: Academic Perspectives. *Academic Computing*. Print.

Dynamics of Value Creation and Sustainability in a Rapidly Changing Economic System

Purvi Pujari and Priyeta Priyadarshini

1 Introduction

As the world tries to grapple with the aftermaths of the COVID-19 pandemic, it is imperative that we find a solution to the economic and social challenges put forth. Businesses all over the world have to rethink their strategies understanding the implications of their actions on this planet. The COVID-19 pandemic has been an inflection point for economies all over the world. There have been impacts on the businesses that have faced huge economic losses as well the mental stress due to disruptions in the workflow. Society has also faced the brunt of the pandemic as a result of widespread job losses, physical and mental health issues and loss of life. There has been a little positive impact as well due to reduced pollution as the world faced a series of lockdowns in both developing and developed countries. The reduction in vehicular congestion due to factories and offices being shut down had a positive impact on the global climate (Anuj and Nishu 2021). This brings a need to examine the way businesses are conducted and create a paradigm shift in terms of the way value is created for the planet as a whole and sustainability is entwined into each and every business practice.

2 Research Methodology

The research's nature will be descriptive and exploratory because the researchers describe and explore the link between value creation and sustainability. The research data has been taken from secondary sources. After a detailed literature review,

P. Pujari (✉) · P. Priyadarshini
Bharati Vidyapeeth's Institute of Management Studies and Research, Mumbai, India
e-mail: drpurvipujari@bvimsr.com

R. N. Subudhi et al. (eds.), *Future of Work and Business in Covid-19 Era*,
Springer Proceedings in Business and Economics,
https://doi.org/10.1007/978-981-19-0357-1_27

the objectives of the paper were identified. This being a relatively new subject, the research methodology adopted for the paper is a detailed exploratory study of secondary data like research papers, articles and Websites. The objectives of the paper are:

1. To understand and explore the concept of value creation
2. To understand and explore the concept of interlink between value creation and sustainability

3 Literature Review

The detailed literature review of the subject has reflected a growing interest in the concept of value creation. The researchers have undertaken a detailed literature review on the subject to understand the concept of value creation and sustainability (Table 1).

The literature review of the research in this field has helped the authors to identify the connected fields with the subject of sustainability. Most of the research in this field state that there is a strong interlink between the fields of sustainability and circularity. Circularity has been defined as an economic system that replaces the "end-of-life" concept with reducing, alternatively reusing, recycling and recovering materials in production/distribution and consumption processes. It operates at the micro-level (products, companies, consumers), meso-level (eco-industrial parks) and macro-level (city, region, nation and beyond), with the aim to accomplish sustainable development, thus simultaneously creating environmental quality, economic prosperity and social equity, to the benefit of current and future generations (Kirchherr and Hekkert 2017). Sustainability has always been connected with economic functions. Andersen (2007) Impact assessment of resource utilization should be done to understand the economic aspect of sustainability. Most of the researchers argue that logistics and supply chain are the domain which should be the prime focus of the organization aiming to bring sustainability (Pravin and Kumar 2021; Dey et al. 2020). Sustainability also encompasses the field of circularity (Rincón-Moreno 2021, Raphaelle and Monia 2018). Any organization aiming to be sustainable has to ensure adoption of innovative business practices (Pieroni Marina et al. 2019).

4 Value Creation

New value is created when firms develop/invent new ways of doing things using new methods, new technologies and/or new forms of raw material. The long-term aim for most of the organization is to create value for its stakeholders and establish a sustainable business model. Value for stakeholders involves value for customers, shareholders and above all the owners as well as the society. From a financial perspective, creating value for its customers and owners is at the core of any business strategy.

Table 1 Literature review

S. no	Authors	Argument regarding value creation and sustainability
1	Andersen (2007)	The paper discusses the link between the global resources and their economic functions. It also discusses the role of these in achieving the aim of sustainability
2	Dey et al. (2020)	This paper focuses on the adoption of sustainable practices in supply chain of SMEs. The researchers advocate the implementation of circular logistic processes in SMEs
3	Rincón-Moreno (2021)	The researchers in this paper have analyzed the indicators for Spanish firm in terms of creating CE. The researchers conclude that the indicators for assessing the performances of businesses in terms of circularity can be used at macro-as well as micro-level businesses
4	Molina-Moreno (2017)	The authors of this paper have concentrated on the assessment of adoption of circularity in the cattle industry. It throws light on how the effluents are converted into resources in the farms which is a way to imbibe circularity in the whole process
5	Sumter et al. (2021)	The authors have identified the knowledge and skills required to achieve circularity. It also assesses the business in terms of model followed by the firm to achieve circularity
6	Pravin and Kumar (2021)	The paper discusses the link between logistics domain of the businesses and sustainability. The researchers put forward the argument that supply chain is one of the areas where circularity can be enhanced
7	Raphaelle and (2018)	The authors have explored the details of sustainability as applicable to the business world, especially FMCG companies. They identified that there is a need to address the issue of CE and sustainability together. The firms need to integrate CE practices in the product packaging and supply chain management domain of their business practices
8	Pieroni Marina et al. (2017)	This research focuses on the CE and sustainability. The authors have emphasized the need of bring innovation into business practices to enhance the circularity in the company
9	Kirchherr and Hekkert (2017)	This is one of the fundamental researches in the field of circularity and brought forward multiple dimensions of sustainability as well as CE

(continued)

Table 1 (continued)

S. no	Authors	Argument regarding value creation and sustainability
10	Welfens et al. (2017)	This research is underlining the link between circularity and factors of production utilized by the businesses to bring sustainable practices. According to them, optimum utilization of resources is one of the main way of bringing circularity

Source Own compilation by authors

A successful strategy will be one that focuses on creating value for society. Value creation process for any organization has the value which the business creates is for its customers. Customers are the main recipients of any value which is provided by the goods and services of the business. Value for employees comes from the positive contribution toward career development, learning, work-life balance and emotional well-being of the employees. Value for owners comes through active participation and creating a sustainable value model. Value for society is becoming more and more important in the current times (Fig. 1).

Value creation for customers, employees, country and owners is definitely the core aim of any organization. This is the primary focus to achieve stability and growth. If the business wants to grow in the long-term and create sustainable value, it has to work toward, creating value for society. Traditional methods of assessing created value by any business rely on financial measures. The value creation for society can be measured through measures like impact investment and steps taken toward creating a circular economy. Creating shared value (CSV) and triple bottom line

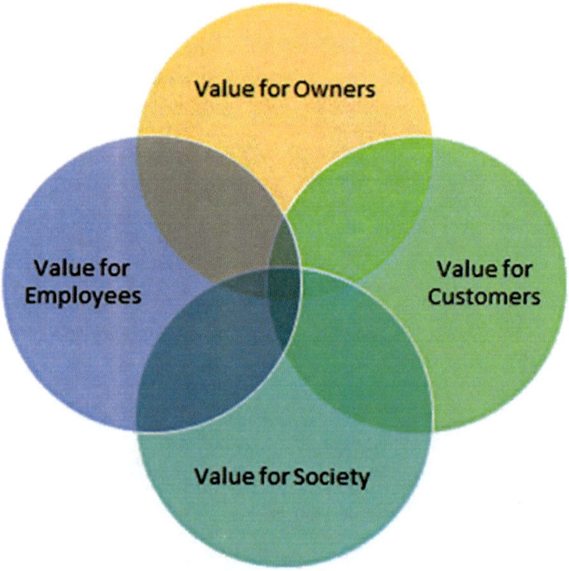

Fig. 1 Value creation strategy *Source* Own conceptualization by author

(TBL) have been the standard measures that have been popularly used by businesses for a long. Value creation ensures stakeholder engagement and paves way for stability and growth.

In the long-term, businesses need to focus on creating circularity. Circular economy has been the paradigm shift that has happened across the globe.

5 Sustainability

It refers to the concept that assists long-term economic growth influencing the social, environmental and cultural outlook of the community, without any negativity. The broad concept of "sustainable evident, showing that sustainability is fast development" was first widely publicized by the World Conservation Strategy (IUCN, 1980). "Sustainable development is development result in the various concepts of that meets the needs of future generations sustainability not being achieved; without compromising the ability of future generations to meet their own needs." (Pezzy 1989). Sustainable development is a type of development that meets the present needs without compromising with the needs of future generations (Fig. 2). (Our Common Future (Brundtland Report) Report of the World Commission on Environment and Development, 1987).

The three pillars of sustainability are:

1) Social
2) Environmental
3) Economic

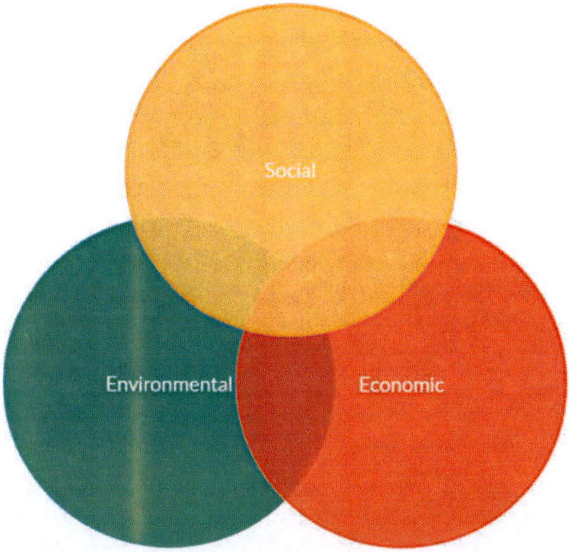

Fig. 2 Three pillars of sustainability *Source* Own conceptualization by author

In order to achieve sustainability, there should be balance and harmony between social, economic and environmental sustainability.

5.1 Environmental Sustainability

It implies that we are living inside the avenue of our natural assets. To live in genuine and actual natural sustainability, we have to be guaranteed that we are expanding our natural assets, such as materials, land, water, energy, fuel, at a sustainable rate. A few resources are more abundant than others, and thus, we ought to consider material scarcity, the harm to the environment from extraction of these materials, and in case the asset can be kept inside circular economy standards. We have to try to net-zero carbon and then move eventually to accomplish positive climate standards. Environmental sustainability should not be confounded with full sustainability which moreover has to be adjusted for financial and social components.

5.2 Social Sustainability

It is something related to identification and management of business impacts, both positive and contrary, on individuals. The nature of an organization's connections and commitment with its partners is basic and important. Truly speaking, organizations influence, what befalls representatives, laborers in the value chain, clients and nearby networks, and it is imperative to oversee impacts proactively.

Any business can flourish with social sustainability efforts. If an organization lacks in social development, including poverty, inequality, it will definitely hamper its operations and growth.

5.3 Financial/Economic Sustainability

Economic sustainability allows an organization or nation to use its capital wisely and responsibly in order to be able to function in a sustainable manner to generate operating profit consistently. A business cannot maintain its operations without an operating profit. A business would not be able to maintain itself without behaving professionally and using its capital effectively.

6 Findings

After the detailed literature review and study of the subject, it can be clearly stated that value creation for society demands businesses to identify the ways in which sustainable methods can be adopted in the various domains such as manufacturing and supply chain, etc. More the value created for the society, easier it is for the business to achieve the aim of sustainability. A sustainable business is the need of the hour and by bringing circularity in the economy, it ensures returns for the economy as a whole. Circularity as a strategy requires a huge amount of planning and rethinking the way operations are conducted in any company. Sustainability is imperative to create long-term high value for any organization. Sustainable value creation requires comprehensive strategic intent in order to maximize total value captured. There is a need to better understand how companies can improve sustainable value creation. The dynamic business environment, active and informed stakeholders and ever-increasing emphasis on social responsibilities of firms has increased the need for sustainable value creation. Growing threats from environmental and social challenges across the globe as well as increasing opportunities from the information technologies that are fueling a move toward value creation and sustainability.

7 Conclusion

For any firm, the process of value creation is one of the most critical one. The value creation potential of any business determines its returns to the business's stakeholders. Among different ways to create value for its stakeholders, businesses must focus on value creation for society. Value creation for society can be done through following the principles of shared value and triple bottom line (TBL). The principle of sustainability necessitates the businesses to adopt the circular economy processes. The idea is to ensure that whatever waste is created in the business processes follows a complete loop and is optimally utilized as a resource for the same business. Better resource utilization through following the principles of circularity results in the returns to the complete economy. In the post COVID-19 world, it is imperative that firms focus on the long-term strategy of social value creation. (Ratten 2020) The best way to create value for the planet is to imbibe sustainable practices and bring circularity in every business domain. The concept of value creation has to be integrated with all the systems. Transdisciplinary systems have to be created to reduce costs and create an atmosphere of value creation.

References

Andersen, M.S. 2007. An introductory note on the environmental economics of the circular economy. *Sustanabilty Science* 2: 133–140.

Anuj, Kumar, and Ayedee Nishu. 2021. An interconnection between COVID-19 and climate change problem. *Journal of Statistics and Management Systems.*

Dey, P.K., et al. 2020. Circular economy to enhance sustainability of small and medium-sized enterprises. *Business Strategy and Environment*, 1–25.

Kirchherr, Julian, Reike, Denise, and Marko Hekkert. 2017. Conceptualizing the circular economy: An analysis of 114 definitions. *Resources, Conservation and Recycling* 1270921–3449: 221–232.

Molina-Moreno, V., J.C. Leyva-Díaz, F.J. Llorens-Montes, and F.J. Cortés-García. 2017. Design of indicators of circular economy as instruments for the evaluation of sustainability and efficiency in wastewater from pig farming industry. *Water* 9: 9–653

Pezzy, John. 1989. *Economic Analysis of Sustainable Development.*

Pieroni Marina, P., T.C. McAloone, and C.A. Pigosso Daniela. 2019. Business model innovation for circular economy and sustainability: A review of approaches. *Journal of Cleaner Production* 215: 198–216.

Pravin, Kumar, Singh Rajesh Kr., and Kumar Vikas. 2021. Managing supply chains for sustainable operations in the era of industry 4.0 and circular economy: Analysis of barriers. *Resources, Conservation and Recycling* 164

Ratten, V. 2020. Coronavirus (covid-19) and social value co-creation. *International Journal of Sociology and Social Policy*

Raphaelle, Stewart, and Niero Monia. 2018. Circular economy in corporate sustainability strategies: A review of corporate sustainability reports in the fast-moving consumer goods sector. *Wiley Online Library*

Rincón-Moreno, J., M. Ormazábal, M.J. Álvarez, and C. Jaca. 2021. Advancing circular economy performance indicators and their application in Spanish companies. *Journal of Cleaner Production* 279:123605

Sumter, D., et al. 2021. Key Competencies for Design in a Circular Economy: Exploring Gaps in Design Knowledge and Skills for a Circular Economy. *Sustanability* 13: 776.

Welfens, P., R. Bleischwitz, and Y. Geng. 2017. Resource efficiency, circular economy and sustainability dynamics in China and OECD countries. *International Economics and Economic Policy* 14 (2): 377–382.

COVID-19 Outbreak: A Paradigm Shift in Food and Beverage Industry with Context to Delhi-NCR

Ajay Jain, Shruti Bansal, and Shobha Bhardwaj

1 Introduction

Due to corona epidemic, almost all types of businesses have been badly affected. But, the food and beverage business has been much more affected because the market movement of people has reduced very much. A number of research papers have been written showing the conditions of these businesses that are described below.

A report on food and beverage industries encompasses the companies engaged in the activities of the food materials, packaging, distribution, which also includes the finished and packaged foods including alcoholic beverages also. Before COVID-19 pandemic, people used to go to eat food in a large number of restaurants that were the chief contributing element that was considered before this pandemic for the development of food and beverages industries. Further, steady increase in per capita income and population with upgraded lifestyles are some other contributing developmental components of food and beverages industry (Newswire 2020).

Food and beverage enterprise in India has been turned into the fifth-biggest region in manufacturing. The growth of food industry is at full pace in India, thereby growing considerable growth possibilities for not only present but to new enterprise players as well (Kasad 2017).

In Fig. 1, it is shown that the revenue in the food and beverages segment is projected to reach 22.2% in 2021 and 8.2% by the end of year 2024 (Statista Report 2020). The reason for these drastic fluctuations is due to the hit of COVID-19 pandemic all over the food industry, which resulted in shutdowns of many restaurants because they are unable to bear the extra increase in their daily expenses such as sanitation costs. The important elements that have affected the meals and beverage enterprise after the pandemic mainly consist of shutdown of the restaurants and cafeterias. The

A. Jain (✉) · S. Bansal · S. Bhardwaj
Faculty of Management, Delhi-NCR Campus, SRM Institute of Science and Technology, Ghaziabad 201204, India

R. N. Subudhi et al. (eds.), *Future of Work and Business in Covid-19 Era*,
Springer Proceedings in Business and Economics,
https://doi.org/10.1007/978-981-19-0357-1_28

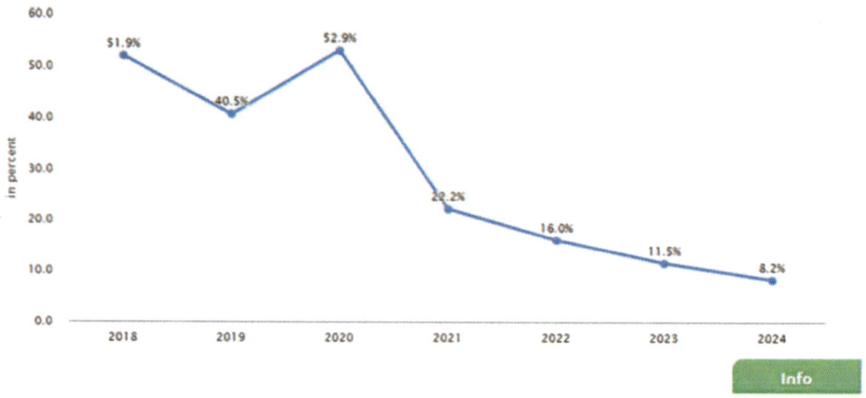

Fig. 1 The food and beverages segment is expected to show a revenue growth of 22.2% in 2021. *Source* Statista forecast report on COVID-19 (June' 2020)

pandemic COVID-19 has affected the meals and beverage enterprise in nearly all areas such as North America, Europe, Asia–Pacific, and other parts of the globe. One major impact of corona that is widely observed in Indian restaurant industry is that very few purchasers or consumers available in the market are willing to take the risk of buying the food or beverage items from outside.

In this research study, the researcher did not take any particular focused food and beverage industry. In fact, the researcher collected the responses based on their convenience and availability of consumers in different food places in the market.

2 Literature Review

2.1 *Impact of COVID-19*

The researcher highlighted the present state of advancement of coronavirus in India and the precautionary actions or measures taken by the government to minimize the effect of this disaster. The Government of India offers various characteristics and trends with the aid of statistical references from numerous country sources of India and the Ministry of Health & Family Welfare (Gupta et al. 2020).

World Health Organization has already announced the outbreak of coronavirus disease in the form of a worldwide pandemic by considering the data of hundreds of infections and deaths received daily. But, this report explores the meals structures inside the technology of the COVID-19 pandemic crisis. The most important objective of this paper is to locate the meals structures inside the epoch of the COVID-19 crisis (Galanakis 2020).

2.2 Impact of Covid-19 on Food Industry

Food industry is a complex but major industry in the whole world. As its name depicts, it supplies food devoured by the greater part of the individuals in the world. Everybody relies on the food business on this planet except farmers who grow crops for their food needs and hunters who chase for their survival. These days, a major and serious issue has been looked by all food industries whether it is large or small in size, i.e., coronavirus pandemic (Bansal and Sadhana 2020).

This research study aimed to explore the effect of lockdown on individuals. In addition, the transition made by human beings regarding the crisis and the way they maintain their daily life has shifted to a great degree. Lockdown state of affairs has altered their actions and manner of residing in the given population. Nowadays, most of the company's allow their employees to work from home by considering their safety point of view in this corona pandemic (Kumar and Dwivedi 2020).

The epidemic of the COVID-19 is a remarkable surprise to the economy of our country. The goal of the study is to have a look at awareness at the effect of coronavirus on numerous sectors of the economy. The sectorial evaluation has additionally helped to examine the beyond consequences with the existing state of affairs and additionally examine the state of affairs inside the country in terms of losses and opportunity costs (Saini 2020).

A pandemic is not a novel occurrence in human history; mankind has faced numerous pandemics throughout history. The goal of this study is to offer information about the COVID-19 outbreak's impact on the food supply chain, as well as a summary of the steps done to mitigate such consequences. The study concluded that maintaining supply in the agriculture and food sector in the pandemic is critical for avoiding a food crisis and minimizing the negative impact on the global economy (Aday and Aday 2020).

2.3 Impact of COVID on Food Safety

The rapid unfold of COVID-19 has brought to light many agencies either nationally or internationally to take emergency steps to minimize their effect globally. The worldwide financial recession creates large negative impacts on people's earnings and their meals safety, nutritions. Among real assets, COVID-19 also created the worst effect on large labor, people's prime asset (Unhale et al. 2020).

Since past 2019, a plague of the coronavirus disorder 2019 (COVID-19) has been unexpectedly unfolding everywhere in the world that creates difficulties for the sustainability of international agro-meals markets. COVID-19 pandemic impacted almost all the sectors of the economy, inclusive of agriculture also. Farmers, meals processors, storekeepers are confused about what further trouble will he get from this corona pandemic disease (Jambor et al. 2020).

3 Research Methodology

3.1 Research Gap

All the above-mentioned literature examination gives researcher a motivation and insight knowledge to investigate on this topic. The research gap has been identified by the researcher in the above-mentioned literature and has been proved helpful in leading this study. After conducting an exhaustive literature review, it is observed that there is a lack of analysis on basically three main parameters, which are consumer behavior, safety measures, and food quality during COVID-19 in the restaurant industry. So, it is the need of the hour to examine deeply on these variables to get better results.

3.2 Research Objectives

- To examine present and future behavior of customers during this COVID-19 regarding their food habits in restaurants.
- To identify the hygiene-based satisfaction level by comparing the restaurants foods and home-cooked meals.
- To identify safety components and other influencing factors that can affect the customers' decision to dine out again.

3.3 Hypotheses of This Study

H1: There is a relationship between customer's current and future food habits behavior in restaurants in COVID-19.
H2: There is a relationship between degree of satisfaction level based on hygiene between restaurant foods and home-cooked meals.
H3: Safety components have an effect on customer decisions to dine out again.

3.4 Data Collection

The first-hand data or primary data has been gathered from the customers of various restaurants in Delhi-NCR to know their opinions regarding the effects of COVID-19 on the food industry. A five-point standard Likert scale-based structured questionnaire used for collecting the responses from the respondents. Secondary data is collected from various journals and online websites of various reputed journals. The researcher based on their convenience and availability of respondents collected 100 responses from Delhi-NCR, which is also the sample size of this study.

3.5 Empirical Context

Factors and their items used in this study

Factor 1: Consumer Behavior

Items: Hospitality sector impact, waiters and chefs availability, income fall, restaurants condition, restaurants dine situation.

Factor 2: Selected Factors and Safety Components

Items: WHO decision, current COVID-19 cases, vaccines approval, local vaccine availability, family and friends influence, proper sanitation, social distancing, timely sanitization, gloves and face masks, customers/staff temperature check, outdoor seating availability, hand sanitizer stations, no touch bathrooms, disposable utensils.

Factor 3: Customer Satisfaction

Items: Hygiene, customer services, order time, ambience, advertisement, better quality, low pricing, cleanliness, ingredients used to cook food, preservatives in eatables, food quality, ambience/surroundings.

Some Other items—Annual income, qualification of the customers.

There are total 39 items have been taken by the researcher in this study to prove their hypothetical assumptions.

3.6 Reliability Analysis

Based on the SPSS software results, the reliability of all items is stated in Table 1

In Table 1, the Cronbach's alpha value is 0.731, which actually reflects high reliability of the measuring instrument or questionnaire. It shows high level of internal consistency with the sample.

Table 1 Reliability statistics

Cronbach's alpha	Number of items
0.731	39

Source SPSS output table, compiled by author, based on primary data collected by authors

3.7 *Validity Analysis*

Validity of the data has been checked to identify that whether all items in the questionnaire are valid or not, and one should check the value of the significance. The items validity of this study also been checked and identified that calculated values of sig (2-tailed) are lesser than their 0.05 threshold value, i.e., 0.000 < 0.05. So, it is cleared that all items presented in the questionnaire are valid.

4 Data Analysis and Interpretation

Proving Objective 1

For proving our Objective 1, chi-square analysis has been conducted in order to find out the results.

From the above Table 2, it is to be seen that the Pearson chi-square value of significance is 0.005, which is much smaller the standard value of alpha, i.e., 0.05. Hence, this means that there is the relationship between people visiting the restaurants before COVID-19 and people going to visit restaurants after COVID-19.

Proving Objective 2

To explore about the degree of satisfaction of hygiene via restaurants comparative to home-cooked meal. To prove this objective, one sample test has been used by the researcher.

From the above Table 3, it is found that obtained value of sig. is 0.000, which is smaller than their significance level 0.05. Therefore, null hypothesis is clearly rejected, and alternative hypothesis has been accepted. So, there is positive relationship based on degree of satisfaction between quality food provided via restaurants comparative to home-cooked meal.

Proving Objective 3

To identify the major factors and safety components that can affect the customer's decision to dine out again. To prove this objective, KMO, BARTLETT'S, factor analysis, and Friedman test have been used.

KMO Test and Bartlett's Test

The value of KMO must lies between 0 and 1, and value of KMO > 0.5 shows that the sample is adequate. In Table 4, KMO = 0.797, which represents the sample adequacy and preference for factor analysis.

Factor Analysis

From the above Table 5, it is identified that people highly entrust over WHO recommendations, and this factor is obtained the highest loading value out of all other

Table 2 Chi-square calculation

	Value	df	Asymp. sig. (2-sided)	Monte Carlo sig. (2-sided)			Monte Carlo sig. (1-sided)		
				Sig	99% confidence interval		Sig	99% Confidence interval	
					Lower bound	Upper bound		Lower bound	Upper bound
Pearson chi-square	31.857[a]	12	0.001	0.005[b]	0.003	0.006			
Likelihood ratio	31.193	12	0.002	0.002[b]	0.001	0.003			
Fisher's exact test	28.759			0.000[b]	0.000	0.001			
Linear-by-linear association	0.117[c]	1	0.732	0.767[b]	0.756	0.777	0.385[b]	0.373	0.398
No. of valid cases	100								

Source SPSS output table, compiled by author, based on primary data collected by authors

Table 3 Sample test results

	Test value = 0					
	Value	df	Sig. (2-tailed)	Mean difference	95% Confidence interval of the difference	
					Lower	Upper
Analyze the degree of satisfaction of quality food provided via restaurants comparative to home-cooked meal	42.981	99	0.000	3.720	3.55	3.89

Source SPSS output table, compiled by author, based on primary data collected by authors

Table 4 KMO and Bartlett's tests

Kaiser–Meyer–Olkin measure of sampling adequacy		0.797
Bartlett's test of sphericity	Approx. chi-square	287.45
	Df	15

Source SPSS output table, compiled by author, based on primary data collected by authors

Table 5 Component matrix[a]

Major factors	Component
	1
When World Health Organization say that it is ok	*0.897*
Data showing that new cases curve is flattening	0.848
Proven and available vaccine	0.528
Widely available local testing	0.679
As soon as family/friends start dining again	0.783
Proper sanitization facilities are available	0.788

Source SPSS output table, compiled by author, based on primary data collected by authors
Extraction method: principal component analysis
[a],1 components extracted

factors. Overall, it means that the most significant factor for influencing customer's decisions to dine out again is WHO recommendations.

Friedman Test

This test has been conducted to identify the major impacting safety components that can influence the customer dine out decision (Table 6).

In Table 7, hygiene is identified as Rank 1 factor, while at the same time, adver-

Table 6 Test statistics[a]

N	100
Chi-square	14.203
Df	6
Asymp. sig	0.027

Source SPSS output table, compiled by author, based on primary data collected by authors
[a]Friedman test

Table 7 Rank identification

Safety components	Mean rank	Ranking
Hygiene	3.66	1
Customer services	3.77	3
Order time	4.10	5
Ambience	4.03	4
Advertisement	4.53	7
Better quality	3.67	2
Low price	4.27	6

Source SPSS output table, compiled by author, based on primary data collected by authors

tisement ranked 7. It is concluded that almost all the customers appeared that the maximum vital component is hygiene, which affects their choice to dine out again.

5 Findings

1. All restaurant staff need to be aware about this disease's early symptoms and about their preventive measures that should be taken by anyone immediately after getting infected to avoid the chances of spreading it to others.
2. Restaurants workers and caterers must wear a face shield while interacting with their customers. Such face coverings and face shields should be wiped and cleaned from time to time.
3. Discourage employees from the frequent touch and usage of different employee's phones, desks, offices, or different painting tools and equipment such as pens, pencils, test holders.
4. Prohibit handshaking and different needless individual-to-individual touch practices inside the workplace.
5. Mention a poster at entrance gate that no one is allowed inside the restaurant who is having above normal body temperature or showing any of the symptoms of COVID-19 infection.

6. Redesign a seating plan to make certain distance of at least six (6) feet of separation between the all tables.

6 Limitations

1. **Sampling Error**: The small size of sample, i.e., 100 that has been used by researcher to represent the whole Delhi-NCR population which may create sampling error.
2. **Limited time**: The time to conduct this study was restricted. It was very difficult to get into detail because of the restricted time frame.
3. **Inadequate data**: The information received from the respondents may not be exactly correct and sufficient due to which the researcher confronted many issues in their exploratory study.

7 Recommendations and Suggestions

Based on this study, the following recommendations are as follows:

1. Restaurants should follow the COVID-19 safety factors properly so that the customer will start to dine out again.
2. Restaurants should try to make food more hygienically in order to attract the customers again.
3. Try to use best quality food ingredients to prepare the high quality nutritional food for the customers.
4. Restaurants should try to assure few good habits in their daily working styles such as use gloves while preparing food, sanitize the table, utensils properly after every visit of the customers.

If all the above-mentioned factors are followed by restaurants properly, they can achieve high customer satisfaction level as well as high chances to survive in this corona crises.

8 Conclusion

To conclude, there has been a difficult and challenging time for every food and beverage industry in India, to the extent that its mere survival is a question now. The coronavirus pandemic is a worldwide crisis. There are exceptionally huge worldwide stresses over the coronavirus that have a drastic negative impact over the global functioning food and beverage industry and also the mindset of the consumers, given them the major health risks. Individuals are afraid to accumulate in gatherings. Not even a single expert or government official perceives how long it will last, nor what a definitive monetary harm will be.

References

Aday, Serpil, and Mehmet S. Aday. 2020. Impact of COVID-19 on the food supply chain. Food Quality and Safety 4 (4).

Bansal, Ashima, and Rajiv Sadhana. 2020. *A Study on the Impact of Corona Virus (Covid-19) On The Global Food Industry*. June 2020, pp. 2321–1784.

Galanakis, C.M. 2020. The food systems in the era of the coronavirus (COVID-19) pandemic crisis. *Foods* 9 (4): 523.

Gupta, Rajan, Saibal K. Pal, and Gaurav Pandey.2020. A comprehensive analysis of COVID-19 outbreak situation in India. *medRxiv* (2020): n. pag. *medRxiv*. Web.

Jámbor, Attila, Péter Czine, and Péter Balogh. 2020. The impact of the coronavirus on agriculture: First evidence based on global newspapers. *Sustainability (Switzerland)* 12 (11): n. pag. *Sustainability (Switzerland)*. Web.

Kasad, Aashish. 2017. *High Growth Segments of the Delicious Indian Food and Beverage Industry*. November 21, 2017. https://www.forbesindia.com/blog/technology/high-growth-segments-of-the-delicious-indian-food-and-beverage-industry/.

Kumar, Mahendra, and Sachin Dwivedi. 2020. Impact of coronavirus imposed lockdown on Indian population and their habits. *International Journal of Science and Healthcare Research* 5 (2): 88–97. Web.

Newswire, Globe. *Impact of COVID-19 on the Global Food & Beverages Industry Market*. News Paper artical. Dublin: ResearchAndMarkets.com's, 2020. January 23, 2021. https://www.globenewswire.com/news-release/2020/04/15/2016396/0/en/Impact-of-COVID-19-on-the-Global-Food-Beverages-Industry-Market.html.

Saini, Ruchi. 2020. *The Impact of Corona Virus on Indian Economy*.

Statista Report. *Food & Beverages*. (2020). www.statista.com. https://www.statista.com/outlook/253/119/food-beverages/india.

Unhale, Shrikrushna S., et al. 2020. Impact of Covid-19 on food safety and food security. *World Journal of Advance Healthcare Research*.

A Case Study of Rental Management in India Under COVID19

[A Study of Symbiotic Arrangements to Work from Anywhere (WFA) Leading to a Business Model Proposition of Smart Rental Homes Owned by Elderly]

Devashish De and Shalini Mahapatra

1 Introduction

The reflection of a rental tragedy faced by the urban poor in India is aptly reflected in Amazon Prime OTT in the much-discussed web series (Purkayastha 2020) titled 'Gulabo Sitabo'. The storyline of this web series is woven around the life of an aged owner, who rents out his old and worn-out palatial building to a few needy tenants, struggling to meet their ends. In the process the aged landlord faces a series of hardships posed by the tenants. The limitations of both the renter and rentee is an unending saga of mistrust as life goes on a barter and bargain duel. In view of this narration, the ushering of the Draft Model Tenancy Act 2020 is a consequence of awareness on healthy social engagements (Maya 2021) that are desired in the field of Rental Management which otherwise pivots on issues of insecurity. Technically a landlord would like to remain a landlord, but the present legal terms do not wholly favour him (Bhansali 2021). It has become even more prominent ever since the labour laws have incorporated the industry voice of a work from home (WFH) (PIB 2021) requirement. It is the new paradigm shift in the new world order ushered in by COVID19 pandemic scenario. The new norm is much in contrast to the earlier assigned form of eight hours of work only. Today there is a requirement of adding the comfort of office space at home, thus creating the new era of work from home protocol. Rental Management of residential spaces is relooked into the scope of this paper with a prompt for the elderly middle class in India. Thus, they can use the opportunity for attaining a social security income model. The cornerstone of

D. De (✉)
Jamsetji Tata School of Disaster Studies, Tata Institute of Social Sciences (TISS), Bombay 400088, India

S. Mahapatra
KIIT (Deemed To Be a University), Bhubaneswar, Odisha, India

R. N. Subudhi et al. (eds.), *Future of Work and Business in Covid-19 Era*,
Springer Proceedings in Business and Economics,
https://doi.org/10.1007/978-981-19-0357-1_29

such thought was first evinced after the declaration of contraction of GDP by the Reserve Bank of India in November 2020 where it stated the drop in GDP by 23.9%. Economists (Kumar) (PTI 2021a) foresaw the drop up to or beyond 25% in 2021. The said observations and recommendations on prepaid rentals were shared with the Finance Ministry on MyGov portal of Government of India as it sought suggestions on the Budget 2021–22. These suggestions were duly acknowledged by the Ministry of Finance, Government of India, for consideration in the coming times. Describing the social security status of the elderly who survive on meagre pensions, it is observed that with reducing bank interest rates and coupling tax profile, the country would actually lead to mass bankruptcy in near future. Primarily the sustenance of the elderly, may collapse. To avoid the same, a social security system on organized rentals rather than reverse mortgage which is the available option for sustained livelihood was proposed.

There are certain terms of reference which has been spelled out by taking forward a step ahead in stringency of the Government of India multiple communiques (PTI 2020) in the wake of impact of COVID19. They are generic but for emulation of the proposal as brought out in this paper it is important that most of the guidelines enlisted by Ministry of Home Affairs (MHA) holding the incident command mechanism of COVID19 in India with certain more from Ministry of Housing and Urban Affairs (MoHUA) are well interpreted. The crafting of the paper is in favour of the landlord or rentee and is a contention expressed as a matter of hypothesis. This article is such since the identity of the renter is shifting and is a temporary identity. Also, all gains and mathematics is pivoted on the property of the landlord (Contributors 2019), who is the only person to open the gates of prosperity for shifting identities. This way the public exchequer gets to benefit from an individual's investment of a lifetime. This paper is thus an attempt to undo the GDP contraction (Daniyal 2020) of 23.9% which India suffered due to COVID19—the worst ever for India. Other states across the world can benefit from the emulation of the transcription presented in the paper. Initial results indicate that the role of landlord could only be of provision of space, but for all other events accruing from the use of space, the renter could be made solely responsible. The aim of this paper is to streamline Apartment Rental Services as a delightful experience (Haider 2020) much in sync with the call of अतिथि देवो भव!(The Visitor is God!).

Renting Arrangements being a sensitive topic, initially a discussion with their colleagues and peers in their workplaces was conducted which on one side was having a set of individuals in the working salaried class who needed rental space at affordable costs in Tier-1/2 cities in India. The evening get-together near a Building Society was the second place where random opinions generated among residents, easing out in Lockdowns, were noted. Some observations were noted from the WhatsApp platforms of societies which have a seperate social and formal group for expression and communication. A series of Newspaper Articles were collated as Secondary Data which were composed on the issues of Rental Mismanagement. *The conclusion was that present arrangement of Rental Agreement was not conducive for Senior Citizens in India due to social ills and lack of awareness of their asset value returns which they could accrue.* In addition, lack of support from Society Management in general due to incomprehension of Rental management as a source of income may have been the supporting reason as well. Inability to address the new dimensions opened due to WFH conditions, by both residents and society management, became the research gap leading to framing a set of parameters which could be transformed as a mobile-based application to facilitate government, societies, renters and rentees among whom the rentees constituted primarily the left out lot of senior citizens. This reserach thus serves as an evolutionary study only.

2 Literature Review

The Transition of WFH to Work from Anywhere. Pandemic has ushered in a spate of job losses and pay cuts. Enveloped by the stringency of COVID19 protocols of institutional and home quarantine, most of the gaining employees of firms had to put in more from a new domain which were their own homes. The change brought in a form of disturbance. As per Economic Times (Basu and Philip 2020) the high-profile performers who were retained by their firms had to constantly take calls and had to follow up on interviews and web conferences. Time zones of office timings got dissolved and it's not sure whether allowances for extra time bonuses were made from the coffers of cash-stripped firms or not. With denatured privacy, pets became an obstruction as much as quality time took a backseat. With anxiety and depression partially setting in due to lack of assured internet speeds leading to fledgling performances, clinical psychologists saw a rise in cases by 40–50%. With reduction in commuting time WFH is a win–win situation for many. Firstly, apartment requirements now have larger carpet areas to cater for life at home which come from rental inventory now held by senior citizens in India. A reduction in commutation will help the government in meeting the energy requirement projections of the nation. Online sales have boosted as much as online food start-ups. Induced boredom due to lack of social life will trigger tourism (Philip 2021) which has become pivotal in augmenting the scope of short spell rentals. The scope adds as the patient list of doctors managing lifestyle diseases has increased. With management interaction and boardroom updates just a click away, the scope of taking a bungee jumping the moment the web interaction would end has become a reality. For those having 'Fatima Mahal' (taken from the reference of Gulabo Sitabo in the introductory lines in this paper) or apartments with compelling views and experiences, this is an opportunity for 'Home as a Hotel' livelihood model. So, while serviced apartments always existed, revival of rental business from underutilized inventory is an opportunity. This way the senior citizen will now focus on a Start Up model from their real estate asset.

Psychological relief requirements induced by Work from Home or Anywhere is a set of aberrations. While condom sales may have increased (PTI, Economic Times 2020) there are also noteworthy news features which are representations on the spike in Domestic Violence (Taskin 2021). Some more of these are isocations (Bureau 2020), solocations, self-isolation, coronavirus divorces and rejuvenating getaways, etc.

Till date in the World Order there has never been a documented contingent condition (BBC 2020) when productive manpower of the society with varied skills have been forced to emulate a term of reference of doing everything as before, but withholding themselves in their residential environment. Till date corporate office spaces never got restricted to homes. There have been fewer studies in all probability when the schedules of office timelines have concurrently run along with home cooking. Comparative studies on closed businesses and new initiatives due to pandemic are yet to formalize. In a fledgling economy, due to the need of larger carpet areas in residential homes, the scope of rental management of empty inventory thus is being looked into, now. People holding it are those who created their asset against the dreams of retirement without having a clear idea of how they were to face the realities of a time, decades ahead.

Problem Areas. Apartment Rental Services (Estrade 2020) are based on the forced accommodation requirement generated by the call of earning livelihood, dislocation from home set-ups, inadequate bank balances which prevents the unfurling of full comfort levels for most individuals in lower- to middle-income group and may be in limited space as opportunity of sightseeing and exploration. The imposed costs which actually translate into the earnings of one or many may be a squeeze for the one who has to dish out the money. These sets of paying individuals are mostly young students and professionals. Due to the setting frustration or greed, many try to grab the asset by force and by not paying up in time. Others try to perpetrate disturbance in neighbourhood by unethical (Press) (PTI 2020) practices which are abhorrent (CommonFloor 2020), namely to include loud parties, promotion of immoral relationships, consumption of spurious material, ogling and gesturing acts at residents (I. E. PTI 2016), etc. A system of mutual gains in principle, translates into an avoidable event leaving a bad taste, as per actuals. The angry renter deviates to damage the settings of a beautiful house when he or she disfigures the walls and the electrical set-up, punctures the electric metre and other soft-covered items as water heater or even the air conditioner. Neighbours (Aggarwal 2017) can be instigators due to factors of jealousy caused by the gains of others and this social truth is better not overlooked. In many places they may even usher in fraudulent dealers to sell their adjacent vacant flats which leads to a litigation and complications. More instigations or unlawful policing may be seen when community differential comes in. In recent times the rush in registrations by slashing the Stamp Duty charges (Adimulam 2020) of Maharashtra Government from 6 to 3% applicable from 01 September 2020 to 31 December 2020 even saw the fraudulent attempt at the Aga Khan Palace (Jadhav 2020) of Pune. With the advent of rent or property management services, the performing executives of the firm have tried to build on these loopholes wherein unsuspecting and civilized renters are charged fines by deceit (Gooptu 2019; Salman 2020), since due to their primary orientation, they fail to suspect foul play when they ward off a fine hairline crack in the washbasin or a loose lock and the list can go on. This experience is more or less recurring with others as well. A careful thought will establish that, the criminal acts of outgoing tenants may actually put on edge the threat of life to future inhabitants for whom the fear of culpable homicide will become real like short circuits leading to fire, etc.

The lack of social security (Guide) (GPG 2020) in the absence of a pension which can match the high cost of living, forces elderly citizens to rent out their spaces. Similarly, law-abiding docile citizens also sublet their space which has otherwise deep sentimental value for them. For some it may be the rooms of their children who may have gone out, or their ancestral property or even their dream house built out of a lifetime of savings towards which they had sometimes calculated the prospect of earnings to sustain their golden years or the corpus that they require for their social security. By promulgating a Model Rent Control Act, the government is setting up centralization when in principle, they had promulgated decentralization by the way of 74th Amendment. However, the renter verification exercise as mandated under Section-188 of the Indian Penal Code (IPC) is generally not being practised when landlords take renters one on one through a newspaper classified or through an internet service. The star system which can caution other landlords has somehow not been formalized in India. Then there are stories where a politically connected renter who is a social goon opens up a sex brothel. This makes it necessary to put the landlord in a security web as against the renters.

Secondary Landlords. This problem statement is being written about since the current government of the day is making provisions for migrant labourers by the way of affordable housing. But their poverty is the generating factor for secondary deviations. For example, there are a very few administrators with the clue as to how the space is being used when the migrant labourer sets out to work and how this 12 h of the day transforms the space. Here, the renter becomes the secondary landlord or rentee. The space is being used for terrorist hideouts, prostitution (Narayanan 2020; TFI Post News Desk 2021), drug abuse meets, antisocial and power delving meets and so on and so forth. Unless these private spaces are guarded by intrusion check arrangements, the policy of affordable housing plans may set off a huge administrative disorder which will be a nightmarish experience.

2.1 Research Gap

After studying the Literature Review it is implied that there is a dearth of research on the proposed topic, 'A Case Study of Rental Management in India under COVID19; A Study of Symbiotic Arrangements to Work from Anywhere (WFA) leading to a Business Model Proposition of Smart Rental Homes owned by Elderly'.

As the WFH concept is a novel trend in the present times that is largely being accepted by the government and private companies pertaining to the COVID19 pandemic situation, not much research has been done on gains possible from property rentals of the elderly, social security and prepaid renting in the pandemic.

The new norm of work from home (WFH) creates the requirement of transparent and conducive rental app, renting reforms and rental laws.

Open-ended and fluid legal regulations have created a challenge for the elderly middle-class Indian landlord preventing him/her from safely renting out his/her property.

2.2 Research Questions

Can a mobile application or App work favourably in a changed scope of renting pattern of residential spaces in India? If yes, then what are the parameters which a renter and rentee should know about their spaces?

If the pitfalls have more or less been studied in detail with respect to Renting Management, how could they be obviated to pave the way for a sustainable Business Model?

Are rentee and renter fully conversant with extant government orders, policies, rules and laws on the subject? If no, what are the legal modifications in 74th Amendment, which could empower rentees through their societies without scope of extraneous policing?

Do senior citizens realize that a Leave and Licence Agreement could be more empowering as against a Rent Agreement since it empowers them to get back to their owned spaces where the terms are that of a licensor or licencee?

What can be a quantitative method to assess a location in terms of its advantages? Could a renter assess his future cost of living in his society? If Yes, How?

Could a rentee blacklist a renter who may be registered on a Unique Identification Number (Haider 2021) and vice versa just like the way a star rating is given by both service provider and service seeker in Apps as Uber/Ola and on Urban Company?

What are the society and community reforms which could be placed upfront as a necessity to make a Society of Retirees a joyful enterprise again?

Objectives. Having known the business parameters and the scope of Renting Services as an organized livelihood option the objectives of the discussion will be to frame the following.

To work out the 'Anticipated Cost of Living' in various Tiers of Cities in India. These could factor the index of supportive societies in a Rent Management space preferably on an App. Thereby societies will be marked on the value levels they may provide like incentive for tuitions, child help, doctor's colony, etc.

To identify unsuspecting renters and rentees by a background check method of star rating. Clear and effective eviction processes will have to be devised.

To list out empowering methods of Senior Citizens with Assets so that they can be micro-Start-Ups and Job Providers as much as Enterprise Facilitators of other businesses.

To work out an App based Standard Operating Procedure or SOP for universal compliance.

To work out a Feedback monitoring system to effectively elicit favourable rent targets, usher in more structured home services for strangers, reduce administrative workload of governance at various levels and empower society as a magnet for earning forex in India.

Frame guidelines to sieve out unscrupulous elements in a tripartite method to include rentee, Society Management and Administration.

To work out Rent Management as assured sustained Business Model to meet the Government target of Housing for All.

3 Methodology

The present study is an effort to find out the Rental Management procedures and limitations present in India. It studies the concept of work from home, i.e. largely being followed in the present COVID19 settings. This model of work from home is assumed to continue in the post-pandemic situation also. This offers a viable and sustainable money generation option for the elderly Indian middle class having properties to rent out. While it is a viable source of income, it also has legal limitations and inadequate information is available with the landlord on new trends of renting out properties.

3.1 Techniques, Tools and Data Collection

Technique. Purposive Sampling Technique was followed for the present study. The sampling was done through informal telephonic, social media and one on one interactions.

Sampling Size. The sample size includes 70 educated Indians.

Sampling Topography. The samples include serving and retired persons primarily from the working class and a few students, who are aware of social trends in India.

Tools. Microsoft Word, Google Forms.

3.1.1 Primary Data Collection.

The primary data was collected from 70 educated persons including men and women of various categories living across India. They included serving government servants who may be best called as not from the upper middle class. Women members from corporate HR departments of known companies, NGOs and banks also participated. Some set of postgraduate students from Pune University chose to be part of the survey. Additional members included Indian NRIs and professionals working abroad. Some academicians were kind to respond as much certain Central Government Staff most of whom have a fair realization of Rental Management and issues in India.

3.1.2 Secondary Data Collection Sources

Mainline English, Vernacular media.

Periodicals, Books, Journals and Research Findings.

Electronic and New age media.

Innovativeness. Most of the Real Estate Apps are business oriented. They miss out on integrating utilities. There are appealing measures and mental feel-good boosters which has been added here to lay the blueprint of an App or a Billboard even. There are other safety features of other business practices which has been integrated. So overall the business model proposition is very near to a remake of the existing segmental process of Renting in the current Indian society.

4 Discussion

The discussion (Singh 2020) pivots around an App much as the way society management Apps as MyGate has come up. A lot of start-ups have tried to meet the solutions pertaining to society management piecemeal. Judiciary has promulgated the Leave and License Agreement to ward off the rising files on rent arbitration and settlements. Apropos the Government could also streamline the process by making real a term called as 'prepaid' and 'set duration' pattern based on post 11-month transfers which would usher in secondary employment. A five-time waiver may be made possible on grounds of renters who may be pursuing a treatment or may be affected by academic rotation of their wards. An initial deposit may follow the following cost sheet, which will deter them from vandalism and perpetration of destructive mindset. These could be activated if the market rent charges of an assumed cost of Rs 10,000/- for a 2BHK (in outskirts) is paid first (This is much less than 10% of the market rate of the property at most urban locations of India -which is the ceiling limit of charging the applicable rent. So, the applicable rent for a property with cost of Rs 30 lakhs is actually Rs 3 lakhs and at 1% it is Rs 30,000/- which is more than the cited figure of Rs 10,000/-) (Tables 1 and 2).

4.1 *Costs of Living as Relatable Only in Terms of Rent (Includes* ϭ*)*

Rs 10,000 (House Rent) + Rs 7000/-(ϭElectricity, Water and Gas) + Rs 2000/- (Society Charges) = Rs 19,000-Rs 20,000/- for a 2 BHK. This means that the applicable charge less the refundable deposit is Rs 20,000 ÷ 10 = Rs 2000/- per month.

Table 1 Assessment of Cost of Living based on feedback from Residents of Societies in Navi Mumbai as Tier I city and Bhubaneswar as Tier II city

Service	Essential (A)/Optional (B)/Preferred (C)	Tentative cost* per month (Prices reflected has been quoted from interpolation of experienced costs)	Remarks
Prepaid electricity (Stranger 2020) б	A	Rs 5000/-	Cost of limited air conditioner/Heater Use included. (Read additional notes on National Programme on Advanced Chemistry Cell Battery Storage)
Prepaid water б	A	Rs 1000/-	Part costs refundable
Prepaid gas б	A	Rs 800/-	Part costs refundable
Wi-Fi ж	B	Rs 500/-	PM-WANI/wireline network
Optional furniture Prepaid ж	B	Rs 5000/-	Fridge, Washing Machine, TV (Source: Furlenco)
Optional transport by electric scooter ж	B	Rs 5000/-	Self-drive motor apps (Website 2021) (Reduced prices are suggestive)
Security of fans, lights and air conditioner	A	Rs 25,000/-	Compulsory
Optional cooking services ж	C	Rs 2000/-	Vocal for Local (Inflated costs as the same may be bargained)
Optional cleaning and dusting services ж	C	Rs 2000/-	Star based performance continuation. includes toilet cleaning
Optional laundry and ironing services б	B	Rs 3500/-	Sanitation and security of Damage to clothes may be checked
Optional catering and party services	C	Rs 10,000/-	For 10-person get-together to include party games, decoration, drinks, music and meal of choice @ Rs 1000/- per person (Reduced prices)

(continued)

Table 1 (continued)

Service	Essential (A)/Optional (B)/Preferred (C)	Tentative cost* per month (Prices reflected has been quoted from interpolation of experienced costs)	Remarks
Optional milk, egg and processed poultry ж	B	Rs 2500/-	Meant for a family of four (Generic)
Optional vegetable and grocery services ж	B	Rs 10,000/-	Meant for a family of four (Generic)
Compulsory inspection of asset	A	Rs 30,000/- (annual/ security deposit)	To be done at the time of leaving the space or gaining the space. Visit charges @Rs 2000/- per visit. Will certify asset taken over and asset handed over as correct. Aggregated payment can only be released if landlord approves. Star rating to be given by landlord once a year. Those with three star or less may be liquidated. Compulsion of Inspection may be as per ticket generated from computer
Add-Ons (Prime 2020a)	C		Home Schooling Services, Nursing Services, School Bus Services, Employee Pick Up and Drop, Pest Control, Taxi Services, Sight Seeing guides, Itinerary planners and ticket makers, Creche maids to move along in office spaces along with mothers, Security Services, Beauty and cosmetic services and so on and so forth

Source Primary data, collected by authors

Table 2 Cost–Benefit Ratio of Office Tables versus WFH tables (for Corporates—Indicative only)

Notes	Office table (Dependents)	Cost per person per day	WFH (Dependents)	Cost per person per day	Elaboration
A rough indicative cost of office space applicable to one person is being put forth in columns on the right. It can be seen that due to part increase in establishment costs the WFH is slightly more costly than using an office space set-up on an everyday basis	5 Cups of Tea @Rs 10/-	Rs 50	Courier Boy for Two Snacks/Meal, Grocery, Home service	Rs 30/- × 4 = Rs120/-	
	Office Cleaner charges per table	Rs 30/-	Home Garbage Collector	Rs 10/-	
	Press and laundry	Rs 30/- to Rs 100/-	Home Helps	Rs 200/-	Approx. Rs 6000 per month
	Flowers and decoration	Rs 30/-	Maintenance of Air Conditioner, etc	Rs 50/-	Calculated out of a consolidated cost of repair, maintenance and annual maintenance contract's part cost
	Wi-Fi	Rs 10/-	Netflix and other Subscriptions	Rs 15/-	
	Cab service	Rs 200/- to Rs 400/-	Medicines and Additional Requirements of comfort	Rs 150/-	Part cost of establishment settings has been left out
Total	Approximately	Rs 320/- to Rs 620/-		Rs 545/- to Rs 650/-	

Source Primary data, collected by authors

Security Deposit of Rs 25,000/- + Rs 30,000/-(ж) = say Rs 50000/- (for 10 months). Considering one would get back 50% of this only, the same would amount to Rs 2500/- per month.

Consolidated Cost of Living applicable to renter is Rs 2000 (Basic Rent) + Rs 2500 (Part Security) + Rs 10,000 (Grocery) + Rs 10,000 (Vegetables) + Rs 10,000 (Communication and Lifestyle) + Rs 6000 (House Helps) + Rs 5000 (Commutation) = Rs 45,500/-per month. (Generic Calculation not based on Absolute values).

Target: Those, whose 80% earning may amount to Rs 50,000/-

(a) *Families with an earning potential of Rs 75,000/- as carrying home pay including HRA.*

(b) *School and College Excursions /Internship teams separate for males and females.*
(c) *Professionals on Short Tours of a month to three months.*
(d) *Professionals on transferable/ corporate jobs.*
(e) *Families seeking rent near their incomplete housing projects.*
(f) *Employees as Bankers.*
(g) *Shopkeepers looking for stocking cloth bales and spices, etc. (if applicable).*
(h) *Start-Up teams looking forward to quiet co-working spaces with computers only. Video Editors, Photographer teams seeking occasional studio spaces, television serial cast seeking actual homes for a theatrical set-up.*
(i) *Foreign groups seeking to stay amid Indian Community.*
(j) *Career counsellors, practising psychologists to whom people may not visit in an open address/ market place. Astrologers and cooks who have their own shows in a closed community of believers.*
(k) *Organizations who may have to meet due to societal call in a foreign place as Kerala Samaj or even Bengali Society who practice for stage plays, Danseuse who may like a residential space for practising dance forms, women fitness enthusiasts who may find home space appealing, Classical Music practitioners seeking serene spaces with sound proofing provided a declaration is made in advance with respect to such ventures to enable surprise visits by law enforcing agencies, with waiting room separate for parents and companions.*

4.2 Incentives by Society Communities (ULBs/Empowered Agencies)

Suggested involvement of societies could include book coves at corners, garden upkeep and duck swarms, cycling tracks, storytelling sessions by elderly, welcome visits by local craftsmen as musicians, snake charmers, sportsmen coaches, city walks (The Department of Tourism is currently registering event programmers), visit to heritage sights, bird and other fauna sighting opportunities, etc.

Property eviction duties in case of defaulters with the help of local police and administration at the request of the landlord are something that society administration will have to undertake. However, ULBs will not police the renters or landlord as per the Court Judgement (Deshpande and Tembhekar 2020) except for undertaking eviction proceedings and gathering dues from the renter and similar legal measures which includes affording parking spaces to the renter as well in societies where it has not been marked as per another Court Judgement (Thomas 2018) (Fig. 1).

Eviction Process: Since a notice giving and notice acceptance process hinges primarily on rent payment and antisocial behaviour, so a forced payment or non-renewal of leave and licence ticket should enable an intimation to the society chairman and security who in lieu will stop the free movement of the former renter as an unauthorized person which will include cessation of electricity and light in two days'

Fig. 1 Suggested Advertisement of a Staycation Location on Real Estate portals as conceived through inputs (addresses, etc., put up are purely coincidental and do not refer to any landlord or renter in specific.) *Source* Own conceptualization by author

time frame and additional services on forthwith mode. These two days should be the process of asset handing over and allocation to next parties in line who should be able to do it online, besides establishing a connect by going to the society, police station and the landlord for an approval. The present suggestion of a Rent Tribunal in the District Office as suggested in the Draft Model Tenancy Act 2020 may be an initiator of corruption practices and avoidable power play. This may not help in reducing the trust gap between landlord and renter. A decentralized control by ULBs and Society Leadership in diffusing these solutions may be apt for emulation. Societies may charge a facilitation to the landlord at about 1% of the rent gains of the landlord. So, for Rs 10,000/- charged as Basic Rent the cost accruable to the society is Rs 100/- per month per flat /house which will be a huge corpus cumulatively.

4.3 Gains

The rental market will bloom from 2% of the underutilized inventory (Babar 2015) to higher figures which will help the exchequer in gains by the way of income tax (inventory overhang of a period beyond 30 months is a loss to the exchequer as well).

Renters may get the incentive to start secondary business as tuitions, research work, sightseeing, art and skill classes, work from home incentivization based on the available technical platform.

Societies as Urban Local Bodies (ULBs) may gain from society contribution of water and cleaning services. Vacant Inventories may start getting utilized. During emergencies the younger working renters can help out the elderly (this will have to be part of the agreement document). This will augment community resilience. A large number of elderlies may get to see children more often, which may help them psychologically. Single women in cities may feel more secure in a community set-up and may be absolved of the pains of privacy traps in hotels.

Larger families can move out on trips of longer duration (Quint 2020).

BPL families will be integrated due to assured work arrangements.

The possibility of terrorist hideouts in urban set-ups may drop due to larger public interface and accountability of all gaining stakeholders. Community Policing may become effective.

Augmented Property tax slabs may fall due to assured returns in small numbers from multiple gainers.

4.4 Losses

A popular rental destination may cause increase in rental prices (Tourist 2020) and prevent the locals from making gains of the popularity. This can directly be proportional to Taxi Rates and Cost of Living which will require a check. This will mean more influx of forex, in due course, which will benefit the government only, one way.

Renting Companies might misuse (Thanawala 2020) the KYC documents of the customer, which has to be guarded against like mobile number, bank statement, Aadhaar card number, e-mail, etc.

During market revival a number of brokers in connivance (Khan and Babar 2020) with greedy landlords may keep properties vacant so that with artificial scarcity, the prospective renters could be charged higher rates for lucrative properties.

4.5 Key Pointers

Rent Arrangements are made between May to August.

Rent Seekers have location on their mind.

Rent Seekers then look for neighbourhood comforts and ease.

Young People Rent. Old People should have been settled.

Some Family members /tenants get larger families in the rented space without intimation.

4.6 Critical Questions

See Table 3.

Table 3 Suggested FAQs (E. T. Prime 2020b) for landlords pursuing affordable properties

1. While buying the property is your EMI more than 25% of your carry home pay/ consolidated earnings?	This may be indicative of your urgency to get a renter which in lieu will spell out your vulnerability
2. Do you realize what are the Recurring Costs after buying your property? (2BHK)	Property Tax (Rs 40000/- annually), Electricity and Water Bills (Rs 5500per month), Society Maintenance Charges (Rs 35000 annually). Say 1,41,000/- in a decent locality
3. To obviate recurring charges is Rent option @Rs 15000/- for 10 months is an option under Leave and License Agreement to cut out the tax load spelled in 5.8.2?	It may be realized that the property may not be with the same renter for more than three years preferably so that one is not surprised
4. Do you realize that all your Rent agreements have to be Leave and License Agreements of a period not more than 10 months?	If you do a Rent Agreement, one may not be able to evict the renter in case of a misinterpretation of terms, death of owner and other issues
5. Do you have a Landlord Community System to have a firm Business Community?	Isolated and Elderly Women may be able to get help
6. Do you believe in Bulk Insurance?	With many beneficiaries, one may not stand isolated for claims

Source Primary data, collected by authors

4.7 *Rent Arrangement Cards*

See Table 4.

4.8 *Rent Giver*

See Table 5.

4.9 *Service Provider Based on a Prepayment Model*

See Table 6.

5 Findings

Many respondents to whom this idea was suggested came out openly with the fact that a house owner is really very sentimental about his/her property. They confided that the fear of damage to their property or forceful occupation was the primary

Table 4 Location advantage for Rent Assessment by Rent Seeker in terms of cost and time. Rent Seeker: 10-Best, 5-OK,0-Poor, A-Location 1, B-Location 2, C-Location 3

Location	Close to office (a)	Close to market/home delivery options (b)	Connectivity with Ola and Uber/Bus /Auto (c)	Security of locality (d)—grown up children can go to School	Freedom and parking (e)
A					
B					
C					

Neighbourhood tolerance (f)	Cordial support for creche and tuitions (d)	Clean house help services/office support mechanism	Garbage collection	Garden/entertainment	Peace/previous experience
A					
B					
C					

Source Primary data, collected by authors

reason due to which inventories across the board are lying vacant. This dissuaded the renting process which is a viable investment option. At some places brokers do take the key of the flat and work around a good business, year after year. But then there were places where people have been cheated when their houses on rent have been locked and arbitration cases have been ensuing year after year. Some even confided that renting processes were without documentation where monies were collected in cash by permitting a stay. A large number of respondents were enlightened with the fact that '11-month contract' was technically a Leave and License Agreement. The difference between a Rent/Lease Agreement and the one stated in previous line was not known to most. Some critical and empowering questions were asked and most of the respondents from cities of Bhubaneswar, Bangalore, Kolkata, Delhi, Nagpur, Pune, Mumbai and outside India responded in equal measure. Some retired professionals were wary of their dream project and instead wanted to live in a rented accommodation till their final hours, rather than getting into a business venture. They had turned into forced caretakers of their assets for which they were not very pleased. The responders also confided that Societies though are empowered, but slowly they are more even with regular residents as against owners. An extraneous policing was seen in power play. The fault line of disaffection was more pronounced if the owners who are not regular residents stayed away or were culturally different. The Society members exhibited varying degrees of officiousness which was probably insidious in carriage. Some of them were upfront in a quarrel. People are not amenable to the

Table 5 Rent Suitability for Contenders at the time of allotment of Space. Family-8, Girls-6, Boys-5. Against Renewable Leave and License Agreement

Star Rating from previous renter	5	4	3	2	1
Interested in Changing House (Leave and License Agreement Process to ensue)	Within three years	2 years	One year	5 years	5–10 years
Professional	Corporate	Transferable government	Student	Local	Uncertain
Has Changed Places in last 5 years	–	Every two years	Fresh	Every Year	Shorter than a year
Police Verification	Written and Available	Lodged	On corporate letterhead	Feedback from Maid	Google search on adverse character
KYC	Ready	Willing	Substitute	Witness	False
Security Deposit	3–5 months	Willing to compensate after 2 months of security	–	Pending	Ready to pay for all prepaid/done (Desperate to get a house)
Education	Average but steady	doctor	Teacher/researcher	Not well educated	Merchant/Lawyer (Those knowing how to twist the law may not be welcome)

Source Primary data, collected by authors

fact that an investment of a lifetime made over decades, could not probably realize the dream due to several new realities years later.

Limitations of Paper. This paper has been made on an 'as is where is' format. It does not give clue to enable a way out for old societies with broken infrastructure with very old people who are practically owners, but incapable to take on a business venture due to frailty and poor shape of their health for which a separate research is desired. This paper also doesn't address those societies who are mired in volumes of litigation and related issues.

In view of all the above organized and supplemented Rent Management was seen as a way of assured secondary income which could support a plethora of businesses

Table 6 Vulnerability Parameters of Service Providers as related to Service Seekers

	Benefits accruable to Service Provider	Tentative issues likely to be raised by service seekers
Milk and everyday grocery	Retention of Overpayment in Wallets	Seekers may only demand convenience from Branded Products which will converge resources to Original Equipment/Product Manufacturer (OEM) as Omfed
Furniture	Scope exists for 'Vocal for Local'. However very sturdy and low value inventory may be maintained. Reuse of used furniture may not invite clientele	Natural Material and Environment Friendly products may be in demand which may empower local artisans. Society may formalize contracts and penalty for unauthorized dumping
Repair agencies	Overpayment extracted on the ignorance of service seeker like charging Air Conditioner gas every time	Star rating processes will continue to empower
Transport facilitators	The OLA/UBER Ad on Woman's Safety is an indicator of vices in the field	Empowered societies can make available their own transport
Cooking and cleaning services	Somewhere the scope of prostitution and secondary deviations in practice of honourable Social Life must end where these people become vectors of unethical practices. Crime reporting serials are becoming suggestive	Empowered societies can take out a tender of house helps and similar service providers for bracketing out unscrupulous entities
Inspection services (cumulative costs can help societies gain corpus for major repair of infrastructure as lifts)	They should not get hands in glove with profit-making agencies	Board of members to include fair representation of women members may help bring transparency. It could be done through draw of lots
Food delivery boy	In the recent past there are a few individuals who have played up the religion card on Twitter	One of the existing skills set with Indian Senior Citizen could be harnessed for house management processes as well which renters may subscribe to
Home schooling and itinerary planners	Must be on a budget	One of the existing skills set with Indian Senior Citizen could be house management processes as well to include education which renters may subscribe to

Source Primary data, collected by authors

and did hold the promise to revive a fledgling economy ushered in by COVID19. This could lead to Atmanirbhar Bharat.

6 Conclusion

This article has been sketched out of the pandemic effect and the new world order set by COVID19. With work from home ideology coming in practice, and sheer loss of jobs and monetary security, there are certain things of the previous world which people are missing. This is their window-shopping urge and their social life which was woven around their offices and establishments. With little money in their pockets and freedom to move out anywhere, the working class is looking for short getaways where longer spells could be spent in residential co-living spaces which can offer periodic rent arrangements, where sightseeing, city walks, and storytelling sessions could be the forefront of a fulfilling life in the new-found freedom (Dave 2020). Hotels continue to remain expensive and could be unaffordable (Press Trust of India 2021b). A bit of careful assessment by the government can help streamline Rental Management to give the Visitors that feel at a much lesser cost with the profit-sharing models well shared among multiple stakeholders.

Acknowledgements The trigger for writing this paper is based on the personal experience of a fellow classmate at TISS.

References

Adimulam, Sweety. 2020. *Now, Pay Stamp Duty Fees by Dec 31 and Register Properties by April*. Published by the Free Press Journal on 14 December 2020 and available at https://www.freepressjournal.in/mumbai/now-pay-stamp-duty-fees-by-dec-31-and-register-properties-by-april. Accessed on December 15, 2020.

Aggarwal, Nikieta. 2020. *How to File a Harassment Complaint Against a Neighbour*. Published on 07 February 2017 in IPleaders and available at https://blog.ipleaders.in/harassment-complaint-against-neighbour/. Accessed on December 15, 2020.

Babar, Kailash. 2015. *Ready-to-Occupy Flats form 3.5% of Unsold Inventory; Navi Mumbai Worst Hit*. Published by ET Realty on 09 July 2015 and available at https://realty.economictimes.indiatimes.com/news/residential/ready-to-occupy-flats-form-3-5-of-unsold-inventory-navi-mumbai-worst-hit/47997947. Accessed on December 15, 2020.

Basu Sreeradha D., and Lijee Philip. 2020. *Crucial to Keep Home Away From Work From Home*. Published by the Economic Times on 27 June 2020 available at https://economictimes.indiatimes.com/news/company/corporate-trends/crucial-to-keep-home-away-from-work-from-home-experts/articleshow/76655000.cms. Accessed on January 24, 2021.

BBC. 2020. *Coronavirus: How the World of Work May Change Forever*. Published on 23 October 2020 by BBC and available at https://www.bbc.com/worklife/article/20201023-coronavirus-how-will-the-pandemic-change-the-way-we-work. Accessed on May 25, 2020.

Bhansali, Aradhana. 2021. *Tenants Paying Rent Regularly may have a Stake in the Property*. Published by the Mint on 20 January 2021 available at https://www.livemint.com/money/ask-mint-money/tenants-paying-rent-regularly-may-have-a-stake-in-the-property/amp-11611073437691.html. Accessed on January 22, 2021.

Common Floor. 2020. *Why Police Verification of Tenant is Important & How it's Done?* Published on 16 March 2020 available at https://www.commonfloor.com/guide/why-police-verification-of-tenant-is-important-how-its-done-56285. Accessed on December 15, 2020.

Daniyal, Shoaib. 2020. *When Will India's Economy Show the Green Shoots of Recovery?* Published by Quartz India on 01 December 2020 available at https://qz.com/india/1939948/indias-economy-will-take-years-to-recover-from-covid-19-damage/. Accessed on December 15, 2020.

Dave, Sachin. 2020. *About 48% of Indians Planning to Spend More in the Coming Months: Local Circles survey*. Published by ET Bureau on 15 December 2020 and available https://economictimes.indiatimes.com/news/economy/indicators/about-48-of-indians-planning-to-spend-more-in-the-coming-months-loclecircle-survey/articleshow/79737969.cms?from=mdr. Retrieved on December 17, 2020.

Deshpande, Swati, and Chittaranjan Tembhekar. 2020. *Mumbai: Housing Societies Can't Take on Role of Cops, Ban Maids, Say Jurists*. Published by the Times of India on 21 June 2020 and available at https://timesofindia.indiatimes.com/city/mumbai/mumbai-housing-societies-cant-take-on-role-of-cops-ban-maids-jurists/articleshow/76491934.cms. Accessed on December 15, 2020.

Desk, B.Q. 2020. *Holiday Homes Are Oyo's New Play as Customers Seek Shorter Getaways, Says Founder Ritesh Agarwal*. Published by Bloomberg Quint on 12 December 2020 available at https://www.bloombergquint.com/business/holiday-homes-are-oyos-new-play-as-customers-seek-shorter-getaways-says-founder-ritesh-agarwal. Accessed on December 15, 2020.

Estrade. 2020. *Model Tenancy Act, 2020—India Gears Up to Implement Rental Housing Policy*. Published by the Estrade on 30 November 2020 available at https://www.estrade.in/model-tenancy-act-2020-india-gears-up-to-implement-rental-housing-policy/. Accessed on December 15, 2020.

ET Bureau. 2020. *Sheen Goes Off Staycations: Isocations or Solocations to be the Next Tourism Trend?* Published by the Economic Times on 18 April 2020 and available at https://economictimes.indiatimes.com/magazines/panache/sheen-goes-off-staycations-isocations-or-solocations-may-be-the-next-tourism-trend/articleshow/75215726.cms. Accessed on January 24, 2021.

ET Contributors. 2019. *What Kind of Residential Real Estate can get you Higher Rental Return on Investment? Find Out*. Published by ET Wealth on 22 April 2019 and available at https://economictimes.indiatimes.com/wealth/real-estate/what-kind-of-residential-real-estate-can-get-you-higher-rental-return-on-investment-find-out/articleshow/68962479.cms?from=mdr. Accessed on December 15, 2020.

ET Prime. 2020a. *Urban Company Widens Lead in Home Services Focussing on the Beauty Segment, But There is a Trade-off*. Published on 15 December 2020 available at https://economictimes.indiatimes.com/prime/consumer/urban-company-widens-lead-in-home-services-focusing-on-the-beauty-segment-but-theres-a-trade-off-/primearticleshow/79727297.cms. Accessed on December 15, 2020.

ET Prime. 2020b. *8 Tricks Builders use to Lure Home Buyers and 10 Questions to Ask Yourself Before Buying Property*. Published by ET Prime Wealth and available at https://economictimes.indiatimes.com/wealth/real-estate/8-tricks-builders-use-to-lure-home-buyers-and-10-questions-to-ask-yourself-before-buying-property/articleshow/79813219.cms. Accessed on December 22, 2020.

Gooptu, Biswaroop. 2019. *OYO China Fires 25 Employees for Unethical Practices; Issues Warning to 110 More*. Published by Economic Times on 18 April 2019 and available at https://economictimes.indiatimes.com/small-biz/startups/newsbuzz/oyo-china-fires-25-employees-for-unethical-practices-and-misconduct-issues-warning-to-110-more/articleshow/68922985.cms. Accessed on December 14, 2020.

GPG. 2020. *Pro-tenant Laws in India Often Inhibit Rental Market*. Published on 20 June 2006 by Global Property Guide and available at https://www.globalpropertyguide.com/Asia/India/Landlord-and-Tenant. Accessed on December 15, 2020.

Haider, Faizan. 2020. *Most Indian Employees Now Want to Head Back to Office, Feel Work From Home Less Enjoyable: Survey*. published by Economic Times on 28 October 2020 available at https://economictimes.indiatimes.com/news/company/corporate-trends/most-indian-employees-now-want-to-head-back-to-office-feel-work-from-home-less-enjoyable-survey/articleshow/78908170.cms. Accessed on December 15 2020.

Haider, Faizan. 2021. *Investment in Residential Properties to Increase in UP After the Tenancy Ordinance*. Published in the Economic Times on 20 January 2021 and available at https://economictimes.indiatimes.com/industry/services/property-/-cstruction/investment-in-residential-properties-to-increase-in-up-after-the-tenancy-ordinance/articleshow/80366657.cms?utm_source=contentofinterest&utm_medium=text&utm_campaign=cppst. Accessed on January 24, 2021.

Jadhav, Mrunal. 2020. *Pune: Three Arrested for Selling Property with Forged MoU*. Published on 29 October 2020 in Punekar News and available at https://www.punekarnews.in/pune-three-arrested-for-selling-property-with-forged-mou/. Retrieved on December 20, 2020.

Khan, Sobia., and Kailash Babar. 2020. *Residential Rentals Take a Hit on Job Losses, WFH model*. Published by the Economic Times on 19 December 2020 and available at https://economictimes.indiatimes.com/industry/services/property-/-cstruction/residential-rentals-take-a-hit-on-job-losses-wfh-model/articleshow/79809727.cms. Accessed on January 24, 2021 (Comment by Sumit Choudhary).

Maya, M. 2021. *Rental Housing in India Is on the Verge of Entering a New Orbit*. Published in Money Life on 14 January 2021 and available at https://www.moneylife.in/article/rental-housing-in-india-is-on-the-verge-of-entering-a-new-orbit/62651.html. Accessed on January 22, 2021.

Narayanan, Vivek. 2020. *Fearing Anti-social Elements, Residents Leave Tenements*. Published by The Hindu on 23 January 2020 and available at https://www.thehindu.com/news/cities/chennai/fearing-anti-social-elements-residents-leave-tenements/article30628792.ece. Accessed on May 24, 2021.

Notes on National Programme on Advanced Chemistry Cell Battery Storage by Clay Stranger, 'Batteries—A cornerstone of the future of India's economy'. Published by Economic Times on 12 November 2020 and available at https://energy.economictimes.indiatimes.com/energy-speak/batteries-a-cornerstone-of-the-future-of-india-s-economy/4625. Accessed on January 24, 2021.

Philip, Lijee. 2020. *Alibag is the Plush WFH Destination for Well-Heeled Mumbaikars in this Pandemic*. Published by the Economic Times on 06 December 2020 and available at https://economictimes.indiatimes.com/news/company/corporate-trends/alibag-is-the-plush-wfh-destination-for-well-heeled-mumbaikars-in-this-pandemic/articleshow/79582583.cms. Accessed on January 24, 2021.

Press Information Bureau Release 1685527 dated 02 January 2021. Accessed on February 02 2021.

Press Trust of India release IDs (Release ID: 1623663), (Release ID: 1612458) and available at https://pib.gov.in/PressReleseDetail.aspx?PRID=1623663; https://pib.gov.in/PressReleseDetail.aspx?PRID=1612458; https://www.mha.gov.in/media/mha-press-releases (199 notifications from 28March 2020 till 17 January 2021); https://labour.gov.in/whatsnew/advisory-secretary-ministry-housing-and-urban-affairs-ease-hardship-being-faced-workers-due. Accessed on January 23, 2020.

PTI. 2020. *Delhi Court Says that Obscenity Against Women Cannot Go Unpunished*. Published in the Indian Express on 29 August 2016 and available at https://indianexpress.com/article/india/india-news-india/delhi-court-says-that-obscenity-against-women-cannot-go-unpunished-3002147/. Accessed on December 15, 2020.

PTI. 2020. *Intimacy in the Time of Corona: Home-bound Couples Find Love as Sale of Condoms Go Up*. Published by Economic Times on 20 March 2020 and available at https://economictimes.indiatimes.com/magazines/panache/intimacy-in-the-time-of-corona-home-bound-couples-find-love-as-sale-of-condoms-go-up/articleshow/74793351.cms. Accessed on January 24, 2021.

PTI. 2021. *Indian Economy May Contract 25 per cent in Current Fiscal: Economist Arun Kumar*. Published by the Economic Times on 17 January 2021 and available at https://economictimes.indiatimes.com/news/economy/indicators/indian-economy-may-contract-25-per-cent-in-current-fiscal-economist-arun-kumar/articleshow/80312742.cms. Accessed on January 22, 2021.

PTI. 2021. Domestic hospitality industry to contract by 65% in FY21: Report. Published by Money Control on 12 January 2021 and is available at https://www.moneycontrol.com/news/business/domestic-hospitality-industry-to-contract-by-65-in-fy21-report-6336781.html. Accessed on January 23, 2021.

PTI. 2020. *Risk of Unethical Conduct in Corporate India Magnifies Due to COVID19 Disruptions: Survey*. Published by Business Insider India on 25 Jun 2020 available at https://www.businessinsider.in/business/news/risk-of-unethical-conduct-in-corporate-india-magnifies-due-to-covid-19-disruptions-survey/articleshow/76624591.cms. Accessed on December 15, 2020.

Purkayastha, Pallabi Dey. 2020. *TNN, Gulabo Sitabo Movie Review : A Well-crafted Satire that Evokes a Riot of Emotions*. Published on Jun 12, 2020 and available at https://timesofindia.indiatimes.com/entertainment/hindi/movie-reviews/gulabo-sitabo/movie-review/76328770.cms. Accessed on January 22, 2021.

Salman, S.H. 2020. *Nestaway Struggles to Refund Tenants as Thousands Vacate Due to Covid Outbreak*. Published by the Mint on 21 July 2020 and available at https://www.livemint.com/companies/start-ups/nestaway-struggles-to-refund-tenants-as-thousands-vacate-due-to-covid-outbreak-11595333740732.html. Accessed on December 14, 2020.

Singh, Pankaj. 2020. *Smart Rental Homes see Surge in Demand Post-COVID19 Lockdown*. Published in the Financial Express on 07 August 2020 and available at https://www.financialexpress.com/money/smart-rental-homes-see-surge-in-demand-post-covid-19-lockdown/2047943/. Accessed on December 15, 2020.

Taskin, Bismee. 2021. *Increased Work, Domestic Abuse—How Covid Lockdown was Especially Hard on Women in India*. Published by The Print on 09 February 2021 and available at https://theprint.in/india/increased-work-domestic-abuse-how-covid-lockdown-was-especially-hard-on-women-in-india/601328/. Accessed on May 24, 2021.

TFI Post News Desk. 2021. *Ghettos in Most Indian Cities are Breeding Grounds of Anti-social Activities*. Published on YouTube published on 03 July 2019 and available at https://tfipost.com/2019/07/ghettos-in-most-indian-cities-are-breeding-grounds-of-anti-social-activities/. Accessed on May 24, 2021.

Thanawala, Hiral. 2020. *Renting Furniture: Is it Really Cost-Effective?* Published by Money Control on 05 November 2020 available at https://www.moneycontrol.com/news/business/personal-finance/renting-furniture-is-it-really-cost-effective-6069241.html. Accessed on December 15, 2020.

Thomas, Shibu. 2018. *Flat Owner Entitled to One Parking Space: Bombay HC*. Published by The Times Of India on 17 September 2018 and available at https://timesofindia.indiatimes.com/city/mumbai/flat-owner-entitled-to-one-parking-space-bombay-hc/articleshow/65835134.cms. Accessed on December 15, 2020.

The Invisible Tourist. 2020. *Should You use Airbnb, 8 Troubling Issues You Didn't Know*. Published in Unpopular Truths on 06 December 2020 and available at https://www.theinvisibletourist.com/why-you-shouldnt-use-airbnb-issues-you-didnt-know/ retrieved on December 15, 2020.

Tracxn Website. 2021. Available at https://tracxn.com/d/trending-themes/Startups-in-Two-Wheeler-Rentals. Accessed on May 21, 2021.

Business Innovations and Change: Lessons from Pandemic

Jaya Rani Das and Monoj Kumar Chowdhury

1 Introduction

1.1 COVID 19 and Its Impact on Society

COVID-19, which is announced as a global pandemic, has truly affected every general public of our society. Because of its quick spread, nations had to stop their worldwide travels and individuals secured themselves inside their homes. Public awareness, personal hygiene, utilization of facemask as well as social distancing have been perceived as the controlling techniques to stop this pandemic. In the midst of lockdown, multiple issues related to social, educational, financial, political, agricultural, psychological levels and many more have been identified, which has created the devastating impact on the lives of the people.

India has been put in lockdown for 3 months (approximately) continuously to stop the spread of rapid coronavirus. People have been advised to remain inside; however, for many daily wage earners, this is not a final solution. Official information says that in India, total 42 crore individuals are working in the unorganized sector, including agricultural laborers, hawkers, cart pullers, transport drivers and tea garden laborers. Some of them are migrant workers, who got stuck in some distant cities, couldn't move to their native villages due to suspended vehicle. As a result, they had to spend sleepless nights thinking about their livelihood without money for the days to come. Moreover, many construction workers, painters, people working in various outlets, etc. lost their jobs during the time of COVID-19, leaving these people helpless. In

J. R. Das (✉) · M. K. Chowdhury
Department of Business Administration, Gauhati University, Guwahati, India
e-mail: jayaranidas@gauhati.ac.in

M. K. Chowdhury
e-mail: mkc@gauhati.ac.in

R. N. Subudhi et al. (eds.), *Future of Work and Business in Covid-19 Era*,
Springer Proceedings in Business and Economics,
https://doi.org/10.1007/978-981-19-0357-1_30

many cases, people got stuck in cities without food and shelter, and in many cases worries of inability to feed their family members haunted them day and night.

In India, up to 53% of organizations have indicated a certain measure of effect of shutdowns caused due to COVID on operations, according to FICCI review in March/2020. By 24th April, the unemployment rate had expanded almost 19% within a month, arriving at 26% unemployment across India, as indicated by the "Centre for Monitoring Indian Economy". Around 14 crore Indians lost work during the lockdown. Over 45% families across the nation revealed an income drop as compared to the previous year.

It has been said that "Emergency brings forth the progressions which were pending for a long time". The situational crisis which was arisen during the hour of pandemic demonstrated this line as true. Things have been changed to address the issues of general public—a thing that the public authority had been making a decent attempt to execute for a long time. Significant changes were observed in case of online education as well as judiciary.

The pandemic has allowed ideas to thrive, grow and take shape. During this time, people got a lot of time to nurture their ideas, use their innovative minds in some productive work. The official employees also saved their time as they were working from home. They spent their quality time with their family and did innovative work. Though to save many lives, entire countries had to shut down, imposing quarantine for the non-essential workers, but fortunately science and technology helped at that time and allowed hundreds of people in affected areas to remain connected, productive and healthy.

1.2 Need of the Research

The pandemic caused by coronavirus has left the whole world in the worst state ever. Initially, scientists couldn't recognize the characteristics of the virus and even countries were also not ready to fight against this deadly virus with the current medical infrastructure. As a result, the entire countries had to shut down all business operations except some of the emergency activities. Lockdown was forcefully imposed, and workers of non-essential sectors had to stay inside their houses. At the same time, many people lost their jobs as companies couldn't bear their salary expenses without any production operation. It was undoubtedly the greatest challenge faced by human civilization. The consequences were observed to be vulnerable, in terms of public health crisis as the direct impact, and social, economic and political system can be considered as the indirect impact. Moreover, a sharp declination was observed in case of economic growth curve due to the remarkable amount of reduction in gross national income. At this stage, innovation has attracted a lot of attention as a means of dealing with these challenges. This kind of research is required to know—"how innovation made for the development efforts in pandemic era, became savior for the whole world, and how people accepted and adapted with the changes in different sections that occurred due to pandemic." It is also required to study "how the new normal will actually look like".

1.3 Objectives of the Study

- To study the impact of COVID pandemic in various sectors
- To study situational innovations in different areas during the pandemic
- To focus on the lessons learnt during this pandemic.

1.4 Research Methodology

This research paper is a form of explanatory study to analyze various changes observed during COVID pandemic.

1.5 Data Collection

The study is based on secondary data collection. The data has been collected from various published sources like books, journals, magazines, reports, publications, etc.

2 Discussion

2.1 What is Business Innovation

Innovation implies coming up with a new method of getting things done. Business innovation incorporates those better approaches for getting things done, which are introduced with the objective earning more money in business. Business innovation can be of many forms, namely product innovation, process innovation, marketing innovation and organizational innovation. In many cases, R & D (Research and Development) is often used as a synonym for business innovation. But this term is usually used in a broader sense than what we understand in the business context. According to Bloomberg Innovation Index, in the year 2020, countries like Germany, South Korea and Singapore led all other nations with reference to their overall growth in terms of economy, technology and society.

2.2 Situational Innovation Created During Pandemic

After COVID-19 broke out, the lives and lifestyle of people have been changed dramatically. Not only the personal lives but also social life of every person has changed. Accordingly, the business scope has also altered from offline to online mode. The scope of some of the online business portals also emerged in the time of lockdown, which were not so active in offline era. The concept of digitalization has been implemented in true sense, and it has become popular with common people. Though the economic activity in the global scenario put many forms of business into a vulnerable position during COVID pandemic, but the crisis is a golden time for tech companies, as technology has become the only way to communicate. Other non-state actors, big corporations have come forward to help frontline workers and support government with financial support. Both public and private sector enterprises have worked together to find innovative ways to minimize the adverse impact of pandemic on nation's health and economy.

There is a deep-rooted saying that ***Necessity is the Mother of Innovation***. During the COVID pandemic circumstance, the entire world came together on a war footing to respond to it. The *triple helix model of innovation* worked well in this situation, and it was the need of great importance to use endeavors between college, new companies and the government. Collaboration among big companies, universities and skilled young talents consistently assists with establishing a rich climate for age of groundbreaking thoughts which are viewed as building blocks. Big companies encouraged other research institutes to do some scientific research by giving them monetary help throughout the process. As pandemic brought trade restriction worldwide, the active involvement of industry and engineering volunteers brought indigenous scientific discoveries, and furthermore encouraged a culture of independence and entrepreneurship in India.

Specialists from both private, public sectors, technical and clinical experts came forward to share their insight and worked in a common loop to fight against COVID in this unprecedented situation. Technology and other innovative methodology help in tracing, isolation and treatment of the disease, which were the primary response strategy. Data collection and dissemination of information are done through application of Internet and telecommunication, and it strengthened the country's response toward COVID. The collaboration between department of health and family welfare, responsible for primary health care and department of medical education, looking after the curative aspects of health through tertiary healthcare centers, education and training of doctors, nurses and paramedical workers helped in streaming a quick response to this pandemic.

The table given below will provide the details regarding innovation during pandemic. But we cannot say about the commercialization of these products because all these ideas are in nascent stage, and most of them (e.g., medical innovations) are generated on the basis of demand of this time. So, the future will tell whether these ideas are suitable for general present market condition or not (Table 1).

Table 1 List of innovations during the pandemic

S. No.	Sector	Name of product/service idea	Description
1	Medical Science	Screening and diagnostic test of Novel Corona Virus	It is a huge achievement for Mylab Discovery Solutions, Pune on the innovation of RT-PCR and rapid diagnostic test by authorized COVID testing laboratory. It is the first indigenous RT-PCR-based molecular diagnostic test for detecting typic genetic material of novel coronavirus within 2.5 h
2		Covaxin and Covishield vaccines	These two COVID vaccines are locally made by pharma company Bharat Biotech. After performing series of test on human body and getting good immune response, drug regulator has given green signal for its application and also ready to ship these vaccines to neighboring countries. Some of them (for instance, Nepal, Bhutan, Maldives, Bangladesh, Myanmar) have already got its first dose
3		AnuPath	Centre for Nano Science and Engineering at IIS, Bengaluru, came with the innovation of handheld biosensor to quickly measure vital parameters for diabetes, chronic kidney failure, anemia and malnutrition with a finger-prick blood sample. It is a technology designed to perform sensitive antibody test using COVID-19-specific antibodies
4		Novel preventions	N9 blue nanosilver—As a part of Nano mission program, Department of Science and Technology, IIT Delhi, has introduced a novel material—N9 blue nanosilver—as an antimicrobial coating for face masks and personal protective equipment. The nanolayer coating provide an extra layer of protection from accidental contamination by virus-carrying droplets and aerosols under different storage conditions, humidity and temperature to validate its shelf life

(continued)

Table 1 (continued)

S. No.	Sector	Name of product/service idea	Description
5		SAANS Pro, (InnAccel Bangalore)	An Indian bio-design medical breathing support system that can be used in ambulances to transport patients and in rural tertiary care centers where ventilators are in short supply
6		RespirAID	A portable breathing support system developed by Bio-design Innovation Labs with an aim to meet the shortage of ventilators in India and abroad
7		A wearable RFID (Radio frequency Identification) anklet (Divij Kinger, Research associate, Tata Institute for Genetics and Society)	A prototype to track, monitor and store information about the doctors, patients and administrative support staff within makeshift hospitals
8	Technological innovation	Gun-mounted drones	Hyderabad-based Binford Robotics has signed an MoU with Bharat Dynamics Ltd to develop next generation combat drone which will mount guns that can be helpful in small wars as a force multiplier. They have worked as active frontline fighters to spray disinfectant during peak pandemic. The company has also tied up with the Uttar Pradesh government to spray pesticides in agricultural fields
9	Ground Level Innovations	Home-made masks and sanitizers	During the time of lockdown and for excessive cost cutting, people have been coming up with indigenous ideas of fashionable home-made masks and hand sanitizers. People became aware, highly conscious of their food habits and increase the use of medicinal leaves like Neem leaves, Tulsi leaves and locally available spices like turmeric, ginger, etc. These indigenous things were used to prepare sanitizers, concoctions as well as food preparations to strengthen a good immune system

(continued)

Table 1 (continued)

S. No.	Sector	Name of product/service idea	Description
10	Digital innovations	Digital gadgets to reduce physical contact	To avoid physical contact with surfaces in public places, some sensor-operated gadgets were designed
11		A full-body walkthrough disinfection chamber for personnel sanitization, mobile tracking application for surveillance of infection suspects, low-cost portable ventilators, comprehensive COVID 19 stations with facilities like thermal screening, pedestal-operated hand-washing, soap dispensers, hand driers, helium balloons attached with cameras for surveillance and many more	DRDO has designed a full-body disinfection chamber and a full bodysuit to stop contamination through the coronavirus IIT Roorkee has developed tracking application with state-of-the-art features and portable ventilators to support the frontline workers
12		Arogya Setu Application	Under Government of India Initiative, smart phone users were encouraged to install this mobile phone application, which can track COVID-19 positive people around and also provide free health advice. People with feature phones get extra benefit with Inter-active Voice Response service
13		Electronic Vaccine Intelligence Network (eVIN)	It is a technological solution aimed at strengthening immunization supply chain system by sharing information of stocks and flows of vaccines. This system has been used for customized services like immunization and protecting children and pregnant mothers against vaccine preventive diseases

Source Own compilation by authors

2.3 Some Changes Observed During Pandemic

Due to the extended lockdown in several nations, most of the business units confronted extreme loss and an unprecedented downfall in revenue and operations. Some industries like travel and aviation, retail and hospitality sector recorded the highest loss in the year 2020 due to limitations in movements, travel and tourism as well as customer spending. But, even amidst this economic crisis, some of the special sectors have not only managed to keep their position in the market but also witnessed trend-defying growth. Capitalizing on the new normal, these sectors have recorded an increase in their revenue and customer base. Some of the niche sectors that are enjoying a booming business despite the economic fall are listed below.

1. **EdTech**

   EdTech has been the savior of students, teachers and parents during the time of lockdown. Innovative and interactive teaching methods such as live classes, on-the-spot doubt clearance and practice papers offered during the time of pandemic helped students a lot. Because of raise in demands for skill-based and knowledge-based online courses among students and professionals, the growth of Ed-tech is accelerating.

   Distant learning programs and open educational applications and platforms have been used by schools and teachers to reach learners remotely and prevent the disruption of education. Colleges have scrambled to find creative solutions to teach students online, in-person but socially distant, or in a hybrid format. During the time of pandemic, popularity of Webinar has also increased. Due to lockdown, people had enough time to explore and learn new things, and webinars on various topics organized by government, semi government and private educational institutes have given scope for this. International seminars in online mode also reduced traveling, boarding-lodging cost; at the same time, they seem to be very effective as participants can attend these events in relax mode at home according to their convenience. So, it can be said that the pandemic taught Android phone users to utilize it in proper way and that too at the optimum level.
2. **Online Gaming**

   COVID pandemic has offered a boost to the gaming industry. During the lockdown, when people were forced to remain inside their houses for the sake of maintaining COVID protocol, online gaming was the only solution to get rid of their boredom.
3. **Agri-tech**

   Digitalization of agricultural markets has been a remarkable success in this era. Due to lockdown restrictions, people couldn't step outside their homes, and at that time online grocers had turned to digital mandis to fulfill the demand for fresh vegetables as well as fruits. It boosted the level of confidence among the rural farmers to produce more and thus become a contributor to the country's earned revenue.
4. **Med-tech**

   Innovation in medical science during pandemic can't be ignored. From infrared thermometers to lifesaving ventilators, med-tech has changed the medicine industry at every step. Cloud-based storage solution and telemedicine have made life easier to both health consultants and patients. With the help of telemedicine, patients from the rural areas, tier II and tier III cities may consult with the doctors virtually, which saves both time and money and also reduce physical contact with others.

5. **Role of Indian Ayurveda, Siddha, Nature Cure and Homeopathy**—India has been known for its abundance of biodiversity including herbs, vegetation and spices. Since ages, Ayurveda and homeopathy have been using these raw indigenous products to prepare medicines which have gained popularity across the world. Recently during the time of pandemic, Kerala government accepted its good results and decided to classify people into seven categories based on spread of the deadly virus and advised Ayurvedic treatment to some classes of people. Common people also can't deny the usefulness of products of some commercial Ayurvedic brands like Patanjali, Himalaya, etc.
6. **Online Media**
   COVID 19 has brought the biggest boom into the digital world, especially to OTT platforms like Netflix, Amazon Prime and Hotstar. A significant increase in viewers was observed in the time of lockdown, as there were restrictions in physical visit to movie halls, theaters, etc. Other social networking sites like Facebook, Instagram, and Twitter have also played a vital role in this crucial time by spreading valid information and awareness globally.
7. **Role of Television, FM Radio**—This COVID 19 pandemic again proved the growing value of media among common people which have been considered the primary source of critical information during the time of disaster and emergencies. Responding to the situation, popular broadcasters kept people updated with the current scenarios by streaming live reporting, daily updates and special reports on COVID, breaking news coverage, daily interviews with elected officials and public health experts, regular announcements to educate citizens to stay healthy. They kept us entertained by launching new family-friendly serials, shows (related to cooking class, yoga class in the morning), repeat telecast of old and popular religious mega-serials like Ramayana, Mahabharata, Jai Hanuman, Shri Krishna, etc., Concerts to raise fund from public, celebrations of the healthcare professionals on the frontline were organized to encourage them. Though various online learning tools (e.g., smart phone, laptops, and tablets) were used widely to reduce the gap created during the pandemic, students couldn't take those opportunities many a time due to low network connectivity. In this case, many television/radio channels came forward to extend help to those remote learners by streaming live classes based on course content. Thus, television and radio platforms kept people updated and mentally contented with positivity and distracted them from depressing news.
8. **E-banking**—To avoid crowd at banks, common people opted for impersonal digital transactions through online and mobile channels during COVID-19 pandemic. People of digital India have now become more dependent mostly on mobile banking for online shopping, money transfer, paying electricity bills, mobile recharge, etc. for its cost effectiveness and 24/7 services. But it can't be denied that unconscious use of many online applications in the smart phone has also increased cybercrime, and hackers have used to steal money from the bank accounts by tracing the transactions by customers.

9. **Emergence of Online Shopping**—Though the option for online shopping was available prior to the days of pandemic, people used to enjoy window shopping and moving from one shop to another in search of the best possible product at low cost. But this scenario has changed totally after the rapid spread of COVID-19 virus. Nowadays, common people don't want to go out and roam about the crowded market in general. They opt for online shopping for various essential items, grocery, fruits, vegetables, electronic gadgets, apparels and many more. Another benefit of online shopping is that at a very low delivery charge, associated vendors carry the ordered products to the doorstep of customers. It even facilitates cashless transactions which reduce the chances of physical connection between two people.

2.4 *Lessons Learnt in This Pandemic*

- Over the last several months, some massive changes have been observed in terms of priorities of lives. People have become more conscious about their spending. They give importance on optimum utilization of every possible resources available at home and realized the need of savings for the time of possible emergency. They have even curbed their expenses by organizing their family and religious functions in a very simple manner.
- Sales of healthy food, fruits, vegetables, etc. have gone high. On the other hand, sales of clothes, makeup, luxury cars, etc. have decreased because people have come to know that they don't need this stuff to spend a healthy life, and this pandemic has acted as an eye-opener to them.
- Taking care of oneself is very much necessary to lead a disease-free life. Before the pandemic, people didn't give much importance to take proper care of themselves due to lack of time. Their whole life had become like machines, and it was solely dedicated to work. People didn't devote enough time to themselves, and it created too much stress in everyday life. But during the lockdown, self-isolation has given one that opportunity to take care of those things which make people actually happy. People nowadays engage in meditation, yoga and other practices to heal and remove mental stress.
- Our lives were put on pause during lockdown. Many were forced to work from home, and few people used to traveled unless it was necessary. As a result of this, common people got enough time for their creative thinking. Many of them came up with some brilliant ideas which can be useful for the well-being of a society. Most of them lost their jobs during pandemic, and it forced them to think of some new ideas of entrepreneurship which would not have been possible in the formerly busy life.
- It is the good news that India was successful in controlling the rapid spread of coronavirus across the nation to some extent compared to the many other countries with the help of selfless hard work of frontline workers, sincere duties of doctors/nurses and strict government rules. The financial system of our economy seems to be

stable, and foreign investors have shown trust to invest in Indian market. During the pandemic, when the world was struggling on channeling investments, India received a noticeable amount of FDI. Moreover, to keep this position in front of foreign countries, the nation has also increased their domestic investment.
- An uncountable number of lives and wealth had got destroyed during this time. To bring normalcy to the world again, some points should be always kept in mind. Firstly, we should preserve nature as it has been a life saver all the time. Secondly, people should never take their health and safety for granted. Thirdly, people should give attention to proper nutrition and cleanliness to boost up their immune system. God forbid, if another wave comes, common people would be more innovative in their own way and take all precautions religiously.

3 Conclusion

COVID 19 has created one of the toughest challenges for government, business and society in recent history. The effects of this virus are not only limited to health and safety of the human race; even economy and social life cycle have collapsed. National GDP growth has gone down below zero (negative 23.9%) which has been the lowest in the history of independent India. The pandemic has created an alarming call for many business enterprises to come up with the new plan to deal with all these disruptions. In this case, technological advances and innovations have played a major role to revive different sectors like healthcare, telecommunication, agriculture, etc. In public healthcare institutions, technology and artificial intelligence helped to predict and forecast epidemics as well as control the supply chain of medicines and related appliances. Similarly, technology helped to connect people during lockdown period, and it has made e-learning and remote-working a little bit easier. Moreover, digitalization strengthened our food supply chain and retail market, as a result of which it can serve people in a more responsible and sustainable way. It is well-known that our economy is affected by the operations of enterprises and businesses. It only survives with the adaptation of industry leaders with the changing times. In order to sustain in the competitive world, the industrial leaders must be innovative and resourceful. Entrepreneurs are considered to be the innovators for an economy. The importance of innovation in entrepreneurship was very much realized during the time of pandemic which brought some new creative ideas to produce any product or solutions. The "New normal" will definitely bring a new age of some innovative startups or entrepreneurships, and time will reveal the hidden opportunities stored in them.

References

Big Tech Companies and Other Non-state Actors. https://www.jstor.org/stable/resrep24924.12.

BT MindRush 2021: Challenges and Opportunities for Startups in the COVID-19 Pandemic (businesstoday.in).

Budget 2021: Here's Everything for Startups and MSMEs FM Sitharaman Announced in the First Digital Budget—The Financial Express.

Chearavanont, Suphachai. 2020. CEO, CP group, *Agenda of World Economic Forum*, August 11, 2020.

Covaxin and Covishield: What we Know About India's Covid Vaccines—BBC News date—January 22, 2021.

Covid-19 Reshapes the Future. https://www.jstor.org/stable/resrep25198.

Early-stage Startup Investments up 100% in 2020: LetsVenture|VCCircle by Shubham Sharma, January 25, 2021.

Gupta, Akash. 2020. *Youth Ki Awaaz*, November 1, 2020.

Gupta, Mayank. 2020. *Charter Accountant & Columnist*, April 23 2020.

How Digitization and Innovation can Make the Post-COVID World a Better Place.

https://yourstory.com/2021/01/disruption-fuelled-growth-indian-tech-startups.

Hyderabad Startup to Build Gun-mounted Drones—The New Indian Express published: February 6, 2021, 9.47 am.

Innovations by Indians During the COVID-19 Pandemic—www.organiser.org.

Sahasranamam, Sreevas. *India: How Coronavirus Sparked a Wave of Innovation.* The Conversation Newsletter.

Singh, Vanshika. 2020. *Innovations to Make India Self-reliant in Tackling COVID-19.* Health& Medicine, Biotechnology and COVID 19.

Technological Innovation, Partnerships and Holistic Approach Guided the COVID-19 Response in Karnataka. News Details published on World Health Organisation-India, September 17, 2020.

The Innovations Indian Startups are Coming up with to Combat Covid-19. Industrial Automation, December 2020.

Will an Entrepreneurial Spirit Become Part of the "New Normal" Post Pandemic?